# Shepherding Nature
## The Challenge of Conservation Reliance

Globally, more and more species are at risk of extinction as the environment and climate change. Many of these species require long-term management to persist—they are conservation reliant. The magnitude of this challenge requires a rethinking of how conservation priorities are determined and a broader societal commitment to conservation. Choices need to be made about which species will be conserved, for how long, and by whom. This volume uses case studies and essays by conservation practitioners from throughout the world to explore what conservation reliance is and what it means for endangered species management. Chapters consider threats to species and how they are addressed, legal frameworks for protecting endangered species, societal contexts and conflicts over conservation goals, and how including conservation reliance can strengthen methods for prioritizing species for conservation. The book concludes by discussing how shepherding nature requires an evaluation of societal values and ethics.

J. MICHAEL SCOTT was a Research Biologist with the US Fish and Wildlife Service for 37 years, leading research programs on forest birds of the Hawaiian Islands and the California condor. He served as Cooperative Fish and Wildlife Research Unit Leader and Professor of Wildlife at the University of Idaho, where he is an Emeritus Distinguished Professor. His research has emphasized conservation, endangered-species policy, and landscape ecology.

JOHN A. WIENS is an Emeritus University Distinguished Professor at Colorado State University and an Adjunct Professor at the University of Western Australia. After 36 years in academia, he served for 6 years as Lead/Chief Scientist with The Nature Conservancy and then for 4 years as Chief Scientist with PRBO Conservation Science in California. His research on landscape ecology, conservation, and the ecology of birds has led to many publications.

BEATRICE VAN HORNE was a professor for 17 years at Colorado State University, where her research focused on population biology of terrestrial vertebrates. Subsequently she was a National Program Leader in areas related to wildlife, fisheries, climate change, and wildfire for the US Forest Service and the US Geological Survey. Most recently she led the Northwest Climate Hub for the US Department of Agriculture.

DALE D. GOBLE is an Emeritus University Distinguished Professor and the Margaret Wilson Schimke Distinguished Professor of Law at the University of Idaho. His research interests are in natural resource law (including public land law and wildlife law), natural resource history, and torts. He has coauthored several books on the Endangered Species Act and a comprehensive primer on Wildlife Law.

The Critically Endangered Araripe manakin occurs in a small area of evergreen forest on the slope of the Chapada do Araripe in Brazil. Although efforts to protect its habitat have been successful, the species remains conservation reliant.

Photo: Ian Thompson.

# Shepherding Nature
## The Challenge of Conservation Reliance

J. MICHAEL SCOTT
*University of Idaho*

JOHN A. WIENS
*Colorado State University*

BEATRICE VAN HORNE
*US Forest Service*

DALE D. GOBLE
*University of Idaho*

*With Essays by Michael J. Bean, P. Dee Boersma, Christopher G.R. Bowden, Brian Gratwicke, Jianguo "Jack" Liu, Loyal A. Mehrhoff, Joseph Y. Oatman, Camille Parmesan, Barbara Taylor and Lorenzo Rojas-Bracho, Timothy H. Tear and Simon Nampindo, and John Woinarski*

CAMBRIDGE
UNIVERSITY PRESS

# CAMBRIDGE
## UNIVERSITY PRESS

University Printing House, Cambridge CB2 8BS, United Kingdom

One Liberty Plaza, 20th Floor, New York, NY 10006, USA

477 Williamstown Road, Port Melbourne, VIC 3207, Australia

314–321, 3rd Floor, Plot 3, Splendor Forum, Jasola District Centre,
New Delhi – 110025, India

79 Anson Road, #06–04/06, Singapore 079906

Cambridge University Press is part of the University of Cambridge.

It furthers the university's mission by disseminating knowledge in the pursuit of
education, learning, and research at the highest international levels of excellence.

www.cambridge.org
Information on this title: www.cambridge.org/9781108421829
DOI: 10.1017/9781108377898

First published 2020

Printed in the United Kingdom by TJ International Ltd, Padstow Cornwall

*A catalogue record for this publication is available from the British Library.*

*Library of Congress Cataloging-in-Publication Data*
Names: Scott, J. Michael, author. | Wiens, John A., author. | Van Horne, Beatrice,
  author. | Goble, Dale, author.
Title: Shepherding nature : the challenge of conservation reliance / J. Michael Scott, John
  A. Wiens, Beatrice Van Horne, Dale D. Goble.
Description: Cambridge ; New York, NY : Cambridge University Press, 2020. |
  Includes bibliographical references and index.
Identifiers: LCCN 2019038341 (print) | LCCN 2019038342 (ebook) | ISBN
  9781108421829 (hardback) | ISBN 9781108434331 (paperback) | ISBN 9781108377898
  (epub)
Subjects: LCSH: Wildlife conservation–Case studies. | Nature–Effect of human beings
  on–Case studies. | Wildlife conservation–Philosophy. | Human ecology–Philosophy.
Classification: LCC QL82 .S359 2020  (print) | LCC QL82  (ebook) | DDC 333.95/416–
  dc23
LC record available at https://lccn.loc.gov/2019038341
LC ebook record available at https://lccn.loc.gov/2019038342

ISBN 978-1-108-42182-9 Hardback
ISBN 978-1-108-43433-1 Paperback

# Contents

Color plates can be found between pages 210 and 211.

# Preface

This is a book about conservation reliance—the need of many declining and imperiled species for ongoing, long-term conservation and management. It is also about shepherding nature—the need for a broad acceptance of the responsibility of humans to act as good shepherds. These are things that the four of us have spent much of our careers thinking about.

Our approach to this challenge has been shaped by our experiences and interests, so we should tell you a little about who we are. Three of us, J. Michael Scott (Mike), John A. Wiens (John), and Beatrice Van Horne (Bea), are scientists who have focused on ecology and conservation; the other, Dale D. Goble (Dale), has dealt with environmental law and its applications. All of us reside in the western United States. Mike grew up in California and received BS and MA degrees from San Diego State University, before moving north for a PhD from Oregon State University. Bea spent her early years in Oregon, the San Francisco Bay area, and Arizona, with undergraduate and advanced degrees (MS, PhD) from the University of California Santa Cruz, Oregon State University, and the University of New Mexico. Dale grew up in southern Idaho, not far from where his great grandparents had homesteaded. He went east for a philosophy degree from Columbia College and then returned west for a law degree from the University of Oregon Law School. John spent his younger years in Oklahoma and then obtained graduate degrees (MS, PhD) from the University of Wisconsin Madison.

After being suitably educated, we followed different but related career paths, mixing experiences in government, academia, and non-governmental conservation organizations. The experiences followed from and deepened our research interests in birds (Mike and John), mammals and populations (Bea), and policy and law (especially the

Endangered Species Act; Dale), eventually converging on conservation.

Mike joined the US Fish and Wildlife's Endangered Species Research Program in Hawai'i and then directed the California Condor Research Program in California before moving to the University of Idaho as leader of the Cooperative Fish and Wildlife Research Unit and Professor of Wildlife.

John held faculty positions for 36 years at Oregon State University, the University of New Mexico, and Colorado State University before joining The Nature Conservancy as a Lead and Chief Scientist. He was subsequently Chief Scientist with Point Reyes Bird Observatory (PRBO) Conservation Science in California. He also spent time in Australia with the University of Sydney, the Commonwealth Scientific and Industrial Research Organisation (CSIRO) Division of Wildlife and Ecology in Darwin, and the University of Western Australia.

Bea was on the faculty of Colorado State University for 17 years before moving to the Washington, DC, area, first as the National Program Lead for Wildlife Research with the US Forest Service and then as the Ecosystems Coordinator for the US Geological Survey. She returned to the west as a Program Manager for the Pacific Northwest Research Station of the Forest Service and then Director of the Northwest Climate Hub for the US Department of Agriculture.

Following Law School, Dale spent 3 years with the US Department of the Interior in Washington, DC, and then returned west to become a Professor in the University of Idaho School of Law, where he was named a University Distinguished Professor and the Margaret Wilson Schimke Distinguished Professor.

All of us are now retired, and still in the West. Mike and Dale live in Moscow, Idaho, and John and Bea live in Corvallis, Oregon.

This is not our first book, nor our first collaboration. In addition to many papers, books, and monographs, Mike and Dale co-edited (with Frank Davis) *The Endangered Species Act at 30* (two volumes, Island Press, 2006); John wrote *Ecological Challenges and*

*Conservation Conundrums: Essays and Reflections for a Changing World* (Wiley, 2016); Bea co-edited (with Deanna Olson) *People, Forests, and Change. Lessons from the Pacific Northwest* (Island Press, 2017); and Dale wrote (with Eric T. Freyfogle) *Wildlife Law. A Primer* (Island Press, 2009)[1] and edited (with several others) *Wildlife Law. Cases and Materials* (Foundation Press, 2017).

Enough about us; how about this book? We build the book around a series of case studies—stories, really—because these are more compelling than a litany of facts and figures, and because they illustrate the many ways in which people, by struggling to save imperiled species, show how closely nature and human communities are intertwined. We draw freely from the places and organisms with which we are most familiar—Hawai'i, the American West, and Australia; terrestrial habitats; birds and mammals. Because two of us have been immersed in the US Endangered Species Act and its applications for decades, we focus on species that are listed under the act. But because conservation reliance is a global challenge, we also bring in stories from elsewhere in the world. To help us out, we have enlisted colleagues from several countries to contribute essays from their own perspectives.

We have aimed to make this book readable as well as informative. Our narratives are science based but not science dense. To that end, we have minimized our use of references and citations, including them where we think a reader might wish to delve more deeply into a topic or example. The internet provides plenty of resources for those who might want more. We found the Red List website of IUCN (www.iucnredlist.org/) and those of nations that have threatened species statutes (e.g., www.fws.gov/endangered/) particularly helpful. In the tradition of legal writing and the humanities, we have made frequent use of footnotes to reduce interruptions to the flow of the text. Scientific names of species mentioned in the text are given in Appendix B.

---

[1]  A second edition was published in 2019.

# Acknowledgments

We have been thinking about the issues we address in this book for most of our adult lives. But we haven't done it alone. Our work and thinking has intersected that of many others. When it came time to put our thoughts and experiences together in this book, we called on many of these people for help and advice. They responded enthusiastically and constructively. Consequently, our list of acknowledgments is long.

Begin with Kyra Wiens and Kathryn Ronnenberg. Kyra read multiple drafts of the chapters, always finding ways to tighten and clarify our writing and bringing better organization to our sometimes-wandering prose. She understood what we were trying to say and often showed us a better way to say it. Kathryn looked over the book as a whole, checking references and style details and bringing a sharp eye to the resolution, layout, composition, and production of the figures. That the color-plate section is both instructive and visually stunning owes much to her senses of design and artistry.

Several other individuals deserve special mention. Sharon Scott read drafts of the entire book, catching cryptic errors that had avoided our attention and alerting us to confusing passages. Loyal Mehrhoff and John Woinarski read many of the chapters, offering thoughtful and unfailingly helpful suggestions based on their long experience with imperiled species in Hawai'i (Loyal) and conservation issues and approaches in Australia (John). Allen Thompson helped us better understand the philosophical and ethical contexts of conservation in frequent discussions over morning coffee. Pat Malatsi introduced John and Bea to the challenges and opportunities of conservation in Botswana. And several colleagues from around the world (listed on the title page) have contributed essays that give conservation a personal touch.

Many other friends and colleagues provided information, insights, and commentary on our case studies, writing, and thinking: Debbie Anderson, Carter Atkinson, Donna Ball, Paul Banko, Michael Bean, Diego Bermeo, Gerard Bertrand, Pete Bloom, Carol Bocetti, Sandy Bowman, Joseph Brandt, Brad Bridges, David Brown, Vernon Byrd, Shawn Cantrell, Christopher Caudill, Alan Channinig, Kevin Clark, Jamie Rappaport Clark, Jack Connelly, William Conner, Nathan Cooper, Charles (Chip) Corsi, Deborah Crouse, Frank W. Davis, David Duffy, John Engbring, David Ewert, Megan Fairbank, Chris Farmer, John Fay, Nancy Ferguson, C. Scott Findlay, Joshua Fisher, Erica Fleishman, Holly Friefield, Megan Gairbank, Ginny Garton, Edward (Oz) Garton, Leah Gerber, Prudence J. Goforth, Jessie Grantham, Noah Greenwald, John Gross, Craig Groves, Joe Grzybowski, Jackie Guadioso-Levita, Aaron Haines, John Hall, Jan Hamber, Brett Hartl, Patricia Heglund, Paul Henson, Steve Hess, Jennifer Hiebert, Malcolm Hunter, Jim Jacobi, Lacrecia Johnson, Justin Jones, Brian Kelly, Steve Kendell, Cameron Kepler, Lloyd Kiff, Steve Kimple, Richard Knab, Shawn Lantrell, Dawn Lawson, David Ledig, Ya-Wei (Jake) Li, David Lindenmayer, Ryan Long, Carl Lundblad, Tim Male, Tom Maloney, Sheri S. Mann, Bruce Marcot, Peter P. Marra, Larry Master, Bryce Masuda, William Mautz, Jasmine McCulligh, Kathryn McEachern, Joseph Mendelson, Robert Mesta, Virgil Moore, Scott Morrison, Peter Moyle, Kim O'Connor, Joe Oatman, Serda Ozbenian, Rob Pacheco, Heather Paterson, Eben Paxton, William Pearcy, Jim Peek, Steve Perlman, Brand Phillips, Anna Pidgorna, Hugh Possingham, Thane Pratt, Janet Rachlow, Fred Ramsey, William Rapai, Kent Redford, Kerry Reese, Mark Reynolds, Sarah E. Rinkevich, Daniel Roby, Lorenzo Rojas-Bracho, Nora A. Rojek, Julie Savidge, John Schmitt, Gwendolyn Scott, Jocelyne Scott, Kevin Scott, Chris Servheen, Gregg Serveheen, Mark Shaffer, Cliff Smith, William J. Snape, Marc Stalmans, Mendel Stewart, Steve Strickland, Paul Sykes, Barbara Taylor, Timothy Tear, Stan Temple, Michael Tewes, Hillary Thompson, Robyn Thorson, Charles Van Riper, Sarah Vickerman, Lisette Waits, Anne Walker, Seanna Walsh,

Robin Waples, Rick Warshauer, Dick Wass, Mike White, David Wiens, Taryn Wiens, Sandy Wilbur, David Wilcove, Heather Williamson, Roland Williamson, Clark S. Winchell, Jim Witham, Lindsay Young, and Kelly Zenkewich. We apologize to any we may have missed.

Special thanks go to the photographers who shared their work with us: Leon Berard, Dee Boersma, Chris Bowden, Paola Branco, Joseph Brandt, Renauld Fulconis, Greg Golet, Brian Gratwicke, Joe Grzybowski, Bryan Harry, Jodi Hilty, Jack Jeffrey, Larry Jones, Dennis Jongsomjit, Maya Legrande, Wei Liu, Lindy Lumsden, John Magera, Elizabeth Neipert, William Newmark, Mustafa Nsubuga, Paula Olson, Aaron Penny, Zach Penny, Don Reeser, Michael Singer, Ian Thompson, Eric Vanderwerf, Ken Wood, and Mark Ziembicki; and to these organizations: Australian Wildlife Conservancy, Galapagos National Park, Habitat INFO, Los Angeles Times, National Library of Australia, Queensland Department of Environment and Heritage Protection, Wilderness Safaris, and the Wildlife Conservation Society.

To all of these individuals and organizations, our heartfelt thanks. You willingly and kindly responded to our frequent requests for information, discussions, and critiques. You forced us to think and rethink about the nuances of conservation reliance, and the book is the better for it.

# 1 Extinction and the Challenge of Conservation Reliance

Let's begin with a story, a true story, about toads.

> The toads were there, just where the people in the village had told them they would be. The scientists and their guide struggled up a muddy trail to a ridgeline. And then they saw them. First one, then a few, then hundreds, shining like amber amid the dark humus of the forest floor. Golden toads. A species new to science.
>
> This was in 1964. It turned out that the golden toad occurred only in a tiny, high-elevation area in the Monteverde cloud forest in Costa Rica. A reserve was established to protect the species within its known range. Surveys over the following years indicated a stable population of 1,000–2,000 toads. Then, suddenly, there were fewer than a dozen in 1988, and only one solitary male a year later. The species has not been seen since.
>
> Why did the toad disappear so suddenly? Perhaps it was a drying of breeding sites accompanying El Niño, or a shift of the cloud layer to higher elevations (both perhaps related to climate change), or fatal fungal infections. Regardless of the cause, the golden toad was extinct.[1]

It didn't have to be that way. Conservation's agenda is to avoid such extinctions, to reverse the trends that bring plants and animals to the brink of extinction and return them to secure self-reliance. In this book, we will share stories and case studies to demonstrate how such outcomes can be achieved and the consequences if they are not.

---

[1] The saga of the golden toad and the controversy over what led to its disappearance are recounted in McMenamin and Hannah (2012). The golden toad is shown in Figure 1.1.

FIGURE I.I. The golden toad, discovered in Costa Rica in 1964, was briefly conservation reliant. It is now extinct. (A black and white version of this figure will appear in some formats. For the color version, please refer to the plate section.)
Photo: Charles H. Smith, US Fish and Wildlife Service.

There have been some real conservation successes. Peregrine falcons, once endangered in the United States, now soar through the skyscraper canyons of New York and other cities, picking off pigeons as they go. Although the Guadalupe fur seal was twice thought to be extinct and remains threatened, it is now abundant on Guadalupe Island off the coast of Baja California. With intensive management, populations of the giant panda are no longer endangered (although they are still considered vulnerable). Garnett et al. (2018) tell the stories of multiple Australian taxa that are well along the road to recovery, including the spiny rice-flower and the Lord Howe Island stick insect.

For most imperiled species, however, success is elusive.[2] We humans are largely responsible. We have hunted and harvested them; destroyed their natural habitats; altered the physical environment; introduced alien predators, competitors, and pathogens; created novel ecosystems to which they are not adapted; and accelerated climate change. For many species, the threats are so pervasive and immutable that the best we can hope for is to mitigate the effects. We must care for and watch over these species. We must shepherd nature.

Because the threats persist, management to conserve many vulnerable and imperiled species must continue. We call such species *conservation reliant*. *A species is conservation reliant if it is vulnerable to threats that persist and requires continued management intervention to prevent a decline toward extinction or to maintain a population.* The golden toad was fleetingly conservation reliant, dependent on the protection provided by a reserve. But when new threats emerged, the protection was no longer adequate and the species disappeared.

We should clarify several nuances of this definition:

- The threats persist. They cannot be completely eliminated, at least over the short term. Consequently, conservation and management actions must be ongoing, recurrent, or take a long time to complete, even if a species' population is otherwise considered to be secure.
- The management actions are intended to increase or stabilize population size and distribution or reduce the rate of decline; without intervention, the species would decline more rapidly.
- The concept applies to imperiled species: species that are at risk of extinction or are declining rapidly in distribution and abundance. If a species is not vulnerable to extinction in the first place, then simply being managed to sustain recreationally or commercially viable populations does not make it conservation reliant.[3]

---

[2] In *Wild Hope*, Andrew Balmford (2012) chronicles how difficult it can be to achieve conservation success.

[3] If such species become imperiled, however, management could shift from exploitation to conservation, and they would become conservation reliant. Chinook salmon, Atlantic cod, and Columbian white-tailed deer are examples.

- A species is conservation reliant if it *requires* continuing management to slow or reverse population declines, whether or not actions are actually taken to reduce the threats.
- If the threats are eliminated or reduced so that specific conservation actions targeted on a species are no longer required, then the species is no longer conservation reliant.

The key elements of conservation reliance, then, are the extinction risk and population trajectory of a species, whether the threats can be eliminated or mitigated, and the duration and intensity of the necessary management. Although many species that are listed under various statutes or categorizations are conservation reliant, so also are many species that meet these conditions but have not been afforded special legal protection. The New England cottontail rabbit, Georgia aster, and western pond turtle in the United States are examples. All are conservation reliant. Needed management efforts are supported by a diverse coalition of citizens, non-governmental institutions, zoos, botanical gardens, and government agencies. For many such species, a desire to keep species from being listed under the US Endangered Species Act is a motivating factor.

The elements that characterize conservation reliance vary, so it is not a fixed either/or condition for a species or population. Conservation reliance is dynamic. Consequently, there are degrees of conservation reliance, which we consider in the following chapter.

Conservationists recognized some time ago that some at-risk species might require ongoing management. In 1994, Version 2.3 of the International Union for the Conservation of Nature (IUCN) Red List used a designation of "Conservation Dependent" for species that were of Lower Risk of extinction but depended on conservation efforts to prevent them from becoming Threatened. IUCN dropped this designation in Version 3.1 of the Red List in 2001, primarily to avoid confounding the status of a species with its need for management.[4] Others have used a "conservation dependent" designation to include

---

[4] www.iucnredlist.org/resources/comparingredlistversion

species that may require some form of management but generally have self-sustaining populations. They are typified by species that have significant commercial value and will remain threatened by overexploitation for the foreseeable future (Redford et al. 2011). Instead, we use "conservation reliance" more broadly to apply to species covering a range of conservation statuses and degrees of management intervention required.

The implications of conservation reliance are sobering. There are some 8–9 million species of plants and animals on Earth, perhaps more. Of these, a quarter of the assessed species may be at risk of extinction, many within decades. The Intergovernmental Science-Policy Platform on Biodiversity and Ecosystem Services (IPBES) projects that around 1 million species may already face extinction unless rapid actions are taken (IPBES 2019). Many of these species will likely be conservation reliant. In the United States, some four-fifths of the species listed as Threatened or Endangered under the Endangered Species Act are conservation reliant (Scott et al. 2010). Species in other parts of the world are similarly challenged. The funding and social will needed to support continued management for so many species are unlikely to be available. In the absence of such support, tough decisions will need to be made about how best to prioritize the allocation of resources. We—society as a whole—will need to decide which species are at the most immediate risk of extinction, which have the best chance of survival, and which to leave on their own.

The magnitude of the challenge of conservation reliance requires fresh thinking and new approaches to conservation. This is the challenge we address in this book. Our overriding purpose is to make the tradeoffs and factors underlying prioritization more transparent so that choices can be made in an informed and rational context. Because commitments to the management of conservation-reliant species are generally long term, we aim to shed light on the factors that drive the costs, benefits, and risks that go along with supporting conservation-reliant species.

To do this, we will first develop the concept of conservation reliance (Chapters 1–3) and discuss the threats that drive species toward extinction (Chapters 4–5). Then we consider the legal and policy contexts of conservation reliance (Chapter 6) and the tools that can be used to manage conservation-reliant species (Chapters 7 and 8). We follow with a discussion of some of the socioeconomic forces that affect actions to reduce conservation reliance (Chapter 9) and the problem of how to prioritize conservation efforts (Chapter 10). Finally, we close by considering some components of a way forward and placing conservation reliance in a broader philosophical and ethical context (Chapter 11).

## THE SPECTER OF EXTINCTION

Extinction is forever. It is the dying gasp of a species that will be no more. Extinction tears at the fabric of ecological communities and ecosystems, permanently altering the world we share.

Nearly all extinctions since the Industrial Revolution have been direct or indirect consequences of human actions. In some cases, species that were once abundant, such as the passenger pigeon, were hunted or harvested until, almost without warning, too few were left and the species disappeared. The same fate nearly befell the American bison in North America and Père David's deer in China. More often, species that were already rare or restricted to one or a few places, such as the golden toad, suddenly went missing.

Confirming the absence of something—that a species is in fact extinct—is more problematic than determining its presence. There are enough rediscoveries of species long thought to be extinct—so-called "Lazarus" species[5]—to give one pause. The Banggai crow, which had not been seen since 1900, was rediscovered in Indonesia in 2007. Since 1889, over 350 species of amphibians, birds, and

---

[5] After the Gospel of John, in which Jesus raised Lazarus of Bethany from the dead. The term was originally applied to species in the fossil record that were long thought to be extinct only to be "rediscovered" in more recent deposits (Flessa and Jablonski 1983) but is now applied to the rediscovery of recently extinct species.

mammals that were thought extinct have been rediscovered (Scheffers et al. 2011). Most of these species are tropical, have small geographic ranges and population sizes, and remain highly threatened.

Species may be overlooked for a variety of reasons: they are secretive or occur in remote locations, the locations in which they were formerly found were poorly recorded so we don't know where to look for them, they occur in areas of armed conflict that cannot easily be searched or on private property to which access is denied, they are difficult to distinguish from other species, or there are simply so few individuals remaining that they are unlikely to be encountered. Baumsteiger and Moyle (2017) have addressed this problem by recognizing several levels of extinction, ranging from species that no longer occur in portions of their range ("regional extinction"), to those maintained only in captivity ("wild extinction"), to those that have not been observed over a defined waiting period ("global extinction"). Before declaring a species globally extinct, they suggest waiting for a period of one generation (i.e. longer for a long-lived mammal or tree than for a short-lived fish or annual plant). Similarly, IUCN declares a species extinct only after exhaustive surveys throughout its historic range over a time period appropriate to the species' life history have failed to record any individuals.

Regardless of the definition, there are clear consequences of declaring a species extinct. Management efforts may diminish or cease, funding to support conservation disappears, and the impetus to maintain habitat set aside for the species wanes. If the species still survives, the curtailment of conservation efforts may doom it to eventual extinction. Understandably, many conservationists prefer to hold out hope.

Such hope fueled the excitement that accompanied reports of a sighting of the ivory-billed woodpecker in the Big Woods of Arkansas in 2004 (Fitzpatrick et al. 2005). The species was widely believed to be extinct, but then a beguiling but inconclusive video set off a massive search effort. Teams of observers scoured the backwaters of the Big Woods and other places for several years in search of firm evidence that the species still existed. Federal funds were diverted to support a recovery effort and lands were purchased to preserve potential habitat. There were enough tantalizing hints—fleeting glimpses of a large woodpecker, distant calls reminiscent of old recordings, unusually large woodpecker excavations in trees—to encourage searchers to continue. But no conclusive evidence has been found. If the ivory-billed woodpecker is not extinct, it is extraordinarily elusive.

Extinction is not a new phenomenon, of course. The story of life on Earth is one of species arising, evolving, persisting for some period of time, and then disappearing. Humans have been pushing species across the extinction threshold for millennia. Many large mammals—short-faced bears, saber-tooth cats, wooly mammoths, giant ground sloths, giant beavers, and dozens of other species and genera—became extinct in North America at the end of the Pleistocene. Although several hypotheses have been offered to account for this pulse of extinctions (Koch and Barnosky 2006; Meltzer 2015), a role for humans is suggested by the coincidence of the extinctions with the arrival of humans some 10 000–15 000 years ago.[6] A similar disappearance of many large mammals from Australia occurred as much as 50 000 years ago, again coinciding with the arrival of humans on the continent (Miller et al. 2005).

More recently, the spread of Polynesians across the Pacific over the past four millennia was accompanied by the extinctions of as many as half the bird species on individual islands or archipelagos—collectively, thousands of species (Steadman 2006; Duncan et al. 2013). Europeans also eradicated species as they explored and colonized new lands. The impacts of people were especially great on islands that had no prior human presence. Species living on such islands had no fear of people and were easily killed; this was the fate of the dodo

---

[6] A recent claim that humans were present in North America 130 000 years ago (Holen et al. 2017) is controversial.

on Mauritius, the moas of New Zealand, and the flightless waterfowl of Hawai'i (e.g. Allentoft et al. 2014).[7] Loehle and Eschenbach (2012) estimated that fully 95% of the extinctions of birds and mammals since 1500 were on islands, largely due to humans and the herbivores and predators they introduced.

The history of human expansion and exploration is littered with the memories of extinct species. What is different now is that we humans have so altered the environment that some recognize a new geological epoch, the Anthropocene (Crutzen and Stoermer 2000).[8] Nature and humans are no longer separable, and the growing domination of people over the planet is pushing even more species toward extinction. By some accounts, the rate of extinction of species is now perhaps tens to hundreds of times higher than over the past 10 million years (IPBES 2019). And it is accelerating. Much of this increase may be brought on by the direct and indirect effects of climate change (Urban 2017).

The distribution and abundance of many more species are declining, putting them on the pathway to extinction. IUCN provides the most comprehensive information on the conservation status of the world's species. Of the 105 500 species of plants and animals reviewed by IUCN (as of 2019), over one-quarter are considered to be

---

[7] In their beautifully illustrated book, *A Gap in Nature*, Flannery and Schouten (2001) describe the fate of 103 mammals, birds, and reptiles that became extinct after 1500, all of them at the hands of humans. IUCN lists 784 well-documented extinctions (over a broad array of taxa) since 1500, but acknowledges that the actual number may be much greater. Lawton and May (1995), Quammen (1997), and Cokinos (2000) provide additional perspectives on extinctions.

[8] Based on markers of human actions that appear in geological strata, Lewis and Maslin (2015) suggest that the Anthropocene began in 1610, coinciding with a global dip in atmospheric carbon dioxide. Noting the sudden appearance of synthetic chemicals and radiocarbon from nuclear bomb tests in the environment, Zalasiewicz et al. (2015) and Waters et al. (2016) suggest a beginning in the mid-twentieth century. One could argue instead that the Anthropocene was set in motion when humans began to modify the environment, as indigenous Australians have been doing by managing fire for tens of thousands of years. The onset, or even the appropriateness, of the Anthropocene as a geological epoch is a matter of continuing debate (Finney and Edwards 2016).

currently threatened with extinction.[9] The percentage of threatened species varies widely among taxa for which sufficient information is available: 25% of mammals, 14% of birds, 40% of amphibians, 34% of conifers, 31% of sharks and rays, and 30% of reef corals are at risk of extinction.[10] The magnitude of endangerment also varies among countries. Based only on the numbers of taxa formally listed by government agencies, there are over 1800 taxa of native plants and animals and 774 ecological communities at risk of extinction in Australia;[11] the Endangered Species Act in the United States lists 1662 plant and animal taxa;[12] the Species at Risk Act (SARA) in Canada lists 769 taxa;[13] and the Threat Classification System in New Zealand lists 799 taxa as Nationally Threatened (Hitchmough 2013). What is truly sobering is that these tallies do not include the many taxa that have not been assigned a specific legal status, so they substantially underestimate the actual number of at-risk species (Wilcove and Masters 2005).

Many conservationists regard extinction as the most alarming manifestation of a broader erosion of global biodiversity. They argue that species teetering on the brink of extinction most urgently need our help. But not everyone considers extinction to be a crisis. Stewart Brand has argued that a preoccupation with extinction may be counterproductive, diverting attention from the widespread decline of much of the Earth's biological diversity (Brand 2015; see Wiens 2016a). Populations of even once-common species are dwindling and their ranges shrinking (Ceballos et al. 2017). This, and the extent of conservation reliance among imperiled species, suggests that the demand on limited resources for conservation may be much greater than we thought.

---

[9]  See www.iucn.org/theme/species. Potential future extinctions due to global changes are not included in these figures.
[10]  www.iucnredlist.org/     [11]  soe.environment.gov.au/frameworks/state-and-trends
[12]  ecos.fws.gov/ecp0/reports/box-score-report
[13]  www.registrelep-sararegistry.gc.ca/species/schedules_e.cfm?id=1

## A FRAMEWORK FOR CONSERVATION RELIANCE

Our definition of conservation reliance embraces considerable variation in the circumstances of conservation-reliant species. It is useful, therefore, to delve in greater detail into what may (or may not) lead to conservation reliance. In Figure 1.2 we offer a framework for thinking about conservation reliance. The figure is the foundation of much of this book, so we'll describe the steps.

Figure 1.2A shows the sequence that leads to conservation reliance. The process usually begins with an assessment of a species' status. Is the species declining in its distribution and/or abundance, does it occur in only a restricted area, is the range fragmented, or does it have a small population? These conditions make a species vulnerable to extinction. The species may then be designated as threatened, endangered, or some equivalent category by international organizations or governments. Implementing action to conserve the species requires that threats—the factors that have led to its imperilment—be identified.

At this point, conservation or management actions may or may not be implemented. Ideally, management to address the threats is initiated before the species is in crisis mode. If the actions are successful in sufficiently mitigating or eliminating the threats, the species may recover and become self-sustaining in the wild. This is the outcome for which conservationists strive. In some cases, however, nothing may be done, for a variety of reasons: the threats cannot be managed, societal or financial support for actions is lacking; the species is considered "unimportant" or low priority and its decline to extinction is ignored; its decline is so rapid that the threat of extinction is not recognized; management intervention is considered too risky; and so on. If there is no diminishment of the threats and no management actions are taken, the species may be doomed to continue its slide to extinction. In other cases, the precarious status of the species may be recognized and actions initiated, but they may prove insufficient. The interventions are too little or come too late, the threats persist, and the species remains at-risk or continues to decline. One outcome is extinction. The other is that the species depends on

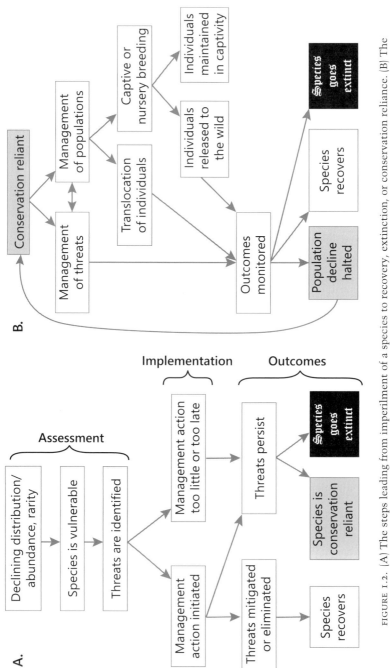

FIGURE I.2. (A) The steps leading from imperilment of a species to recovery, extinction, or conservation reliance. (B) The management steps that can lead to a conservation-reliant species recovering, becoming extinct, or continuing to be conservation reliant.

continuing, long-term management intervention to prevent further decline—it is conservation reliant.

Conservation reliance acknowledges a continuing need for monitoring and management (Figure 1.2B). Management of threats is continued through actions such as habitat restoration, predator eradication, establishment of protected areas, or a variety of other measures (see Chapters 7 and 8). These efforts may be augmented with more intensive direct population management. If suitable habitat exists elsewhere, individuals may be translocated to another area where the threats are absent or can be managed. Translocations often require frequent replenishment to establish new populations. In some cases, individuals may be brought in from the field and placed in a captive-breeding or nursery-propagation program. Captive breeding may fail for a variety of reasons: too few individuals of the right sexes, constraints on social behavior, pollination difficulties, inadequate funding or facilities, lack of public support, inadequate understanding of the species' biology, and so on. Even if the breeding program is successful, it may not be possible to re-establish the species in the wild, perhaps because suitable habitat is not available, other threats have not been anticipated, regulations prohibit reintroductions, funding is inadequate, or there is public resistance to reintroductions. Ideally, however, individuals can be released back into the wild, survive, and reproduce.

Gauging the success of management actions requires monitoring. Monitoring is necessary, for example, to determine if threats have been reduced sufficiently that captive-reared individuals will have suitable habitat or not be eaten by predators when they are released. Monitoring can detect changes in the threats or the emergence of new threats, allowing management efforts to be adjusted. Monitoring can also reveal whether the population is continuing to decline, perhaps to become extinct. If the threats have diminished sufficiently or the translocated individuals have become established or adapted to the threats, the species may recover and no longer be conservation reliant. If the threats persist, the species may remain conservation reliant even if the population decline has been halted or numbers have increased.

Even without management, circumstances may change. A species may undergo behavioral or evolutionary changes, adapting to existing threats or developing new habitat preferences. In Australia, invasive cane toads have contributed to population declines of several species that are highly susceptible to the venom they ingest when they try to eat the toads. Some northern quolls (a carnivorous marsupial) avoid the toads, however. The trait is seemingly inherited, giving hope that releasing resistant quolls might spread avoidance through the population. On the other hand, new threats may emerge, shifting the pathway from recovery to increasing conservation reliance. This is what's happening to northern spotted owls where they co-occur and compete with closely related barred owls in the Pacific Northwest of the United States. Such changes will become more likely as the effects of climate change unfold.

## WHAT MAKES A SPECIES CONSERVATION RELIANT?

The concept of conservation reliance applies to species whose distribution and/or abundance are declining or are rare or occur in only one or a few locations—species that are vulnerable to extinction. Thus, a need for ongoing management does not by itself make a species conservation reliant. Populations of American elk, for example, may benefit from supplemental feeding during winter, and stocks of trout in mountain lakes are often replenished by releases of hatchery-reared fish. Habitat for migratory waterfowl is created and maintained by state and federal wildlife agencies in many countries.[14] Management of such game species is intended to ensure that populations are maintained at levels sufficient to support recreational hunting and fishing, rather than avoid extinction. Similarly, management of species that damage crops or prey on livestock does not mean that the species is conservation reliant; such management actions are intended to

---

[14] Many National Wildlife Refuges in the United States were established primarily to provide habitat for migratory waterfowl; see www.fws.gov/refuges/history/, although more recently several have been created for specific endangered species; see en.wikipedia.org/wkik/List_of_National_Wildlife_Refuges_established_for_endangered_species.

protect human interests from the species rather than to protect the species from human influences.

Species differ in their susceptibility to threats and their potential to respond to management actions. Species with specialized diets or narrow habitat preferences may be more vulnerable and difficult to manage than generalists. If a target species depends on other species for parts of its life history, those other species (e.g. pollinators, seed dispersers) may also need to be managed. Migratory or nomadic species that move over great distances and occupy different habitats in different places pose different challenges than do species like the golden toad that are resident in a small area. Species with low reproductive rates or short lifespans may respond differently than fecund or long-lived species. Species also differ in their responsiveness to breeding programs; specialized pollinators or animals with more complex social behavior are especially challenging. Achieving sustainable wild populations also depends on the availability of suitable habitat; habitat loss and fragmentation may have driven a species to imperilment in the first place.

Management decisions are also affected by the nature of the threats, how a species responds, and the ability and capacity of management to deal with those threats. Managing a single threat is usually more feasible than addressing multiple threats. Threats are more easily addressed in a restricted area that is ecologically isolated, such as a small island, than in large areas like a continental mainland. Some threats are more important than others; those that could lead to the extinction of a species or forestall its recovery should elicit the most immediate actions. Threats differ in the directness, immediacy, or severity of their impacts. Many conservation success stories involve species that were imperiled by only one or a few threats that could be eliminated. For example, the distribution and abundance of American alligators in southeastern United States and saltwater crocodiles in northern Australia expanded dramatically once the primary threats of hunting and harvesting were tightly regulated.

Additionally, some threats are more amenable to management than others. The local effects of cowbird nest parasitism on imperiled songbirds can be reduced by removing the cowbirds from nesting areas. On the other hand, the widespread threat to many marine invertebrates of increasing ocean acidity cannot be directly or quickly managed. We are then left to consider options for managing the indirect effects and the affected population more locally, although this may not be feasible with widespread and pervasive threats. In these situations, conservation reliance is likely to persist.

Conservation and management operate in complex social, economic, and political contexts. Management decisions depend on the availability of financial and human resources, and the perception of costs, benefits, and risks of actions, especially when human livelihoods are affected. Even if societal commitments to conservation increase, the growing queue of conservation-reliant species will strain resources. Consciously or not, we humans are already making decisions about which species merit attention, where conservation should be focused, and which management approaches may be appropriate.

At this point, an example may help to illustrate the challenges of conservation reliance. There may be no better example than the ongoing saga of the California condor.

## A CASE STUDY: THE CALIFORNIA CONDOR

*Pessimism has long prevailed about the ability of the California condor to survive as man takes more thorough control of the country within its range. The condor can not live with man, some people have said; though harmless, it can not survive the changes brought about by him; it is a passing remnant of the Pleistocene. But through several decades of such an attitude of defeatism the condor has hung on as though to prove it could, yet threatened at every turn with extinction and indeed doomed should a few unfortunate accidents take place and a further invasion of its stronghold is allowed. – Alden Miller, prefacing Koford (1953).*

The California condor (Figure 1.3) has been a focus of conservation activity for nearly a century.[15] Condors are relicts of an earlier age; their fossils have been found in the Pleistocene deposits of the La Brea

---

[15] Detailed treatments of condor conservation are provided by Snyder and Snyder (2000), Walters et al. (2010), and USFWS (2013).

FIGURE 1.3. An Endangered California condor soaring in Bitter Creek National Wildlife Refuge, California. All free-ranging birds are individually marked (note the wing tag) and monitored. (A black and white version of this figure will appear in some formats. For the color version, please refer to the plate section.)
Photo: US Fish and Wildlife Service Pacific Southwest Region.

tar pits of California (Syverson and Prothero 2010). When large herbivores disappeared some 10000 years ago, condors were forced to scavenge elsewhere and their distribution and abundance shrank. Over the last two centuries condors have been confronted by a changing array of new threats—shooting by ranchers who (mistakenly) thought condors preyed on calves; collecting of eggs and adult birds; habitat loss; collisions with power lines; and poisoning from strychnine-laced carcasses used by ranchers to kill animals that harassed or preyed upon their livestock. Coupled with the leisurely reproductive rate of condors (perhaps one chick every 2 years), these threats led the population to wither away. By the mid-twentieth century, condors were restricted to a tiny portion of their former range (Figure 1.4).

The plight of the condor was not ignored. The San Diego Zoo proposed to breed condors in captivity in 1952, but concerns about excessive intervention stymied the program. By the time Carl Koford published the results of his monumental study of condors in 1953, he estimated that only 60 condors remained in the wild. The species was listed as Endangered in 1967. By 1982, only 21 birds remained in the wild. By the summer of 1983, there were 19 condors in the wild, and 15 by 1984. Six birds died in the winter of 1984–1985 alone, leaving 9 by 1985. These losses occurred despite a substantial increase in knowledge since Koford's time about the habitat requirements, behavior, and life history of condors and the threats they faced.

Consultations with geneticists, raptor specialists, zoo biologists, and other experts made it clear that the remaining birds had little chance of surviving in the wild. The only hope of increasing the number of condors lay in establishing a viable captive-breeding population. All remaining birds in the wild would need to be brought into captivity to forestall extinction and increase the chances of future reestablishment of a free-flying condor population.

The decision to bring all remaining condors into captivity created deep divisions among conservationists. Some suggested the condor was "almost certainly doomed" and pleaded that the species be allowed to "die with the dignity that has always been yours" (Pitelka 1981; Stallcup 1981). Others argued for taking the "ultimate risk" of bringing the remaining individuals into captivity, depriving

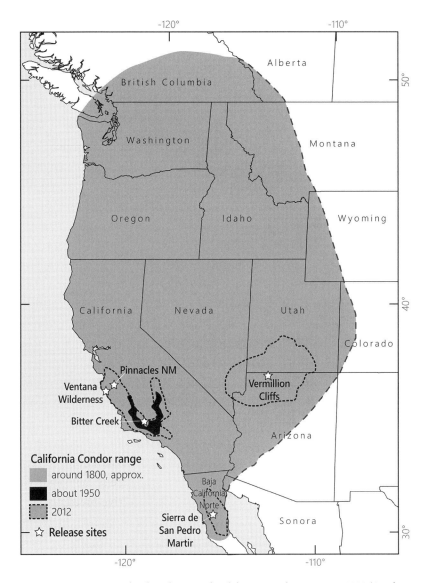

FIGURE 1.4. The distribution of California condors in circa 1800 (Snyder and Snyder 2005), 1950 (Koford 1953), and 2012 (dashed lines, distribution approximate). Captive-reared condors were released at several sites beginning in 1992. From USFWS (2013).

them of their freedom in the interests of saving the species (Ripley 1981). Legal action to prevent taking the last individuals into captivity was rejected by the courts and the last free-flying condor was captured on Hudson Ranch (later to become the Bitter Creek National Wildlife Refuge) on Easter Sunday in 1987. The species was now extinct in the wild.[16]

But would the condors breed in captivity? If they did, how would eggs be incubated and nestlings reared without them imprinting on or habituating to humans? How would juvenile birds be cared for so that they could themselves breed in captivity? Would birds be able to survive and breed in the wild, and what continuing management would be needed?

Ultimately, these challenges were overcome and captive breeding was successful (but expensive). The first captive-reared birds were released back into the wild in January 1992. Additional captive-breeding programs were established and more condors were released in several locations in California, Arizona, and Utah, and in Baja California, Mexico (Figure 1.4). Many of the threats that previously imperiled the species remained, however, and released birds continued to die from lead poisoning, trash ingestion, powerline collisions, shooting, and other causes (Rideout et al. 2012). Rearing and release methods were improved and the number of condors living in the wild gradually increased. At the end of 2017, there were 463 California condors: 290 in the wild and 173 birds still in captivity (Figure 1.5).

This success must be tempered with realism. Although 27 nesting attempts in 2017 successfully fledged 10 young condors, 17 free-flying birds died that year. Natural reproduction is failing to keep ahead of mortality.[17] Condor populations in the wild are

---

[16] The final days of the last wild-living condor were recounted in the March 23, 1987 issue of *Sports Illustrated*; www.si.com/vault/1987/03/23/115061/last-chance-for-the-condor-with-only-one-of-the-species-left-in-the-wild-a-remarkable-bird-struggles-for-survival.

[17] www.fws.gov/cno/es/CalCondor/PDF_files/2017-CA-condor-population-status.pdf

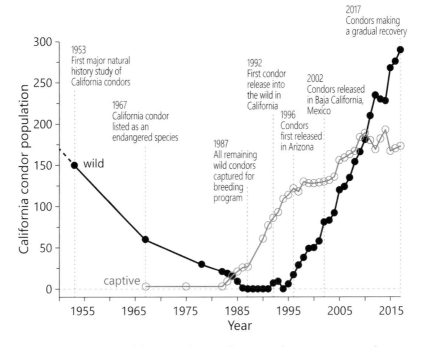

FIGURE 1.5. California condor population trends, 1953–2017. Condor numbers declined precipitously during the 1960s, but numbers have increased in captivity and in the wild as a result of captive breeding and releases since the 1990s. Important events are noted.
Source: US Fish and Wildlife Service data.

maintained almost entirely by continued releases of birds from breeding centers and supplemental feeding. To identify individual condors, each bird is marked with a highly visible number on wing tags (Figure 1.3).

Ensuring the survival of free-living birds requires extraordinary management interventions. Nestling condors are vaccinated against West Nile virus and receive annual booster shots. Nest sites are visited monthly to remove trash and plastics brought in by adults and to check nestlings; if necessary, nestlings are removed for a day to surgically remove ingested trash. Poisoning from lead ammunition fragments remaining in carcasses killed by hunters contributed to the historic decline in condor numbers and continues to be a chronic problem (Finkelstein et al. 2012).[18] To counter this threat, birds must be captured annually or semiannually to be treated with chelation or surgery to remove ingested lead particles. In 2007, California enacted the Ridley-Tree Condor Preservation Act,[19] which banned the use of lead ammunition within the California range of the condor. Subsequent legislation in 2013 extended the ban statewide (to be fully implemented by 2019).[20] Enforcement, however, has been difficult. A 5-year review of the status of the condor (USFWS 2013) concluded "condors would not survive in the wild if they were not regularly trapped, tested, and treated for lead exposure." Condors are not yet outpatients; they still require intensive care. Even so, condor management is gradually shifting from a focus on individual birds to an emphasis on populations. Supplemental feeding and clinical treatment of birds for lead poisoning are being scaled back and the savings are being applied to bolster efforts to reduce the use of lead ammunition and increase the numbers of captive birds released into the wild.

These efforts come at considerable expense. In 1997, it was reported that some US$20 million had been spent on the condor. At that time, it was anticipated that by 2015 another US$30 million would have been spent, by which time it was hoped that the condor could downlisted. As of 2019, however, the condor was still listed as Endangered under the Endangered Species Act and Critically

---

[18] From the first releases of captive-bred birds into the wild in 1992 until the end of 2012, 42 of the 123 (34%) condor deaths where a cause was known were from lead poisoning, more than twice the next highest cause of death (predation) (Rideout et al. 2012). Five of the 15 recorded deaths of birds in the wild during 2016 were associated with lead poisoning.

[19] www.leginfo.ca.gov/pub/07-08/bill/asm/ab_0801-0850/ab_821_bill_20070910_enrolled.html

[20] A similar ban on the use of lead ammunition on US National Wildlife Refuges was overturned by the newly installed Secretary of the Interior on his first day in office in 2017. Laws and regulations are vulnerable to politics.

Endangered by IUCN. Efforts to track, feed, capture, treat, and release birds are becoming more costly, raising concerns about the long-term sustainability of the captive-breeding-release program.

There are several broader lessons of the condor story. One is that selecting one species for intensive conservation efforts can have consequences for other vulnerable species. During the time that millions of dollars were being spent to bring the condors back, eight species of Hawaiian birds disappeared and another, the 'alalā (Hawaiian crow), became extinct in the wild. An unknown number of invertebrates and plants in Hawai'i have also become extinct. These choices have not been made deliberately or even knowingly, but they were choices nonetheless. Conservation involves value judgments, whether they are made consciously or not.

The story of the California condor also shows what can be done when there is public support and cooperation between government agencies and the private sector and dedicated individuals take on the challenge. Public support for conservation is much more likely for iconic species such as condors—or bald eagles, giant pandas, or tigers—than for plants or for small or "insignificant" species such as slugs or worms or lice (Box 1.1).[21] Commercially valuable or recreationally important species, such as salmon, attract far greater attention and funding than species with little apparent value, such as the snail darter or Delta smelt that we discuss later in this book.

---

[21] Thus, although invertebrates comprise 75% of the estimated number of described species in the world, they account for only 11.6% of the species listed under the Endangered Species Act (ecos.fws.gov/ecp0/reports/box-score-report) and 22% of the taxa included on the IUCN Red List (cmsdocs.s3.amazonaws.com/summarystats/2017-1_Summary_Stats_Page_Documents/2017_1_RL_Stats_Table_1.pdf).

---

BOX 1.1. **The Fate of the California Condor Louse**

Seemingly "insignificant" species rarely attract attention, so few mourn (or are even aware of) their passing. This is especially true for parasites, which are often viewed with distain. Most species support a community of parasites, some of which are endemic to their host species. If the host becomes extinct, so also do the parasites. This is referred to as "co-extinction" (Koh et al. 2004).

Even if the host species is saved, the parasites may still be lost. Such was the fate of the California condor louse, a species of feather louse that parasitized only California condors. In keeping with captive-breeding practices, when the wild condors were brought into captivity they were treated with pesticides. In the process, the last remaining condor lice were eradicated. The California condor louse is now extinct. The condors may not miss the lice, which caused them no harm. Whether we, as conservationists, should be concerned about their passing is a matter of values and ethics.

---

The condor represents an extreme case of conservation reliance, but not all conservation-reliant species require such massive management interventions. Depending on which pathways are followed (Figure 1.2), conservation reliance can take a variety of forms, as we will see next.

# 2   The Conservation Spectrum

The California condor is on the road to recovery. It's a torturous, twisting road, paved with extraordinary management interventions and with no end in sight.

Many other species will require management for a very long time. These are conservation-reliant species—and there are many of them. Not all conservation-reliant species require such massive management interventions as the condor, however. Whether or not a species is conservation reliant depends on the species, the threats, and numerous other factors. These factors affect which of the pathways depicted in Figure 1.2 are taken. They also determine the intensity and cost of management necessary for conservation.

It is useful to think of conservation as a spectrum (Figure 2.1). The spectrum is bounded by two outcomes: species that are no longer imperiled—they are self-sustaining in the wild and are no longer conservation reliant—and extinction. In between are various degrees of conservation reliance. These species range from those that require only occasional management interventions to those that are constantly dependent on human interventions for survival and known to occur only in captivity.[1] For conservation-reliant species that still occur in the wild, management may include regular monitoring, population supplementation from captive-bred or nursery stocks,[2] translocations, supplemental feeding, medical intervention, control of competitors or predators, habitat management, genetic

---

[1] Redford et al. (2011) use the terms "lightly managed" and "heavily managed."
[2] We use "captivity" or "captive breeding" as shorthand to include maintaining or propagating plants in nurseries.

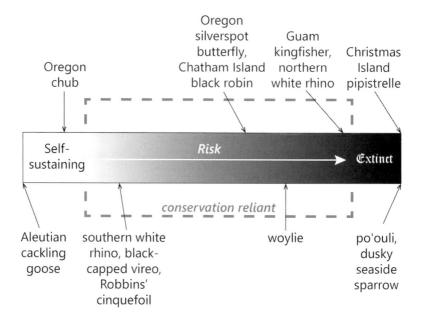

FIGURE 2.1. Conservation can be thought of as a spectrum bounded by two outcomes: species that are no longer imperiled, and extinction. In between are various conservation-reliant species, including the 13 shown in this figure that are presented as case studies in this chapter. Species inside the dashed box are conservation reliant.

manipulation, or other actions. These actions differ in their cost and probability of success and species may move from one position on the spectrum to another depending on the effectiveness of management actions, environmental changes, or the emergence of new threats.[3]

To illustrate points along this conservation spectrum, we tell the stories of the species mentioned in Figure 2.1 and depicted in Figures 2.2–2.14. Let's begin with the most encouraging end of the spectrum: successful emergence from conservation reliance.

[3] The conservation spectrum is a gradient of dependence of species on management interventions; similar gradients could be used to show risks of extinction, as in the IUCN categories (Extinct to Least Concern).

## THREATS ARE MITIGATED AND THE SPECIES RECOVERS

When conservation efforts reduce the factors that threaten a species to a point where the threats no longer impede recovery and the population becomes self-sustaining in the wild, the species no longer needs targeted management and is no longer conservation reliant. This is the story of the **Oregon chub** (Figure 2.2).

The Oregon chub is a small, minnow-like fish endemic to the Willamette Valley of western Oregon. Historically, the chub occurred in a variety of floodplains, side channels, sloughs, and slow-moving backwaters. However, dams and channelization altered the hydrodynamics of the river, non-native predator and competitor fish moved into the remaining habitat, and chemical contamination from agriculture and timber harvesting affected water quality. By 1993, there were

FIGURE 2.2. An Oregon chub. The chub was declared recovered and removed from the US endangered species list in 2015. (A black and white version of this figure will appear in some formats. For the color version, please refer to the plate section.)
Photo: Rick Swart, Oregon Department of Fish and Game.

fewer than a thousand individuals occurring in only a few known locations and the chub was listed as Endangered under the Endangered Species Act.

As often happens, listing prompted increased research and field studies. New surveys led to the discovery of several previously unknown populations. Chub were also introduced at several locations on privately owned property, whose landowners established long-term conservation easements under the US Wetland Reserve Program.

These measures were a resounding success. By 2013, nearly 160 000 chub occurred at 77 locations. The primary threats (contaminated water, invasive predators, and competitors) had been mitigated and the species was abundant and well distributed throughout much of its historical range. In 2015, the Oregon chub became the first fish to be removed from the endangered species list due to recovery rather than to extinction.[4]

One of the stated recovery criteria, however, was that management "must be guaranteed in perpetuity" (USFWS 1998: 27–28). This sounds a lot like what we mean by conservation reliance. However, because the needs of the chub are met by existing management practices and regulations that are likely to continue into the foreseeable future, no additional management is required specifically for the chub. The species is no longer conservation reliant.

Is it possible for recovery efforts to be *too* successful, to move a species from conservation reliance to requiring control? **Aleutian cackling geese** (Figure 2.3) were once abundant, breeding throughout the Aleutian Archipelago and wintering in the Pacific Northwest. During the eighteenth and nineteenth centuries, however, fur traders introduced Arctic foxes on many islands in the Aleutians. Geese and their eggs and goslings were easy prey and their numbers plummeted. By the middle of the twentieth century the goose was thought to be extinct. However, a population of a few hundred birds was discovered in 1962 on a remote island in the Aleutians. The species was listed

---

[4] Federal Register 80 FR 9219: 9125–9150.

FIGURE 2.3 The Aleutian cackling goose, a species once thought extinct, has recovered to become an agricultural pest. (A black and white version of this figure will appear in some formats. For the color version, please refer to the plate section.)
Photo: Elizabeth Neipert, ERDC, US Army.

under a precursor to the Endangered Species Act in 1967 and a recovery plan was drafted. Translocations of wild birds, removal of foxes from breeding islands, closure of hunting seasons in California and Oregon, habitat protection through agreements with landowners, and establishment of wildlife refuges to manage foraging areas on the wintering and migration areas resulted in a dramatic increase in the goose population. The recovery goal of 7500 birds was quickly surpassed and the species was delisted in 2001.

Goose numbers continued to increase. By 2011, the population was estimated at nearly 112 000 birds. Well before that, it had become apparent that grazing by the thousands of geese gathering at spring migratory stopover areas in California and Oregon was damaging newly emerging pasture grass and crop vegetation. Birds roosting overnight on offshore islands were degrading habitat in seabird breeding colonies. To protect their lands, landowners began hazing birds to drive them off their fields. An Agricultural Depredation Plan to address the goose problem replaced the recovery plan (Mini and LeValley 2006; Mini et al. 2011). There is now a hunting season. These measures have reduced pressures on private lands by shifting the geese onto nearby public lands. The current objective is to maintain a population of 60 000 birds, but even with control and hunting, reducing the population to this level will be difficult. In 2018, the population was estimated at over 171 000 birds and had been growing by approximately 8% each year for a decade.[5] A species once thought extinct and then struggling to survive has, in the space of 50 years, become an agricultural pest.

## SPECIES IS MAINTAINED OR INCREASES IN THE WILD WITH MANAGEMENT

Short of full recovery, the most satisfying conservation outcome is when an imperiled species responds to management and populations stabilize or increase. A species may increase to a point where it can be considered legally recovered and no longer requires the protection of specific legislation. Even then, however, the species may require continuing management to prevent it from backsliding into imperilment. Here are three stories that describe variations on this theme.

The **southern white rhinoceros** (Figure 2.4)[6] was thought to be extinct in the late nineteenth century, but a small population was discovered in Kwazulu-Natal, South Africa, in 1895. South Africa and several international groups developed a management plan and helped establish multiple populations on public and private properties. The management plan included incentives to maintain populations for selective trophy hunting, which entailed breeding to enhance traits desired by trophy hunters, moving rhinoceroses from one population to another at least once a generation to maintain genetic diversity,

---

[5] www.fws.gov/migratorybirds/pdf/surveys-and-data/Population-status/Waterfowl/WaterfowlPopulationStatusReport18.pdf

[6] We'll tell the story of its sister species, the northern white rhino, later in this chapter.

FIGURE 2.4. An adult southern white rhinoceros and calf, considered Near Threatened by IUCN. (A black and white version of this figure will appear in some formats. For the color version, please refer to the plate section.) Photo: Renauld Fulconis, Awely.

and establishing a commercial market for taking, viewing, and photographing rhinoceroses. Although one can debate whether this husbandry has produced a domesticated version of the rhinoceroses, these activities have become a major source of funding for ongoing management, which involves extensive fencing to keep populations secure. The species was listed as Near Threatened by the IUCN in 2002, with an acknowledgment that continuing management intervention will be needed if that status is to be maintained. In 2016, the overall population numbered around 20 000 individuals.

Poaching for the illegal trade in rhinoceros horns remains a significant threat. Poaching declined in South Africa from the hundreds that were killed in the mid-twentieth century to a low of 13 in 2007. As the demand for rhinoceros horn increased in recent years, however, poaching has become more sophisticated. It is financed by highly organized international gangs using automatic weapons, helicopters, satellite radio communications, and bribes—what Lunstrum (2014) calls "green militarization." Rhinoceros kills by poachers reached 1000 in 2013 and have remained at that annual level.[7]

South Africa has responded by mobilizing a well-equipped and well-trained force of armed rangers to seek out poachers and protect the rhinoceroses. As long as economic growth in China and Southeast Asia creates more wealth, demand for rhinoceros horn will remain high and buyers will continue to reward illegal poaching. The southern white rhinoceros is likely to remain conservation reliant until the threat of poaching and the demand that drives it are abated.

Our second story is about the **black-capped vireo**, a small, strikingly colored songbird (Figure 2.5). The vireo breeds in parts of Oklahoma, Texas, and northern and western Mexico and migrates to Mexico's Pacific coast during winter (Grzybowski 1995; Smith et al. 2012).[8] Historically, fires maintained its woody and scrubland breeding habitats. During the mid-twentieth century, vegetation succession resulting from fire suppression, disturbance by grazing and browsing livestock, and conversion of breeding habitat to development and agriculture led to habitat loss. Nest parasitism by brownheaded cowbirds further threatened the species. By the 1980s, the population in over half of the known breeding range was greatly reduced and confined to small pockets; brood parasitism by cowbirds was very high. Only 350 individuals were located in a range-wide search.

The species was listed as Endangered under the Endangered Species Act in 1987. Federal, state, military, and non-governmental organizations (NGOs) and private landowners launched an intensive

---

[7] www.savetherhino.org/rhino_info/rhino_population_figures/

[8] A personal digression: John Wiens well remembers accompanying Jean Graber as an aspiring young birdwatcher on one of her trips to the field in central Oklahoma as she conducted her PhD studies on black-capped vireos (Graber 1961). The birds were common in the right habitat, and their melodious songs and tidy hanging nests were delightful to behold. It all made a lasting impression, one of the building blocks of a subsequent career as an ornithologist, ecologist, and conservationist.

FIGURE 2.5. The black-capped vireo, formerly listed as Endangered, was removed from the endangered species list in 2018, although the species remains conservation reliant. (A black and white version of this figure will appear in some formats. For the color version, please refer to the plate section.)
Photo: Joe Grzybowski/US Army.

management program to protect and recover the vireo. The two primary threats, habitat loss and cowbird parasitism, were addressed through prescribed burning to enhance habitat and trapping of cowbirds to reduce the incidence of nest parasitism.

These management actions were effective. The population stopped declining and vireos returned to portions of their historic range. By 2014, vireos occurred in multiple populations, of which the five largest (four of which are on wildlife-management areas or US military installations) supported more than 14 000 adult male vireos. By 2018, the vireo had met all recovery goals and regulatory assurances were in place to deal with continuing threats; the species was delisted in May 2018. It is still covered by the US Migratory Bird Treaty Act.

Does delisting mean that the black-capped vireo is no longer conservation reliant? Although the threats of habitat loss and cowbird parasitism continue, they have been reduced in magnitude by collaborative conservation actions. The US Fish and Wildlife's delisting proposal acknowledged, "[It] is likely that conservation actions, in the form of habitat and cowbird management, are needed for persistence of breeding populations in a portion of its range."[9] Habitat management through prescribed burning is likely to continue for a variety of purposes unrelated to black-capped vireo management, particularly on the publicly managed areas where most of the vireos currently breed. Given the high incidence of cowbird parasitism prior to the initiation of control programs (more than 90% in some areas of Texas; Grzybowski 1991), dealing with the threat posed by cowbirds is essential. A subsequent proposal[10] acknowledged the need for continuing cowbird control through a cooperative management agreement with multiple partners. The black-capped vireo has met recovery goals, but it is still conservation reliant.

Our third story shows how a species can be very close to self-sufficiency but still be conservation reliant. **Robbins' cinquefoil** (Figure 2.6)[11] is a small perennial plant that occurs only above the tree line in the White Mountains of New Hampshire. It was rare when discovered in the early nineteenth century, but it had the misfortune to grow alongside the Crawford Path, one of the oldest and most

---

[9] 50 CFR Part 17; Federal Register 81 (241): 90762-90771, December 15, 2016.

[10] 50 CFR Part 17: Federal Register 83: 11162-11164, March 14, 2018.

[11] Details are given in the final delisting document: Federal Register / Vol. 67, No. 166 / Tuesday, August 27, 2002 / Rules and Regulations: 54968-54975; ecos.fws.gov/docs/federal_register/fr3937.pdf

FIGURE 2.6. Robbins' cinquefoil, originally listed as Endangered, was declared recovered and delisted in 2002. It remains conservation reliant. (A black and white version of this figure will appear in some formats. For the color version, please refer to the plate section.)
Photo: US Fish and Wildlife Service.

heavily traveled mountain trails in the eastern United States. Over the years, plant collectors removed some plants, but the main impact on the plants and their habitat came from foot traffic on the trail. By the early 1970s, only a few thousand individuals remained, most of them in a single 0.4-ha area. The species was designated as Endangered under the Endangered Species Act in 1980 and management and restoration efforts were soon initiated under a partnership between federal agencies and public non-profit organizations. The Crawford Path was relocated, the main population was fenced off, and a viewing garden was created to allow hikers to see the plant without disturbing its habitat. Plants were propagated and transplanted to establish two additional populations.

These efforts paid off. The plants thrived and, in 2002, the species became the first plant to be removed from the endangered species list. There are now more than 14 000 plants growing in the wild. Since delisting, private organizations have stepped in to ensure that the viewing garden and the enclosure that protects the main population are maintained, as foot traffic remains a persistent threat. Nursery propagation, transplanting, and monitoring continue. With delisting of the species, the most intensive management wound down, but it has not stopped and the cinquefoil remains conservation reliant.

## RELEASES FROM CAPTIVITY OR TRANSLOCATIONS SUSTAIN A SPECIES IN THE WILD

The goal of captive-breeding programs is to be able to re-establish populations in the wild so that they become self-sustaining. Translocations of individuals to new areas serve a similar purpose. Both approaches are difficult, expensive, and require a long-term commitment, so they are usually a last resort in species recovery programs (Snyder et al. 1996). In some cases, however, they can be hugely effective.

Butterflies are particularly good candidates for captive breeding. Although their multi-stage development requires careful husbandry, the techniques of rearing lepidopterans are well established. Even so, successfully re-establishing populations in the wild is challenging, especially for a species with a spotty distribution.

Historically, the **Oregon silverspot butterfly** (Figure 2.7) occurred in a narrow band along the Pacific coast of Oregon, barely extending into Washington and California. Populations were patchily distributed in salt-spray meadows and stabilized vegetated dunes close to the shoreline or in similar montane grasslands a few kilometers inland. The larvae feed exclusively on leaves of the early blue (hookedspur) violet, which further restricts suitable habitat.

Given its distribution and habitat preferences, the species was probably never abundant. Numbers declined to perilously low levels in recent decades as suitable habitat was lost to development and disturbed by off-road vehicles, livestock grazing, and altered fire regimes. Habitat underwent succession to brush and woodland (Black and Vaughan 2005). The silverspot was listed as a Threatened species under the Endangered Species Act in 1980. It is now found in only five locations.

FIGURE 2.7. The Oregon silverspot butterfly is listed as Threatened under the Endangered Species Act. (A black and white version of this figure will appear in some formats. For the color version, please refer to the plate section.)
Photo: NatPar Collection/Alamy.

Recovery of the butterfly relies in part on managing the habitat. In the absence of grazing by wildlife (primarily American elk) and the occasional wildfires that maintained open coastal prairie habitat in the past, active management (mowing and controlled burning) is needed to keep succession at bay. Human access to areas of critical habitat has been restricted to reduce disturbances, and native violets are planted to enhance larval food sources. However, these measures have not been sufficient to stabilize the populations.

In 1999, a conservation NGO, a college, and two zoos began a collaborative captive-rearing program.[12] Each year a small number of wild female silverspots are provided to the zoos, which care for the

_____

[12] As an additional partner in the collaboration, Pelican Brewing, in Pacific City, OR, donates a portion of its proceeds from sales of its Silverspot IPA to the conservation efforts.

eggs and caterpillars through their development to pupae and then release them back into the wild. Captive rearing and releases will need to continue in order to stabilize and increase the populations, but the efforts have forestalled the likely extinction of the butterfly from several locations. Additional conservation efforts are underway: in 2017 and 2018, silverspots were translocated and reintroduced to two natural areas in northwest Oregon, and The Nature Conservancy (TNC) and US Fish and Wildlife Service are working with private landowners to connect protected areas by restoring silverspot habitat on their properties.

Translocations of individuals are often used when a species is imperiled by threats that cannot be controlled in one place but another similar habitat is available that lacks those threats. Translocation has been particularly useful when dealing with threats posed by predators such as rats or cats on islands (Fischer and Lindenmayer 2000; Seddon 2010), as in the case of the **Chatham Island black robin** (Figure 2.8) (Butler and Merton 1992).

A small songbird endemic to the Chatham Island group of New Zealand, Chatham Island black robins are vulnerable to predation by introduced rats and cats. By the late nineteenth century, the species occurred only on Little Mangere Island. Habitat loss and continuing predation further reduced its numbers; only seven birds remained by 1976. These individuals were captured and moved to predator-free Mangere Island. The five individuals still alive in 1980 included one breeding pair. By cross-fostering eggs and young from this pair with a similar species,[13] robin reproduction was enhanced and the population slowly increased. Attempts to establish populations in predator-free areas on other islands in the Chatham group have met with varying success, but by 2013 there were over 250 black robins on two islands.

---

[13] Eggs were taken from first-brood nests of the robins to replace those of a similar species, the Chatham Island tomtit, which incubated the robin eggs and raised the nestlings to fledging. The black robins re-nested with a second brood, roughly doubling their reproductive output.

FIGURE 2.8. The Chatham Island black robin is considered Endangered by the IUCN. (A black and white version of this figure will appear in some formats. For the color version, please refer to the plate section.)
Photo: Leon Berard.

As the black robin population began to recover, however, some females started laying eggs on the rims of nests. These "rim eggs" failed to hatch, but when the eggs were placed back inside nests they produced offspring. Yet the frequency of laying rim eggs in the population continued to increase. Analyses revealed that laying rim eggs was a heritable trait, so by repositioning the eggs and allowing them to hatch, investigators were inadvertently promoting the spread of a maladaptive trait in the population. When repositioning rim eggs was stopped, natural selection was allowed to do its job and the frequency of rim eggs in the population rapidly declined (Massaro et al. 2013). In this instance, a well-intentioned management intervention was actually increasing the need for more intervention.

Although the Chatham Island black robin is still regarded as Endangered by IUCN, intensive management (including a halt on repositioning rim eggs) has mitigated the threats in some areas and brought the species back from the brink of extinction. Management continues, with the aim of reintroducing the species to other islands, including returning it to Little Mangere Island. Because introduced predators, competitors, or pathogens can wreak havoc on island ecosystems, however, monitoring to detect invasive species must continue, along with a rapid response should such species appear.[14] The robin is recovering but remains conservation reliant.

## SPECIES DECREASES IN THE WILD DESPITE MANAGEMENT EFFORTS

In some instances, management of wild populations does not sufficiently mitigate the threats (or new threats emerge) and the species continues to decline. **Woylie**s (brush-tailed bettongs; Figure 2.9) are small nocturnal Australian macropods.[15] At the time of European colonization, they were widespread over much of the continent and occurred in a variety of habitats. By the 1920s, however, the species was extirpated over most of its former range, largely as a result of clearing of land for agriculture, grazing by introduced livestock, and predation by introduced red foxes. Numbers continued to plummet and by the 1970s it had become one of Australia's rarest mammals, occurring in only a few remnant habitats in Western Australia. The IUCN listed the species as Endangered in 1982.

Subsequent conservation efforts focused on trapping and poisoning red foxes, protecting a few areas with predator-proof fences, and reintroducing woylies to fox-free areas. Woylie populations responded dramatically and the species was removed from threatened species lists in 1996. By the turn of the century, population estimates ranged from 40 000 to as many as 225 000—lots of woylies. So far, so good.

But the success was short-lived. The population crashed in 2001, dropping by as much as 90%. The species was relisted as

---

[14] Nest predation by introduced European starlings is now the major threat, although there is evidence that black robins that have suffered nest predation can adjust their nest-site selection in subsequent breeding attempts to reduce predation risk (Lawrence et al. 2017).

[15] Marsupial mammals, such as kangaroos and wallabies.

FIGURE 2.9. The woylie (brush-tailed bettong) is considered Critically Endangered by the IUCN. (A black and white version of this figure will appear in some formats. For the color version, please refer to the plate section.)

Photo: © Wayne Lawler/AWC.

Critically Endangered by IUCN in 2008. The reversal in the woylie's fortunes was almost certainly due to a new threat from feral cats, whose numbers increased as red foxes decreased with extensive and ongoing conservation efforts (Wayne et al. 2015, 2017). Controlling one threat allowed another to emerge. Since 2008, woylies have been translocated to several fenced areas. Numbers are again increasing, but the species requires continuing management.

## SPECIES IS EXTINCT IN THE WILD BUT IS MAINTAINED IN CAPTIVITY

Acrimonious political, cultural, and legal battles are often waged about the need, wisdom, ethics, and legality of removing individuals of an imperiled species from the wild to prevent its extinction.

FIGURE 2.10. Armed rangers keeping watch over Sudan. Until he died in 2018, Sudan was the world's last male northern white rhinoceros. (A black and white version of this figure will appear in some formats. For the color version, please refer to the plate section.)
Credit: Martin Harvey/Gallo Images/Getty Images Plus.

Nonetheless, protecting the few remaining individuals in zoos or preserves may be a way to buy time while exploring how to rescue a species.

The story of the **northern white rhinoceros** in Africa is starkly different from that of the southern white rhinoceros (Knight et al. 2015).[16] Historically, the northern white rhinoceros (Figure 2.10) occurred in several countries in east and central Africa south of the Sahara. In the 1960s, some 2300 northern white rhinoceroses

---

[16] The two white rhinoceroses were until recently considered sister subspecies. Groves et al. (2010) presented genetic and morphological evidence to support their proposal that the two be recognized as separate species. Their results are not universally accepted and IUCN continues to treat the northern and southern white rhinoceroses as subspecies. Given the status of the northern white rhino, the argument is largely academic.

lived in the wild. By the 1980s, poaching had decimated the population and only 15 individuals remained, all in Garamba National
Park in the Democratic Republic of the Congo. The species was
declared Critically Endangered by IUCN in 1996. Subsequent conservation efforts in the Park doubled the population, but then
nearby armed conflicts and rampant poaching resulted in a catastrophic decline in the population. Only four animals could be
found in 2004 and the last wild rhinoceros was reported in 2006.
Although captive northern white rhinoceroses had been held in
zoos (with limited breeding success) for several decades, by
2016 only one male and two females (both descendants of the male)
remained in captivity, none capable of breeding. The species was
extinct in the wild. When the male (Sudan) died in March 2018 at
the age of 45, the northern white rhinoceros became extinct for all
practical purposes.

Some still hope to rescue the northern white rhinoceros. An
international consortium of veterinarians has proposed using novel
stem-cell technology, *in-vitro* fertilization, and embryo implants in
female southern white rhinoceroses to resurrect reproduction (Callaway 2016; Saragusty et al. 2016). Restricting conservation efforts to
sperm and eggs from the northern population would create a genetically pure but highly inbred northern white rhinoceros population. For
this and other reasons, this proposal has generated considerable controversy (Callaway 2016).

Other species have not been so unlucky. In some situations,
captive breeding has rescued a species from the brink of extinction—
but still fallen short of re-establishing the species. This brings us to
the story of the **Guam kingfisher**. It is also Mike Scott's story, so we'll
begin there.

In early 1981, Mike and his colleagues had just completed the
Hawaiian Forest Bird Survey, a 7-year census of some of the world
rarest birds—the kāma'o (large Kaua'i thrush), nukupu'u, and Kaua'i
'ō'ō—all with populations estimated to be fewer than 100 individuals.
That information was used to develop new management approaches

and set priorities for conservation of Hawai'i's endangered forest birds
and habitats (Scott et al. 1986). A short time later, Mike and three
colleagues went to Guam to meet with the Guam Department of
Agriculture Division of Aquatic and Wildlife Resources to discuss
possibilities of using the same methods to assess population sizes of
the forest birds of Guam.

Guam is a heavily forested, 54900-ha tropical island in the
Central Pacific that is in some ways similar to Hawai'i. Guam was
once home to 14 native forest birds (including two endemic species
and five endemic subspecies), including the Guam kingfisher
(Figure 2.11). For unknown reasons, the kingfisher and other birds of
Guam were declining rapidly. Mike and his colleagues hoped that a

FIGURE 2.11. A male Guam kingfisher, listed as Endangered under the
Endangered Species Act. (A black and white version of this figure will
appear in some formats. For the color version, please refer to the plate
section.)
Photo: Eric Savage/Creative Commons.

census of the birds of Guam could provide information to help determine what caused those declines and suggest possible management
responses and priorities for action.

Later that year, a survey of birds on the northern end of the
Island estimated more than 3000 Guam kingfishers—many more than
had been expected. It seemed that there might still be time to save the
kingfisher and perhaps many of the other imperiled forest birds
of Guam.

This hope was soon shattered. The kingfisher and three other
Guam forest birds were listed as Endangered in 1984. One year later,
4 years after completion of the bird survey, there were only 56 kingfishers left in the forests of Guam. Three years after that, Guam
kingfishers were extinct in the wild.

The primary cause of the decline and eventual loss of the
Guam kingfisher in the wild was predation by the brown tree snake,
a species native to parts of Australia, Indonesia, New Guinea and
adjacent archipelagos, and the Solomon Islands (Savidge 1987). The
snakes had probably arrived on Guam after World War II on cargo
ships, and they quickly spread throughout the island. The snakes
have had severe effects on 17 of the 18 native birds on Guam;
12 species have been extirpated (Wiles et al. 2003). One endemic
species, the Guam flycatcher, was last seen in 1985 and is now
thought to be extinct; another, the Guam rail, is now extinct in the
wild.[17]

But all has not been lost. In 1984–1986, just before the kingfisher went extinct in the wild, a collaborative effort between Guam
Department of Fish and Aquatic Resources and the Association of
Zoos and Aquariums captured 22 kingfishers and sent them to
17 cooperating institutions. These birds became the founding parents
of multiple insurance populations for the kingfisher. By 2016, there
were 146 individuals in those populations. Unfortunately, those institutions were at their full capacity to raise and maintain kingfishers

---

[17] www.guampedia.com/a-native-forest-birds-of-guam/

and the populations were facing a bottleneck forced by limited space. It was time to begin returning kingfishers to the wild if they were to have a chance for survival.

Multiple groups drafted conservation plans and provided guidance for management actions to restore kingfishers to their island home. Everyone agreed that the brown tree snake would have to be eliminated from the areas where the birds were to be reintroduced. The biggest challenge, however, was the inability to scale up management actions to match the scale of the threat. Small, snake-proof plots would not allow the kingfisher adequate space to thrive. Because they were unable to eradicate brown tree snakes from fenced areas large enough to sustain a viable population of kingfishers, researchers turned their attention to other, snake-free islands in the Central Pacific as possible sites for translocations.

Cocos Island, a short distance offshore of Guam, is one possibility. A similar effort there involving the Guam rail is having some success. However, Cocos Island is small and can support only a few pairs of kingfishers. A recent assessment of 239 Central Pacific islands to identify possible new homes for the Guam kingfisher found five islands to have suitable ecological conditions to sustain a viable population (Laws and Kesler 2012). It remains to be seen whether birds will be moved to one or more of those islands from insurance populations in North America and Guam. Currently, funds are insufficient to conduct and follow up on such introduction efforts.

Meanwhile, work continues to find a way to eradicate the brown tree snakes.

### WHEN CONSERVATION EFFORTS COME TOO LATE

Unlike several Hawaiian forest bird species that have gone extinct owing to neglect, the plight of the **po'ouli** (black-faced honeycreeper) (Figure 2.12) was recognized and it did receive needed management attention, but too late to save it from extinction (Powell 2008).

The po'ouli was one of many species of Hawaiian honeycreeper. When it was first discovered in the Ko'olau Forest Reserve on Maui in

FIGURE 2.12. The extinct po'ouli. (A black and white version of this figure will appear in some formats. For the color version, please refer to the plate section.)
Photo: Paul E. Baker, US Fish and Wildlife Service.

1973, there were perhaps 200 individuals. Despite its rapid listing as Endangered under the Endangered Species Act, the population declined by over 90% through the mid-1980s owing to habitat loss (particularly due to feral pigs), mosquito-borne disease, predation by introduced mammals, and a decline in the tree snails that it favored for food. In 1986, the state established Hanawi Natural Area Reserve, a 3030-ha area centered on the site at which the po'ouli was known to occur. Management efforts were delayed by inadequate funding and bureaucratic inertia, but a pig-free exclosure was built in 1989, and the first fenced parcel was ungulate free by 1992. By 2000, the entire reserve was pig free (although removal of rats and cats continued). By then, however, only three po'ouli were known to exist. Last-minute efforts to establish a captive-breeding program failed. The last bird died in 2004 and the species has not been seen since. It was declared extinct in 2005 (Elphick et al. 2010), although it remains listed as Critically Endangered by IUCN.

A similar story can be told about the **dusky seaside sparrow** (Figure 2.13), although in this case recovery efforts were overwhelmed by human actions that hastened the species' demise. Dusky seaside

FIGURE 2.13. The extinct dusky seaside sparrow. (A black and white version of this figure will appear in some formats. For the color version, please refer to the plate section.)
Photo: P.W. Sykes, US Fish and Wildlife Service.

sparrows were restricted to *Spartina* salt marshes on Merritt Island and along the St. Johns River in Florida, and consequently were particularly vulnerable to habitat loss (Sykes 1980; Walters 2007). Populations were already declining in the late 1950s, largely as a result of the aerial spraying of insecticides to control mosquitoes. Although spraying was reduced in the 1960s, it was not stopped. At Merritt Island, management for mosquito control replaced the marshes with open ponds, destroying sparrow habitat. Management and agricultural practices also disrupted the wet–dry seasonality to which the birds were attuned. The sparrows nested near the ground during the spring–summer rainy season when the marshes flooded shallowly. When flows in the St. Johns River were reduced by upriver irrigation diversions for agriculture, much of the marsh area remained dry except during wet years. Upland predators such as snakes and mammals then had access to sparrow nests, reducing recruitment. The dry marshes were also susceptible to fires used to improve nearby pastures for cattle, causing additional habitat loss. To provide additional habitat for the sparrows, a reserve was established in a nearby marsh, but construction of a highway through that marsh and its subsequent drainage for real-estate development left little remaining habitat.

By 1979, only six dusky seaside sparrows were known to exist, all of them males.[18] Attempts to use crossbreeding to recreate the subspecies through progressive hybridization with females of a closely related subspecies ran afoul of legal interpretations of what "species" and "subspecies" mean in the context of the Endangered Species Act (James 1980) and the program was stopped. In 1983, the four remaining birds were taken to a reserve at the Walt Disney World Resort, where the last individual died in 1987.

## WHEN NO CONSERVATION ACTION IS TAKEN

Perhaps the most distressing conservation stories are those where it is known that a species is rapidly declining and is on the brink of extinction, but nothing is done. This is the fate that befell the **Christmas Island pipistrelle** (Figure 2.14), a small insectivorous bat that was historically widespread and abundant on Christmas Island (Woinarski 2018).

Christmas Island is a 135-km$^2$ Australian territory in the Indian Ocean, 350 km from Java and Sumatra and 1550 km from the Australian mainland. As is often the case on isolated oceanic islands,

---

[18] The assumption that for each singing male there was also a female proved to be unfounded. The final efforts to save the species in the wild are chronicled in a US Fish and Wildlife Service Endangered Species Technical Report, available at www.fws.gov/endangered/news/pdf/1980%20Apr%20Special%20Report.pdf.

FIGURE 2.14. The extinct Christmas Island pipistrelle. (A black and white version of this figure will appear in some formats. For the color version, please refer to the plate section.)
Photo: Lindy Lumsden.

endemic species evolve and they often then disappear. Christmas Island, for example, once had five endemic mammal species. Four of these are likely now extinct. Maclear's rat and the bulldog rat became extinct early in the twentieth century and the Christmas Island shrew was last seen in 1985. The Christmas Island pipistrelle joined this gallery of extinctions in 2009.[19]

Perhaps if action had been taken, the pipistrelle might have survived, but numbers began to drop rapidly starting in the 1980s. Monitoring devices used to detect the bat's ultrasonic echolocation calls documented a 90% decline in abundance between 1994 and 2006, along with a further retraction in distribution (Lumsden et al. 2010). The pipistrelle was listed as Endangered under Australian legislation in 2001 and a recovery plan was drafted; the species' status

[19] The remaining endemic mammal, the Christmas Island flying fox, is listed as Critically Endangered by IUCN and continues to decline.

was changed to Critically Endangered in 2006. By January 2009, how-ever, pipistrelles were present at only a single roosting site and the total population was estimated to be fewer than 20 individuals. In August 2009, an array of bat detectors recorded only one individual. The last echolocation call of this individual was detected on the evening of August 26. The extinction of the Christmas Island pipi-strelle was witnessed by those listening as the bat detectors fell silent.

Across the decades of the pipistrelle's decline, researchers were unable to identify the principal cause of its loss. Habitat loss was unlikely, as the island largely remained forested, much of it in a conservation reserve. Without knowing what factors were causing the decline, it was difficult to fashion a targeted recovery or manage-ment plan to address the threats. In retrospect, the most likely cause of the loss matches that of the Guam kingfisher described earlier in this chapter: predation by an introduced snake, in this case, the Indian wolf snake (Woinarski 2018)

Some have argued that the extinction of the pipistrelle could have been avoided had officials responded to the urgency of the situ-ation (Martin et al. 2012; Woinarski et al. 2017). Based on findings of the January 2009 survey, Lumsden and Schulz (2009) warned "with-out urgent intervention there is an extremely high risk that this species will go extinct ... within the next 6 months." Researchers desperately sought approval to capture the remaining individuals to initiate a captive-breeding program, but the government procrastin-ated. Instead of responding quickly, it established an Expert Working Group to study the problem. Only after the group had issued its report, 6 months later, was permission given to capture the remaining pipi-strelles. By then, however, only the single bat remained and it evaded capture until it disappeared. As Tim Flannery lamented, "[S]aving the bat wasn't an impossible mission. It's just that the government and the people of Australia—one of the richest countries on earth—decided it wasn't worth doing" (Flannery 2012a).

The Christmas Island pipistrelle was conservation reliant, but appropriate actions were not taken for several reasons: Australian legislation did not focus on avoiding extinctions, it was unclear who was accountable for acting, resources for conservation were inadequate, and there was no public involvement and little advocacy for an uncharismatic species occurring on a remote island (Woinarski et al. 2017). More precisely, the *right* actions were not taken. Attempts were made to control one putative threat, the introduced yellow crazy ant, but these actions did little to help the pipistrelle.

Unfortunately, such failings are not restricted to a remote island or to Australia. In the absence of evidence to identify the causes of a species' decline, managers may do something that is ineffectual or wait for more information and do nothing. Such situations are distressingly common. Other species (particularly among invertebrates, plants, or fungi) may wink out of existence without ever having been discovered or described (e.g. Régnier et al. 2009).

## DEGREES OF CONSERVATION RELIANCE

These stories illustrate how the circumstances and outcomes of conservation reliance can vary. Whether a species becomes self-sustaining in the wild, continues to slide toward extinction, or becomes conservation reliant may hinge on the balance between the long-term costs of conservation and the probability of success. This balance may determine the willingness of society to invest in conservation.

Threats are the main drivers of conservation success or failure. In some situations, the threats can be eliminated or at least substantially reduced. In other situations, the threats persist and so too must management, creating conservation reliance. Sometimes, however, the threats persist and rescue efforts are too little, too late, or non-existent, perhaps because people don't even realize that a species is in trouble

Whether or not a particular threat can be alleviated depends on characteristics of the threat (as we discuss in Chapters 4 and 5). The success stories generally involve a single primary threat: habitat loss for the chub, trampling for the cinquefoil, or predation for the black robin. The situation becomes more challenging when a single threat cannot be mitigated in a realistic time frame, as with brown tree snakes on Guam, or a species is affected by multiple threats over a broad spatial scale, as with the northern and southern white rhinoceroses. Unanticipated threats and unforeseen consequences of management are likely to appear more often as the human population continues to grow, more habitat is lost, and climate change and its effects gain force.

Although threats are a primary driver of the position of a species on the conservation spectrum, the ecology and life history of the species are also important. Species with a naturally restricted range, low abundance, and/or narrow food or habitat preferences are more likely to be imperiled in the first place. On the other hand, species that are widespread, produce many offspring, and are long lived are better able to respond rapidly to management, allowing more time and opportunity for managers to develop and implement effective management responses. Oregon chub females lay several hundred eggs; woylies mature at 6 months, breed often, and live 4–6 years; and Aleutian cackling geese lay large clutches and may live a decade or more in the wild. In contrast, black robins do not begin breeding until they are 2 years old, have only one breeding attempt per year and lay only two eggs, and normally have a life expectancy of 4 years.[20] Po'ouli had a similarly low reproductive potential.

For most of these species, the initial management was undertaken by government agencies. In some of the success stories, however, conservation reliance was reduced or eliminated through substantial participation by private individuals or groups. For example, landowners made places available for Oregon chub introductions. Several NGOs partnered with federal agencies or the military to protect habitat for the Robbins' cinquefoil, Oregon silverspot butterfly, and black-capped vireo. Private reserves have been essential

---

[20] Recovery of the species was possible because the last breeding female ("Old Blue") lived for over 14 years.

for the recovery and continued protection of southern white rhinoceroses.

This theme—that citizen participation is a vital element in dealing with conservation reliance—reappears often in the following chapters. But mobilizing broad support for imperiled or conservation-reliant species depends on the species being noticed. The white rhinoceros attracted worldwide attention, in part, because it is large and spectacularly strange. The Robbins' cinquefoil was noticed because it was next to a popular hiking trail. The Oregon silverspot butterfly excited lepidopterists. Unfortunately, recognition of a species' status by IUCN or governments does not by itself ensure that conservation actions will be taken. The Christmas Island pipistrelle and po'ouli were not accorded a conservation priority until there were too few left to save the species.

Conservation reliance is not an either/or categorization. Not all conservation-reliant species pose the same challenges or demand the same level of commitment and resources. Rather, conservation reliance varies across the broad spectrum of conditions we have described in this chapter. The position of a species on this spectrum is largely determined by the threats the species faces; how the species responds to those threats; and the success of management in eliminating, mitigating, or circumventing the threats. A species can shift positions on the spectrum as management actions take effect or its population continues to decline; the conservation spectrum is dynamic.

Considering conservation reliance across a spectrum of circumstances raises additional issues: How do we even understand what constitutes a species, when there may be hybrids or geographically or genetically distinct populations? Is there a difference between habitat, range, and potentially suitable habitat? How can we be sure a species has "recovered," and is there agreement about what that means? Such questions are the focus of our next chapter.

# 3 The Genesis of Conservation Reliance and the Language of Conservation

Conservation often focuses on species that are formally recognized as being at risk of extinction. These species represent only the tip of the iceberg. Populations of many other species are declining, and the queue of species of conservation concern is bound to lengthen as current and future environmental changes play out. Many of these species will be conservation reliant.

To deal with conservation reliance and its implications, we must understand the attitudes people have about nature and what "conservation" actually means. What is it that conservationists are trying to conserve? What do they mean when they talk about "habitat" or "recovery," and what do they consider "success"?

These are the topics of this chapter. But let's start at the beginning.

## WHERE DOES THE CONCEPT OF CONSERVATION RELIANCE COME FROM?

The idea of conservation reliance began with the experiences of one of us, Mike Scott, in dealing with the challenges of conserving birds listed under the US Endangered Species Act. Shortly after completing his PhD studies (under the direction of another of us, John Wiens), Mike joined the Endangered Species Research Program of the US Fish and Wildlife Service in Hawai'i. Hawai'i is the epicenter of endangered birds in the United States. Inspired by the first steps toward recovering the endangered nēnē,[1] Mike and his colleagues set out to answer

---

[1] The nēnē depended then, as it still did until recently, on continuing predator control and releases of captive-reared birds into the wild. Its recovery was so successful that the nēnē population on Kaua'i became a nuisance at an airport and golf course. Birds are now captured and translocated to Maui or the Big Island to be released in reserves.

FIGURE 3.1. An Endangered palila selects a seedpod from a māmane tree high on the western slope of Mauna Kea, Hawai'i. (A black and white version of this figure will appear in some formats. For the color version, please refer to the plate section.)
Photo: © Jack Jeffrey Photography.

some key questions about the endangered forest birds of Hawai'i: Which species are still extant and how many of them are there? What are their habitat associations and who owns the land? What threats do they face? Answers to these questions could help managers identify where new protected areas might best be located and which management actions might yield the greatest benefits.

The research began with the first range-wide census of the palila (Figure 3.1). The palila is a honeycreeper found only on the dry, upper-elevation māmane-naio forests on Mauna Kea. It was threatened by a loss of habitat from browsing by feral and domestic cattle, sheep, and goats, which had been introduced in the late 1700s. Attempts to limit the damage to native forests were initiated in the 1930s. Thousands of sheep and other ungulates were removed and the forest began to recover. It is unlikely that the palila would have survived without these early eradication efforts.

Control of ungulates in palila habitat was halted after the end of World War II to meet demands from hunters for a higher quality hunting experience. Mouflon sheep were introduced in the 1960s. They bred with feral sheep and the hybrid population increased; damage to palila habitat by ungulates continued. Following the dictates of the Endangered Species Act, federal courts ruled (twice) that the sheep must be removed.[2] Hunting groups and the Hawai'i Department of Land and Natural Resources countered that recreationally viable populations of sheep should be maintained in critical habitat of the palila (Banko et al. 2014). Their efforts prevailed. Palila numbers continued to decline.

It was not until 2009 that the state committed to removing the sheep from critical habitat for the palila. The work went slowly, but by the summer of 2018, more than three decades after the judge's decision that all sheep be removed in 2 years, all but a few kilometers of the core habitat had been fenced. Sheep (and goats) remain, albeit in much reduced numbers. However, other threats, including predation by feral cats and rats and the invasion of māmane-naio forest by exotic grasses that increase fire susceptibility, have increased. Until the fencing is completed, sheep and goats will remain a threat. Palila are listed as Critically Endangered by IUCN. It is not that researchers and managers did not identify the threats to the palila, nor where management opportunities existed, nor what needed to be done and how to do

---

[2] The palila has the distinction of being the first species to have legal standing in a US court case, in *Palila v. Hawaii Department of Land and Natural Resources* (852 F.2d 1106, US 1988).

it. The shortcoming was a failure to implement management actions at a scale that would mitigate or eradicate the threats.

As Mike and other researchers extended their work to other species of Hawaiian birds,[3] they saw the same thing time and again. The size and ruggedness of many islands meant that the threats could not be eliminated. Other threats—habitat destruction by feral sheep, goats, pigs, deer, and cattle; disease; predation by rats, cats, and mongooses—posed additional challenges. Management would need to be ongoing, perhaps in perpetuity. But sustaining such efforts would require substantial social and political support and funding (Juvik and Juvik 1984).

The Hawaiian Forest Bird Survey revealed that eight species with precariously low numbers would not survive without the establishment of captive flocks (Scott et al. 1986). However, only one such flock, for the 'alalā, was established. Efforts to save the other species were stymied by concerns about costs, technical challenges, a lack of basic natural history information, and an unwillingness of most agencies or organizations to take responsibility for a program with such a high likelihood of failure.[4]

When Mike later moved to California to lead research efforts to conserve the California condor, he saw first-hand how conservation reliant the condor really was (Chapter 1). In spring 1985, a rancher had seen an ill or injured condor at a water trough on a ranch in the southern Sierra Nevada foothills. The bird was one of 15 remaining in the wild. Thinking it might still be alive, Mike and others from the condor research program, Los Angeles Zoo, National Audubon Society, and California Department of Fish and Game left immediately. They drove through the night to the ranch and then rode on horseback and hiked miles into the rugged mountains. They found the bird still alive. The veterinarian on the crew immediately began to administer

---

[3] In the Hawaiian Forest Bird Survey mentioned in the Guam kingfisher story in Chapter 2.

[4] Plans to establish a captive-breeding program for one other species, the po'ouli, were never implemented because only three birds remained by the end of the planning process (Chapter 2).

antibiotics to the bird, but it died while it was being treated. Mike rode back with the dead condor lying across the back of his saddle. An autopsy revealed that it had died of lead poisoning from ingesting bullet fragments in an animal carcass. The bird did not carry a transmitter; if it had, rescue might have come in time to save it.

This bird was one of six that died that winter. The precariousness of the situation led to the decision to capture the nine birds remaining in the wild and bring them into captivity. A captive-breeding program was successful and birds were later released back into the wild, less than 5 years after the last wild condor was captured. Although numbers have increased, the condor remains conservation reliant.

Mike was struck by the disparities in attention and funding between the condor and the Hawaiian birds. While millions of dollars were being spent annually on restoring condors to the wild, seven species of Hawaiian birds that had been seen during the Hawaii Forest Bird Survey—the 'ō'ū, Kaua'i 'ō'ō, kāma'o, 'alauahio (O'ahu creeper), Maui 'akepa, Maui nukupu'u, oloma'o (Moloka'i thrush), and po'ouli—became extinct.

Mike's experiences prompted several observations. First, conservation was subject to social and political forces, which could initiate, redirect, or overwhelm science-based management plans. Second, planning how to recover an endangered species took time; in the meantime, planning paralysis could preclude any chances for recovery of a rapidly declining species. Third, the factors that threatened species and led to their imperilment could not easily be eliminated or mitigated at conservation-relevant scales, so continuing intervention would be needed to ensure the species' survival. Fourth, some species might be beyond saving because numbers had dropped too low or access to critical areas was not possible. The notion of conservation reliance was beginning to take form.

The concept crystalized when Mike moved to the University of Idaho and began a long-term collaboration with Dale Goble. Dale's knowledge of wildlife law and the Endangered Species Act provided complementary depth and a legal context for Mike's experiences in the trenches of conservation management. Together, Mike and Dale added flesh to the bones of a developing concept. Long discussions led to conferences, workshops, and publications (e.g. Scott et al. 2005, 2010; Goble et al. 2012; Reed et al. 2012) that have coalesced into the chapters of this book.

In the United States, conservation reliance has usually been cast in the context of the Endangered Species Act. It is easy to see why. Mike's experiences and Dale's legal focus emphasized the act and its implications. Management approaches for endangered species in Hawai'i and California were deeply tied to the provisions of the act (and remain so). Moreover, the species listed under the act included many of those most critically imperiled and those species commanded the greatest attention from conservationists and the public. Conservation reliance could pose a significant impediment to their recovery and eventual delisting.

The tight coupling of conservation reliance with the act, however, has led to criticism that the concept may confound a biological problem (how to deal with the threats that imperil a species) with the legal and policy issues of the act itself (how to remove a species from the act's protection) (Rohlf et al. 2014a). In this book, we define conservation reliance strictly in biological terms. We base our definition on the need for management intervention to ensure persistence of a species in the wild. When conservation reliance becomes too entangled with the Endangered Species Act or any other at-risk species law, we risk focusing only on listed species. Unlisted species would then receive insufficient attention, even though many may also be conservation reliant (Wiens and Gardali 2013). Entangling biology with legal strictures also shifts attention from dealing with species and threats to addressing the legal issues of categorizing, listing, and delisting species.

WHAT DOES "CONSERVATION" MEAN?

The title of this book implies that conservation compels us to be good shepherds of nature. But what does "conservation" mean? It depends on one's perspective on nature.

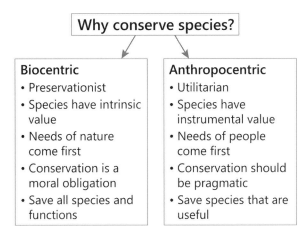

FIGURE 3.2. Attributes of the different philosophical positions on the conservation of species. The differences influence which conservation efforts people support or oppose.

For simplicity, we can identify two contrasting sets of conservation values: a *biocentric* perspective and an *anthropocentric* perspective (Figure 3.2). The biocentric perspective emphasizes the ecological, environmental, and aesthetic values of species and nature. The goal is to protect and preserve as much of the Earth's biodiversity—its species, habitats, ecological functioning, genetic diversity, and evolutionary potential—as possible. "Save all species" is the mantra. This perspective is manifest in religious edicts to protect all God's creatures and in the preservationist views that lie at the foundations of many conservation and environmental organizations. It reflects a philosophy that emphasizes the *intrinsic* value of nature. According to this view, species and ecosystems have value in and of themselves. It is therefore morally incumbent upon us to protect nature from ourselves. Most people who identify themselves as conservationists or environmentalists have some variation of this perspective and philosophy. Aldo Leopold (1949) advocated a "land ethic." E.O. Wilson has written extensively and eloquently from this perspective (e.g. 1984, 2002) and it is a recurrent theme in the writings of Paul

Ehrlich (for example, in Bradshaw and Ehrlich 2015) and Tim Flannery (2012a), among others.

The anthropocentric perspective, in contrast, is explicitly utilitarian. Many environments and the species, natural communities, and ecosystems they contain have economic value; the goal of conservation is to protect and preserve these benefits for humans. "Save species that are worth saving" is the mantra. Proponents of this perspective adhere to a philosophical position that emphasizes the *instrumental* value of nature— the benefits derived by humans.[5] We manage natural resources (such as forests or fisheries) to maximize sustained yield and we enhance ecosystem services (such as pollination, pharmaceutical applications, flood control, or recreation) to maximize their benefits to us. This is the perspective advocated by Robert Costanza (1991), Gretchen Daily (1997), Peter Kareiva (e.g. Kareiva et al. 2007), and Chris Thomas (2017), among others.

Debates over biocentric versus anthropocentric perspectives and intrinsic versus instrumental values of nature have been going on for more than a century (Rolston 2012; Wiens 2016b; Gardiner and Thompson 2017). To those dedicated to environmental preservation, people are the primary threats: human overexploitation of fisheries and forests and desertification of grazing lands (e.g. Flannery 1994; Kurlansky 1997; Diamond 2005) violate the very meaning of "conservation." To others, such ardent preservationist views ignore the reality of the Anthropocene: that people subsist off of the environment, human impacts are pervasive, and the needs of people come first. These two perspectives also suggest different time scales for achieving goals. Preservation, such as establishing conservation easements, tends to regard conservation as being for all living creatures in perpetuity. Utilitarian management, such as slash-and-burn agriculture or ranching, tends to be short term—a few years to a few human generations.

---

[5] Sandler (2012) delves more deeply into the philosophical and ethical aspects of how people value species. We return to this topic in Chapter 11.

Like most dichotomies, that between preservation and human use ignores a vast middle ground. Many people use natural resources while recognizing the need and value of conserving those resources and the ecosystems that contain them. They consider aspects of each perspective depending on circumstances. A manager of a national park or wildlife refuge in the United States or Australia, for example, must balance public demands for recreation and other uses with demands to protect the biodiversity and intrinsic nature of those lands. A farmer or rancher can manage a property to be economically profitable while ensuring that it will also be ecologically sustainable. A game manager strives to ensure that populations of game species remain sufficient to support hunting and fishing. Many human activities embody both a desire to preserve nature and a need to benefit from nature.

Indigenous people are often among the most ardent advocates for environmental preservation *and* sustainable use. In the Pacific Northwest, for example, tribes such as the Nez Perce have been active in drawing attention to Chinook salmon. They have subsisted on the salmon for millennia and attach great cultural and spiritual importance to sustaining salmon runs (see Essay 3.1 by Joseph Oatman). Chinook salmon are also a multi-million dollar commercial resource and are prized for recreational fishing. Now, 18 salmon runs are endangered, limiting commercial and recreational uses. The different ways of valuing salmon often conflict. If the history of California can be written in gold and water, that of the Pacific Northwest and Alaska is written in salmon.

The distinction between preservation and ecosystem use (or between intrinsic and instrumental values) blurs as societal and economic forces come into play. These forces are expressed in policies, laws, and regulations, which establish a formal structure for pursuing a particular philosophy. They determine how natural resources may or may not be used and whether they merit legal protection.

ESSAY 3.1    **Nez Perce and Salmon: Ensuring Fish Are There for Future Generations**

*Joseph Y. Oatman*[6]

The Nez Perce live in the heart of salmon country, in the Snake River Basin, along the Salmon, Snake, Grande Ronde, Imnaha, Clearwater, and Tucannon rivers in Idaho, Oregon, and Washington. Historically, these rivers were major salmon and steelhead producers, supporting an important part of our year-round trade and subsistence economy. Nez Perce culture revolves around fish and water, and many of the traditional Nez Perce calendar months are named after fish species and fishing times.

The Nez Perce reserved the right to harvest fish in our Treaty of 1855 with the United States. The US negotiators at the Treaty Council assured Nez Perce leader Chief Looking Glass that tribal members could catch fish at any of our usual and accustomed fishing areas, and remarked that the rivers within Nez Perce Country contained the best fisheries. Reserving our rights to fish was essential because each and every tribal member, from their youth to old age, ate salmon. At the time, Nez Perce caught and consumed 300 to 564 pounds of fish (136 to 256 kg) per person—amounting to an annual harvest of 150 000 to 282 000 fish. Harvest at these levels translates to an average of 69 adult fish per person annually.

Today, salmon and steelhead runs, along with many other important fishes in the Snake River Basin, are nowhere near as abundant or productive as they were when the treaty was written. All of our salmon populations have declined to extremely low levels and are no longer found in areas where they once thrived. Historic salmon and steelhead escapement to the Snake River Basin was estimated to range from 0.5 to 2 million and has since declined to a low of 50 000 fish in recent years. This is a result of the dramatic and wide-scale changes that have occurred within and outside our treaty territory over time. Thousands of miles of rivers and streams have been blocked and altered as a result of dams and other human development: hydropower, fishing, logging,

---

[6] With thanks to Dave Johnson, Becky Johnson, Emmit Taylor, Jay Hesse, and Jason Vogel.

ESSAY 3.1    **(cont.)**

mining, irrigation, agriculture, grazing, and urbanization. Snake River Chinook salmon (spring, summer, and fall runs), as well as sockeye and steelhead, are listed under the Endangered Species Act[7] and coho salmon have been extirpated. In addition, other key anadromous species of the Snake River Basin are in trouble. Lamprey are on the verge of extirpation and sturgeon cannot navigate the fish ladders of the eight dams they must pass to spawn in their natal rivers.

To address the threats the fish encounter throughout their life cycle, the Nez Perce are involved in a massive multi-decade, multi-generational management effort to help salmon survive, recover, and persist in our rivers. We manage our treaty-reserved resources through traditional ecological knowledge, guided by a spiritual/cultural sense of respect and duty and blending in modern scientific techniques. The tribe executes this management approach through its Fisheries Department, which implements a broad suite of fish recovery and restoration actions with multiple aims: to rebuild fish runs and our fisheries; to maintain diverse and productive ecosystems with species distributed throughout historically used tributaries; to address the impacts of dams and human development; to maintain genetic diversity of these fish, allowing for population persistence and adaptation; to practice a "ridge-top to ridge-top" approach for watershed protection and restoration of rearing and spawning habitats and protection of water quality; to use hatcheries to "put fish in the rivers," allowing them to spawn as well as provide for harvest; to protect water flows and passage for upstream and downstream migrants; to participate in ocean and in-river harvest management forums; to co-manage adult returns and sharing of harvest with our non-Indian neighbors; and to monitor our activities and the runs to determine how things are faring and respond when intervention is needed.

---

[7] Under the Endangered Species Act, the Snake River Sockeye Salmon Evolutionally Significant Unit (ESU) is listed as Endangered. The Snake River spring/summer Chinook salmon ESU, the Snake River fall-run Chinook salmon ESU, and the Snake River basin steelhead Distinct Population Segment are listed as Threatened.

ESSAY 3.1    **(cont.)**

An example of the Fisheries Department's activities is the use of fish hatcheries. The tribe manages two hatcheries and 10 acclimation sites and co-manages one of the nation's largest federal hatcheries, releasing over 13 million salmon and steelhead annually. The tribe's efforts account for some 32% of total fish production in Snake River Basin. The tribe's Snake River fall Chinook and Coho salmon restoration program are two examples of using hatcheries as a modern management strategy to restore diminished or lost salmon populations. Fall Chinook salmon returns have rebounded from a low of 300 fish in the 1980s to nearly 60 000 in 2014. Coho salmon, which were extirpated in the Snake River Basin, numbered over 18 000 recently and were abundant enough to provide for a tribal treaty and non-tribal sport harvest for the first time in anyone's memory. Since 2000, tribal fishing for spring and summer Chinook salmon has expanded to more "usual and accustomed" fishing areas than were available to previous generations of tribal members (Figure E3.1.1).

FIGURE E3.1.1. Aaron Penney, a member of the NimíiPuu (Nez Perce Tribe), dip-net fishing for Chinook salmon in the Middle Fork of the Salmon River, Idaho. (A black and white version of this figure will appear in some formats. For the color version, please refer to the plate section.) Photo: Zach Penney.

ESSAY 3.1 **(cont.)**

Despite this effort, the Snake River Basin still does not provide the fisheries to support our people as it once did. The threats to and impacts on fish directly affect the health, well-being, culture, and economy of the Nez Perce people by limiting the amount of fish that we eat. A recent fish-consumption survey of Nez Perce tribal members found that for half of our membership the current consumption is about three fish per person annually, a small fraction of historic consumption levels.

Our predicament is clear: salmon, from their birth in Nez Perce Country to their journey through the Snake and Columbia rivers to the Pacific Ocean and back home again, face an increasingly difficult survival challenge. On average, only one adult salmon returns for every 200 juveniles that start the journey. Management throughout this life cycle then becomes an exercise in balancing a diverse and often conflicting set of human activities and benefits. The real question is: Of all the people and their activities that affect or kill salmon, who is responsible for the conservation burden?

At Treaty Council, the Nez Perce chiefs were promised that our fisheries and fishing places would be preserved in perpetuity. The tribe believes the conservation of these fish should not be left to our tribal members alone, to further restrict and reduce our harvest and sacrifice our fishing-based way of life while others profit and thrive on this land. We have made sacrifices for multiple generations. Now is the time for the region to treat our needs as a paramount objective to achieve. These other non-fishing activities and actions that threaten or kill the fish that we depend upon must carry more of the conservation burden to help restore these species to healthy, self-sustaining levels. Those conservation actions that are in place today to benefit these species of fish must continue into the future. We must also learn how to respond to our changing environment and to take new actions as we adapt to those changes.

A Nez Perce ethic and the tribe's treaty-reserved rights have been instrumental in reversing and tempering the human-centric impacts to natural resources and altered landscapes. Respect, care, and reliance on the natural environment, along with a time-immemorial sense of place, makes the Nez Perce Tribe's work indispensable to our region's

ESSAY 3.1    **(cont.)**

management of its natural resources. As a seventh-generation direct descendant of Chief Looking Glass, I, along with others, have a responsibility to help protect, conserve, and maintain our fish for the benefit of the current generation and the generations that follow. Our children's children will inherit this land and its resources, and it should be all of our calling and our duty to improve on what we leave them.

In the United States, the intent of policy is to regulate certain practices to ensure safety standards exist (such as air and water quality), avoid actions that might harm species or their habitats, or achieve other objectives. In principle, laws are intended to remain in force indefinitely (unless they contain an expiration or renewal clause). In practice, however, laws and policies are subject to the ebb and flow of political interests and funding to support their implementation.

How do these two perspectives (and the middle ground between them) relate to conservation reliance? Conservation reliance is a problem determined by the status and attributes of a species and the threats that imperil it; by biology and the environment. But what is *done* about it through management, conservation, and policy depends on how people view the problem. Biocentric conservationists may consider the long-term investment required to manage a conservation-reliant species justified if the species is in imminent danger of extinction. Anthropocentric conservationists may think management is worthwhile only if the species provides critical ecosystem services or is otherwise culturally or economically important. These differences lead to different decisions about how to prioritize species for conservation, which criteria to use, and how to weight the criteria. Conservationists with different perspectives would probably differ in their views about how (or whether) to address conservation of the species whose stories we told in Chapter 2. To be successful, conservation must blend the biocentric and anthropocentric perspectives.

## WHAT IS A "SPECIES"?

Just as there are multiple perspectives on what "conservation" is, there are multiple viewpoints on what it is we are trying to conserve. From a biocentric perspective, conservation aims to protect, preserve, and restore Earth's biodiversity, the "living parts of the multifarious ecosystems of the world" (Wilson 1997: 1), including genes, species, biological communities, and ecosystems.

Our focus in this book is on species. Most conservation efforts are directed toward species (and the habitats that support them), especially when the emphasis is on avoiding extinctions. Genes may disappear from a gene pool through selection or genetic drift and communities and ecosystems may change as species come and go, but only a species can become extinct. Species also seem more tangible, bounded, and identifiable in ways that resonate with the public. Birdwatchers and butterfly collectors tally lists of species.

There is some uncertainty, however, about what exactly "species" means in the context of conservation and management. A biological species concept emphasizes the boundary (interbreeding) that maintains species as discrete, fixed categories. Ernst Mayr (1942) defined biological species as "groups of interbreeding natural populations that are reproductively isolated from other such groups." This definition has evolved over the decades, including in Mayr's own writings (Beurton 2002; de Queiroz 2005). Alternatively, some scientists support a phylogenetic species concept that emphasizes the evolutionary history and patterns of divergence of taxa. The phylogenetic concept considers the character traits that distinguish species as evolving (and changing) entities. The distinction is more than academic. Using the phylogenetic approach, Barrowclough et al. (2016) estimated that there may be over 18 000 bird species rather than the 11 000 or so described using more traditional criteria.

Rather than taking sides in this debate, it may be more useful to consider how the Endangered Species Act defines species. The act includes in the definition of species "any subspecies of fish or wildlife or plants, and any distinct population segment of any species of vertebrate fish or wildlife which interbreeds when mature."[8] Laws in other countries follow a similar approach. Australia's Environment Protection and Biodiversity Conservation (EPBC) Act refers to species and communities, although subspecies and populations are also included. The Canadian Species at Risk Act (SARA) refers to species, but the list also includes subspecies and populations. SARA's criteria for status assessment are patterned after the IUCN scheme (Mace et al. 2008) and delineate "wildlife species" using the concept of a "designatable unit" (Green 2005). These units meet the criteria used to identify distinct population segments or evolutionarily significant units under US law (Fraser and Bernatchez 2001). Vertebrates, invertebrates, and plants are covered in New Zealand and European Union regulations and law.

The emphasis on categories such as "subspecies" and "distinct population segments" in legislation has contributed additional ambiguity and controversy.[9] Subspecies are taxonomically defined units, so they are subject to the classification practices in vogue for a particular group (e.g. plants vs. beetles vs. birds) or at a particular time (e.g. splitting vs. lumping taxa). Some (e.g. Ripley 1981) have argued against applying the Endangered Species Act to any units other than full species, but others (e.g. Patten 2015) have advocated strengthening the definition of subspecies to include both morphological and genetic distinctiveness. Under the act, many full species are listed as threatened or endangered whereas others are partitioned into subspecies, only some of which may fall under the act's protection. As an example, two of the three recognized subspecies of spotted owl (the northern spotted owl and Mexican spotted owl) are listed as Threatened, whereas the other (the California spotted owl) is not.

[8] ESA Sec 3(15). Note the inherent taxonomic biases: the explicit emphasis on fish, the passing mention of plants, the use of "wildlife" to include mammals to (apparently) invertebrates, and the absence of organisms other than animals or plants.

[9] Gleaves et al. (1992) discuss the legislative history of debates about what "species" means in the context of the Endangered Species Act.

A "distinct population segment" is an arbitrary designation created by the United States Congress, perhaps with the aim of protecting the evolutionary potential of distinct lineages. The Florida population of the northern crested caracara, for example, is geographically separated from populations in the southwestern United States and Central America. The Florida population is listed as Threatened, but the same subspecies is common throughout the main part of its range and the listing status applies only to the Florida population.[10] Pacific salmon exhibit an array of life histories and migratory pathways within single taxonomically defined species. Accordingly, the National Marine Fisheries Service has adopted "evolutionarily significant units" to recognize both the degree of isolation and the evolutionary history and potential of a population segment. Using this categorization, the seven species of salmon and steelhead found in California and the Pacific Northwest include 58 evolutionarily significant units, many but not all of which are listed under the Endangered Species Act (Waples 1991, 2006). This approach accords with the phylogenetic approach advocated by Barrowclough et al. (2016). Different criteria have been applied in efforts to conserve the endangered Florida panther subspecies, which has been cross-bred with individuals of a different subspecies from Texas to bolster genetic diversity (Johnson et al. 2010) rather than maintain evolutionary distinctiveness. Use of "distinct population segments" or "evolutionarily significant unit" as categories is restricted to vertebrates.

How the units for protection or conservation are defined continues to be debated. Detailed knowledge of life history and ecology, phylogeny, or even molecular genetics is needed to determine what constitutes a "distinct population segment" or an "evolutionarily significant unit" (Moritz 1994). After reviewing several approaches to defining "evolutionarily significant units" for conservation, Fraser and Bernatchez (2001: 2742) offered their own definition: an evolutionarily significant unit is "a lineage demonstrating highly restricted

---

[10] https://ecos.fws.gov/docs/five_year_review/doc2507.pdf

gene flow from other such lineages within the higher organizational level (lineage) of the species."[11] This approach requires knowledge of the phylogenetic relationships among lineages, which is often not available.[12]

Uncertain specifications of the units to be conserved may open the door to legal challenges. In such situations, using taxonomically defined units such as species or subspecies may make sense. Doing so, however, may ignore fundamental ecological differences among groups within a species that may require different conservation and management approaches. Management practices appropriate for winter-run Chinook salmon in the Sacramento River, for example, may not be appropriate for spring/summer-run Chinook salmon in the Snake River.

The challenge of defining the entities on which conservation and management should be focused is made more complex by hybridization and introgression (Allendorf et al. 2001). Individuals in a small or sparsely distributed population may have difficulty finding mates and may interbreed with other closely related species (the "desperation hypothesis"; Hobbs 1955). This can progressively erode the genetic distinctiveness of a population, erasing species boundaries and potentially leading to extinction via hybridization (Rhymer and Simberloff 1996) or to the emergence of new species (Grant and Grant 2014). Current efforts to manage red wolves, for example, are aimed largely at protecting the species from a loss of identity through hybridization with coyotes (Gese et al. 2015; Waples et al. 2018)—never mind that the red wolf may itself be an evolutionary derivative of hybridization between coyotes and gray wolves a few millennia ago (Reich et al. 1999; but see NAS 2019). In Africa, the endangered great sable antelope is interbreeding with the sympatric roan antelope as populations of both species have decreased owing to the Angolan civil

---

[11] See Waples and Gaggiotti (2006) for additional review of this issue.

[12] Gumbs et al. (2018) have proposed a method for estimating the evolutionary distinctiveness of species that have not been incorporated into phylogenetic analyses.

war and subsequent poaching (Vaz Pinto et al. 2016). All surviving hybrids and sable antelope females in one of the two remaining populations have been captured and are now confined in large enclosures. Managers bring in sable bulls and females from the other population, which has restored the genetic distinctiveness of the sable antelope. Both antelope species (and their hybrids) remain conservation reliant.

Political boundaries may also affect how we define the species we want to conserve. Laws and regulations apply to political entities such as states, provinces, territories, or nations, not to the geographic ranges of species. It makes sense to focus national conservation efforts (and funding) on species endemic to a country, such as the Robbins' cinquefoil in the United States or the Araripe manakin in Brazil, or on the many species endemic to single islands in the Galapagos, Hawaiian, Malay, or Philippine archipelagos. In some cases, however, a species may receive special conservation attention because the periphery of its range occurs in a state or nation, even though it is widely distributed and abundant elsewhere (Peterson 2001). Thus, a subspecies of the ferruginous pygmy-owl was listed as Endangered under the Endangered Species Act in 1997 based on its precarious status in the Sonoran Desert of Arizona. Because the subspecies is widespread through the lowland tropics of Mexico and Central America, however, the listing was challenged and the Arizona population was delisted in 2006 with the rationale "original data in error."[13]

Populations at the periphery of a species' range are often sustained only by immigration of individuals from more central parts of the range. These so-called "sink" populations (Liu et al. 2011) are vulnerable to local extinction, but they may also be sources of evolutionary novelty and are an important element of metapopulation dynamics (Wright 1940; Hanski and Gaggiotti 2004). Range edges shift as species move about, so what is peripheral at one time may become a core part of the range (or be unoccupied) at another time. One can argue either position: that investment of time and resources in the

---

[13] ecos.fws.gov/ecp0/reports/delisting-report

conservation of peripheral populations is a questionable strategy (Peterson 2001), or that species that are rare locally merit special protection even if they are common elsewhere (Hunter 1993). The arguments become murkier when the peripheral population is also a recognized subspecies and therefore a potential target for protection under the Endangered Species Act.

Rather than attempting to weave our way through the multiple (and sometimes contradictory) perspectives about what it is we aim to conserve, we will use the term "species" to refer to a population of individuals that is or could be a target of conservation and management actions and to which the concept of conservation reliance can apply. Thus, "species" may be a distinct group defined by phylogeny (evolution), geography, systematics (taxonomy), or genetics.

How do the various perspectives on "species" relate to the issue of conservation reliance? Laws and regulations, such as the Endangered Species Act in the United States and similar statutes elsewhere, define the units of protection and conservation by policy (which, to varying degrees, may be biologically informed). However, if the intent is to deal with imperilment and prevent extinctions, then the focus should be on units that are biologically realistic, be they full species (woylies or Chatham Island black robins), distinct subspecies (northern spotted owls), or evolutionarily significant units or distinct population segments (winter-run Chinook salmon in the Sacramento River). It would make little sense to deal with the northern white rhinoceros (IUCN Critically Endangered) and the southern white rhinoceros (IUCN Near Threatened) in the same way. Different segments of the same or closely related species may be exposed to different threats, have different life-history attributes, and exhibit different degrees of conservation reliance.

Debates about the appropriate units for conservation reflect differing perspectives and philosophies about what is important. The Endangered Species Act takes a biocentric perspective, explicitly valuing species over economic concerns. To those with an anthropocentric perspective, this emphasis may seem misguided or wrong.

Why should an endangered local population or subspecies restrict human activities or economic development when the species as a whole is doing fine elsewhere? California gnatcatchers are listed as Threatened under the Endangered Species Act where they occur in a limited but rapidly urbanizing area of southern California (Chapter 5). Provisions of the act have restricted development, leading to legal conflicts. Yet, the gnatcatcher is common south of the border in Mexico.[14] As a species, the gnatcatcher is doing well; it is only the peripheral portion in California, defined by a political boundary, that is imperiled. Gray wolves are another example: they are imperiled (but recovering) in the United States but are common in the boreal forests of Canada and globally are considered a species of Least Concern by IUCN.

Conservation reliance may intensify such debates and conflicts because it raises the prospect that investments in conservation and management will be long-term and continuing. Why should we invest time and resources in a conservation-reliant population (or species) that is of little economic value? On the other hand, we may believe that every species has intrinsic value and merits whatever commitment is necessary to conserve it. Such questions lie at the heart of the socioeconomic and cultural context of conservation reliance.

## WHAT IS "HABITAT"?

Then there is the issue of "habitat." Loss of habitat is a primary cause of imperilment for many species. In order to alleviate the threat of habitat loss and understand how habitat management relates to conservation-reliant species, we must know what we mean by "habitat."

Ecologists have grappled with defining "habitat" for decades. This has produced "a large collection of literature full of muddled

---

[14] Based on its status in Mexico, the species is considered of Least Concern by IUCN. The distribution in the United States, however, is fragmented into a northern and southern population separated by the Los Angeles urban sprawl. Cooper et al. (2017) describe the difficulty of defining the northern limits to the species' distribution.

terminology" (Mathewson and Morrison 2015: 3). Part of the confusion is about whether "habitat" is used to refer to an attribute of a species (e.g. spotted owl habitat) or a feature of the landscape or target of management (e.g. old-growth forest habitat). Most people define habitat by dominant vegetation—the trees when we look at a forest or the grasses when we look at a prairie. Dominant vegetation lends itself to classification and mapping, especially as it is readily detected and displayed by remote sensing. Such a definition facilitates landscape-based management. The goals of habitat protection or habitat restoration, for example, can be framed in terms of a dominant vegetation type (at least in terrestrial landscapes).

Such landscape-based classifications may not accord well with how a species of interest views "habitat." This was brought home to one of us, Bea Van Horne, when she studied Pacific wrens in Oregon. Wrens established territories and bred successfully in dense shrubbery near water. This habitat occurred in the understory of old-growth coniferous forest with towering trees, but the wrens also occupied the same habitat in alder-dominated 10-year-old second growth—vegetation that a plant ecologist or forest manager would regard as a totally different type. To the wrens, they were apparently the same. Because our focus in this book is primarily on species, we consider "habitat" from the perspective of the species.

Even within such a species-centered perspective, however, there are different views on "habitat." For example, Mathewson and Morrison (2015: 5) define habitat as "an area with a combination of resources ... and environmental conditions ... that promotes occupancy by individuals of a given species (or population) and allows these individuals to survive and reproduce." In the same volume, Van Horne and Wiens (2015: 34) define habitat as encompassing "the local environmental conditions in which a species of interest lives."

The first definition ties habitat to survival and reproduction, the second only to living there. The former would seem to preclude conditions in which reproduction does not occur but that are nonetheless essential to a species' life history. For example, birds, monarch butterflies, and other migratory species often use the same stopover sites year after year. These stopover sites are essential to the species survival, but may not be where the species breeds. Or consider places in which the last remaining individuals of a species live but do not reproduce, such as the last two northern white rhinoceroses (both females) mentioned in Chapter 2; their habitat would not be considered as such by the first definition. The second definition, however, implies that a species must actually be living in an area for it to be considered habitat, precluding consideration of places that are potentially suitable but not currently occupied. In the remainder of this book, we will use a modified version of the second definition: habitat encompasses *the local environmental conditions in which a species of interest lives or could live.*

It is easy to see why "habitat" has become a muddled term. From a conservation perspective, it is also important to consider whether habitat is *sufficient*: Is the area of habitat adequate to allow a population to remain stable or expand? If available habitat is insufficient, some form of ongoing habitat management will be needed to sustain the species. If a species continues to decline after its habitat is protected and adding more protected habitat is not an option or is not effective in halting the decline, then the species will be reliant on conservation actions undertaken to support survival and reproduction. These might entail the continuous removal of invasive plants or predators, supplemental feeding during seasonal "crunches," hydrologic management, maintenance of early successional habitat, creation of suitable nest sites, or capture and translocation of individuals to other areas with suitable habitat.

There is an added wrinkle, however. What constitutes sufficient habitat is dynamic, varying over space and time. Spatial variation creates a mosaic of habitat and non-habitat patches across a landscape.[15] Environmental changes may shift conditions in a particular

---

[15] The places also differ in "habitat quality," a concept that continues to be debated. Van Horne (1983) suggested a mechanistic framework for how one might understand habitat quality; but see also Johnson (2007) and Guthery and Strickland (2015).

location from suitable for a species to unsuitable. For example, Piute ground squirrels in Idaho shrubsteppe survived and reproduced more successfully in habitat dominated by a native bunchgrass (Sandberg bluegrass) during three relatively wet years than in habitat dominated by native shrubs (big sagebrush), but the situation reversed during a year of severe drought when the bunchgrasses dried out very early in the season (Van Horne et al. 1997). Suitable habitat may also change as a result of catastrophic events such as landslides or flooding. More gradual changes may occur through invasion of non-native plant or animal species, increased human use, ecological succession, or consequences of climate change.

Adopting a species-centered perspective on habitat compels us to consider habitat on scales relevant to the species of interest, which may not be the same as the scales on which management operates (Figure 3.3). It also compels us to consider places a species does not occupy now but has in the past or could in the future. A species that is declining, has recently suffered a range contraction (e.g. because of a severe winter freeze or climate change), or has a metapopulation structure may not always occupy all places that contain adequate resources and suitable environmental conditions. Many species occupy different habitats at different life-history stages, so critical areas may be occupied at some times but not at others. There are methodological issues as well: occupancy of an area is related to the detectability of individuals, which depends on the species and its behavior (e.g. raucous displays versus cryptic skulking), population density in an area, and the thickness of vegetation, among other factors.

A species-centered perspective has implications for how habitat is managed for a species, especially if the species is conservation reliant. Protecting a species' habitat is often the primary goal for conservation: Unless there is habitat for a species, all other efforts will ultimately fail. Ideally, a protected area or nature reserve should be of sufficient size and quality that a target species can persist or recover. However, because the boundaries and sizes of such areas are usually administratively rather than ecologically determined, the

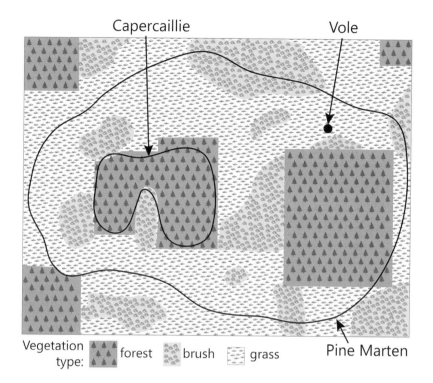

FIGURE 3.3. Habitats scale in different ways for different species. The challenges of managing multiple species in a landscape are apparent in this hypothetical depiction of habitat occupancy by a European pine marten, western capercaillie (a grouse), and northern red-backed vole in a Norwegian landscape. The three species have different home-range sizes and different habitat preferences: the vole a small area of grassland, the capercaillie a larger area of forest, and the marten a much larger area that includes a mixture of vegetation types. "Habitat" in the same landscape is thus both species-specific and scale-dependent. Resource management in such a landscape may occur at yet a different scale (e.g. the rectangular area of forest on the right).
From Wiens et al. (1993).

habitat the species needs in order to thrive may be truncated or severed. Species that roam beyond the protected area, such as mobile species or ones that disperse widely, may stray far from a secure place. Indeed, most protected areas are habitat islands in an otherwise anthropogenic landscape.

The importance of a definition of "habitat" was brought home by a US Supreme Court decision in November 2018. The court ruled unanimously[16] that critical habitat for an endangered species (a legal designation) must be places where the species could currently live. In the words of Chief Justice Roberts, critical habitat "must also be habitat." The Court passed the question of what constitutes "habitat" back to a lower court. Jurists seem to wrestle with this issue as much as ecologists and conservationists.

Understanding how a species uses its habitat will help to identify which aspects of habitat are most important, although the dynamics of both the habitat and the target species mean that habitat designations must be flexible. So long as "habitat" remains a muddled term, however, there is a risk that it may become a panchreston, a word that, in an attempt to include everything, loses its meaning.

## WHAT IS "RECOVERY"?

The objectives of conservation and management of imperiled species are usually stated as first, to avoid extinction, and then, to ensure recovery. Defining "extinction" is clear enough: the species no longer exists. Defining "recovery" is more problematic (Goble 2009a). The general meaning of "recovery" among conservationists is that an imperiled species is drawn back from the brink of extinction and made secure; it is "viable" and sustainable in the wild. This is the perspective that is incorporated into many laws and regulations. For example, the Endangered Species Act considers a Threatened or Endangered species to have recovered when the act's protection is no longer necessary to ensure the species' persistence. According to the act, to be declared "recovered" a species must meet both biological and legal requirements (Goble 2009a; Neel et al. 2012). Biologically, the threats to the species must have been eliminated or neutralized[17] and the

---

[16] In *Weyerhaeuser Co. v. US Fish and Wildlife Service.*

[17] Documents supporting delisting proposals also refer to threats being "satisfactorily minimized" "ameliorated," or "reduced to the point where [the species] no longer

species' abundance and distribution must have increased to levels at which the species can persist in the wild. Legally, the species must have met or exceeded recovery goals; it no longer requires protections provided by the Endangered Species Act because sufficient regulatory or conservation mechanisms are in place to assure that the species will not again become imperiled once the act's protection is removed (Doremus and Pagel 2001). Both the biological and legal elements are necessary: providing habitat to a species to offset habitat loss, for example, may not lead to recovery if there are other threats that still require targeted legal or regulatory protection.

Recovery can also be gauged by a reduction in risks or costs to some acceptable level. The closer a species is to extinction, the greater the risk that it may be pushed over the edge by a sudden storm, loss of habitat, interactions with an invasive species, or some other threat. Conservation of an imperiled species can also be expensive, so there is an incentive to reach a point where costs can be reduced. This may be especially important for conservation-reliant species, for which management (and therefore cost) is usually long term, weakening the willingness of society to keep on paying the bills.

A different perspective on recovery is embodied in laws and regulations that deal with the environmental impacts of chemical releases, oil spills, or other environmental accidents. Natural Resource Damage Assessment (NRDA) regulations in the United States define recovery as "the return of injured natural resources and services to baseline," where baseline is "the condition of the natural resources and services that would have existed had the incident not occurred."[18] Although this perspective acknowledges that environments may vary and the baseline might have changed over time if the accident had not occurred, recovery has often been interpreted as a return to conditions at the time of the accident (Wiens 2013). The

meets the definition of an endangered species or a threatened species under the Endangered Species Act."

[18] US Code of Federal Regulations 15 CFR § 990.30.

underlying assumption is one of a stable system in which the condition of a natural resource (such as the abundance of a species) does not vary much and was not declining at the time of the incident. In other words, NRDA ignores threats other than the event and does not consider whether additional management may be necessary once a species has returned to pre-incident levels. The NRDA perspective on recovery addresses the effects of an incident, not the status of a species as it existed beforehand: If the species was imperiled or conservation reliant before the incident, it will continue to be so after it has "recovered."

## WHAT IS "CONSERVATION SUCCESS"?

How we think about the language of conservation—terms such as "conservation," "species," "habitat," or "recovery"—leads to different perspectives on what constitutes "conservation success." To many conservationists, avoiding extinction by saving even a small number of individuals is success. The success stories that people like to hear, however, are those in which a species rebounds to the point where it has recovered and no longer needs special management. To Redford et al. (2011), success is achieved when a species is "fully conserved": the species maintains multiple populations across its range in representative ecological settings, with replicate, self-sustaining, and genetically robust populations in each setting—and it does so without human assistance. In other words, the species has made it to the left-hand end of the conservation spectrum of Figure 2.1.

The perspective on success offered by Redford et al. is by their own admission aspirational. It establishes a goal that is unlikely to be achievable for many imperiled or conservation-reliant species. By this measure, many conservation actions may be unable to achieve success, no matter how great the effort. But conservation of an imperiled species is a process that entails multiple steps, each of which has goals and measures of success. If the goal is avoiding extinction, isn't it a success if the species is still around? If a species has met recovery goals but is still conservation reliant, isn't that a success? Recognizing that there can be many successes along the way to self-sustaining populations sends an encouraging yet realistic message.

There are different perspectives about what conservation means and hopes to achieve. How one views a threat and decides what to do about it depends on whether one is trying to conserve a species, subspecies, evolutionary potential, or something else and whether one wants to conserve it for its intrinsic or instrumental value, or both. Whether the long-term investments needed to conserve a conservation-reliant species are considered worth the effort and expense hinges on which perspectives hold sway. Different perspectives lead to different conclusions and priorities. No single perspective is best in all circumstances.

# 4    What Are the Threats?

Conservation strives to eliminate or blunt threats to a species so that special management attention is no longer required. If the threats persist, however, ongoing management may be needed to ensure that the species is not on a pathway toward extinction.

To understand what makes an imperiled species conservation reliant, we begin with the threats. In this and the following chapter, we ask: What are the threats and why do some threats require long-term management but others can be diminished so the species can live long and prosper without dedicated management? How this question is answered holds the key to solving the problem of conservation reliance. Implementing management to address the threats can be impeded by several factors, so we then ask: What factors make it difficult to eliminate threats and perpetuate conservation reliance?

We begin with a story that illustrates how threats that interact over multiple scales may be hard to eliminate, leading to long-term conservation reliance. The Kihansi spray toad (Figure 4.1A) is a small, insectivorous amphibian that lives only in the spray zone at the base of Kihansi Falls in Tanzania—a total range of 2 ha (Channing et al. 2006; Nahonyo et al. 2017). It was described as a new species in 1999. The following year, the Kihansi Dam began operation upstream to help provide hydroelectric power to Tanzania's 57 million people. The dam greatly reduced spray from the falls and the toad's habitat disappeared.

To mimic the species' habitat, a gravity-fed sprinkler system was installed below the falls in 2001 (Figure 4.1B). For several years after their discovery the toads were abundant, varying between 11 000 and 21 000 individuals. But the population crashed in 2003, coincident with a breakdown of the sprinkler system during the dry season, the

FIGURE 4.1. (A) A Kihansi spray toad with a toadlet. The species is considered Extinct in the Wild by the IUCN. Photo: Julie Larson Maher © Wildlife Conservation Society. (B) The sprinkler spray system at the Mhalala Bridge over the Kihansi River, Tanzania. (A black and white version of this figure will appear in some formats. For the color version, please refer to the plate section.)
Photo: William Newmark.

appearance of a fungal pathogen (amphibian chytrid fungus), and a brief opening of the dam to flush out pesticide-laden sediments. Only three individuals could be found in early 2000 and there were no confirmed records thereafter. The species was declared extinct in the wild by IUCN in 2009.

Management of the spray toad to prevent its demise in the wild was confounded by multiple interacting threats that occurred at different spatial scales and were driven by different forces. The spray toad persists today because of rapid collaborative actions. The extinction of the spray toad in the wild had been anticipated. Three years before the toad population crashed, the Tanzanian government had established a captive-breeding program in collaboration with the Toledo Zoo, the Bronx Zoo, and the Wildlife Conservation Society, and the World Bank funded installation of the sprinkler system. A partnership between the government and the power company that operates the dam now ensures sufficient stream flows, The Wildlife Conservation Society continues to support the breeding program. An additional captive population has been established at the University of Dar es Salaam. Several thousand individuals have been released back into the wild and the species is slowly re-establishing itself at the sprinkler-sprayed base of Kihansi Falls.

## CLASSIFYING THREATS

Conservationists have devoted considerable attention to categorizing threats, assessing the impacts of threats, dissecting the sources of threats, and analyzing which threats may be most important in particular ecosystems. The threat classification used by IUCN, for example, recognizes 12 threat categories, 45 subcategories, and 73 sub-subcategories.[1] More generally, Wilson (1992) identified four major global threats, which he called the "mindless horsemen of the

---

[1] www.iucnredlist.org/resources/threat-classification-scheme. By this system, the spray toad is threatened by the sub-subcategories of renewable energy, large dams, invasive diseases, and herbicides and pesticides.

environmental apocalypse": human exploitation and overkill, habitat destruction, introduced species, and disease. We would add two more to Wilson's list: alteration of natural processes such as stream flows or fire regimes, and pollution—and, of course, there are the many consequences of global change. In addition to these anthropogenic threats, species also face natural disasters, such as volcanic eruptions, tsunamis, and hurricanes, that occur less frequently but can be devastating when they do occur.

## WHEN A SINGLE THREAT DOMINATES

When a species is imperiled by a single threat that dominates all others, a simple solution may sometimes be possible. As many of the case studies or stories in this book illustrate, habitat loss is often the primary cause of species' imperilment. Here the story of the Araripe manakin is instructive for what it tells us about the effects of habitat loss on a specialist species with a tiny distribution.

The Araripe manakin (Frontispiece and Figure 4.2) was discovered in 1996 in a small area of moist evergreen forest on the slope of the Chapada do Araripe (Araripe Plateau) in Ceará, Brazil. When the species was listed as Critically Endangered by IUCN in 2000, there were fewer than 50 individuals (although later surveys estimated a population of perhaps 800).

The primary threat was habitat destruction, first from development for housing and agriculture in the surrounding lowlands and then from deforestation on the slopes of the Chapada. Potentially suitable habitat became restricted to a narrow band on the slope of the Chapada (Linhares et al. 2010). In 2000, a large recreational water park (replete with asphalt roads and parking lots) was built in the area where the species was first discovered. Fires later destroyed the forest in one nesting area. The springs that fed the streams supporting the species' habitat were diverted for recreation and agriculture. Although the population apparently remained stable, suitable habitat was shrinking. The species seemed destined to follow the fate of the po'ouli and dusky seaside sparrow we described in Chapter 2.

FIGURE 4.2. An Araripe manakin, considered Critically Endangered by the IUCN. (A black and white version of this figure will appear in some formats. For the color version, please refer to the Frontispiece.)
Photo: Ian Thompson.

At this point, however, the stories diverge. In 2014, a 57-ha reserve was established through the joint efforts of a local conservation organization (Aquasis) and the American Bird Conservancy. A neighboring landowner set aside an additional 11 ha as a protected area. The conservation work hasn't stopped there. Native tree saplings are being planted to restore the forest in the reserve and collaborations with other local stakeholders may expand the conservation and reforestation to other areas of remaining moist-forest habitat on the Chapada. Although the protected areas must be maintained and the manakin population monitored to ensure that it remains stable or grows, the outlook for the species is good. The manakin has moved toward the left end of the conservation spectrum in Figure 2.1, although it is still conservation reliant.

Progress was possible in this case because the manakins occupied a small area, so habitat could be protected and restored at a scale that matched that of the threat. There were no bureaucratic or legal impediments, so governments and local citizens could collaborate in an effort to save the manakin. People responded quickly once the status of the manakin and the threat became known. Local communities are now using the Araripe manakin to promote ecotourism. In Essay 4.1, Dee Boersma provides an example of the role of ecotourism in promoting the conservation of penguins in Argentina.

Like habitat loss, disease can pose a single overpowering threat to species. This is especially true if the disease (or its vector) is not native to the ecosystems in which a species has evolved. In the Hawaiian Islands, for example, both avian malaria and its vector (the southern house mosquito) were inadvertently introduced in the nineteenth century. Native bird species, particularly Hawaiian honeycreepers, are highly susceptible to malaria. The disease has eliminated nearly all endemic bird species from lower elevations (<1200 m), where temperatures are not too cold for the mosquito vectors. As temperatures warm with climate change, the mosquitoes will survive and breed at higher elevations, bringing the threat into the remaining refugia of native birds (Paxton et al. 2016). One Hawaiian bird species, the 'amakihi, may be evolving resistance to avian malaria (Foster et al. 2007). Such evolutionary adaptation may help a species escape the grip of conservation reliance.

Efforts are now underway to find ways to control or eradicate avian malaria in Hawai'i. This would create opportunities for native birds to reoccupy suitable habitat in the low- and mid-elevation mosquito zone (although they would still face threats from predation by non-native species, habitat degradation, and disrupted food webs).

ESSAY 4.1   **Penguins of Punta Tombo, Argentina**

*P. Dee Boersma*

Penguins are scientifically interesting and, of course, endlessly fascinating. They are sentinel species, telling us about what is happening to the environment and motivating us to alter our behavior to reduce human-caused impacts. They are increasingly dependent on our conservation efforts and the science that informs our actions.

When I first went to Argentina in 1982 to study Magellanic penguins at Punta Tombo, it was because a company wanted to harvest penguins to turn their skins into high-fashion golf gloves, protein, and oil. Fortunately, the people living near the penguin colonies in Chubut, Argentina, protested to the military government to block the harvesting of penguins. With the help of William Conway and the Wildlife Conservation Society, I began what turned into a 37-year (and still counting) study. The Magellanic penguins at Punta Tombo now greet over 100 000 tourists during each breeding season from September until April (Figure E4.1.1). No longer do any businesses,

FIGURE E4.1.1. Magellanic penguins are curious about and tolerant of the thousands of tourists who visit Punta Tombo, Argentina, every year. (A black and white version of this figure will appear in some formats. For the color version, please refer to the plate section.)
Photo: P.D. Boersma.

ESSAY 4.1  **(cont.)**

government officials, or local residents talk about harvesting or killing penguins.

The land for the Chubut Provincial Reserve, donated by a local landowner, is making money for people and the government of Chubut. Punta Tombo is a wild place, where the winds howl, dust dances across the landscape, and penguin brays fill the air. What was once the largest breeding colony for Magellanic penguins in the world is now a mecca for people to see penguins. Visitors drive over 150 km into the steppes of Patagonia to see penguins, petrels, and other wildlife. The landscape at this "tourist attraction" is now encumbered with boardwalks, buildings, bathrooms, trails, and fences to accommodate people who want to visit a penguin's world. Fortunately, penguins are hardy creatures and have tolerated the intrusion, although it is clear that people are out of balance with nature at Punta Tombo. For example, as it is a desert, all the potable water has to be delivered in trucks and all the garbage has to be driven back to town. But nature persists. Humans need to live in better balance with nature if we are to retain places like Punta Tombo.

There are no places on Earth that are untouched by humans. Whether it is a garden, forest, or the sea, the human footprint is heavy and it will get heavier. Hopefully, technology will help lighten the human footprint, although there are no easy technological fixes for too many people and their unending consumption. For penguins at Punta Tombo, there are monumental challenges. What needs to be done to allow penguins to live more successfully with so many tourists visiting them on land? That is likely the most tractable problem because people can be educated to do the right thing. Visits by people can be restricted to midday, when most penguins are not traveling to and from their nests. Limiting trail extensions into the colony and elevating trails so penguins can walk under people and people over penguins are relatively simple accommodations that can be made. Other threats, such as climate change with increasing temperature and rainfall on penguin breeding grounds and inadequate food for penguins in the ocean, are not so easy to address.

What can or should humans try to do to manage and ensure penguins thrive for generations to come? We need to know what to do, where to

ESSAY 4.1   **(cont.)**

do it, and have the means to check to make sure that what we do works. We need science, long-term studies, and the political will to do the right thing for nature, wildlife, and, in the long term, for our planet.

When I went to Argentina, it took only took one trip to the beach at Punta Tombo to realize that oil pollution was a problem for penguins. There were literally hundreds of old mummified carcasses of penguins covered with petroleum. My Argentinian students and I obtained funds to walk beaches for a decade to look for oiled birds. We started in 1982 and counted dead penguins with and without oil on their feathers. We went to government hearings to publicize the problem. People saw live and dead penguins covered in petroleum on TV and in the newspapers. Finally, the provincial laws were modified in 1997 to require tankers to travel farther offshore and less petroleum was dumped illegally along the coast. Few penguins are now oiled along the Chubut coast. The government took steps that changed human actions—the dumping of petroleum nearshore is now rare. Nonetheless, it took over a decade of data, public hearings, and political support to get the tanker lanes moved and reduce the amount of petroleum dumped.

At Punta Tombo, we have followed the lives of individual penguins for 37 years. These data first showed the alarming adverse effects of petroleum. The penguin population at Punta Tombo has declined by about 1% per year for at least 30 years. The population in the 1970s probably reached 400 000 breeding pairs but is now les than 200 000. The sex ratio has become more and more biased toward males. Currently, there are nearly three males for every female at Punta Tombo. Mortality in the non-breeding season has been higher for females than males in every year we have studied the colony. When we do our breeding survey we look at nests that are occupied, so we are likely underestimating the decline of the population because if a penguin is at a nest we count it active. We now realize that we count a lot of males that never find a mate. We know of one male that is now at least 14 years old, has a high-quality nest with lots of shade, but has had only one female keep him company for only a few hours of one day in all those years.

ESSAY 4.1  **(cont.)**

So, what is happening to the females? In the non-breeding period penguins migrate north and winter from northern Argentina to southern Brazil, eating anchovy, which is considered an "underexploited" fishery. As the climate has changed and fishing pressure has increased, starvation has become the major cause of death for penguins during the non-breeding season. Additionally, when the Rio de la Plata Current in northern Argentina is strong, females return to Punta Tombo late, in poorer body condition, and lay smaller eggs.

The threat of starvation or demographic changes caused by diminished food availability is exacerbated by what may be the biggest problem—climate change. The frequency and severity of rainstorms have increased over the last 30 years at Punta Tombo. In one year, a single storm killed half of all the chicks in less than a day. More often, heat kills an adult or a few chicks here and there. Even when an extreme event occurs and many chicks die, it goes largely unnoticed. The impact of that one storm killing half the chicks may not be seen for 5 to 7 years, as that is how long it takes for a chick to return to the population to breed.

What can humans do to make sure penguins at Punta Tombo and elsewhere thrive for generations to come? If we want Magellanic penguins to succeed at Punta Tombo, we need to protect their food in the non-breeding period, as well as during the breeding season. There is no marine protected area on the non-breeding grounds of Magellanic penguins. There should be. The challenge will be for three nations (Brazil, Uruguay, and Argentina) to agree to a marine protected area so that penguins and other predators have plenty of food in the non-breeding season.

Solving the problems that face penguins and, more fundamentally, humans and society, requires good science, knowledge founded on long-term studies, and the political and societal will to mitigate human rapaciousness. Societal priorities will need to shift to valuing education, the natural world, and other creatures more, not less. Whether penguins will continue to share the planet with us depends on our knowledge and our willingness to use it.

Similar efforts are being made to halt the spread and manage the effects of the amphibian chytrid fungus and salamander chytrid fungus that have decimated amphibian populations in many places around the world, as well as the fungus that causes white-nose syndrome, which has led to massive mortality in bat populations in eastern North America. It remains to be seen whether these efforts will be successful.

Eradicating a disease is a daunting task, but the history of rinderpest shows that it is possible. Rinderpest was an often fatal viral disease that infected a wide range of domestic and wild even-toed ungulates, from cattle in Asia and Europe to buffaloes, giraffes, and antelope in Africa. It altered the ecology of entire ecosystems (Spinage 2003; Holdo et al. 2009). By the 1980s and 1990s, rinderpest had become the focus of an intense global eradication campaign that was ultimately successful. The last confirmed case occurred in 2001 and the disease was declared globally eradicated in 2011.

Several factors contributed to the elimination of rinderpest, including public support for protecting domestic cattle and coordinated campaigns joining national governments with multinational organizations. In the end, however, the disease was controlled through medical technology, which developed an effective vaccine to prevent transmission of the virus.

Like disease, pesticides and contaminants may pose a single overwhelming threat that can be controlled or eliminated. In this case, laws and regulations that restrict or ban their use are most effective; such bans typically occur only when alternatives are available to control unwanted pests, parasites, or pathogens. The classic example is DDT. Following World War II, organochlorine pesticides, especially DDT, became widely used in North America. Concentrations of DDT in the food of several bird species caused eggshells to thin and break. Reproduction failed and bird populations rapidly declined.

Peregrine falcons (Figure 4.3) were especially vulnerable. By 1964, peregrines no longer nested in the eastern United States. The species was listed as Endangered in 1970. In response to health and environmental concerns (many captured in Rachel Carson's 1962

FIGURE 4.3. A peregrine falcon. (A black and white version of this figure will appear in some formats. For the color version, please refer to the plate section.)
Photo: Roy W. Lowe, US Fish and Wildlife Service.

book *Silent Spring*), the United States and Canada banned the use of DDT in 1972.[2] An aggressive program of breeding peregrines in captivity was initiated. Captive-bred birds were reintroduced to many areas, and eggs and nestlings were transferred into nests in the wild. Breeding success was high, populations recovered, and the species re-established itself in much of its former range (Burnham and Cade

[2] The Stockholm Convention on Persistent Organic Pollutants, which came into force in 2004, aims to eliminate or restrict the production and use of persistent organic pollutants (including DDT) worldwide. Despite its leadership in banning DDT, the United States has not joined the 181 other nations and the European Union that are parties to the Convention, stating that it "currently lack[s] the authority to implement all of its provisions." To control vectors of malaria and other diseases, DDT remains heavily used in some countries, particularly India. The search for alternatives to DDT is coordinated by the United Nations (www.unenvironment .org/explore-topics/chemicals-waste/what-we-do/persistent-organic-pollutants/ alternatives-ddt).

2003). By 1998, there were 1650 known breeding pairs in the United States and Canada, well above the recovery goal of 632 pairs. The American peregrine was delisted in 1999 and populations have continued to increase.

Vultures are a different story. Vultures are obligate scavengers and are vulnerable to contaminants in their food. In India, Pakistan, and other areas on the Indian subcontinent, white-rumped, slender-billed, Indian, and red-headed vultures have experienced massive declines since the 1990s; all are considered Critically Endangered by IUCN. The primary cause is feeding on carcasses of livestock that have been treated with veterinary diclofenac, a non-steroid drug used to treat pain and inflammation in cattle and other animals (Green et al. 2004).[3] Vultures that ingest even small quantities of diclofenac suffer kidney failure within a few days. The loss of vultures has had secondary effects on human health: feral dogs have multiplied as competition with vultures over carcasses has decreased, leading to a higher incidence of rabies mortality among people than would be the case if vultures remained at their earlier, far-higher population levels (Markandya et al. 2008).

Veterinary use of diclofenac was banned in India, Pakistan, and Nepal in 2006 and in Bangladesh in 2010. Although comprehensive enforcement is difficult, vulture populations are slowly beginning to rebound (Prakash et al. 2012), in part because there are alternative veterinary medications (e.g. meloxicam) that are safe and have similar properties. Some other drugs that are increasingly being used in place of diclofenac are toxic, however, so the story may not yet be over unless use of these drugs can also be brought under control. Spain, which hosts the greatest numbers of vultures in Europe, continues to permit veterinary uses of diclofenac. In Essay 4.2, Chris Bowden describes some of the complex issues surrounding the diclofenac ban.

---

[3] Unlike Old World vultures (Accipitridae), New World vultures such as the turkey vulture (Cathartidae) can tolerate much greater concentrations of diclofenac.

ESSAY 4.2 **Reflections on the Asian Vulture Crisis**

*Christopher G.R. Bowden*

I've spent my 35 year career addressing threats to endangered species. Initially, I conducted research on nationally rare woodlarks and nightjars in the United Kingdom, but then went on to Cameroon montane endemic birds through developing local rural-development initiatives. It was my many years based in Morocco working on northern bald ibis where my role evolved into one of not just collecting vital information, but nurturing the wider conservation and governmental communities to work together to implement priority conservation actions.

The bald ibis community was about as diverse as you can imagine, varying from passionate individuals, zoo groups, conservation NGOs, and university and animal behavioral researchers to national park staff and government officials from countries like Syria, where conservation and western involvement were quite novel. It has been satisfying to see how coordinating these groups and developing action plans and agreed priorities with all these parties have resulted in the first recorded population increase for the species in Morocco. Northern bald ibis have now been downlisted from Critically Endangered to Endangered by IUCN—a wonderful acknowledgment of progress. But it was in March 2004, when the conservation director for the Royal Society for the Protection of Birds called me to his office to ask me to accept an even greater coordination challenge: for Asian vultures. This was a month or two after the revelation that diclofenac was the main driver of the unprecedented declines. I was both flattered and daunted by the scope of the challenge involved, but I agreed to take it on, at least for 3 years. And here I am, 15 years later, still immersed in the issue.

The priority actions for Asian vultures were initially to identify a safe alternative drug as a prerequisite for pushing for a veterinary diclofenac ban, something we always knew would be a tough call. Meanwhile, we also needed to develop an *ex situ* breeding and release program while there were still sufficient birds in the wild to be a safety net for the species. This had never been done for these species.

ESSAY 4.2   **(cont.)**

Identifying meloxicam as a viable alternative drug was a massive breakthrough. Together with concerted advocacy efforts spearheaded by the Indian BirdLife Partner, the Bombay Natural History Society, as well as other national and international NGOs, this resulted in India, Pakistan, and Nepal all banning the production, sale, and use of veterinary diclofenac in 2006. As it was for the ibis, the array of players was extremely diverse. The challenge of maintaining a clear, scientifically grounded message that could be heard by governments while avoiding the pitfalls of local rivalries and competing interests resulted in us creating a consortium to provide a transparent umbrella and context for developing an agreed regional action plan. We called this consortium 'Saving Asia's Vultures from Extinction' (SAVE). It now has 24 partners and meets and reports annually, reviewing and reporting against the regional action plan (see www.save-vultures.org). The SAVE consortium provides a transparent, agreed voice of recognized expertise and regional representation to set the key priorities. This helps guide funders and decision makers to support those priority actions. The Convention of Migratory Species recently developed a multi-species action plan for all Old World vultures; for Asia, this fully endorses and builds on the SAVE regional action plan. A lot of my time now is devoted to communicating with and coordinating this partnership and the related reporting.

Since the initial diclofenac bans in 2006, there have been several further steps that have been key additional measures: the gazettement (official publication) of the 2006 bans in 2008, the mandatory labeling of veterinary supplies of diclofenac as 'not for veterinary use,' and the Bangladesh ban in 2010. By then, it had become clear that human diclofenac (the same formulation as veterinary) was being bottled in larger vials that facilitated illegal veterinary use and, in 2015, the Indian Government agreed to restrict vial size to 3 ml. It was in 2011 that we received the latest results from India- and Nepal-wide vulture road-transect surveys, and we saw that these measures had really stemmed the declines. What a day that was! This result, more than any other in my career, was a clear signal that all the efforts were paying off and that the future releases could really become a viable

## ESSAY 4.2   (cont.)

contribution to vulture population recoveries. These birds may now not be going extinct (Figure E4.2.1)!

Despite the relative simplicity in this case of a single major threat, dealing with it has been complicated by the fact that birds die days after ingesting diclofenac, so it is very much an invisible cause. Consequently, many conservationists and biologists remained skeptical that this was really the main problem. The tests are highly sophisticated and specialized, and can give unreliable results, adding to speculation that other competing causes may be responsible and diluting the urgency to continue addressing the veterinary drugs threat. The fact that other toxic and untested drugs are now also emerging in veterinary use means we can't yet relax, and the vulture release and safety-testing programs still have an important role to play. The vultures are still conservation reliant.

It is to the great credit of the South Asian governments that the bans were put in place as quickly as they were, and to the dedication of some

FIGURE E4.2.1. White-rumped vultures attending a cow carcass in Nepal. (A black and white version of this figure will appear in some formats. For the color version, please refer to the plate section.)
Photo: Chris Bowden/RSPB.

ESSAY 4.2  **(cont.)**

key individuals such as Vibhu Prakash and his team. Vultures are very unlikely to be as super-abundant as they were prior to this problem. It will ultimately be down to the upholding of these regulatory changes to save Asian vulture populations from extinction.

## MULTIPLE THREATS MULTIPLY THE CHALLENGES

Threats such as habitat loss, disease, pesticides, and other contaminants can be eliminated if there is a single dominant threat and the threat is controllable. Conservation efforts can then advance. When species face multiple threats, however, controlling or eliminating all threats becomes much more difficult and the species are more likely to depend on long-term management.

In Africa, populations of most vulture species are declining precipitously. Although the most critical threat is poisoning, it takes different forms and affects species differently in different areas (Botha et al. 2017). For example, bearded and white-backed vultures are killed when they feed on poisoned bait actually intended for predators or problem animals. Other species, such as hooded, Cape, or lappet-faced vultures, may be intentionally poisoned by poachers, who lace carcasses of illegally killed rhinoceroses, elephants, and lions with poisons to kill carrion feeders that might act as sentinels to attract the attention of law-enforcement personnel. Vultures are also killed for body parts that are used in various belief practices or trade crafts. Electrocution or collisions with energy infrastructure also threaten many vulture species.

These threats are hard to mitigate, enforcement is problematic, and coordination among different countries and cultures is challenging. The factors that drive poisoning, for example, vary geographically: Belief-based poisoning is prevalent in parts of west and central Africa, whereas poisoning of sentinels is a problem where poaching occurs in southern Africa (Figure 4.4). As multiple vulture species are

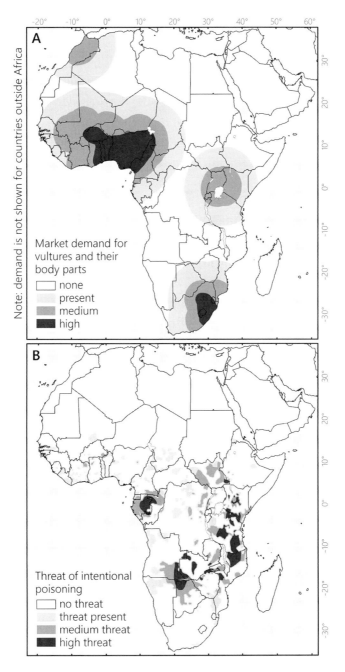

FIGURE 4.4. The geographic distribution of poisoning threats to vulture species in Africa. (A) Poisoning for belief-based use of vultures and their body parts. (B) Poisoning to kill vultures that might act as sentinels of illegal poaching activities.

*Source*: redrafted after Botha et al. (2017)/Habitat INFO.

imperiled by similar threats it makes sense to consider multiple species together; because the affected species range across many countries, a coordinated, comprehensive approach is needed. We describe one such multi-species action plan in Chapter 8.

Even when a species appears to be threatened by a single factor, threats are often intertwined, so resolving one may allow another to emerge (Zavaleta et al. 2001). Here is an example. Introduced European rabbits posed a major threat to the habitat of nesting seabirds on Macquarie Island in the southern Pacific Ocean. A program to eliminate rabbits by introducing myxomatosis was initiated in 1979. Over the next decade, rabbit numbers were reduced by 90%, but the program stopped before all the rabbits were eliminated. In the meantime, feral cats, which had preferred to eat rabbits, switched to preying on nesting seabirds as rabbits became scarce. The impact of cats on seabirds prompted another eradication program, which led to the elimination of cats from Macquarie by 1985. Success? Not quite. During the cat-eradication campaign, there was an unanticipated increase in rabbits, rats, and house mice, which led to a significant reduction in vegetation cover, which increased predation on seabirds and altered food webs. Dealing with one threat at a time wasn't working. Finally, a fully integrated management plan was implemented to eliminate rats, mice, and rabbits from Macquarie (Bergstrom et al. 2009a, b; Dowding et al. 2009). Macquarie Island was declared pest-free in 2014. Although the seabird species on Macquarie (17 of them Threatened) have moved closer to the recovery end of the conservation spectrum of Figure 2.1, they remain conservation reliant because of the need for continuing monitoring to ensure that the threats of cats, rabbits, rats, mice, or other invasive species do not reappear.

Sometimes multiple threats appear sequentially: once measures to address one threat have been implemented, a new, unanticipated threat appears. Such is the story of the northern spotted owl. Spotted owls are closely tied to the old-growth coniferous forests that were once widespread from the Pacific Northwest to northwestern California (Olson and Van Horne 2017). These forests are prized for their timber, and many communities in the Pacific Northwest used to depend on harvesting and milling timber. Between the early 1900s and 1940, older forests in Oregon and Washington decreased by 24%. Following World War II, the combination of timber harvesting, wild-fire, and housing development led to an additional loss of almost half of the older forests by 2012 (Davis et al. 2017). With the disappearance of old-growth habitat, the spotted owl populations crashed. The species was listed as Threatened under the Endangered Species Act in 1990. A court order halted logging in national forests in 1991. To stem the tide of habitat loss that threatened the owl, the 1994 North-west Forest Plan established a conservation strategy for the owl and associated wildlife on federal lands and coordinated management among federal agencies (USDA and USDI 1994).

Neither conservationists nor the timber industry was satisfied with the compromise proposed by the plan. Although demand for timber was already declining and automation was replacing some jobs, the closure of many timber operations and loss of jobs in the region was widely blamed on the owl and overreaching environmental protection by the federal government. Older forest habitat on federal lands managed under the plan decreased only slightly between 1993 and 2012, but logging continued on the private lands that were not subject to the restrictions of the plan. The owls were increasingly confined to protected forests on federal land and owl populations continued to decline (Figure 4.5; Dugger et al. 2016).

Then a new threat emerged. Closely related barred owls, histor-ically inhabitants of forests in eastern North America, began disper-sing westward early in the twentieth century and had reached British Columbia by mid-century. They had expanded through west-coast forests by the 1980s (Livezey 2009).[4] As barred owl numbers rapidly

---

[4] Livezey suggested that the range expansion of the barred owl was aided by the control of fires and expansion of woodlands across the prairies of the Great Plains. Whether this expansion was "natural" or facilitated by human activities is debated (Monahan and Hijmans 2007; Livezey et al. 2008). The fact remains that the owls did it without direct human assistance.

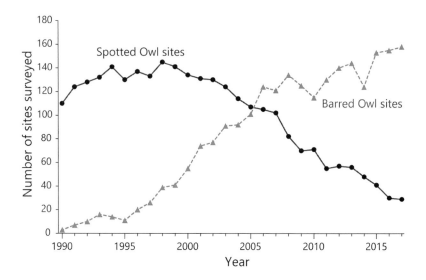

FIGURE 4.5. Proportion of northern spotted owl sites in which barred owls and spotted owls were detected on an Oregon Coast Range study area, 1990–2017.
From Lesmeister et al. (2018).

increased, they began to pose a significant competitive threat to spotted owls in old-growth forests. Barred owls occupy the same forest conditions as spotted owls but are larger and more aggressive, occupy smaller territories (and can therefore attain greater population densities), take a wider variety of prey, and have a greater survival and reproductive potential; in short, they are superior competitors. Barred owls displaced spotted owls from breeding territories and excluded them from remnant patches of old-forest habitat protected under the Northwest Forest Plan (Lesmeister et al. 2018).

To counter this emergent threat, an experimental program was implemented to remove barred owls from areas previously favored by spotted owls (Wiens et al. 2018). Pilot studies in California demonstrated that removing barred owls, when coupled with habitat conservation, could slow or even reverse population declines of spotted owls (Diller et al. 2016). Whether similar results can be obtained in other areas with different forest conditions, greater densities of barred owls, and fewer remaining spotted owls is unclear. Regardless, the population densities of barred owls, coupled with their high survival and reproductive potential, suggest that continued control of barred owl numbers will be necessary until more effective management tools are developed if the northern spotted owl is to survive.

The case of the spotted and barred owls highlights how long-term conservation plans must not only address multiple interacting threats, but also have the capability to quickly respond to new threats as they emerge. The story is still being written. Both owl species now face the additional threat of poison used to control rodents on illegal marijuana operations in the forests. Marijuana production and use are now legal (at least under state laws) in Washington, Oregon, and California, but illegal use of rat poison continues. The conservation reliance of spotted owls is increasing as threats proliferate and owl populations continue to dwindle.

## LAWS AND REGULATIONS CAN HELP AND HINDER

The plight of the spotted owl has been addressed in part through legal and regulatory mechanisms. The Endangered Species Act provides protection to the owl and the Northwest Forest Plan articulates policies and guidance for managing owl habitat. Although these legal and bureaucratic measures have helped, they have not addressed the continuing loss of habitat on private lands or anticipated the magnitude of the emerging threat from barred owls (or rat poison).

There is little doubt that legal and bureaucratic measures have been effective in addressing, and sometimes eliminating, threats to some imperiled species. By providing legal protection and fostering recovery planning, the Endangered Species Act has played a pivotal role in the conservation of endangered species in the United States, as have similar laws in other countries. Peregrines recovered because laws mandated a halt to the use of DDT. American alligators and Aleutian cackling geese recovered in part because hunting those species was banned. International treaties or organizations can impose limits on killing or harvesting species that move across national boundaries or roam over the open ocean. For example, in 1949 the International Whaling Commission established a moratorium on commercial harvesting of whales, allowing several imperiled species to rebound (Punt and Donovan 2007).

When the major factor threatening a species can be regulated or outlawed, a pathway for avoiding extinction and escaping conservation reliance may open, but bureaucracies may move too slowly relative to a species' needs, as with the extinction of the golden toad or the rapid relapse of the woylie. The story of the Christmas Island pipistrelle is one of bureaucratic dithering while a species declined to extinction. The process of listing a species under the Endangered Species Act is arduous and almost always generates lawsuits, further delaying conservation action. Removing invasive species such as rats, cats, or goats from an island usually requires permits from multiple sources and is also likely to face legal challenges. Experimental removals of barred owls to benefit spotted owls faced legal challenges despite years of public and stakeholder outreach before the experiments began.

Laws and regulations may also restrict management actions that might aid in the recovery of an endangered or conservation-reliant species. 'Alalā historically occurred only on the island of Hawai'i. The 'alalā was threatened by a variety of factors—predation by introduced rats, cats, and Javan mongooses; deforestation; illegal shooting; avian malaria; and loss of habitat to invasive plants and development. The last report of a free-living 'alalā was in 2002; the species was extinct in the wild.

A captive-breeding program had been initiated in the 1990s, however, and 27 birds were released while the species still existed in the wild. This attempt at reintroduction failed. Released birds were threatened by disease (toxoplasmosis) and native and non-native predators, including the 'io (Hawaiian hawk), which is also listed as Endangered under the Endangered Species Act. The future of the species rested on the 40 birds remaining in captivity. By 2016, there were over 125 birds living in captive-breeding facilities and another attempt at reintroduction was made at a different location. This attempt also failed, for many of the same reasons. The rearing and release program was redesigned to release birds in an area with no known breeding pairs of 'io and at a more favorable time of year. Young birds were trained to avoid predators. A third attempt to establish a free-living population of 'alalā was made in 2017: of the 11 birds released, 10 were still alive a year later, when an additional 10 birds were released. Groups of 'alalā have been seen mobbing 'io and at least one pair has initiated nesting activities. Efforts by the 'Alalā Project mean there is still hope for the 'alalā.

During recovery planning, it was also suggested that 'alalā be released on other Hawaiian Islands where the 'io or other threats do not occur (and where fossils record that the 'alalā or its ecological equivalent once occurred). Although this might have enabled the 'alalā to begin recovery in the wild decades ago, the suggestion was rejected because such actions would conflict with efforts to protect other Threatened and Endangered species. Translocations to other islands would also be likely to require an Environmental Impact Statement under the provisions of the National Environmental Policy Act (NEPA; see Chapter 6).

Sometimes the only way to rescue a species is to circumvent rules and bureaucratic inertia. The Owens pupfish was once common in water bodies in the Owens Valley of California. Water diversions drained its habitat and, by the 1940s, it was thought to be extinct. A small population was rediscovered in one small spring in 1962 and the species was listed as Endangered in 1967. Conditions in the sole pond in which the species existed continued to deteriorate. By August 1969, vegetation was depleting oxygen in the pond and the pond was drying up. Faced with the prospect of losing the species, and despite warnings from his supervisors, a California Fish and Game biologist, Phil Pister, took action. He scooped up the remaining pupfish and walked away from the only place where the species could be found with all the remaining individuals in two buckets. Pister released the fish in several nearby spring-fed ponds. The species is still threatened by encroachment of cattails and by native and non-native predators and competitors and it is still considered Endangered, but the threats are being managed. By 2009, thousands of individuals could be found in several locations. The Owens pupfish owes its existence to one individual who ignored the rules and took action. Phil Pister recounted the story of rescuing the Owens pupfish in an essay in *Natural History* magazine (Pister 1993).

Unfortunately, there are others who also ignore the rules, but with different intentions. Most nations have policies and laws that regulate the exploitation of plant and animal species; such restrictions are particularly stringent for imperiled species. Laws and regulations are effective only when they are enforced, however. Wherever there is a strong financial incentive, there is likely to be pressure for illegal trade in endangered wildlife (or their body parts) on the black market. Thousands of animals are killed every year to satisfy demands for traditional medicines, exotic foods, or as status symbols to demonstrate wealth and success. It is a lucrative business. A kilogram of rhinoceros horn (used for traditional Chinese medicines or to make dagger handles) is currently valued at US$60 000–$100 000. Such amounts are an overpowering incentive for poachers and criminal syndicates, especially in areas where people struggle in poverty. Countering this threat requires a combination of local conservation efforts and enforcement of existing laws or treaties, such as the Convention on International Trade in Endangered Species (CITES) (Fabinyi and Liu 2014).

The story of the Tibetan antelope shows how law enforcement can counter the threat of poaching. Tibetan antelope (known locally as chiru) (Figure 4.6) inhabit the steppe of the Tibetan Plateau in Tibet and northwestern India (Leslie and Schaller 2008). Antelope coats are highly valued for their exceptionally soft and fine underfur, *shahtoosh*, an adaptation to the frigid high-elevation (3500–5500 m) environment. The wool is used to make shawls that can sell for thousands of dollars. Three or more Tibetan antelope must be killed for the wool to make a single shawl, leading to rampant poaching. International

FIGURE 4.6. Tibetan antelope in Zanda County, Tibet Autonomous Region, China, 2015. (A black and white version of this figure will appear in some formats. For the color version, please refer to the plate section.) Photo: Panda Eye/Alamy.

trade in shahtoosh was prohibited by CITES in 1979, but poaching drove a continuing decline in the antelope population from as many as a million in the early twentieth century to fewer than 75 000 in the mid-1990s. At the peak of antelope poaching in the 1980s and 1990s, perhaps 20 000 antelope were being killed each year for their wool.

Several actions were taken to protect the Tibetan antelope from poaching and reduce the driving force of market demand for shahtoosh shawls. The Chinese government established the Chang Tang Reserve in 1993, strengthened trade restrictions, and initiated ranger patrols.[5] Wildlife Conservation Society scientists conducted surveys and publicized the peril of the antelope. To ban sales of the shawls in the United States, the species was listed under the Endangered Species Act (although the shawls are still sold openly in some other countries). The reserve, already the second largest in the world ($334\,000\,\text{km}^2$), was linked to a network of other reserves to enable the antelope to migrate between summering and wintering grounds. The conservation efforts paid off (Leclerc et al. 2015). Well over 100 000 antelope now roam the Tibetan Plateau.

Poaching is still rampant where the species occurs in India and Kashmir. The IUCN regards the species as Near Threatened, noting: "the current status can only be maintained with continued high levels of protection in its natural range and strict controls on trade and manufacture of the shawls made from its underfur; any relaxation in the protection regime are [sic] predicted to result in a rapid population decline due to commercial poaching."[6] It would be hard to find a clearer statement of conservation reliance than this one.

Overexploitation and poaching of imperiled species are not confined to animals. The decline of Robbins cinquefoil, described in Chapter 2, was in part due to plant aficionados collecting plants from the tiny area in which the species occurred. Overexploitation of plants favored by horticulturists can be especially damaging: supply–demand economics tells us that as a resource becomes increasingly scarce, demand increases and drives up the price. This cycle has caused the decline of mahogany in Central American tropical forests, sandalwood in the Hawaiian Islands, and many threatened species of cactus in the Americas (Goettsch et al. 2015). As with animal exploitation, the problem usually is not a lack of laws but the challenge of providing sufficient enforcement.[7]

---

[5] The challenge of stopping illegal poaching was highlighted in the 2004 Chinese film, *Kekexili: Mountain Patrol.*

[6] www.iucnredlist.org/details/15967/0.

[7] For instance, apprehending poachers and smugglers in the desolate, arid environs favored by cacti is challenging. Phippen (2016) gives a fascinating account of efforts to enforce these laws and catch cactus poachers in the act.

GETTING TO THE ROOT CAUSES OF THREATS

Conservation often pits the interests of a species against those of people, leading to controversy and conflicts that impede management efforts. Most threats are consequences of human activities, so there is almost always a socioeconomic driver behind the threats. This may lead to conflicts over what is valued, by whom. Some actions that threaten species, such as subsistence hunting for wildlife, clearing forests, or diverting rivers for irrigation of food crops, may be essential to people's livelihoods. Controlling the feral pigs that destroy remnant native forest in Hawai'i can create conflicts with hunters who value pigs as a recreational resource or with native Hawaiians who view pigs as part of their cultural fabric. On Lord Howe Island in the Tasman Sea, proposals to eradicate rats to save the endemic Lord Howe stick insect and other species are championed by some residents and condemned by others[8]. When a species is conservation reliant and the management and investment must be ongoing, conflicts may become more intense.

Here, the story of Mexico's vaquita porpoise is apropos (Bessesen 2018). The vaquita (Figure 4.7) lives only in the northern Gulf of California (Sea of Cortez), a highly productive marine ecosystem surrounded by severe desert. The villages next to the vaquita's habitat rely on fishing with gillnets, which accidentally entangle and drown vaquitas. Vaquitas were only described as a species in 1958, were never abundant, and were listed as Critically Endangered by IUCN in 1996. By 1997, estimates of the numbers of vaquitas killed in gillnets and the number of vaquitas remaining (around 600) indicated that the kill rate was unsustainable. An international recovery team (Comité Internacional para la Recuperación de la Vaquita, or CIRVA), established in 1997, advised the government of Mexico that gillnets needed to be banned if vaquitas were to survive and that alternative fishing methods and livelihoods needed to be developed. No actions

---

[8] After years of planning and delays the eradication program was finally launched in 2019; see https://science.sciencemag.org/content/364/6444/915/tab-pdf.

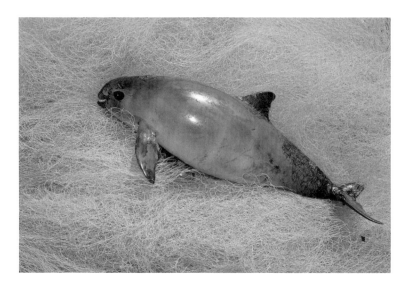

FIGURE 4.7. A vaquita, the world's most endangered marine mammal, entangled in a gillnet. (A black and white version of this figure will appear in some formats. For the color version, please refer to the plate section.)
Photo: Flip Nicklin/Minden Pictures.

were taken, the number of fisherfolk and the amount of net increased dramatically, and by 2006 only 245 vaquitas remained.

The plight of the vaquita worsened with the resurgence in 2011 of an illegal fishery for totoaba, a large fish listed as Critically Endangered by IUCN. Swim bladders of totoaba are dried and smuggled to China, where they are a prized delicacy in soup and widely believed to have medicinal benefits. A single swim bladder may command thousands of dollars on the black market. Gillnet fishing was finally banned throughout the vaquita's range in 2015, but illegal fishing for shrimp and totoaba continues in spite of deterrence efforts by conservation organizations and the Mexican navy. This added vaquita mortality resulted in a catastrophic decline and by 2016 only 30 vaquita remained (Thomas 2017). In September 2018, scientists observed only six vaquitas (Jaramillo-Legoretta et al. 2019) and estimated that fewer than 19 remained. The vaquita is the world's most endangered marine mammal.

The vaquita is conservation reliant, but even massive conservation efforts have not stemmed its plunge. The finding in 2018 that vaquitas could give birth annually (Figure E4.3.1) offers a glimmer of hope. But saving vaquitas (and many other small cetaceans with declines caused by gillnetting) depends on using alternative fishing methods and developing markets that pay the true costs of fishing sustainably. The vaquita example also illustrates that even with a single threat (gillnets), the issues that make it difficult to eliminate the threat can be very deep rooted. For example, switching from gillnets to alternative gear requires good governance, and stopping illegal activities requires adequate laws, enforcement, and stopping corruption. Saving the vaquita depends as well on addressing the socioeconomic drivers of fisherfolk trying to make a living and a market demand halfway around the world, as Taylor and Rojas-Bracho illustrate in Essay 4.3.

In many rivers and streams of the world, the primary threat is altered hydrology, often resulting from dams. People harness waterways for irrigation, agriculture, industrial and domestic uses, and hydropower. Perhaps a third of the world's freshwater fish are at risk from dams in just three of the world's most biodiverse major river drainages: the Amazon, Congo, and Mekong (Winemiller et al. 2016). Upstream dams on major rivers in the Amazon basin, such as the Tucuruí dam in Brazil, have altered the "floods of fortune" that formerly replenished the vast floodplains that nurture both people and a rich diversity of plants and animals (Goulding et al. 1996). If the dams proposed for the Mekong are constructed, not only could they cause the loss of over a third of the fish species in the system (International Center for Environmental Management 2010) but they will also jeopardize the well-being of some 40 million people who depend on the river for agriculture and fisheries.

The greatest threats of dams on the Mekong lie in the future. Major rivers in most developed parts of the world were dammed long ago, and the devastating ecological effects have been clear for some time.

ESSAY 4.3   **The Lessons of the Vaquita**

*Barbara Taylor and Lorenzo Rojas-Bracho*

Mexico's vaquita porpoise is the world's most endangered marine mammal (Figure E4.3.1). Fewer than 22 individuals remain. Numbers have declined precipitously over the past decades due to the accidental bycatch in illegal gillnets described in this chapter. To date, efforts to save the vaquita have failed, but there are some important lessons to be learned.

The decline of vaquitas began during a fishery for a large fish called the totoaba. By the mid-1980s, both were declared endangered under Mexican law. As the totoaba fishery became economically unviable, the main fisheries in the region converted to gillnet fisheries for finfish and shrimp. The international recovery team (Comité Internacional para la Recuperación de la Vaquita, or CIRVA), established in 1997, repeatedly stressed that if the vaquita was to survive, use and possession of all gillnets must be banned throughout its range. A protected area, the Vaquita Refuge, was established in 2005. The use of gillnets was banned in about half of the vaquita's range. However,

FIGURE E4.3.1. An adult and juvenile vaquita photographed in the Gulf of California on October 18, 2018. Adults with calves were again sighted in autumn 2019 (Barbara Taylor, personal communication). (A black and white version of this figure will appear in some formats. For the color version, please refer to the plate section.)
Photo: Paula Olson/NOAA.

ESSAY 4.3 **(cont.)**

enforcement was at best inconsistent and the refuge remained essentially unmanaged. The species' total population declined by around 57% between 1997 and 2008. It was not until 2015 that gillnet fishing was banned (on paper) throughout the shrinking range of the vaquita. The *in situ* approaches were not working.

Illegal fishing of totoaba never stopped, despite the closure in 1975 and the banning of totoaba gillnets in 1992. In about 2011, a large illegal totoaba fishery resurged and the resulting catastrophic decline of vaquitas was quickly apparent from the acoustic monitoring methods put in place in the hope of documenting the recovery of vaquitas resulting from the Vaquita Refuge (Jaramillo-Legorreta et al. 2016). Up to this point, CIRVA had rejected *ex situ* options because members had concluded that the animals had a better chance of surviving in the wild than in captivity.

Despite emergency actions announced by the Mexican government, the measures were not properly implemented and the continued documented vaquita decline, plus high numbers of illegal gillnets being removed from their habitat, led CIRVA to reconsider whether *ex situ* actions were needed. In 2014, CIRVA started to develop a step-by-step plan for learning to capture and care for vaquitas in captivity. However, by 2016 it was estimated that only 30 animals remained. Eight dead vaquitas were recovered in 2016 and 2017, with the cause of death determined to be entanglement in gillnets, and the Vaquita Conservation, Protection, and Recovery (VaquitaCPR) consortium was formed. CIRVA recognized that "the risks of capture and captive management are high, but these are greatly outweighed by the risk of entanglement in illegal gillnets in the wild."[9] They concluded that the only hope for the species was to abandon step-by-step approach and immediately capture as many vaquitas as possible so that they could be brought into a safe haven, away from the gillnets and under human care until their natural environment became threat free.

---

[9] Report of the Ninth Meeting of the Comité Internacional para la Recuperación de la Vaquita (CIRVA-9) (2017). Available at: www.iucn-csg.org/index.php/downloads/.

ESSAY 4.3    **(cont.)**

In early 2017, planning for the VaquitaCPR field program began with a clear understanding of the risks related to gaps in knowledge about the species and the possibility that vaquitas could die during capture, handling, and movement. Vaquitas are shy animals that tend to keep well away from motorized vessels. No one had ever attempted to catch vaquitas and hence no body of experience with handling or housing this species existed.

The VaquitaCPR team, which included 90 researchers, technicians, animal handlers, and veterinarians from nine countries, faced many challenges: just finding vaquitas in view of how few remained; safely capturing and transporting them; and establishing appropriate sea- and land-based housing facilities (Rojas-Bracho et al. 2019). Two vaquitas were captured in the autumn of 2017. The first, an approximately 6-month-old female, did not deal well with the stress of being captured and was released soon after it was captured. The second, a 15-year-old non-lactating female, initially appeared to adjust to the confined environment but shortly died of capture myopathy. With so few vaquitas remaining, the risk of additional deaths was deemed too high to proceed. Further capture attempts were immediately suspended.

The failure to stem the vaquita's decline despite years of *in situ* research, direct interventions, negotiations with government agencies, and the VaquitaCPR emergency *ex situ* effort, provides important lessons for other rapidly declining species reduced to small population sizes and facing similar anthropogenic threats that could lead to extinction.

Setbacks such as the death of an animal are likely to be inevitable during the early stages of an *ex situ* program. Allowances for such costs should be factored into contingency planning, so that a single death does not derail or delay the larger initiative to save a species.

The establishment of an *ex situ* population is difficult and the learning curve is steep. The VaquitaCPR effort was hampered by significant gaps in information that could have been filled many years earlier, when there were hundreds of vaquitas in the population. The behavioral and physiological responses of a species to interventions

ESSAY 4.3  **(cont.)**

necessary to establish an *ex situ* population need to be well understood before a population reaches critically low numbers.

If *ex situ* options are to serve as viable conservation tools, the information critical to success must be gathered when populations are still relatively large. The CIRVA team was concerned that *ex situ* actions could jeopardize *in situ* actions. The lesson from the vaquita case is that managers must be convinced that avoiding extinction requires developing action plans that consider both *in situ* and *ex situ* options when populations still number in the many hundreds. In retrospect, research on vaquitas and their reaction to being captured should have begun as soon as gillnet mortality was recognized to be unsustainable, around 1997.

Finally, many members of CIRVA felt that taking vaquitas into captivity would significantly lessen the political will that was needed to deal with the considerable negative social reaction to the "extreme" measure of banning gillnets in the Vaquita Refuge. The concerns that moving ahead with *ex situ* planning would derail efforts to make the vaquita's natural habitat safe for its continued survival and recovery may have been unfounded. In hindsight, the complexities of working with all stakeholders within government and fisheries were vastly underestimated. Although eliminating gillnets seems like a simple problem, in reality the task involved major social changes to develop alternative fishing gear and maintain livelihoods within a political and social structure known to be rife with both corruption and a large and well-organized criminal element. In the final analysis, conservation energy and resources might have been better invested in developing the knowledge and skills for *ex situ* management of vaquitas.

The vaquita's story serves as a cautionary tale. *Ex situ* options are potentially valuable, but complex, tools for supporting the survival and recovery of populations of small cetaceans. However, building the capacity for *ex situ* actions can take years and should be initiated well before such tools are urgently needed. Populations of threatened species can decline to critical levels in a very short period of time due to unexpected events.

FIGURE 4.8. A Chinook salmon jumps falls at Ship Creek, Anchorage, Alaska. (A black and white version of this figure will appear in some formats. For the color version, please refer to the plate section.)
Credit: Calvin Hall/First Light/Getty Images Plus.

Salmon, lamprey, white sturgeon, steelhead, and bull trout on the Pacific coast of North America have been trying to migrate around dams for decades. The Chinook (or king) salmon is the largest of the North American salmon species. It is migratory, moving from spawning areas in upstream tributaries to the open ocean as juveniles and then returning 3 to 5 years later as adults to spawn in natal streams. To spawn in the Salmon River in Idaho, for example, salmon may travel more than a thousand kilometers and traverse eight dams and reservoirs on the Columbia and Lower Snake rivers. Although most of these dams were constructed with fish ladders to permit migratory fish passage (Figure 4.8), these measures only address restrictions on migratory movements. Movements to most headwater streams are blocked by impassible dams.

Dams interfere with more than migration, however. Water releases from dams are tightly controlled to address multiple interests, among these flood control, hydroelectric power, irrigation, recreation, sedimentation, and municipal uses. Water flows are lower, slower, and less seasonal than what is (or was) "natural." As a result, water temperatures become warmer in summer, testing the thermal tolerance of the fish. In 2014, millions of eggs and recently spawned fry of fall- and winter-run Chinook salmon were killed in the upper reaches of the Sacramento River by warm water and reduced stream flows, wiping out nearly the entire cohort of those two runs. A year later, more than a quarter of a million sockeye salmon (half of that year's returning adults) died from high water temperatures in the Columbia River and its tributaries. Dam operators immediately started to release the cool water stored behind the dams in an effort to reduce temperatures so that later-spawning fall-run Chinook salmon and steelhead would not suffer a similar fate. Such conditions are likely to become more frequent as climate change accelerates.

Dams also create bottlenecks that create easy pickings for predators. California and Steller's sea lions and harbor seals feast on tens of thousands of salmon returning to their upstream spawning grounds. Native predators such as Caspian terns, double-crested cormorants, gulls, and northern pikeminnows and non-native northern pike and smallmouth bass take juvenile salmon by the millions as they move downstream to the sea. Competition and predation from hatchery-reared fish are threats to wild-spawned juveniles on the natal grounds, especially in smaller headwater streams. In the Pacific Northwest, non-native Atlantic salmon are reared in hatcheries, with assurances that they will not be released into the wild where they could threaten the genetic integrity of native salmon stocks, but accidents happen. In 2017, a holding pen at a hatchery collapsed, releasing thousands of Atlantic salmon into Puget Sound.

As long as there are dams, species that move up and down the rivers will remain conservation reliant. Management may be able to address the proximate threats by controlling predators, managing hydrologic flows to control water temperature, or using laws and regulations to limit recreational and commercial harvests and require safeguards for hatcheries, but the dams will remain. Removing a dam to recreate stream flows and allow passage by migratory fish requires multiple permits and government approvals. It is costly and often contentious. The removal of two dams on the Elwha River in Washington to restore natural flows and habitat and allow salmon to reach upstream spawning areas cost about US$325 million.

Dealing with the underlying socioeconomic factors that drive threats is often more difficult than addressing the more immediate threats. When we see condors suffering from lead poisoning or poachers killing Tibetan antelope, the most obvious thing to do must be to deal directly with the threat: chelate the condors to cleanse lead from their blood or send out patrols to catch the poachers. The forces driving these threats are often less obvious and require us to move beyond conserving a species to consider the socioeconomic tradeoffs. Hunters prefer to use lead ammunition because it is more effective than steel shot. People in the supply chain that supports luxury clothing stores selling shahtoosh shawls may depend on the income for their livelihoods.

## WHEN THREATS ACT AT DIFFERENT SCALES

Addressing socioeconomic drivers is also difficult because the cause and the consequences are often separated across space and time. The dam that threatens the Kihansi spray toad is some distance upstream, and buyers in distant markets drive the poaching that threatens the Tibetan antelope and vaquita. Forest fires that destroy habitat vary in size, intensity, and frequency and the impact of a given fire may be greater on a plant or animal with limited mobility or a restricted range, such as an orchid or a salamander, than on a wide-ranging, mobile species, such as a cougar or hawk. If the scale of conservation activities is not aligned with the scale of the threat and the response potential of the species, well-intentioned efforts may fail and conservation reliance may be perpetuated.

Attempts to eradicate invasive species from islands or protected areas often encounter scale mismatches. To be effective at eliminating the threats posed by introduced rats, cats, pigs, snakes, or other invasive species on a large island, every last individual must be removed or otherwise neutralized. A program to eradicate rats from 43-km$^2$ Henderson Island in the South Pacific, for example, came tantalizingly close, but a few rats remained and numbers quickly recovered when the control efforts stopped (Amos et al. 2016). In contrast, a program to eradicate rats from the 7-km$^2$ Palmyra Atoll was successful (and had the secondary effect of eliminating Asian tiger mosquitoes as well; Lafferty et al. 2018). The problem is that the most effective controls of invasive threats—fencing, poisoning, shooting, or sterilization—become exponentially more difficult and expensive as the area to be treated increases or if the invasive pest is small and difficult to find. The largest island from which goats have been removed, for example, is 62 800-ha Dirk Hartog Island, although the successful eradication from the 250 000-ha northern section of 438 000-ha Isabella Island in the Galapagos Archipelago suggests that eradication of ungulates from much larger islands may be possible. Feral cats have been eradicated from Dirk Hartog Island off western Australia, and rats and mice have been removed from the 100 680-ha on which they occurred on 352 800-ha South Georgia (the majority of the island is covered by ice) (Richardson and Croxall 2019).

Conservation efforts on the Channel Islands off southern California show how a constrained area such as an island can facilitate integrated management. There, the island fox (Endangered under the Endangered Species Act) was threatened by introduced pigs. When the pigs were removed, golden eagles turned to preying on the foxes (Roemer et al. 2001). The golden eagles were subsequently captured and removed and bald eagles (a deterrent to the return of golden eagles) were reintroduced. All this was possible because the scale of management of the fox aligned with the scale of the threats. The islands were ecologically isolated and small enough (21 500-ha and 27 200-ha) that removal of the pigs and the golden eagles was possible using available methods. Additionally, a well-trained workforce and a collaboration between the National Park Service and TNC carried the project through to completion. Although the fox is no longer endangered, it remains conservation reliant because of the ongoing need for inoculations to prevent diseases (rabies and distemper) and for other management interventions.

Such alignment of scales is not always feasible. The 'a'o (Newell's shearwater) was thought to be extinct at the beginning of the twentieth century but was rediscovered in 1947 and a nesting colony was found on Kaua'i in 1967. Hurricanes Iwa (1982) and Iniki (1992) devastated the forests on the island in which the shearwaters bred. The 'a'o population declined by 75% between 1993 and 2008. It is now listed as Threatened under the Endangered Species Act and considered Critically Endangered by IUCN; the population continues to decline. In addition to hurricanes, the 'a'o is threatened by predation from introduced rats, cats, pigs, and barn owls; trampling of nesting burrows by pigs and goats; habitat modification by invasive plants; light pollution that confuses young birds on their first flight to the ocean; and collisions with power lines and other structures. A landscape strategy has been developed to coordinate island-wide recovery actions. Efforts to trap, poison, shoot, or fence out the animal threats, however, would be too costly to undertake over the entire island. Kaua'i has an area of 1430 km$^2$; the control efforts so far have focused on areas with dense colonies and cover less than 200 ha, only 0.1% of the island. Matching the scale of the solution to the scale of the threats at the species level may not be possible, so alternative possibilities are being considered. Predator-exclusion fences are planned to protect the largest colonies and individuals are being translocated to initiate breeding colonies inside newly fenced areas.

Where a species is local and isolated, conservation is usually more feasible. The Kihansi spray toad occurs in a tiny area, the Robbins' cinquefoil and Araripe manakin in places not much larger, and the threats to these species can be addressed at those scales. Habitat can be managed or restored in small areas if that is what is needed; restoring habitat over tens or thousands of square kilometers may not be possible logistically or financially. The contradiction, of course, is that it may be easiest to align scales for sedentary species with localized and isolated distributions, but these are also the most likely to be threatened with extinction and the most vulnerable to invaders, habitat loss, disease, and other threats.

Wide-ranging migratory species, on the other hand, occur over vast areas. Many move seasonally between breeding and non-breeding areas or follow the rains: migrations of the red-billed quelea of sub-Saharan Africa or the blue wildebeest of the Serengeti are legendary (Ward 1971; Sinclair and Norton-Griffiths 1979). Neither of these species is imperiled,[10] but many other migratory species are. Monarch butterflies migrate annually between eastern North America and central Mexico, Tibetan antelope historically traversed much of the Tibetan Plateau, and salmon and other anadromous fish may swim hundreds of kilometers between the open ocean and spawning areas in the upper reaches of small tributary streams. Protected areas may be established in specific summering or wintering areas for such species, but they offer little protection during migrations. Establishing larger protected areas or networks of such reserves to encompass more of a species' annual movements, as has been done for the antelope, is generally not feasible in developed regions where much of the land is used or the rivers are dammed. Additionally, enforcement of laws and regulations to protect a species becomes more difficult as resources are spread thin over a larger area, as for the antelope or vaquita.

Time scales are also important. Sometimes a threat can emerge suddenly and quickly cause a species to go extinct before conservationists can act. This is what happened to the golden toad and the Christmas Island pipistrelle. Laysan rails, originally endemic to Laysan Island in the Hawaiian Archipelago, became extinct on the island in the 1920s. They were victims of introduced European rabbits that ate their way across the island and destroyed the rail's habitat. Showing remarkable foresight, managers had already relocated a few individuals to Midway Atoll. The rail was still thriving on Midway in

---

[10] Far from it. In fact, the quelea is arguably the most abundant non-domesticated bird on Earth and is the target of massive pest-control efforts in Africa.

1940, but rats arrived in 1943. World War II hostilities delayed attempts to save the rail. When the island could finally be searched in 1945, no rails were found. It took less than 2 years for rats to finish off the rails (Fisher and Baldwin 1946; Hume 2017).

WHEN THREATS ARE TRULY UNMANAGEABLE

Not all threats are amenable to management actions. Natural events such as hurricanes, earthquakes and tsunamis, epic floods, severe storms, or periods of extreme heat or drought can have devastating effects on a species. An exceptional snowstorm in the Tibetan Plateau of western China in 1985, for example, caused high mortality among the Tibetan antelope and led to its disappearance from some areas (Schaller and Ren 1988). The rabbits that ate the vegetation on Laysan Island nearly wiped out the Laysan honeycreeper as well, but the three remaining individuals died instead in a severe sandstorm. The eruption of Krakatoa in 1883 destroyed nearly three-quarters of the island and the eruption of Mount St. Helens in 1980 devastated a large area, although neither is known to have caused extinctions.

Natural disasters pose an unpredictable and uncontrollable risk to species that are already driven to imperilment by other threats. At one time, millions of short-tailed albatrosses nested on two small volcanic islands south of Japan, but feather hunters killed almost all of them in the late 1800s and early 1900s. Then most of the remaining birds perished in three volcanic eruptions in the 1930s. By 1954, only six pairs were observed in the main breeding colony on Torishima Island. Because of unstable soils in the nesting areas, birds were transferred to other islands and vegetation was planted to stabilize the soil.[11] As a consequence of these and other conservation actions, some 4200 individuals now breed on four islands, with an additional

---

[11] The second nesting island, Minami-Kojima, is currently claimed by both Japan and China. This ownership dispute prevents scientists from studying or managing the birds that nest there. See www.fws.gov/alaska/fisheries/endangered/pdf/STALfactsheet.pdf.

pioneer pair raising young on Midway Island.[12] The species is increasing in numbers, but it is still conservation reliant and remains threatened by volcanic eruptions. Short of moving the colonies to more stable (and predator-free) islands, no long-term management solution seems possible.

Earthquakes make species living in low-lying coastal areas, islands, or atolls particularly vulnerable to inundation by waves and tsunamis. This is what happened on Midway Atoll in March 2011. A 9.0-magnitude earthquake over 4000 km away in Japan generated 2-m waves that washed over most of the three islands comprising the atoll. At that time, there were more than half a million Laysan and black-footed albatrosses nesting on Midway. The tsunami killed perhaps 2000 adults and 110 000 chicks—22% of all chicks hatched that year. On one of the islands, only four chicks remained from the 1520 albatross nests previously surveyed.[13] One of the Laysan albatrosses to survive on Midway (named Wisdom) is the world's oldest wild bird (Figure 4.9). Wisdom has kept returning to Midway and, in early 2019 at the age of 68, hatched yet another chick. Over the years, Wisdom and multiple mates (she has outlived several) have raised at least 30–35 young.

## A FINAL STORY: THE BORAX LAKE CHUB

Conservationists face an uphill climb in dealing with the threats and constraints that produce conservation reliance. But success happens. So we end this chapter with the story of a conservation-reliant species that faced an array of threats. Most have been overcome, but one threat remains, lurking somewhere beneath the surface and sometime in the future.

The Borax Lake chub occurs only in Borax Lake, a shallow, 4.1-ha alkaline lake in the Alvord Basin of eastern Oregon (Figure 4.10)

---

[12] www.iucnredlist.org/details/22698335/0.

[13] The chick of the short-tailed albatross from Torishima Island was washed some distance away from its nest but was found alive and placed back in its nest; it later fledged successfully.

FIGURE 4.9. Wisdom, a Near Threatened (IUCN) Laysan albatross, is the world's oldest known bird, here shown nesting (successfully) on Midway Atoll in 2018. (A black and white version of this figure will appear in some formats. For the color version, please refer to the plate section.)
Photo: Eric Vanderwerf.

(Goble 2010). The lake is fed by subterranean hot springs. Water flowing into the lake often exceeds the chub's thermal maximum, so chub inhabit only cooler areas in the shallow fringes of the lake and adjacent ephemeral wetlands. The chub population fluctuates from thousands to tens of thousands as temperatures in the lake vary. The species is at risk not because of low numbers, but because it occurs nowhere else and its habitat is vulnerable to multiple threats.

Borax Lake is perched 10 m above the surrounding desert on mineral deposits from the spring that have built up over millennia. The lake is susceptible to low water levels if cattle grazing, off-road vehicles, or other disturbances break the fragile shoreline or if water is diverted for irrigation. The lake (and thus the chub) is also threatened by drilling for geothermal energy, which could disrupt the hot spring feeding the lake. It was the prospect of geothermal development that prompted a rapid conservation response. The chub was emergency

FIGURE 4.10. Borax Lake, Oregon, is fed by a thermal vent deep beneath
the surface. The endemic Borax Lake chub (inset) persists along the
margins of the lake despite high temperatures and high levels of arsenic
and lead. (A black and white version of this figure will appear in some
formats. For the color version, please refer to the plate section.)
Photo: The Nature Conservancy.

listed as Endangered under the Endangered Species Act in 1980,
followed by a final listing in 1982; a recovery plan was published
in 1987.

The restricted habitat and distribution of the chub made it
possible to conduct management at an ecologically appropriate scale.
Legislation was quickly passed to make the area surrounding the lake
off limits to geothermal development. The federal government designated the lake and surrounding federal land as critical habitat, removing the threat of irrigation diversions. TNC purchased surrounding
private lands and acquired water rights. Fencing limited access to the
lake, reducing the threat of disturbance.

The chub was proposed for delisting from the federal endangered species list in early 2019. It remains common, although
restricted to Borax Lake. Monitoring of the lake and the chub
must continue and the fencing must be maintained, so the species

and its habitat require continuing management, albeit at a much reduced level.

Another threat, however, is not easily addressed. Borax Lake sits atop a thermal vent in a seismically active area. The entire lake ecosystem, including the chub, is vulnerable to even a moderate earthquake that could alter the subterranean hydrology. Should contingency plans, such as captive breeding or translocation to other hot springs (if such could be found), be pursued? Or should this threat be ignored because, like other unpredictable extreme events, it has a low probability of occurrence? How probable does a threat need to be to justify an allocation of limited conservation resources to its mitigation, especially if the threat itself is beyond management? These are questions that lie at the heart of how we should think about conservation reliance and prioritization.

## DEALING WITH THREATS

Understanding threats and their underlying drivers is key to conserving imperiled species and enabling them to escape the grip of conservation reliance. Many threats are amenable to management constraints and can be overcome, although success depends on matching the scale of management to the scale of the threat and the species' ecology.

Laws and regulations provide an essential foundation for conservation, but they must be rigorously enforced and supported by the public. Laws are in place, for example, to prevent poaching of vaquita, rhinoceros, Tibetan antelope, and other imperiled species, but enforcement is sometimes lacking, sometimes corrupted by bribery, sometimes piecemeal, and almost always understaffed and underfunded.

Successful conservation also may require managing for multiple threats concurrently. Threats are often interconnected, creating a "one thing leads to another" conundrum—the efforts to control rabbits on Macquarie Island are an example. Often the factors that drive threats to a species may be several steps removed and some distance away. The social and economic forces in Southeast Asia and China that drive the poaching of totoaba continue to imperil vaquitas. If the driving forces are not addressed, the threats may require ongoing management. Conservation reliance is perpetuated.

Some threats are inherently unmanageable. In this case, the only management strategies available are either to move individuals away from the threat or to try to maintain the population and hope for the best.

In the future, many of the threats we have mentioned in this chapter will only become more severe. The human population of the planet continues to grow, intensifying conflicts between species and people. Climate change is altering species' habitats and ranges. Weather extremes will become more frequent and more severe. Conservation reliance will grow. It is to these emergent threats and their effects on conservation-reliant species that we now turn.

# 5 Emerging Threats in a Rapidly Changing World

The Earth's environment is changing. Since the Industrial Revolution gases have been building up in the atmosphere, trapping heat and raising the temperature of the planet. Warming soil and increased mortality rates in plants and animals elevate the activity of microbiota, amplifying the emissions of $CO_2$ and other greenhouse gases.

Secondary biological consequences—including new patterns of phenology, the spread of disease and invasive species, disrupted food webs, and many of the threats described in the previous chapter—interact in ways that make conservation much more challenging. For example, drought-stressed trees in boreal forests are more susceptible to the pests and disease that thrive in the altered climate, and the dead trees provide tinder for wildfires, which are also increasing in spread and intensity because of climate changes. Other species may react to the loss of mature forest habitat, disrupting trophic relationships (Parmesan and Yohe 2003).

Global changes in climate, sea levels, and ocean chemistry are well documented.[1] Although there is uncertainty about the magnitude of future changes, there is scientific consensus that the trends we see now will continue for multiple human generations. Scientists expect more species to become threatened or endangered and the rate of extinction to increase (Thomas 2012; IPBES 2019). Climate change and its secondary biological consequences affect people and their

---

[1] Skepticism about the reality and importance of climate change (e.g. Lomborg 2001) is diminishing. A 2018 survey found that 67% of individuals across 23 countries said global climate change is a major threat to their country, up from 56% in 2013. In the United States, views of the importance of the climate change threat diverge sharply along partisan political lines (www.pewglobal.org/2019/02/10/climate-change-still-seen-as-the-top-global-threat-but-cyberattacks-a-rising-concern/).

livelihoods. For instance, the ecological effects of increasing atmospheric $CO_2$ alter the global nitrogen cycle, creating a feedback loop with changing land use and land cover that reduces agricultural production (Vitousek 1994). Rising ocean temperatures are already causing coral bleaching events and changing ocean currents, threatening food sources for millions of people. Environmental refugees are created by drought, rising sea levels, and armed conflict driven by a loss of food and water security.

Tragically, these changes are beyond the ability of direct management to counteract, at least in the near term. To deal with the threats to species and ecosystems, conservation efforts will need to increase concurrently with efforts to sequester more carbon in biological systems while reducing emissions. These efforts will need to encompass local, regional, and global scales and continue for a very long time.

In this chapter, we consider how four forces of global change—climate change, sea-level rise, ocean acidification, and extreme weather—exacerbate the challenge of eliminating threats to species and increase the prevalence and level of conservation reliance. How will these forces alter current threats to species? How can broad-scale changes be countered by local conservation actions? And how can species or managers cope with conditions that they have never encountered before?

## TRADITIONAL APPROACHES MAY NO LONGER WORK

Given the scope of change, conservation management needs to be embedded in a larger framework that addresses species interrelationships, ecosystem processes, and landscape changes over the long term. Certainly, species-specific rescues are called for when extreme weather poses an immediate threat or more gradual changes breach tolerance limits. But we simply do not have the conservation resources to rescue every species endangered by climate change. More and more scientists and concerned citizens are promoting efforts to identify and rank species based on vulnerability to global changes (e.g.

USEPA 2009; Gardali et al. 2012; Moyle et al. 2013). Yet it has been
difficult to incorporate these vulnerability rankings into regulations
and the prioritization of conservation actions. Assessing the vulnerability of a species requires information about its sensitivity, exposure, and ability to adjust behaviorally, genetically, and evolutionarily
(i.e. its adaptive capacity; Foden and Young 2016). All of this requires
time and study, yet the specter of mounting extinctions requires
quick action. The reality of global changes highlights the importance
of coupling a quick response with a more measured analysis of alternatives, costs, and risks conducted in a larger context.

A couple of examples illustrate the need for quick and anticipatory responses. The white form of the lemuroid ringtail possum
(Figure 5.1) has been pushed to the brink of extinction by climate
change.[2] This furry marsupial mammal occurs as a population only
in a small area of cloud forest on the slopes of Mount Lewis in the
Daintree rainforest in Queensland, Australia. It cannot survive temperatures above 30°C for more than a few hours. Most of the population was lost to a severe heat wave in 2005, and surveys a few years
later failed to find any remaining individuals. The white form was
feared extinct until one individual was sighted in 2017. The white
form may be hanging on by the thinnest of threads, but as temperatures continue to warm and heat waves become more frequent, there
is little cause for optimism. Perhaps it could have been rescued
if scientists and managers had anticipated the crisis, initiated
captive breeding, and found a release site with more moderate
temperatures.

The Bramble Cay melomys (Figure 5.2) was a small, mouse-like
rodent that has the distinction of being the first mammal known to
have become extinct as a consequence of climate change (Fulton
2017). The species was discovered in 1845. It occurred only on
Bramble Cay, a 4-ha coral island in the Torres Strait north of

---

[2] The white lemuroid ringtail possum is a distinctive color variant of the lemuroid
ringtail possum, which is considered Near Threatened by IUCN.

FIGURE 5.1. The white form of the lemuroid ringtail possum. This form may be extinct, although the lemuroid ringtail possum as a species is considered Near Threatened by the IUCN. (A black and white version of this figure will appear in some formats. For the color version, please refer to the plate section.)
Photo: Mark Ziembicki.

Queensland. The highest point on Bramble Cay is only 3 m above high tide, which made the melomys vulnerable to inundation from storm surges. Such storm surges have become more frequent as sea levels rise. The population was estimated at several hundred individuals in 1978, 90 by 1998, but only 12 were recorded in a survey in 2004. A fisherman saw one melomys in 2009, but subsequent surveys (including an intensive search in 2014) failed to find any. Most likely, the few remaining melomys were swept out to sea with a storm surge. The species was reported to be extinct in 2016 (Gynther et al. 2016;

FIGURE 5.2. The extinct Bramble Cay melomys lived only on Bramble
Cay, a tiny islet in the Torres Strait north of Queensland, Australia (inset).
Rising seas and storm surges led to its extinction. (A black and white
version of this figure will appear in some formats. For the color version,
please refer to the plate section.)
Photo: Ian Bell, Government of Queensland, Australia, Department of Environment
and Heritage Protection.

Woinarski et al. 2017) and was officially declared extinct by the
Australian government in 2019.

Arguably, the melomys could have been saved if anticipatory
action had been taken. Its perilous state was recognized in the 1990s
and the species was listed as Endangered under the Australian Environmental Protection and Biodiversity Conservation Act in 2000.
However, it was another 8 years before a recovery plan was adopted—
a plan that contained no provision for captive breeding, came with no
funding, and was never implemented. The public expressed little
interest in advocating for an uncharismatic species occurring on a
tiny remote island. By the time an attempt was finally made to
capture individuals for captive breeding in 2014, it had been 5 years
since a melomys had even been sighted (Gynther et al. 2016).

Had the white form of the lemuroid ringtail possum or the
Bramble Cay melomys survived, they would have been conservation

reliant. Managers would have had to somehow recreate the cool condensation of moist air needed to maintain cloud-forest habitat for the possum and either build a barrier around Bramble Cay or relocate the melomys to a different island (where it would probably face other threats, such as invasive predators).

## GLOBAL CHANGES DISRUPT NATURAL COMMUNITIES

The global buildup of greenhouse gases is leading to a loss of habitat, to which managers can respond by restoring or protecting remaining habitat. This may entail maintaining fencing, monitoring population size, establishing breeding sites, increasing soil moisture for drought-sensitive plants, planting food plants for pollinators, encouraging or restricting grazing, building burrows or nesting boxes, controlling the spread of non-native species, and other actions. Managers may also seek to replace the physical processes that have been altered by climate change, such as seasonal fluctuations in stream flows and temperature, or biological processes, such as food-web interactions.

Species in aquatic environments may have greater difficulty adjusting to increased temperatures than those on land because they cannot rid themselves of excess heat unless they have access to cooler water. Warm water temperatures reduce available oxygen in the water and increase the risk of bacterial infections, especially in lakes and ponds with slow or no current and insufficient aeration. Global warming increases the urgency of managing riparian flows for water temperature. Large-scale salmon mortality events in the Sacramento, Klamath, and John Day rivers of the United States have been linked to elevated water temperatures. In Australia, thousands of barramundi were found dead in a small billabong in the Northern Territory in 2017, probably as a result of the combination of heat and a reduction in dissolved oxygen. Such massive fish kills are becoming more frequent in many parts of the world as conditions exceed thermal thresholds. To be effective, actions such as releasing colder water from the bottoms of dams into river systems must be taken before water temperatures reach thermal thresholds. Often, however, fish are most in need of cooler water during the summer— coinciding with the highest demand for water for agriculture and hydropower for air conditioning.

Temperatures in the oceans are beyond management. Oceans absorb some 93% of the heat added by global warming. Scientists have already documented critical changes in ocean circulation and geographic shifts of temperature isotherms. Changes in the seasonal timing of temperature shifts can occur rapidly and affect nutrient and oxygen availability at local to regional scales (Burrows et al. 2011). Like freshwater species, marine species have a limited capacity to tolerate warm water.

One of the most well-known effects of warming oceans is coral-reef bleaching. In warm water, corals expel the algae (zooxanthellae) living in their tissues and turn white. Multiple or sustained bleaching events can lead to widespread mortality. As temperatures have increased in many tropical and subtropical oceans, the frequency and extent of coral-reef bleaching have increased. In 2005, half of the coral reefs in the Caribbean were affected by a single massive bleaching event. Thermal stress was greater than in any of the previous 20 years.[3] In 2016 and 2017, two sequential massive coral bleaching events affected two-thirds of Australia's Great Barrier Reef. Ocean warming is relatively predictable, so if funding were made available conservationists could translocate more coral-reef species and seed new substrates for coral reefs to grow where conditions are expected to be within their thermal tolerances.

Corals are also threatened by ocean acidification. As the oceans absorb $CO_2$ from the atmosphere, they become more acidic. The acidity of ocean-surface waters has increased by about 30% since the late eighteenth century, but by the end of the twenty-first century these waters could be nearly 150% more acidic (Jewett and Romanou 2017). Increased ocean acidity interferes with the calcification by which corals and many other marine organisms (oysters, clams, sea

---

[3] oceanservice.noaa.gov/facts/coral_bleach.html

FIGURE 5.3. Laysan albatrosses and chicks nesting on Midway Atoll. The low elevation of the atoll makes it vulnerable to storm surges, tsunamis, and sea-level rise. (A black and white version of this figure will appear in some formats. For the color version, please refer to the plate section.)
Photo: J. Klavitter, US Fish and Wildlife Service.

urchins, calcareous plankton) form their structure and shells. There is some evidence that corals can acclimate or adapt to increases in ocean acidification (Schoepf et al. 2017) and there is hope that scientists may be able to breed corals more resistant to acidification and warmer temperatures.[4] If successful, wild populations could perhaps be established, although they would likely require ongoing translocations.

Rising sea levels increase storm surges and tidal flooding. The melomys found on Bramble Cay became extinct. Other low-lying islands in the Pacific, many of which contain endemic species, are similarly susceptible (Figure 5.3; Reynolds et al. 2015)[5]. In the

[4] For a summary of management interventions, see NAS (2019).
[5] See also www.usgs.gov/centers/pierc/science/predicting-risks-island-extinctions-due-sea-level-rise-model-based-tools?qt-science_center_objects=0#qt-science_center_objects.

Hawaiian Archipelago, staff from Pacific Rim Conservation and their collaborators are working to replace breeding areas that are already being lost and are translocating Laysan albatross, black-footed albatross, Tristram's storm petrel, and Bonin petrel from low-lying islands to the higher relief of James Campbell National Wildlife Refuge on O'ahu.[6] The need could not be more urgent. In 2018, a hurricane washed across East Island in the French Frigate Shoals, part of Papahānaumokuākea Marine National Monument in the remote northwestern Hawaiian Islands. At 4.5 ha it was the largest island in the Shoals, but following the hurricane only a 46-m-long strip of sand remained above sea level. The island had provided key habitat for endangered Hawaiian monk seals and nesting habitat used by 96% of the surviving Endangered green sea turtles and several seabirds.

In an assessment of 1779 islands in the western Pacific, Kumar and Tehrany (2017) recorded 11 amphibian, 67 mammal, and 72 reptile species that were listed by IUCN as Vulnerable, Endangered, or Critically Endangered. Most are vulnerable to sea-level rise. These species are not recognized as endangered by national governments, lessening impediments to translocation and allowing improved long-term planning that can take global changes into account. Of course, this also means that the species lack some legal protections.

Other coastal habitats, including beaches, dunes, marshes, lagoons, tidal wetlands, and mangroves, are also subject to periodic inundation or tidal intrusion of salt water. Many of these habitats will disappear if sea levels continue to rise as expected (Stralberg et al. 2011). For a species such as the Endangered Ridgway's rail in California, moderate increases in sea level and salinity might actually enhance its tidal-marsh habitat—but more substantial increases could threaten the species with extinction if sedimentation and marsh vegetation fail to keep pace with the rising sea (Zhang and Gorelick 2014). Coastline habitats can be managed to some extent by cultivating marsh vegetation to protect and raise the substrate and by movement

---

[6] www.islandarks.org/.

of sediments through dredge operations. However, these measures do not address the sea-level problem and would require an ongoing commitment.

Management of coastal wetlands can protect coasts from sea-level rise and help to reduce threats to multiple species. Wetlands protect human communities and coastal estuaries. They serve as refugia and nurseries for fish and other marine life and stepping-stones for long-distance migrators. So long as sea levels and ocean chemistry continue to change—which may be for as long as we can imagine—these wetlands and the species that depend on them will be conservation reliant.

## EXTREME WEATHER EVENTS INCREASE RISKS

As the intensity and frequency of torrential rainstorms, hurricanes, heat waves, and droughts increase, such events need to be considered in long-term conservation plans. These events directly threaten species, as do indirect consequences such as flooding, erosion and landslides, or lightning-sparked wildfires. The number of record high-temperature events in the United States has been increasing since 1950 (NAS 2016). In California, 2012–2016 was the driest period since record keeping began in 1895 and its effects were exacerbated by record high temperatures in 2014 and 2015. Over 100 million trees died from the effects of the drought, most of them in the Sierra Nevada. In 2017, Hurricane Harvey inundated some parts of Texas with over 150 cm of rain, leading to unprecedented flooding. One analysis suggested that the intensity of rainfall from Hurricane Harvey was increased by 15% as a consequence of climate change.[7]

Commonly used global climate models underestimate the probability of extreme weather, in part because mean values are easier to describe accurately than more sporadic extremes. Also, it is difficult to capture fine-scale, local physics for any single location in forecast models. This unpredictability complicates attempts to design

---

[7] https://www.climatecentral.org/analyses/hurricane-harvey-august-2017/

conservation actions for imperiled species; some progress has been made, however, in estimating probabilities of tropical cyclones, severe thunderstorms, winter storms, and atmospheric-river events (Kossin et al. 2017).

Knowing the probabilities of extreme events may enable managers to take proactive measures to protect endangered species, especially when a species is restricted to a small area. During a drought in California, supplemental feeding was shown experimentally to be effective in maintaining populations of Endangered giant kangaroo rats; a process for feeding the kangaroo rat and other vulnerable species is now included in California's drought planning. The state's drought planning now also includes provisions for monitoring water volumes of streams and hatchery breeding for rare fish. Maintaining separate populations in places not likely to experience the same event can also reduce the potential effects of extreme events on imperiled species. Such spreading of risks may be a good conservation strategy, although protecting multiple locations adds to management costs over time.

In places where increasingly frequent and severe hurricanes threaten species, managers can sometimes establish insurance populations at safe facilities in advance or can capture vulnerable individuals with enough advance warning. In the Caribbean, hurricanes are frequent and the islands contain many unique and endangered species. One such species, the Puerto Rican parrot (Figure 5.4), was once widespread throughout forests of Puerto Rico, but numbers declined as forests were cleared in the nineteenth and early twentieth centuries. By 1940, the species was found only in the primary forest of El Yunque in the Luquillo Mountains. By the 1950s, only 200 parrots were left in the wild (Snyder et al. 1987). In 1967, the species was listed as Endangered under the predecessor of the Endangered Species Act, and a captive-breeding project began in 1972. In 1975, the population reached a nadir of 13 individuals in the wild. By the time Hurricane Hugo came along in 1989, there were 47 individuals, but half were lost in the ensuing destruction. Between 2007 and 2017, parrot numbers decreased by 8% per year.

FIGURE 5.4. The Puerto Rican parrot is Endangered and is being bred in captivity. It is particularly vulnerable to the increased frequency of hurricanes in the Caribbean. (A black and white version of this figure will appear in some formats. For the color version, please refer to the plate section.)
Photo: US Fish and Wildlife Service.

Puerto Rican parrots are still being bred in captivity and individuals have been released at a second location in Rio Abajo. In 2017, there were some 140 individuals living in the wild at Rio Abajo and another 56 in El Yunque. Then two major hurricanes struck in rapid succession. Most of the Rio Abajo birds survived, but El Yunque was more severely affected and only two parrots have been seen since. The value of establishing an insurance population is obvious, but it requires careful planning and long-term management to maintain a species in the face of hurricanes that can wipe out years of recovery effort in just a few days (Paravisini-Gebert 2018). The parrots are

FIGURE 5.5. An Attwater's prairie chicken male defending its territory at a lek on the Attwater's Prairie Chicken National Wildlife Refuge in Texas. (A black and white version of this figure will appear in some formats. For the color version, please refer to the plate section.)
Photo: John Magera.

clearly conservation reliant and have been since before they were declared endangered half a century ago.

Given enough time and a reliable forecast, scientists and managers can sometimes take emergency steps to protect a species in the path of a hurricane. Emergency measures have been taken twice to protect Endangered Attwater's prairie chickens (Figure 5.5). This ground-nesting species was formerly abundant in coastal grasslands in Texas, but by the late 1930s only a few thousand birds remained. Loss of habitat owing to development, altered fire regimes, and invasion by exotic trees, brush, and grasses led to the species being designated as Endangered in 1967. Despite protections, by 2003 fewer than 50 birds could be found in two small areas of remnant prairie. Captive-breeding programs were subsequently established at several facilities and wild populations began to grow through releases of young birds.

One of the release sites was TNC's 930-ha Texas City Prairie Preserve. Texas City is a major petroleum refining and production center, so the preserve is dotted with nodding oil pumpjacks and is hemmed in on all sides by petrochemical plants.[8] Because the preserve is only 1–2 m above high-tide level along a coastal bayou, levees have been built to mitigate the threat of flooding from Galveston Bay. Urban coyotes regularly patrol the levees. It is hard to imagine a patch of prairie with more inhospitable surroundings.

In 2005, with Hurricane Rita bearing down on the Texas coast, 17 captive-bred birds scheduled to be released in the preserve were herded into a truck and transported inland to escape the storm. After the storm had passed, they were released back at the preserve, joining the 10 birds that had weathered the hurricane in the wild.

Attwater's prairie chickens disappeared from the Texas City Prairie Preserve in 2012, when the recovery team shifted all releases of captive-bred birds to the larger Attwater's Prairie Chicken National Wildlife Refuge. The refuge is also vulnerable to flooding and hurricanes. There were perhaps 100 birds living there by 2014, but heavy spring flooding in 2016 reduced the population to 42 birds. The population was being augmented with captive-bred birds when Hurricane Harvey swamped the refuge in 2017. Only 5 of 29 radio-tracked individuals could be found in a post-hurricane survey. Most birds probably died during the hurricane itself, but others likely suffered predation as both they and their predators were forced to seek refuge together on the few islands of higher ground. Once again, however, the hurricane had been predicted and the 20 captive-bred birds awaiting release were transported inland until the storm passed.

---

[8] The land for the Preserve was donated to TNC by Mobil Oil, which did not want to be responsible for management of an endangered species. Oil production and drilling continued on the Preserve, however, leading to public outcry over how a large conservation organization could justify profiting from oil and gas production on land it protected (Klein 2014). By the terms of the land transfer, however, the Conservancy had no choice in the matter.

A wet winter in 2017–2018 reduced the augmented population to 12 free-ranging birds by April 2018.

Captive breeding of prairie chickens continues to expand in hopes of producing enough birds to enable the wild population to successfully withstand another hurricane. Other management actions include planting food plants, controlling red fire ants, controlling predators during the breeding season, managing cattle, and conducting prescribed burns of several thousand hectares annually. Attwater's prairie chicken may remain conservation reliant for a very long time, however, leading some people to question whether the costs of captive breeding and maintaining wild populations of a species in such a vulnerable setting (much less trucking them away from hurricanes) are justified. Those on the ground who are working daily with the bird are more optimistic. Hope for success endures.

With increases in extreme weather events, species that are already conservation reliant will become even more dependent on emergency measures such as rapid status assessments, new protective structures, translocations, or supplemental feeding. The vulnerability of a species to extreme weather events is generally not a function of the species' inherent traits so much as the location, time, spatial extent, and duration of the events—essentially a matter of being in the wrong place at the wrong time. The immediate direct effects of hurricanes and cyclones may be limited (although the effects on habitat may be long lasting). On the other hand, heat waves and droughts often occur over broad areas and last longer. Climate change alters the calculus for when, where, and how long species will be at risk, which affects the planning, speed, and duration of effective conservation actions.

## KEEPING UP WITH HABITAT CHANGE

As locally abrupt disturbances occur and more gradual and widespread climate changes unfold, habitats in terrestrial systems shift or disappear. Wildfires are already growing larger and more intense in many areas, in part because changing climate is increasing tree mortality resulting from drought and insect invasions. Fires and extreme storms create habitat for species that thrive in disturbed areas but destroy habitat for those dependent on late-successional stages, such as streamside amphibians or species that use the hollows found in large, old trees for nesting or roosting. Because species differ in their responses to global changes and disturbance events, local ecological communities and their complex webs of interrelationships may change. At a broad scale, deserts will continue to expand and woodlands and forests shift to higher latitudes or elevations. Future distributions of birds are likely to be more strongly linked to the distribution of habitat than to temperature and precipitation alone (Matthews et al. 2011).

On average, the Earth's temperature is increasing more quickly closer to the Earth's poles and at higher altitudes. At regional or local scales, the velocity $(km\,yr^{-1})$ at which temperatures change varies with landform (Loarie et al. 2009). Where the thermal and topographic gradients are steep, as on the slopes of mountains, a given amount of temperature change occurs over only a short distance; the velocity of climate change is low. Steep environmental gradients and low climate velocity on mountainsides may allow species to escape warming and drying conditions by moving short distances to higher elevations. Also, valleys or canyons are often subject to cold-air drainage that can counter increasing temperatures. In large, flat areas such as lowlands or deserts, changes may be more widespread and the velocity much greater, so species must move much farther to escape inhospitable local climate conditions.

Scientists are already documenting habitat shifts in mountain areas. The center of the altitudinal distribution of 171 plant species in western Europe shifted upslope at a rate of 29 m per decade during the twentieth century (Lenoir et al. 2008) and plants endemic to the Himalayas showed a similar upward shift (Telwala et al. 2013). In the Sierra Nevada of California, nearly all of 53 bird species that were surveyed early in the twentieth century and then resurveyed nearly a century later had shifted their distributions to keep pace with the shifting climate. The relationships with temperature and precipitation differed, however: rising temperatures pushed species upslope, whereas increasing precipitation pushed species downslope (Tingley et al. 2009, 2012).

There are at least four implications of variability in climate change velocities. First, different management strategies may be required to manage habitat in areas with different climate change velocities. Where the velocity of change is low, species may be able to adjust by moving or being translocated short distances. Where the velocity of change is high, it may be difficult for animals and (especially) plants to keep pace with the shifting climate because the effects will be felt over broad areas. Second, habitats that experience less change may provide refugia for species unable to move or adapt to the altered conditions. Places set aside as protected areas may serve this function, although many of these areas have been established based on historical understandings of species' habitat requirements. As conditions change, these locations may no longer be suitable for the species of greatest conservation concern, although they may become more suitable for other species. Third, because protected area boundaries do not shift with climate changes, protected areas in deserts may need to be larger than those on mountainsides to allow species more opportunity to shift their ranges while remaining protected. Finally, restoring habitats for imperiled species will become a moving target as restoration gains are overwhelmed by rapid climate change.

Western Australia is relatively flat and the climate change velocity is high. Scientists there are attempting to relocate Critically Endangered western swamp turtles. With long generation times and low genetic diversity, the species' adaptive capacity is low. A captive-breeding program that began in 1988 has produced more than 500 turtles, which have been released into fenced areas or sites where red foxes have been removed by baiting. The habitats receiving translocated turtles, however, are drying out. Managers have begun pumping water from underground aquifers at some sites to maintain swamp conditions. Additionally, turtles are being released farther south where moisture and temperature conditions are predicted to be better for them.[9] Managers need to be adaptable.

Even in areas with low climate change velocity, there may be barriers to habitat shifts and changes. The climate regimes currently existing on the tops of ridges or mountains are likely to disappear altogether. The high-alpine zone of mountains in Ethiopia where giant lobelias are endemic is shrinking rapidly. Lobelias produce a flowering rosette stalk that may be 10 m tall (making it attractive to hardy ecotourists). Model projections suggest that less than 4% of the suitable habitat will remain by 2080 (Chala et al. 2016). Because small populations will be confined to just four isolated mountaintops, genetic diversity may narrow dramatically, further increasing the likelihood of extinction.

The effects of climate changes may be exacerbated by changing land uses. California gnatcatchers are small insectivorous birds that inhabit coastal sage scrub in southern California, extending into similar habitat in Baja California and Baja California Sur, Mexico. Populations have declined over the past several decades as habitat has been lost to urban development; the species was listed as Threatened under the Endangered Species Act in 1993. Although the future climate is projected to improve conditions for coastal sage scrub, much of the species' current distribution lies in the rapidly growing Los Angeles–San Diego corridor. When Dennis Jongsomjit and his colleagues (2012) modeled the current and future distributions of gnatcatchers based on current and projected climate and vegetation variables and housing densities, a northward expansion of the distribution of gnatcatchers (Figure 5.6B) was consumed and fragmented by development (Figure 5.6D).[10] In the near future, the gnatcatcher will depend on reserves and management to maintain remnants of its coastal

---

[9]  www.hideaway-haven.com.au/blog/2017/9/4/australian-endangered-species-western-swamp-tortoise

[10]  This example was not included in the published paper.

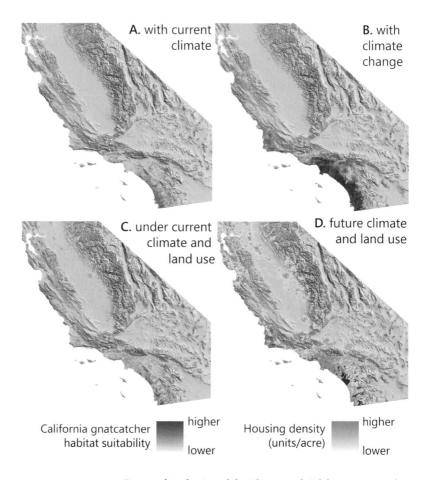

FIGURE 5.6.  Current distribution of the Threatened California gnatcatcher in southern California (A), projected distribution with climate change (B), and current (C) and future (D) distributions with projected changes in land use superimposed. (A black and white version of this figure will appear in some formats. For the color version, please refer to the plate section.)
Source: D. Jongsomjit, Point Blue Conservation Science.

sage-scrub habitat. Over the longer term, coastal sage habitat will need to be restored (or created) in places where projected climate is more suitable to preserve this and other coastal sage species. Not everyone supports such land-use tradeoffs or the costs of revegetation and fire management, however. Developers, for example, have objected to restrictions on the kinds of projects that would produce the growth shown in Figure 5.6D.

The western swamp turtle, giant lobelia, and gnatcatcher illustrate the need to consider the landscape as a whole in identifying and protecting habitat. As conditions change, places not previously thought to be suitable for a species should be included in planning. Global climate models that account for terrain in local areas may help to identify potential refugia, although these models are more accurate in assessing temperature changes than precipitation changes and are more useful for terrestrial than for aquatic systems. Maps of the probabilities of disturbance from extreme events can aid in selecting refugia. Translocations may be necessary to enable some threatened species to reach suitable refugia. Ethiopia's giant lobelia is restricted to the tops of a few mountains, but no higher mountains are available for translocations. Such situations raise difficult questions about how to prioritize the conservation of a species for which no suitable habitat is likely to exist in the future.

## SPECIES RELATIONSHIPS WILL BE DISRUPTED

In many instances, changes in breeding activities, food availability, pollination, or predator–prey relationships will result from the disassembly and reassembly of communities of plants and animals that accompany global changes. Mobile species can shift their occupied range more rapidly than can sedentary species, resulting in the disruption of ecological communities as species expand into new areas or disappear from historic habitats at different rates. Consequently, species will encounter conditions and species (some of them competitors or predators) they have not faced before. Such changes in species distributions will also influence species interrelationships and species functions. Species may become imperiled, for example, if other species that they depend on for food or habitat move elsewhere. Changes in the timing of phenological events such as flowering time or insect emergence can throw relationships such as pollination or the hatching of young birds out of synchrony in both time and space

(Burgess et al. 2018). Globally, increasing numbers of plants are at risk because of this asynchrony or because pollinators such as bats, butterflies, skippers, moths, hoverflies, ants, and flies are absent or their numbers are reduced. Management of threats to pollinators, some of which are themselves imperiled or conservation reliant, may be required to reduce the conservation reliance of these plants.

Some of the most vulnerable species are insects. Not only are they often sensitive to changes in temperature and seasonality, but they also tend to specialize on plant symbionts. As Camille Parmesan describes in Essay 5.1, the Mono checkerspot butterfly developed a preference for laying eggs on a weed associated with ranching in Nevada and nearly died out when cattle grazing stopped.

The reshuffling of communities and ecosystems will lead to no-analog communities or novel ecosystems (Stralberg et al. 2009; Hobbs et al. 2013), creating challenges for conservationists. In some cases, the reshuffling may require people to replace ecosystem processes that have been lost—for example, by mimicking the functions of missing pollinators (Figure 5.7). Whenever humans take over environmental functions necessary to the survival of an imperiled species, conservation reliance follows.

## MANAGING DIVERSE SPECIES RESPONSES TO GLOBAL CHANGES

The effects of changing conditions are likely to be greatest on species with limited adaptive capacity. These include species that are ecological specialists; are large; are top predators; have long generation times and/or low fecundity; are sedentary or immobile; have a small population that is endemic to a small area; are already at their physiological limits; or have little genetic diversity (Foden et al. 2013; Pacifici et al. 2015). In an assessment of the effects of prolonged drought on fish in the Murray–Darling River basin of Australia, for example, Chessman (2013) found that the species that fared worse were significantly more likely to have a narrow rather than broad diet, low age at sexual maturity, small body size, low spawning temperature, long

ESSAY 5.1    **The Specter of Conservation in
a Time of Rapid Change**

*Camille Parmesan*

The species I have worked on have surprised me many times over, teaching me never to succumb to the complacency of thinking that I understand them completely and I can move on to something else. Wild species are more adaptable than we scientists often give them credit for. Back in the late 1990s, experts expected the endangered Quino checkerspot butterfly (a subspecies of Edith's checkerspot) to go extinct as a result of massive urbanization across their range—with Los Angeles and San Diego surging to meet each other—combined with continued warming and drying trends that had already driven many populations extinct, even where habitat still existed. This delicate little butterfly surprised us all by managing to shift its range up the mountains in response to regional warming, a move none of us expected because it required a diet shift to a novel host plant that was not used by other Quino populations.

The diet shift that helped rescue Quino did not require evolution—the butterflies had such weak dietary preferences that they easily added a new plant species to their repertoire. However, study of another subspecies of Edith's checkerspot in Nevada, the Mono checkerspot, showed how its diet is capable of rapid evolution in response to changes in the environment (Figure E5.1.1). In this case, the change was the introduction of a European weed, narrowleaf plantain, brought in by humans and accidentally distributed in hay. By the time of our study, the plantain was well established on "Schneider's ranch," where the Schneider family had raised cattle for more than a century. Edith's checkerspot caterpillars had higher survival on this novel host than on their traditional host, and increasing preference for plantain by egg-laying females was already evolving rapidly between 1982 and 1990.

Once the butterflies had become dependent upon the plantains, they were vulnerable to rapid changes in how the land was managed. After "Uncle Harry" Schneider died, his nephew Joe inherited the large ranch (hundreds of hectares) and did not have the cash to pay inheritance

ESSAY 5.1  **(cont.)**

FIGURE E5.1.1. A Mono checkerspot butterfly, free-flying in its natural habitat. One of the few remaining populations at Schneider's ranch (near Carson City, Nevada) was extinct by 2008 owing to rapidly changing land use. Only five populations of this subspecies are currently known to exist. (A black and white version of this figure will appear in some formats. For the color version, please refer to the plate section.)
Photo: Michael C. Singer.

taxes. The meadow was the most valuable part of the ranch, so it was the obvious part to sell. The entire butterfly population was sold to pay estate taxes and the cattle were removed. Grasses quickly grew up around the plantains, shading and cooling them by around 7°C. The butterfly population went extinct.[11] Humans had created a trap for the insects by providing a wonderful new resource. The trap was set when

[11] See this process illustrated in a very cool puppet show at: www.nature.com/articles/d41586-018-05132-x.

the insects evolved dependence on that resource, then was sprung
when the resource was abruptly snatched away.

Like their cousins in Nevada before the crash, Quino populations
seem resilient to human-caused environmental changes, rapidly
adapting to a shifting climate. However, by 1996, the Quino's small
range in Mexico (extending <250 km south of San Diego) had already
suffered high extinction rates in habitats that looked superficially
healthy but were becoming climatically unsuitable. Computer models
of changing climate predict that in just the next 40 years all of the
Quino's current range in the United States, including the new higher-
elevation populations, will also become climatically unsuitable, lying
outside the range of climates that the Quino occupies today. It seems
likely that these southern range boundaries are at the limits of the
species' physiological tolerances, in which case genetic evolution may
be unable to surmount this ramped-up challenge.

These two butterfly examples highlight the fundamental problem
driving many wild species to the brink of extinction: humans can
change our actions and alter the environment faster than wildlife can
adapt. Europeans have recognized this for some time, and have
developed conservation insights and practices in response to evolved
dependencies of many wildflowers, insects, and birds on traditional land
management. American conservation biologists historically have been
able to focus on fencing and protection to preserve the wild species in an
area. They have only recently come to grips with the fact that
everywhere in the country (absent some places in Alaska) has some level
of human influence that must be recognized and dealt with as part of
conservation planning. In the future, conservation in North America
will increasingly resemble that in Europe, requiring continuation of the
human activities to which wild species have become adapted.

For now, the Quino is protected in its upward range expansion by the
designation of critical habitat around the new colonies. This is a
pioneering response to climate change by the US Fish and Wildlife
Service, one that I hope we'll see more of. But climate change presents
a moving target, so management actions must also track a moving

ESSAY 5.1   **(cont.)**

baseline. Species like the Quino checkerspot will continue to be conservation reliant.

As the pace of climate change ramps up, true adaptive management that embraces flexibility will become essential. Such a stepping-stone approach, in which attention to real-time population dynamics informs managers as to which future (projected) pathway a target species is following, will be key to saving many species. Meanwhile, the butterflies are in a two-step ecological and evolutionary dance, in which one partner (the host plant or the climate) moves and the other partner (the butterfly) responds. The problem for wildlife is that the dance is orchestrated by humans, and we keep changing the score.[12]

spawning season, low fecundity, demersal rather than planktonic eggs, and a low upper thermal limit. Native fish species in California are already more vulnerable to extinction than are non-native, alien species, but climate change accentuates the differences. In an analysis of the vulnerability of 164 California freshwater fish species to climate change and warmer waters, Moyle et al. (2013) found that 82% of the native species were classified as highly vulnerable compared with only 19% of aliens. In fact, most alien species are projected to thrive under future conditions.

Species that are anchored to a substrate, such as corals or mussels, along with most plants, may be incapable of moving rapidly to a better available habitat. With nursery or aquarium propagation, however, propagules can be transferred. In anticipation of climate change, a citizen group has planted seeds of an Endangered conifer, Florida torreya, well outside its historic range.[13] With proper

[12] For more information on Edith's checkerspot responding to global change, see Parmesan et al. (2015) and Singer and Parmesan (2018)

[13] www.torreyaguardians.org/. The torreya pine is also threatened by a fungal blight, which has decimated the population in its restricted historic range in Florida. Use of gene editing technology to create fungus-resistant strains is under consideration (Marinelli 2018).

FIGURE 5.7. Research biologist Maya Legrande uses climbing gear to hand-pollinate an Endangered pua'ala (Moloka'i ohaha) plant growing on a cliff face on Moloka'i in the Hawaiian Islands. There are fewer than 200 individuals growing in the wild. (A black and white version of this figure will appear in some formats. For the color version, please refer to the plate section.)
Photo: Ken Wood/Maya Legrande.

horticulture, plants may become established in new areas. In such situations, transportation by humans may overcome dispersal limitations and enable a species to keep pace with the velocity of climate change. Caution is needed, however, as there is a risk of negative impacts on the recipient ecological community.

When mobile animals cannot move to better habitat on their own, they may also need translocation. However, individuals may choose not to remain where they are translocated and released. Without additional training, captive-bred individuals may also lack appropriate behaviors for avoiding predators or capturing prey needed for successful release back into the wild. Often the most successful translocations are to islands, where individuals can less easily move elsewhere and predators may be absent.

When species remain in place, they may be able to adapt by increasing their physiological tolerance to extreme conditions, changing their life-history features, or adjusting their behavior. These adaptations may be genetic or phenotypic. Various plant and animal species have advanced the seasonal phenology of flowering, breeding, migration, spawning, and emergence in relation to warming climate, particularly at higher latitudes where warming has been greatest. Several stocks of salmon, for example, are starting their spawning migrations earlier in the year as water temperatures have warmed over the past several decades (Waples et al. 2008; Kovach et al. 2013).

Management may help a species increase its adaptive capacity. Exchanging individuals among subpopulations can increase genetic diversity and possibly adaptive capacity. Captive breeding might incorporate selection for individual traits likely to be useful in future environmental conditions. Genomic technology may offer ways to quickly enhance adaptive capacity, although this approach is largely untested and is not without risks.

Management interventions to enhance a species' adaptive capacity are likely to be costly and have uncertain outcomes (Nicotra et al. 2015). To mitigate the risk, scientists require detailed knowledge of a species' physiological limits, ecological relationships, and genetic population structure. Ecological niche models that link the abiotic and habitat conditions a species can tolerate with demographic modeling can help define expected responses to climate change. Such models can also be used to evaluate the possible outcomes of actions such as translocation, habitat management, or creation of protected areas (Fordham et al. 2013). Laboratory experiments can provide insight into a species' ability to adapt to changes in variables such as temperature, although such experiments usually test the capacity of a species to respond to changes in single variables rather than the suites of interacting variables that characterize complex ecosystems.

## GLOBAL CHANGE AND CONSERVATION RELIANCE

The threats to species that conservation has traditionally considered (Chapter 4) become dire and more difficult to manage under global change. The magnitude and extent of driving forces such as sea-level rise, ocean acidification, or changes in precipitation and temperature seem beyond our management capacities. Adaptation to these changes requires local approaches to managing species and ecosystem processes, approaches that are proactive and flexible but can be costly (Donlan 2015). Such approaches depend on monitoring that addresses the effects of both incremental change and abrupt and unpredictable events.

Prioritizing conservation options for addressing emergent threats requires enough data to build realistic scenarios for the locations and species of concern. It also requires extensive knowledge of how changes in essential ecosystem processes are likely to affect population dynamics. As conditions change it will be necessary to re-engage with affected stakeholders and revise conservation plans. Plans must be flexible and transparent about projected future conditions as well as responsibilities and long-term costs of potential conservation activities (Groves and Game 2016). Understanding the scope of conservation reliance across species and through time is essential to developing and prioritizing conservation activities that will be successful.

The institutions and policies that affect imperiled species were largely created before we understood climate change as we do now. Historically, it has been assumed that threats to species are local, static, and reversible and the responses of species are predictable. For example, there are no provisions in the Endangered Species Act for designating critical habitat in a way that accounts for where the species is or could potentially exist as habitats shift and communities are disrupted by climate change (Ruhl 2008; Doremus 2010). Policies generally do not encourage quick response to urgent threats. Conservation laws and management actions should be designed to allow quick and flexible responses as well as foster the long-term commitments needed to maintain ecosystem processes and manage conservation-reliant species.

# 6 The Role of Policy and Law

To conserve at-risk species, nations have developed policies, enacted laws, and signed treaties that are implemented and enforced by government agencies and courts. International organizations have generated listings of imperiled species. Depending on their situation, species are designated as Endangered, Threatened, Vulnerable, Near Threatened, or some other category. These status designations are often accompanied by legal mandates or restrictions on actions that may negatively affect the species. The intent is to prevent extinctions, stabilize declining populations, and enable recovery so that the long-term survival of species in the wild is ensured. Such categorizations of species are well established in legal, scientific, and public discourse.

Conservation-reliant species are generally not acknowledged as a distinct legal category, so they are not accorded any specific legal status. Conservation reliance refers to the condition of a species—its degree of imperilment, the threats it faces, and the form or duration of management needed to mitigate those threats—rather than its conservation status. Conservation reliance takes many forms (Figure 2.1) and may apply to a species regardless of its legal status. Most species at risk of extinction are conservation reliant, but so also are some that are declining but not yet imperiled.

Because conservation reliance is not recognized in policy and law, it can easily be ignored. When an imperiled species is designated for legal protection, it qualifies for targeted management. Often it is only later, when the species is recovering, that its conservation reliance and need for continuing long-term management may be recognized. Conservation reliance may make it difficult to remove special legal protections, even after a species has recovered. It would be better if the conservation reliance of a species and the likelihood that its conservation will require a long-term investment could be considered from the outset.

To assess whether existing policy, law, and treaties provide enough flexibility to deal with the long-term needs of conservation-reliant species, it is necessary to understand how these instruments work. In this chapter, we explore how policy decisions to protect at-risk species are embodied in statutes and regulations of several international organizations and nations, and where in government those responsible for promulgating and implementing regulations reside. The legal approaches we describe in this chapter deal primarily with the status and vulnerability of species. Although the specificity of status designations varies among countries, most relate to the immediacy of the risk of extinction.

## FIVE THEMES FROM THE HISTORY OF AT-RISK SPECIES LEGISLATION

Policies, statutes, regulations, and treaties (Box 6.1) reflect the thinking, agendas, and social attitudes of the time and evolve as these forces change (Doremus 2010). An historical perspective, therefore, may help to explain why current law is as it is.[1]

One emerging theme is a gradual shift from thinking of "wildlife" only in terms of game species to be managed for hunting or fishing to include a broad array of species and their habitats. This focus on nongame species threatened by imminent extinction is now embodied in specific laws, as in the United States and Australia, or it may be embedded in more general "wildlife" laws, as in New Zealand (Appendix A).

A second theme is the widespread recognition that wildlife is a shared resource for the benefit of all people. As such, it may require governmental stewardship. The authority of governments to regulate

---

[1] Barrow (2009) provides a general overview of how environmental legislation emerged and Goble (2006) and Nie et al. (2017) review the history of legal approaches to conservation and management of at-risk species in the United States.

BOX 6.1.   **Policy, Statutes, Regulations, Law, and Treaties**

Ecologists and conservationists often use the words "policy," "law," "regulation," and "treaty" interchangeably, but there are distinctions. We offer a quick glossary.

**Policy** is the body of general principles that guide a government in its management of public affairs. It is a goal, expressed in statutes, regulations, and judicial decisions.

**Statutes** are acts of a legislative body declaring, commanding, or prohibiting something. When the term "policy" is applied to statutes, it denotes the general purposes of the act. The purpose of the Endangered Species Act is to conserve at-risk species. When policy is embodied in a statute, it has legal consequences: Any person who knowingly takes a listed species faces either a civil penalty of up to US$12 000 or criminal penalties up to US$50 000 and a year in prison.[2]

**Regulations,** unlike the term "statute," do not have an agreed-upon meaning. In New Zealand, the term is a synonym for "statute."[3] In the European Union, a regulation is "a binding legislative act [that] must be applied in its entirety across the EU."[4] In the United States and Canada, the term is applied to legally binding rules promulgated by an administrative agency that has been delegated the power to do so. The regulation must be promulgated through specified procedures and have the force of law.[5] In Australia, it is "[a]ny rule endorsed by government where there is an expectation of compliance... [P]ublic servants make rules every day."[6]

The regulations implementing the Endangered Species Act dwarf the act itself. The agencies responsible for administering the act use

---

[2] Endangered Species Act §11(a)-(b).    [3] www.nzlii.org/nz/num-reg
[4] europa.eu/european_union/eu-law/legal-acts-en
[5] Canada, Act and Regulations, https://www.canada.ca/en/privy-council/services/ publications/guide-making-federal-acts-regulations.html#pt3; United States, Administrative Procedure Act United States Code, sec. 553–559.
[6] Australian Government, The Australian Government Guide to Regulation, cuttingredtape.gov.au/sites/default/files/documents/australia_government/guide_ regulation.pdf

BOX 6.1. **(cont.)**

regulations to flesh out the broad statutory language. In doing so, they are embodying policy.

**Judicial decisions:** In deciding cases, courts draw upon a large body of policies, often cloaked in Latin. The court's decisions affect not only the parties before the court: under the policy of *stare decisis*, courts are not to disturb settled precedent. The difficulty, of course, lies in deciding which precedent is applicable—which is the role of the courts.

**Law** is all of the above. Laws have legal standing within the governmental jurisdiction to which they apply.

**Treaties** are agreements among parties (sovereign states, international organizations) that oblige them to written policies and responsibilities. Parties that fail to meet the obligations may be held liable under the terms of the treaty or international law. Because they do not bind the parties, however, treaties can also be abrogated unilaterally.

public lands for wildlife dates back as early as 1066 when William I, as King of England, arrogated to himself the power to designate tracts of land as "forests." In these newly declared forests, the king and his friends had the exclusive right to hunt. To ensure adequate numbers of game, forest laws restricted other land uses. This is the foundation of wildlife law as it developed in England and its former colonies. The New Zealand Animal Protection Act, for example, was modeled on English hunting laws (Galbreath 1993). In many countries (such as Uganda, Tajikistan, and China), ownership of wildlife is vested in the state on behalf of the people. Governmental control over the use of wildlife, however, is expressed in various ways. Some nations, such as Burkina Faso and Botswana, retain ownership of wildlife but grant hunting rights to landowners on their own land, whereas others, such as Zimbabwe, transfer ownership and management of wildlife to private landowners or community councils (FAO 2002).

In a federal system—as in the United States, Canada, or Australia—the issue of who "owns" wildlife has been contentious (Matthews 1986; Freyfogle and Goble 2009; Wojciechowski et al. 2011). When the United States was founded, much of the power and authority, including the ownership of wildlife within a state's boundaries, fell to the states. By the beginning of the twentieth century, however, it was apparent that conflicting state laws and regulations were not adequate to conserve many species of interest, which did not recognize political boundaries. Beginning with fur seals and migratory birds, laws and treaties were enacted that gradually shifted responsibility for conservation of certain wildlife to the federal government (Kannan 2009; Bowman et al. 2010). Later federal statutes have strengthened the protection of endangered species and their habitats, although responsibility for management of most wildlife still resides with the states. The issue of state versus federal ownership of land and management of natural resources remains contentious.

In his 1972 Environmental Message to Congress, President Nixon concluded that federal law "simply does not provide the kind of management tools needed to act early enough to save vanishing species." He proposed that Congress "make the taking of endangered species a federal offense" and authorize "protective measures to be undertaken before a species is so depleted that restoration is impossible." The statute that emerged from the legislative process, the Endangered Species Act of 1973, created a legal structure that stipulated how the status of a species would be determined, a mechanism for developing and implementing actions to recover the species, and what restrictions were necessary to protect it. Despite several amendments and considerable controversy, the act continues to guide the conservation of at-risk species in the United States and has been a model for laws in other countries.

This historical progression of laws illustrates a third theme. Discussions of who "owns" wildlife or bears the responsibility for conserving imperiled species are often explicitly utilitarian. Laws tend to emphasize the instrumental values of nature: species are resources to be used by people. In many countries, laws and regulations are designed to implement CITES, which protects at-risk species by regulating their use in international commerce. On the other hand, the progression of endangered species laws in the United States and elsewhere illustrates a growing concern with intrinsic values:

protection of imperiled species is viewed as an ethical and moral imperative that takes precedence over other societal goals (Goble 2009b; Robinson 2011).

A fourth theme underlying most legal approaches is the implicit assumption (or hope) that if appropriate measures are taken, recovery goals will be met and populations will become self-sustaining. This assumption is founded on an equilibrium, balance-of-nature perspective that was the prevailing paradigm in ecology when the Endangered Species Act was drafted. Ecological thinking, however, has undergone a fundamental shift toward viewing nature as variable and dynamic (Wiens 2016b) and legal approaches and regulations have not kept up (Doremus 2010). The expectation that species will be able to recover to some former state and will no longer need special legal protection has fostered controversy about the usefulness of the laws, or of conservation itself.

A fifth theme is part of our reason for writing this book. The effectiveness of policies, laws, and treaties depends on support for the agencies and organizations that implement and enforce them. Many people and societies are now deeply concerned about the fate of declining or imperiled species. Yet those responsible for developing conservation policies or undertaking conservation actions often occupy different levels of government with different agendas and responsibilities. Funding and support for conservation vary in how closely they are linked to legal instruments.[7] When long-term support is erratic or uncertain, the risk of failure rises with the extent of conservation reliance.

## HOW DO POLICIES, LAWS, AND TREATIES WORK?

Laws that deal with endangered species aim to prevent extinction, stabilize populations, and achieve recovery by reducing or eliminating threats (Box 6.2). Several nations have statutes that address these aims, although in many cases the restrictions are derived from laws aimed to maintain game animals ("wildlife") for hunting or fishing. The organization

---

[7] Goble et al. (1999) and Camacho et al. (2017) analyze the disparities between federal and state support for endangered species conservation in the United States.

---

BOX 6.2   **The Purposes of Threatened Species Laws**

*What do at-risk species laws aim to do?*

- Prevent extinctions
- Stabilize declining populations
- Enable and achieve recovery

*How do laws aim to do this?*

- Solicit support and collaboration among government agencies, scientists, stakeholders, tribal groups, and the public
- Identify at-risk and vulnerable species
- Identify threat factors
- Identify critical habitat
- List species for legal protection
- Prohibit actions that will harm listed species or their habitats ("take")
- Prevent impacts of development, farming, extractive industries, and similar human actions on species and habitats
- Specify penalties for violations of laws
- Direct and implement enforcement
- Provide incentives for actions that promote aims of the laws
- Draft recovery plans
- Implement recovery actions
- Monitor the ongoing status of species and the effectiveness of recovery efforts
- Create a coordinated administrative structure
- Obtain and allocate funding.

---

Endangered Earth has compiled statutes governing the conservation or use of wildlife for 242 governments[8] (see Appendix A for the 101 statutes available in English). To varying degrees, these laws incorporate the conservation intentions and actions listed in Box 6.2. Of course, how a statute is written may not match how it is actually applied.

The most comprehensive statutes explicitly address the conservation of at-risk species. The Endangered Species Act in the United

---

[8] www.endangeredearth.com/endangered-species-laws/

States, the Species at Risk Act in Canada, the Environment Protection and Biodiversity Conservation Act in Australia, and similar statutes in Bermuda, Macedonia, and Vietnam establish processes for listing at-risk species and delegate the responsibility and authority to take recovery and protective actions. Seventeen other countries incorporate protection of at-risk species as a separate category in a broad wildlife-management statute. For example, Armenia includes "vanishing animal species" and Taiwan emphasizes "endangered species, rare and valuable species, and other conservation-deserving species." These statutes lack an explicit directive to undertake recovery actions. Most other countries (e.g. Bhutan, Finland, and Mauritius) have general wildlife-management statutes that include hunting regulations, management of nature reserves, and the like, without recognizing at-risk species as a distinct category. In some cases, wildlife-management statutes focus on specific wildlife: Iceland targets birds and fisheries, whereas South Africa has specific statutes dealing with elephants. Statutes in many other countries have been enacted to comply with CITES: Botswana, Mongolia, and the Solomon Islands are examples.

## INTERNATIONAL CONSERVATION GOALS

Statutes in many countries align with several broad international initiatives that have developed over the past two decades. Two stand out. The United Nations (UN) Millennium Development Goals, signed in 2000, committed the 191 member states to work to achieve eight goals by 2015. The emphasis was on human poverty, education, and health, with the additional goal of significantly reducing biodiversity loss by 2010 (Goal 7B). In 2015, the UN extended the Millennium Development Goals by adopting 17 Sustainable Development Goals. Once again, biodiversity was included: "Take urgent and significant action to reduce the degradation of natural habitats, halt the loss of biodiversity and, by 2020, protect and prevent the extinction of threatened species" (Goal 15.5). The Convention on Biological Diversity (CBD) is a multilateral treaty that recognizes conservation of biodiversity as an integral part of human development programs.

The goals of the CBD, embodied in the Aichi Targets adopted in 2010, include Target 12: By 2020 "the extinction of known threatened species has been prevented and their conservation status ... has been improved and sustained."

Collectively, these broad international agreements highlight the recognition of the magnitude of biodiversity loss and the imperative to take actions to forestall further loss and enable the recovery of threatened species. Nearly all nations support these goals, at least in principle. In addition to these global initiatives, however, many other global, regional, and species-specific treaties and instruments deal with conserving species. In a non-exhaustive list, Trouwborst et al. (2017) highlighted 65 such international measures. The variety reflects the differing influences of social constraints, objectives, and values. The instruments also vary in their legal standing and enforcement. Most emphasize the status of species and prohibit specified actions. CITES, for example, has been largely successful in restricting and coordinating international trade in species. It has fostered the recovery of species such as the Nile crocodile, whose populations in parts of sub-Saharan Africa had been severely depleted by hunting for the leather trade. Most of these instruments, including the two mentioned above, are silent on the need for long-term conservation commitments and thus conservation reliance.

## A GLOBAL AUTHORITY ON SPECIES STATUS

Many statutory approaches are based upon the IUCN categories. The IUCN was established in 1948 as a consortium of governmental and civil-society organizations (Holdgate 1999; Lausche 2008). Its mission is to "influence, encourage and assist societies throughout the world to conserve the integrity and diversity of nature and to ensure that any use of natural resources is equitable and ecologically sustainable."[9] IUCN does not specifically aim to mobilize public support for nature conservation or prioritize species for conservation action. Rather, it tries to

[9] www.iucn.org/about

influence the actions of governments, businesses, and other stakeholders by providing information and advice and by building partnerships.

The IUCN is perhaps best known for its Red List, a global list of
species at risk of extinction that was begun in 1954. The most recent
Red List (version 3.2, 2019)[10] classifies plant, fungi, and animal
species into seven categories ranging from "Least Concern" to
"Extinct" (Box 6.3). The assessments are based on the rate of population decline, size and number of populations, geographic range, and
other factors. The IUCN listings inform people of a species' conservation status and changes in that status. The status of the southern
white rhinoceros, for example, was changed from Vulnerable to Near
Threatened when the species met all the biological standards for that
category, even though it still requires intense human intervention.
Status determinations are made without regard to the nature or duration of management actions that might be taken to conserve species,
so they do not consider conservation reliance.

Importantly, the IUCN has no governmental power to engage in
legal action, so listing a species in one of the Red List categories has no
legal standing. The categorizations become legally relevant only when
they are included in statutes and listings in countries that adopt the
IUCN list. The IUCN encourages, guides, and informs rather than
legislates actions to improve a species' status.

## THE UNITED STATES: THE ENDANGERED SPECIES ACT AND NATIONAL ENVIRONMENTAL POLICY ACT

The Endangered Species Act is one of the world's most robust,
successful, and contentious conservation laws. It is robust because,
despite repeated and ongoing attempts, it has largely withstood political pressures to relax its provisions. It is successful because it has
enabled several hundred perilously endangered species to escape
extinction, stabilized populations of many others, and become a

---

[10] https://www.iucnredlist.org/resources/threat-classification-scheme

BOX 6.3   **Categorizations of At-Risk Species Used by IUCN and Government Agencies in Several Countries**

**International Union for the Conservation of Nature (IUCN) Red List Version 3.2 (2019)**

*Data Deficient*: "inadequate information to make a direct, or indirect, assessment of its risk of extinction"

*Least Concern*: "does not qualify" for any of the following categories; "widespread and abundant taxa are included in this category"

*Near Threatened*: "likely to qualify for a threatened category in the near future"

*Vulnerable*: "facing a high risk of extinction in the wild"

*Endangered*: "facing a very high risk of extinction in the wild"

*Critically Endangered*: "facing an extremely high risk of extinction in the wild"

*Extinct in the Wild*: "known only to survive in cultivation, in captivity or as a naturalized population (or populations) well outside the past range"

*Extinct*: "no reasonable doubt that the last individual has died."

**United States Endangered Species Act (1973)**

*Threatened*: "likely to become an endangered species within the foreseeable future"

*Endangered*: "in danger of extinction throughout all or a significant portion of its range within the foreseeable future."

**Canada Species at Risk Act (SARA) (2002)**

*Data Deficient:* "not enough information is available to determine the species' status"

*Special Concern*: species "may become threatened or an endangered species because of a combination of biological characteristics and identified threats"

*Threatened*: species "is likely to become endangered if nothing is done to reverse the factors leading to its extirpation or extinction"

*Endangered*: species "is facing imminent extirpation or extinction"

BOX 6.3 **(cont.)**

*Extirpated*: species "no longer exists in the wild in Canada, but exists elsewhere"

*Extinct*: species "no longer exists."

### Australia Environmental Protection and Biodiversity Conservation Act (1999)

*Conservation Dependent*: "the species is the focus of a specific conservation program without which the species would become vulnerable, endangered or critically endangered within five years" and is a species of "fish" (which includes some other marine organisms, such as mollusks).

*Vulnerable*: "the species is not critically endangered or endangered but is facing a high risk of extinction in the wild in the medium-term future"

*Endangered*: "the species is not critically endangered, but it is facing a very high risk of extinction in the wild in the near future"

*Critically Endangered*: "the species is facing an extremely high risk of extinction in the wild in the immediate future"

*Extinct in the Wild*: "the species is known to survive only in cultivation or in captivity, or as a naturalized population well outside its past range"

*Extinct*: "there is no reasonable doubt that the last member of the species has died."

### New Zealand Threat Classification System (2002)

*At Risk Species*: "species which are not considered Threatened but could quickly become so if declines continue or if a new threat arises"
Declining: "population declining but still common"
Recovering: "population is increasing after previously declining"
Relict: "small population stabilized after declining"
Naturally Uncommon: "population is naturally small and, therefore, susceptible to harmful influences"

*Threatened*: "likely to go extinct (or be reduced to a few small safe refuges) within the lifetime of those alive today"
Nationally Vulnerable: "facing risk of extinction in the medium term"
Nationally Endangered: "facing high risk of extinction in the short term"
Nationally Critical: "facing immediate high risk of extinction"

*Extinct:* "no longer exists."

vehicle for protecting habitat to the benefit of both listed and unlisted species (Schwartz 2008). And it is contentious because environmentalists and conservationists have used the law to protect the interests of listed species, which often conflict with the utilitarian interests of developers, farmers, industrialists, and many political conservatives.[11]

The purpose of the act is to conserve endangered and threatened species and the ecosystems on which they depend. The act's intellectual model for achieving this goal is seemingly straightforward (Figure 6.1). A species threatened with extinction is listed through a process that identifies the threats to the species. Prohibitions on harming the species and its habitat are imposed. A recovery plan is written and implemented. After the threats to the species are eliminated, the species rebounds, recovery goals are met, and the species is delisted—it no longer requires the specific protection or management provided under the act.[12]

For many imperiled species, however, continued, species-specific management may be necessary to sustain their distribution and abundance—the species remain conservation reliant. The Greater Yellowstone population of the grizzly bear was removed from protection under the Endangered Species Act in 2017, but a year later a federal judge reinstated the species' status under the act, noting that the lack of connectivity with grizzly populations elsewhere threatened the genetic diversity of the Yellowstone population. One day after the court's ruling, a bill was introduced in the US Congress that would reverse the court ruling and shelter further delisting

---

[11] The act was not contentious when it was enacted; it passed the Senate unanimously and the House by a vote of 390–12.

[12] Species not protected under the act or species that have been delisted may still be protected. Most birds, for example, are protected by the Migratory Bird Treaty Act; the Marine Mammal Protection Act protects whales, dolphins, and other marine mammals; and the Sikes Act directs the Department of Defense to develop plans that apply to species on military lands. Forty-six states have laws that complement the Endangered Species Act.

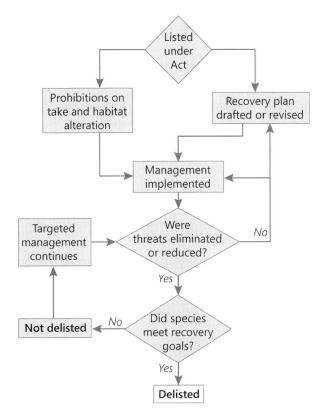

FIGURE 6.1. Key processes for recovering species listed under the US Endangered Species Act.

decisions from judicial review. The legal standing of the grizzly bears may be uncertain, but biologically the bears continue to require trans-locations of individuals at some locations outside the Greater Yellow-stone population to maintain genetic diversity. Other species, such as the island night lizard, similarly may need continuing management even after they have legally recovered (Box 6.4).

The decision to list a species is based on an assessment of the risk of extinction and the contributing threats. The Endangered Species Act recognizes the threats of habitat loss or modification, overexploitation, disease or predation, inadequacy of existing

## BOX 6.4.   The Endangered Species Act Process: The Island Night Lizard

The island night lizard (Figure 6.2) is a small insectivorous lizard that may spend its entire 35-year life in an area smaller than a tiny house. It occurs on three of the Channel Islands off southern California, almost entirely on San Clemente Island. Here is a summary of how the species has been treated under the Endangered Species Act.

1. *Listing:* The Island night lizard is one of seven plant and animal species endemic to San Clemente Island that were listed under the Endangered Species Act in 1977. In listing the species, the US Fish and Wildlife Service

FIGURE 6.2. The island night lizard, a small lizard restricted to three Channel Islands off the coast of southern California, remains conservation reliant. Color patterns vary among islands; this individual is from San Clemente Island. (A black and white version of this figure will appear in some formats. For the color version, please refer to the plate section.)
Photo: Lawrence L.C. Jones.

BOX 6.4.   **(cont.)**

identified habitat losses owing to feral goats and pigs, predation by feral cats, and the introduction of non-native plants as major threats.[13] Fire and disturbance by military activity also threatened the species. Abundance was not estimated at the time of listing, but 2 years later a US Fish and Wildlife Service biologist reported the lizard to be widespread.

2. *Recovery Plan:* The US Fish and Wildlife Service published a collective recovery plan for the endangered and threatened species of the California Channel Islands in 1984. It called for identifying and restoring habitat and ecosystem function, monitoring population size and distribution, removing non-native species, and directing military activities away from biologically sensitive areas. No numeric goals were stipulated for any of the species covered by the plan.

3. *Management Actions:* Feral goats and pigs were removed from the island by 1992. Trapping of feral cats is ongoing, as is a program to control the impacts of non-native plants. Fire is addressed through prevention, containment, and suppression measures. Military activities are managed under the Military Operations and Fire Management program. Restoration of habitat is accomplished through planting of native plants and erosion control.

4. *Species Status:* The estimated population in 2014 was 21 332 899, of which 99% occurred on San Clemente Island.

5. *Delisting:* On April 1, 2014, the US Fish and Wildlife Service delisted the species: "We consider the island night lizard to be 'recovered' because all substantial threats to the lizard have been ameliorated. All remaining potential threats to the species and its habitat, with the exception of climate change, are currently managed through implementation of management plans."[14]

Despite its large population size, the island night lizard remains conservation reliant. The delisting document cited six federal statutes and eight management programs as providing the necessary regulatory assurances to justify removing the species from the protection of the Endangered Species Act. The primary law assuring

[13]  Federal Register 42: 40682-85 (1977)
[14]  Federal Register50CFR Vol. 79, No. 62 18190-18210 FED50CFR

BOX 6.4.  **(cont.)**

continuing management is the Sikes Act,[15] which pertains to military lands (San Clemente Island is owned and operated by the US Navy). Because delisting stipulated the continuation of management activities targeted on the lizard and other at-risk species, they remain conservation reliant.

regulations, or "other natural or manmade factors affecting its survival."[16] The US Fish and Wildlife Service and the National Oceanic and Atmospheric Administration (NOAA) Fisheries are responsible for listing species.[17]

Recovery of listed species under the Endangered Species Act is addressed through preparation of a recovery plan that specifies the management actions necessary to eliminate or mitigate threats, provides specific goals for delisting a species, and estimates the time and cost to achieve the goals. It takes time, money, and information to develop a scientifically sound recovery plan. In urgent situations, conservation actions are often taken without a recovery plan and without a structured process to assess which actions are likely to be most effective. Without a plan (or even with one), a lack of funding, personnel, or initiative may delay conservation efforts even as the condition of a species worsens. This is what happened to the dusky seaside sparrow and the Maui 'akepa, ō'ū, and several other Hawaiian

[15] 1960, 16 USC 670a-670o, 74 Stat. 1052    [16] Endangered Species Act, § 4(a)(1)(B).
[17] The US Fish and Wildlife Service is responsible for most terrestrial and freshwater species. NOAA Fisheries is responsible for most marine species. The listing requirements and procedures are set out in Endangered Species Act, § 4. Agencies are also required to prioritize species for listing and delisting and for development and implementation of recovery plans. As petitions to list species increased, Congress chose not to increase funding and instead amended the Act to authorize the listing agencies to determine that a species' listing can be "warranted but precluded" by other pending proposals (§ 4(b)(3)(B)(iii)). The Act also authorizes listing species not found in the United States or its territories; see Foley et al. (2017) and Van Norman (2017).

bird species that became extinct while waiting for the process to play out.

In addition to recovery efforts, a significant aspect of the Endangered Species Act is to provide protection to listed species through its prohibitions. The act prohibits actions that would harm a listed species or its habitat. Federal agencies are required to consult the US Fish and Wildlife Service or NOAA Fisheries to ensure that agency actions[18] will not jeopardize a listed species or adversely affect its critical habitat. Consultation may lead to a biological opinion that assesses the effects of the proposed action and recommends modifications or alternatives, if necessary. Some regard the consultation process as an onerous requirement that delays or halts economic development. When modifications are required they may be controversial and entail considerable financial costs. Consequently, biological opinions may end up being challenged in court, adding to costs and delays.

When a species is proposed for listing, the responsible agency must also consider whether there are areas of habitat essential to the species' conservation that may require special management or protection. Such areas may be designated as "critical habitat." Critical habitat includes all areas deemed essential to the survival and recovery of a species, whether it currently resides in those areas, historically resided in those areas, uses those areas for movement, or needs them for any other reason. Designation of critical habitat therefore requires a careful examination of the environmental features that are most important to the conservation of a species. This part of the act also restricts federal actions or actions requiring a federal permit, so it can be contentious. As these legal machinations show, ambiguities in what "habitat" means (Chapter 3) come into play.

A decision to list a species under the Endangered Species Act is required to be based only on scientific information, whereas human

---

[18] Any actions that involve federal funding or personnel, require a federal permit, or affect a resource under federal jurisdiction (e.g. lands, waters, protected species)—in short, any action bearing a federal fingerprint.

economic concerns and interests may enter into recovery planning and critical habitat designations, consultations, and Habitat Conservation Plans. The separation is not always clear, however, and where interests of people and a species conflict, litigation often follows. One of the earliest legal challenges to the act involved the snail darter and the Tennessee Valley Authority (TVA).[19] The TVA (a public corporation of the US government) began constructing the Tellico Dam on the Little Tennessee River in 1967. When the National Environmental Policy Act (NEPA)[20] was enacted 3 years later, the lawsuits that followed prompted new research. In 1973, a new species of fish, the snail darter, was discovered in the stretch of river due to be inundated by the dam. The Endangered Species Act was passed a few months later. In 1975, the snail darter was listed as Endangered and the portion of the river that would be affected by the dam was subsequently designated critical habitat. By then the dam was nearly completed.

Opponents of the dam alleged that the act applied to the project even though the dam was nearly finished. In 1978, the case reached the US Supreme Court, which ruled that the facts that over US$100 million had been spent and the dam was largely finished did not override the act's prohibition on jeopardizing endangered species.[21] In response to this decision, the US Congress quickly passed an amendment to the Endangered Species Act to create a high-level Endangered Species Committee with the power to exempt actions from the provisions of the act.[22] By permitting a project to go forward, the decision of this committee could potentially condemn a species to extinction; thus its nickname, the "God Squad."

---

[19] The legal twists and turns of the story are reviewed by Goble et al. (2017: 1024–1037); popular accounts of the controversy are provided by Murchison (2007) and Plater (2014).

[20] We discuss NEPA and its intersection with the Endangered Species Act later in this chapter.

[21] *Tennessee Valley Authority v. Hill*, 437 US 153 (1978).

[22] Endangered Species Act, § 7(e).

The committee met in early 1979 to consider exempting the Tellico Dam project. Unexpectedly, it voted unanimously in favor of the snail darter, denying an exemption for the dam not only because of its impacts on the fish and its habitat, but also because it made no economic sense to continue the project. Undeterred, dam proponents were successful in attaching an exemption for the dam to an appropriations bill that passed Congress in September 1979. Two months later, the (now completed) gates on the dam were closed and the reservoir began to fill. In the interim, however, snail darters were discovered in several new locations and had been successfully translocated to other streams. The species was reclassified from Endangered to Threatened in 1984.[23] Nearly two decades later, less than a quarter of the proposed recovery actions had been implemented. The darter is listed as Vulnerable by IUCN.

Although the Endangered Species Act has a reputation as being rigid and harsh, this characterization is substantially overblown. Congress has carved out numerous exceptions to support human interests; implementation has shifted from regulation toward collaboration. For example, incidental-take permits allow limited take when permitted actions are not likely to jeopardize a species. Other legal tools provide incentives to landowners for conserving imperiled species (Wilcove and Lee 2004; Evans et al. 2016). For example, Safe Harbor Agreements and Habitat Conservation Plans provide assurances to landowners that they will not be held responsible should their activities harm a listed species; in exchange, landowners pledge to undertake conservation actions to benefit the species or minimize the negative effects of their activities (Wheeler and Rowberry 2010). Michael Bean reflects on the importance of incentives in Essay 6.1.

Despite the flexibility provided by these tools, the act's reputation continues to shape its implementation. Although the act's prohibition against federal actions that jeopardize the survival of listed species has garnered notoriety for stopping a few projects (like,

---

[23] Federal Register 49(130):27510–27514.

ESSAY 6.1   **Incentivizing Beneficial Land-Use Decisions**

*Michael J. Bean*

It is a common, but mistaken, belief that the principal cause of wildlife endangerment is ruthless overexploitation to supply a seemingly inexhaustible international demand for wildlife and wildlife products. While it is true that commerce is a major threat to some species, for the great majority of wildlife species throughout the world the most pervasive and important threat comes from a more prosaic cause: the loss and degradation of habitat as a result of human land-use decisions.

If land-use decisions lie at the root of wildlife endangerment, then the challenge facing conservationists is to influence those decisions to achieve enduring landscapes on which people can prosper and wildlife can persist. That is no small challenge, for it entails both rectifying past land-use decisions that have made many species endangered today and ensuring that future land-use decisions will sustain formerly endangered species throughout all the tomorrows that follow.

Although this challenge faces every country in the world, the experience of the United States, which thinks of itself as a world leader in conservation matters because of its Endangered Species Act, may be instructive. Perhaps one of the least-cited provisions of that act is its introductory finding that "a system of incentives" for "interested parties" to develop and maintain conservation programs is key to safeguarding the nation's heritage in wildlife and plants. Given that finding, one might logically expect to find an array of conservation incentives described elsewhere in the act. Yet, a search for incentive provisions in this foundational conservation law turns up nothing. The word "incentives" never appears again in the statute, nor does any provision that has the character of an incentive.

The omission is significant, and potentially debilitating. The act's goal, after all, is not just to stave off extinction of already imperiled species, but to achieve a secure future for them through recovery. If the only tools the act provides are prohibitory in nature—proscribing harmful conduct—it will be exceedingly difficult to bring about an

ESSAY 6.1 **(cont.)**

improvement in the status of such species, particularly those for which the loss or degradation of habitat is the primary driver of endangerment.

What Congress failed to provide, therefore, the administrators of the act have had to create. To encourage the development of ambitious habitat-conservation plans, they offered an assurance of regulatory stability by way of a "no surprises" policy. To elicit voluntary conservation efforts for threatened or endangered species by private landowners, they conceived and offered "safe harbor" agreements. To entice such landowners to make similar efforts on behalf of declining— but not yet threatened or endangered—species, they designed "candidate conservation agreements with assurances." To turn rare species into potential economic assets rather than liabilities, they fostered the practice of "conservation banking."

These policies, agreements, and practices are now part of the daily diet of the federal agencies that implement the Endangered Species Act. Ironically, however, none of them appears in the text of the statute. Instead, they have all been fashioned administratively out of the broadly worded provisions of that law. Born of necessity, these disparate tools today constitute a "system of incentives" that responds to Congress's finding and that, together with the act's stringent prohibitions, offers improved hope for achieving that law's lofty goals.

Despite that improved hope, however, still more is likely to be needed. Given that Congress has not made significant revisions to the law in over 30 years and seems unlikely to do so in the near term, the burden will be on the act's administrators to continue to fashion and test new incentive measures. There is no reason to believe that the existing catalog of incentive measures exhausts the possibilities. Nor is it necessarily the case that other countries will find the same incentive measures that have been helpful in the United States to be similarly helpful elsewhere. For all countries, however, the challenge for the future is to build and continuously expand a catalog of effective incentives aimed at those who own, use, or manage the land for meeting human needs.

ESSAY 6.1  **(cont.)**

Nearly a century ago, Aldo Leopold, in an essay titled "Conservation Economics," offered this pithy two-sentence history of conservation in the United States: "We tried to get conservation by buying land, by subsidizing desirable changes in land use, and by passing restrictive laws. The last method largely failed; the other two have produced some small samples of success" (Leopold 1934)

Almost a century later, Leopold's judgment about the failure of restrictive conservation laws may need to be reassessed, but his conclusion about the importance of incentivizing desirable land use seems especially timely for the United States and for the rest of the world. No greater challenge faces those who seek to preserve the nation's—and the world's—wildlife heritage.

temporarily, the Tellico Dam), it has rarely done so in recent years (Malcom and Li 2015). The designation of land as critical habitat may have little effect on land-use change for development or agriculture (Nelson et al. 2014). Litigation has become a dominant driver in forcing the listing of additional species and shaping implementation of the act by restricting some actions and encouraging others. Although recovery efforts and legal defenses draw on different funding sources, defending listing and conservation decisions may take up staff time that could otherwise be used to recover listed species.[24]

Congress's power over the budgets of federal agencies has also played a crucial role in the evolution of the act. Funding is woefully inadequate to carry out the statute's mandates. For example, in 2015 the US Fish and Wildlife Service reported a backlog of more than 500 species awaiting a determination of whether they warranted

---

[24] Bea and John recall years ago visiting an office of the US Fish and Wildlife Service in Hawai'i. We asked the biologists what they were doing to protect and recover the many listed species under their program. Their reply? "Nothing. We never get out into the field, but spend all of our time in the courtroom responding to lawsuits." Since then budgets and staffing have been reduced, while the status of the listed species has worsened and litigation continues.

protection under the act.[25] Although there are now fewer delays, there were times when it took more than a decade to reach a decision to list a species. In the meantime, declines might continue and more species become imperiled. Between 1973 and 1995, 42 species awaiting a listing decision went extinct (Greenwald et al. 2019). There are also vast disparities in funding to support the recovery of different listed species. In fiscal year 2016, 16 species (1% of listed United States species) received US$557 million of the US$1.3 billion spent on endangered species recovery by state and federal agencies. Eight of those taxa were evolutionarily significant units of Columbia River salmon.

Despite these realities, the Endangered Species Act has had some notable successes: the peregrine falcon, Aleutian cackling goose, American alligator, gray whale, bald eagle, San Miguel Island fox, and Oregon chub come to mind. In all, 53 populations, subspecies, or full species have been delisted because they have recovered since the act came into force.[26] Critics use the small number of delistings to justify their claim that the act has not worked and should be revised or repealed (Mann and Plummer 1995; Seasholes 2007). Easily overlooked, however, are the subtler success stories of declines toward extinction that have been stabilized or reversed (Taylor et al. 2005; Schwartz 2008). For example, in Hawai'i the Plant Extinction Prevention Program has worked with state and federal agencies, universities, and arboretums to prevent the extinction of more than 220 listed plant species that have fewer than 50 individuals remaining in the wild.[27] No known plant extinctions have occurred since that program was launched.

Even more overlooked is the fact that over four-fifths of the species listed under the act are at risk from threats that can be

---

[25] www.biologicaldiversity.org/news/press_releases/2015/endangered-species-act-12-23-2015.html.

[26] ecos.fws.gov/ecp0/reports/delisting-report. (March 21, 2019) Another 21 species were delisted because the original data were in error or there was a taxonomic revision; 11 species were delisted because they became extinct.

[27] www.pepphi.org/

managed but not eliminated. Most listed species are conservation reliant and will require long-term care, even if they meet recovery goals and are delisted (Scott et al. 2010). The act has no provisions that explicitly recognize conservation reliance. A separate policy provision, however, allows consideration of ongoing or proposed conservation efforts to list a species, acknowledging that long-term management may be necessary.[28] The criteria for removing a species from the endangered species list[29] require assurances that other regulations or management actions will continue to provide a species with the necessary protection (Neel et al. 2012). The island night lizard (Box 6.4) and Kirtland's warbler (Chapter 9) are examples.

One way to facilitate delisting species or to avoid listing in the first place might be to broaden stakeholder participation in the management of conservation-reliant species through Conservation Management Agreements (CMAs; Scott et al. 2005, 2010). A CMA represents a legally enforceable contract that gives a conservation manager the authority to provide the necessary conservation for the foreseeable future (Goble and Scott 2006). The conservation manager could be a federal land-management agency; a state, tribal, county, or municipal government; a well-established NGO; or individual(s) with the resources to meet long-term obligations. Under the terms of a CMA, authority for conserving a listed or candidate species and addressing the threats it faces would transfer from the federal wildlife agency to the conservation manager. If a listed species has met the goals in a recovery plan but remains conservation reliant, the commitment of a conservation manager to continue targeted management actions under a CMA may be considered in delisting decisions.

[28] The Policy for Evaluation of Conservation Efforts When Making Listing Decisions (PECE); www.fws.gov/endangered/esa-library/pdf/PECE-final.pdf. The provisions of the policy recognize conservation efforts by State and local governments, Tribal governments, businesses, organizations, and individuals in addition to those undertaken by federal agencies.

[29] Endangered Species Act §4(a).

Species protected under the Endangered Species Act also fall under the umbrella of other laws and regulations. When a proposed federal action would be likely to have adverse effects on a listed species or its habitat that is covered by a Habitat Conservation Plan,[30] the stipulations of the Endangered Species Act intersect with the restrictions of the National Environmental Policy Act (NEPA). NEPA came into effect in 1970. It requires federal agencies to incorporate environmental and economic considerations into their decision making. As implementation of NEPA has evolved, the act has come to mandate an assessment of the potential environmental impacts of any proposed action by a federal agency. Agencies must prepare an Environmental Assessment or a more detailed Environmental Impact Statement (EIS). Generating an EIS can be expensive and time-consuming, as new research may be needed to determine possible environmental impacts of a proposed action (this is what led to the discovery of the snail darter). Indeed, one of the stated aims of NEPA is to "enrich the understanding of the ecological systems and natural resources important to the Nation."

Because the "take" prohibitions of the Endangered Species Act apply to actions that may significantly modify the habitat of a listed species, the legal requirements of both statutes come into play (Cosco 1998). Although the legal requirements of NEPA do not directly affect those of the Endangered Species Act, the reverse is not true. If proposed actions will have significant adverse effects on a listed species or its habitat, those effects must be addressed in an EIS, adding another layer to the NEPA process. Conservation reliance is not addressed in NEPA, but if an affected species is conservation reliant, mitigating the impacts may require continuing long-term management. Because enforcement of NEPA occurs through the court system rather than by civil or criminal penalties, an EIS often provides ample fodder for those with conflicting agendas to engage in legal battles

---

[30] Endangered Species Act §10.

or to challenge the adequacy of the underlying environmental evaluation.

Threatened species laws in several other countries (Appendix A) illustrate the variation in how at-risk species are treated under the law and how (or whether) conservation reliance is acknowledged or addressed. Rather than cast our net broadly, we briefly review the approaches taken in Canada, Australia, and New Zealand.

## CANADA: THE SPECIES AT RISK ACT (SARA)

The Species at Risk Act (SARA) was the legislative culmination of a commitment Canada made under the CBD in 1992. It is rooted in the complementary Accord for the Protection of Species at Risk,[31] a non-binding cooperative agreement among the federal, provincial, and territorial governments. SARA was enacted in 2002.[32] It provides the legal foundation for the Committee on the Status of Endangered Wildlife in Canada (COSEWIC), an advisory body that assesses the biological status of species based on scientific, community, and First Nations peoples' knowledge (Scudder 1999). Following the IUCN Red List, species are listed in seven categories ranging from extinct to not at risk (Box 6.3).[33] The act makes no mention of conservation reliance or similar concepts. Assessments by COSEWIC have no legal standing; the Minister of the Environment and Climate Change makes a recommendation to the Governor in Council, who decides whether to accept or reject a recommendation or send it back for further study.

When a species is listed, killing or harming the species or destroying its "residence" become legally prohibited on federal lands.[34]

---

[31] The National Accord is a two-page agreement that is available at www.registrelep-sararegistry.gc.ca/default.asp?landg=En&n=92D90833-1.

[32] Statutes of Canada 2002, c.29 (available at laws-lois.justice.gc.ca/eng/acts/S-15.3/page-1.html). The Act's provisions came into effect in 2003 and 2004. Smallwood (2003) and Mooers et al. (2010) provide additional information about SARA.

[33] The listing process can be found in SARA §§14–25.

[34] Residence is defined as a "dwelling-place" (e.g. den or nest) occupied by individuals during their life cycle. "Residence" has a more restricted meaning than "habitat" (Smallwood 2003).

Listing triggers the development of recovery strategies and action plans for Endangered, Threatened, and Extirpated species. Both the initial assessment and the development of recovery strategies involve multiple stakeholders. The planning process identifies threats to the species and its habitat, identifies critical habitat, and establishes population and distributional goals for recovery of the species in Canada. Although socioeconomic factors are not considered in the listing assessment, they do enter into the decisions of the Governor in Council and are included in action plans. The prohibitions and designations of critical habitat apply only to federal lands, aquatic species, and birds protected by the Migratory Birds Convention Act (the Canadian counterpart of the Migratory Bird Treaty Act in the United States); no protection is guaranteed for species on private or provincial Crown lands. This is a significant limitation: although 41% of Canada is federal land, only 11% of the federal land is in the provinces bordering the United States, which contain most of the country's endangered species. Despite court orders, the Canadian government has been lax in following through on its responsibility to implement recovery strategies and designate critical habitat (Wallace and Fluker 2016).

Although Canadian provinces are largely responsible for implementing recovery strategies and action plans, only 6 of the 10 provinces have enacted legislation to protect at-risk species and only 2 have revised their statues since the enactment of SARA. Ontario has an act that is generally similar to the US Endangered Species Act, whereas Saskatchewan, Alberta, and British Columbia provide provincial-level protections for endangered species only under general wildlife laws (Wojciechowski et al. 2011; Fluker and Stacey 2012; Olive 2016). The listing process varies from largely discretionary in some provinces to closely following the science-based COSEWIC assessments in others (Wallace and Fluker 2016). SARA does include a "safety net" mechanism that allows the federal government to act when a province or territory is failing to meet its obligations under the act,[35] but the authority has never been used (Olive 2014a).

The United States and Canada share about 6400 km of border (excluding Alaska), but differing statutes result in conservation inconsistencies (Waples et al. 2013). Northern spotted owls, for example, are listed as Endangered under SARA, because they now occur only in a small area of old-growth forest in British Columbia, but they are considered only Threatened under the Endangered Species Act in the United States. Conservation efforts are similar in the two countries: setting aside and protecting habitat and removing barred owls from suitable spotted owl habitat. In British Columbia, however, a captive-breeding program has been initiated through collaboration among the province and several NGOs and business groups.[36] The owls apparently do not take well to captive breeding; as of spring 2019, no birds had yet been released. Although recovery plans for the owl have been drafted in both countries, they draw on different scientific data and the US plan does not reference the Canadian plan, which was completed 5 years earlier.

Collaboration between the United States and Canada is limited. Of 30 species listed as Threatened or Endangered in both countries, the countries worked together to draft a joint recovery plan only for the whooping crane (Olive 2014b). Bureaucratic factors such as restrictions on international travel by agency staff, inadequate budgets, and differences in the legal protections afforded to species among provinces and between the two countries create barriers to crafting shared approaches that could benefit the species and be more cost effective for both countries.

## AUSTRALIA: THE ENVIRONMENTAL PROTECTION AND BIODIVERSITY CONSERVATION (EPBC) ACT

Because of its long isolation, most of Australia's species are endemic: 92% of the plants, 87% of the mammals, 45% of the birds, and 94% of

---

[35] Species at Risk Act §§ 35, 61.   [36] https://www.nsobreedingprogram.com

the frogs are found nowhere else.[37] More mammals have gone extinct during historical times in Australia than on any other continent. Many other species are critically imperiled.

Despite the historical imperilment of its plants and animals, legislation to protect at-risk species in Australia developed slowly. Individual states and territories began to develop conservation programs in the 1970s and 1980s, but the first comprehensive national statute—the Endangered Species Protection Act (ESPA)—was not enacted until 1992 (Woinarski and Fisher 1999). The ESPA was modeled on the US Endangered Species Act but went farther, recognizing the need to protect endangered ecological communities and identify "key threatening processes" (such as habitat loss, invasive species and introduced predators, and disease). The array of state and territorial statutes sometimes conflicted with one another and with the national ESPA, however. Passage of the Environmental Protection and Biodiversity Conservation Act (EPBC) in 1999 aimed to provide a more cohesive framework for legally protecting imperiled species.

The EPBC Act consolidates responsibility at the national level for protection of nine "matters of national environmental significance." These include "Nationally Threatened species and ecological communities" and "migratory species," but the statute also applies to "nuclear actions (including uranium mining)" and "a water resource, in relation to coal seam gas development and large coal mining development." The objectives of the act go beyond protecting threatened species and communities to include assessments of the environmental impacts of projects (similar to NEPA in the United States), promotion of ecologically sustainable development, compliance with CITES obligations, and recognition of the contributions of indigenous people to conservation.[38] Thus, unlike SARA or the Endangered Species Act, the EPBC Act is a broad environmental protection act that combines multiple aims, some of which do not always mesh well together. In

---

[37] www.environment.gov.au/biodiversity/threatened/publications/strategy-home.

[38] www.environment.gov.au/epbc/about

practice, implementation of the act has emphasized oversight of urban and commercial development activities that may affect threatened species rather than dealing directly with the complex array of factors that threaten such species (Woinarski et al. 2017) or considering their long-term conservation reliance.

An independent group of experts, the Threatened Species Scientific Committee, assesses species for possible inclusion or removal under the act by providing recommendations to a single administrator, the Australian Government Minister for the Environment. Species may be listed in one of six categories (Box 6.3). Conservation reliance is recognized as a separate category for "conservation-dependent species," but this category can be used only for fish (with "fish" defined to also include species in some other marine groups, such as mollusks, although not marine reptiles or mammals). The EPBC Act also authorizes listing of threatened ecological communities, such as the critically endangered eucalypt woodlands of the Western Australian wheat belt. Key Threatening Processes can also be listed in a comparable procedure. The relevant minister may require such listed processes to be managed through a Threat Abatement Plan, which generally provides a long-term strategic approach to the management of threats that may affect many listed threatened species. Although these plans have limited legislative clout, they may provide a useful model for management of threats that affect conservation-reliant species.

Listing of threatened species and communities imposes restrictions on activities that might harm species or communities, regardless of who owns the land. The obligatory components of recovery plans, however, apply only to Commonwealth lands or actions carried out by a Commonwealth agency. Moreover, the minister's authority is restricted to the nine matters of national environmental significance. Under the Australian constitution, most environmental matters are the responsibility of individual states and territories, each of which has its own legislation. State interests may supersede national conservation goals (Seabrook-Davison et al. 2010). Thus, although grey-headed flying foxes are protected as a Nationally Threatened species under the EPBC Act, state governments have been allowed to facilitate removal of flying foxes from critical habitat in areas where farmers consider them a pest.[39]

When a species or community is listed under the EPBC Act, a "conservation advice" is mandatory but the minister has the discretion to decide whether to develop a more substantial recovery plan. Recovery plans describe the research and actions needed to protect threatened species and communities and support their recovery. Because habitat loss is a major threat for many species, it figures importantly in recovery plans. One analysis found that 72% of the plans evaluated made mention of critical habitat, although only 10% actually listed critical habitat or prescribed limits on future habitat loss.[40] Designation of critical habitat is not mandatory. A majority of listed species lack recovery plans and the plans that do exist are often delayed. There is no legislative requirement for plans to be implemented, their stipulations are not legally enforceable, and funding is inadequate (Woinarski et al. 2017).

The Australian Government's Threatened Species Strategy, released in 2015, aims to remedy at least some of these problems.[41] The strategy does not replace or amend the EPBC Act, but articulates an approach to lessen delays in implementing the act by building collaborative partnerships and developing a 5-year action plan to prioritize conservation efforts. The action plan goals for 2016–2020 include improving recovery planning and practices, facilitating rapid responses to avert extinctions, and reducing the threat of feral cats (an action woylies will appreciate). A prioritization protocol has been used to select species of mammals, birds, and plants for actions to improve population trajectories.

---

[39] www.hsi.org.au/editor/assets/Flannery%20QE%20Response%20WLT.pdf

[40] www.birdlife.org.au/documents/OTHPUB-Recovery-Planning-Report.pdf

[41] www.environment.gov.au/system/files/resources/51b0e2d4-50ae-49b5-8317-081c6afb3117/files/ts-strategy.pdf

## NEW ZEALAND: THE WILDLIFE ACT AND THE BIODIVERSITY STRATEGY

As in Australia, many New Zealand species are endemic. Prior to human settlement, New Zealand was a land of birds: the only terrestrial mammals were three species of bats (one of which is now extinct and the other two imperiled). Historical extinction rates have also been high: nearly half of the amphibians and one-fifth of the birds have become extinct in the roughly 700 years since humans arrived (Wilson 2004) and nearly 75% of the amphibian species and 30% of the bird species remaining were listed as Threatened or At Risk in the 2013 IUCN Red List.

Like Canada and Australia, New Zealand is a member of the Commonwealth of Nations. Unlike those countries, however, New Zealand is not a federal system of states, provinces, or territories; authority and responsibility reside in the national government alone. Legal approaches to dealing with threatened species in New Zealand also have little in common with those in Canada, Australia, or the United States. The country does not have a comprehensive endangered species act.

Protection of threatened species in New Zealand instead falls under the provisions of the Wildlife Act of 1953.[42] The act states that "all wildlife is … subject to this Act and … is to be absolutely protected"[43] *unless* the species is excluded by one of seven schedules in the act (e.g. "wildlife declared to be game," "partially protected animals," and "wildlife not protected"). Although the act protects some wildlife, it does not require the conservation, management, or recovery of threatened species or their habitats (Wallace and Fluker 2016). The statute does not contain provisions to designate critical habitat, nor does it require the development of recovery plans for threatened species. Consequently, most threatened species lack a recovery plan (Ewen et al. 2013).

---

[42] legislation.govt.nz/act/public/1953/0031/60.0/DLM276814.html
[43] Wildlife Act of 1953, § 3.

There are two more recent statutes that deal with wildlife protection. The Trade in Endangered Species Act of 1989, enacted to comply with obligations under CITES, encourages "the management, conservation, and protection of endangered, threatened, and exploited species to further enhance the survival of those species."[44] It carries no legal authority to enforce these goals. The Resource Management Act of 1991, which deals with the environmental impacts of extractive industries and development, does not specifically address effects on threatened species and may override the Wildlife Act when the acts conflict (Wallace 2009).[45]

New Zealand does have a well-developed system for assessing the extinction risk of plants and animals. The New Zealand Threat Classification System classifies species into nine categories based on population size, habitat area occupied, and population trends (Molloy et al. 2002; Box 6.3).[46] There is no category for conservation-dependent or conservation-reliant species. As of 2011, 799 species were listed as Threatened and 2741 as At Risk; an additional 3940 species were considered "Data Deficient" (i.e. no assessment of their conservation status could be made) (Hitchmough 2013). The Threat Classification System provides guidance by prioritizing species for conservation attention, but it does not have legal force.

In response to the lack of a statute governing threatened species, New Zealand has developed the New Zealand Biodiversity Strategy.[47] The strategy sets out goals and priority actions intended to heighten the engagement of the public in conservation of indigenous species, protect the interests of native people in biodiversity, halt declines in

---

[44] Trade in Endangered Species Act § 2; www.legislation.govt.nz/act/public/1989/0018/latest/DLM145966.html

[45] Wallace and Fluker (2016) consider the lack of linkage between the Wildlife Act and the Resource Management Act as a weakness because it segregates efforts to deal with threats to species; in Australia, where similar statutes are combined into a single act, the weakness is in the implementation and the tendency to defer to economic interests when they conflict with those of threatened species.

[46] www.doc.govt.nz/nature/conservation-status/

[47] www.doc.govt.nz/Documents/conservation/new-zealand-biodiversity-strategy-2000.pdf

indigenous species and their habitats, and maintain genetic resources in economically important introduced species. Actions are proposed to manage threatened, at-risk, or declining species to the extent necessary to minimize extinction risk. Recovery is not an explicit goal. The strategy has a broad agenda, much of which deals more with the social and cultural forces influencing biodiversity writ large rather than the status of threatened species. In other words, it seeks to address the source of threats that imperil species—people and their activities.

Despite New Zealand's lack of hefty legal authority to protect imperiled species, it has shown what can be accomplished with aggressive conservation actions to protect threatened species. New Zealand has pursued a program of eradicating predators from islands and translocating the few remaining imperiled individuals of some species to predator-free islands (Russell and Broome 2016).[48] The Chatham Island black robin is an example. The New Zealand government is now undertaking an ambitious plan ("Predator Free 2050")[49] to eliminate all invasive rats, possums, and stoats from the entire country by 2050 (Russell et al. 2015). The plan is contentious and challenging, and certainly audacious.

## HOW DO CONSERVATION LAWS ADDRESS CONSERVATION RELIANCE?

The measures we have discussed provide a framework within which conservation-reliant species must fit if they are to receive dedicated legal protection. The Endangered Species Act, SARA, and the New Zealand Wildlife Act do not directly address the issue of conservation reliance. Australia's EPBC law does explicitly recognize conservation-dependent species, but of the 1827 species of plants and animals listed under the Australian law, only eight—all fish—are designated as

---

[48] Such actions may be undertaken in part because the existing statutes (and the fact that New Zealand is not a litigious society) place few restrictions on what can be done, in contrast with the situation in the United States.

[49] www.doc.govt.nz/Documents/our-work/predator-free-2050.pdf

conservation dependent. Some of them, such as the southern bluefin tuna (considered Critically Endangered by IUCN), are commercially valuable. Conservation-dependent species are specifically exempted from the requirement to prepare a recovery plan under the uncertain assumption that existing fisheries management legislation and plans will ensure long-term management. Listing species in this way may also remove the possibility that the fishery might be closed to protect the fish.

The IUCN's actions help to explain why categories such as conservation dependent are generally missing from legal acts. The 1994 Red List (Version 2.3) did include a category for "Conservation Dependent" species that needed continuing taxon-specific or habitat-specific conservation efforts. This category was dropped from Version 3.1 of the Red List (2001) because it combined extinction risk with the need for continuing management. The purpose of IUCN and the Red List, after all, is to highlight species at risk of extinction and to assemble the information to justify a listing categorization, not to manage at-risk species. Unlike IUCN, however, governments can implement management in addition to assessing the status of such species. It makes sense, then, for governments to consider both the long-term management needs of species and their population status.

Although the statutes do not recognize conservation reliance, the agencies responsible for implementing them have often implicitly acknowledged the need for long-term management. For example, the northern hairy-nosed wombat is listed as Critically Endangered by IUCN. The conservation actions to be undertaken by the Queensland and Australian governments include controlling predators, setting prescribed burns to maintain grassland, managing predator-proof fences, providing food and water in hard times, translocating individuals, and captive breeding. To the extent that these measures entail long-term investments, the wombat is conservation reliant, regardless of its status category.

A need for long-term management is not directly incorporated into the listing process of the laws we have discussed, but it does become important in delisting decisions. The Endangered Species Act acknowledges that removing a species from the protection afforded by the act may require assurances that its long-term management needs will be met. The EPBC Act specifically prohibits delisting a species if that would result in the cessation of conservation management actions required to keep the species from declining again and becoming eligible for re-listing (as happened with the woylie).

Conservation reliance and the need for long-term management may contribute to a growing reluctance to list additional species, lengthening the queue of species awaiting listing decisions. The Endangered Species Act recognizes such taxa-in-waiting as "Candidate Species"—species for which listing is warranted but is precluded by other, higher-priority listing decisions. Candidate Species are not protected under the Endangered Species Act but are targeted for cooperative conservation efforts through Candidate Conservation Agreements or Candidate Conservation Agreements with Assurances. By agreeing to undertake proactive conservation actions to reduce threats to a species, landowners may avoid additional restrictions should a candidate species later be listed. If implemented, such agreements may make the need to list some species unnecessary. In Chapter 9, we describe the agreement to conserve the greater sage grouse without formally listing it under the act. This agreement was crafted in 2015 as part of a broader collaborative effort involving 11 states, multiple federal agencies, tribal groups, dozens of NGOs, and private stakeholders. The mutual trust on which such agreements are founded can take years to develop but can easily be broken. In late 2018, the US Department of the Interior proposed replacing the sage grouse conservation agreement with a federal plan more favorable to gas and oil interests.

Given their emphasis on the immediate challenges of identifying and protecting at-risk species and avoiding extinctions, it is understandable that most legal systems are silent on conservation reliance. The laws are designed to prevent actions that might worsen the condition of imperiled species and to initiate actions that lead to their recovery. To be effective, these laws and regulations need to be closely tied to financing and enforcement.

Achieving such integration is difficult when regulatory authority is partitioned among agencies or levels of government, as in Canada and Australia. In the United States, the issue of who owns wildlife and is therefore responsible for its management continues to generate debate and controversy. Although cooperation between the states and the federal government is generally good, there can be disagreements over who should provide the staff to implement conservation and who should cover the costs. Dilution of responsibility for at-risk species adds to delays, which may allow imperiled species to be drawn closer to extinction and more species to become conservation reliant.

# 7    What's in the Conservationist's Toolbox: Species-Centered Approaches

The stories we have told in previous chapters describe approaches to eliminate or blunt the factors that threaten imperiled and conservation-reliant species. Often, however, the threats cannot be easily eliminated, so conservation efforts must focus on how we can enable species to avoid or cope with the threats. We move individuals to places where they are less vulnerable. We breed or propagate individuals in captivity and then release their offspring to establish or replenish populations. We track individuals to see where they are going and whether they survive. And we monitor populations to see if it is all working as planned. We do all this, and more, to keep species from sliding into extinction and to restore populations. For conservation-reliant species, these efforts must go on, and on, and on, because the forces that threaten the species persist.

In this chapter, we describe some approaches used to directly manage imperiled species. Increasing the efficiency and effectiveness of these tools could improve the outlook for reducing the long-term needs of conservation-reliant species. We focus on how translocation and captive breeding can assist species in their recovery, how remote sensing can determine where individuals are and where they move, and how conservation directed toward one or a few species can benefit multiple species. In the following chapter, we extend our discussion beyond species to consider conserving the places they need—habitats.

The emphasis on species is appropriate. Species are the axis about which conservation turns. Species resonate with the public. Species are given special protection under the Endangered Species Act, CITES, and other legal instruments. Species are what we use to track the status of biodiversity. By conserving species we preserve evolutionary potential. Species are what we identify as being conservation reliant.

MOVING INDIVIDUALS: TRANSLOCATION

When the threats that affect a species cannot be sufficiently alleviated, one option is to move individuals to other places where the threats are absent or much reduced. Such translocations have been used by conservationists for more than a century. In 1894, several hundred kākāpōs (a large, nocturnal, ground-dwelling parrot) were translocated from mainland New Zealand to Resolution Island to escape predation.[1] Unfortunately, stoats colonized Resolution Island shortly afterward, eliminating the kākāpōs.

As suitable habitat has been lost and threats have proliferated, the use of translocation to establish or re-establish populations in safe areas has become more common. The stories of the Chatham Island black robin and Aleutian cackling goose (Chapter 2) or the short-tailed albatross (Chapter 4) are examples. Conservationists are increasingly looking to translocation as a way to help species keep ahead of shifting environments as climate changes (IUCN 2013).

For some species, such as the cackling goose, translocation is a relatively short-term effort. The plants and animals released to the wild thrive and no longer need intensive management. For other species, translocation may buy time for habitat to be restored or the species to adapt. In Hawai'i, the 'amakihi may be evolving a resistance to avian malaria, and some salmon populations in the Pacific Northwest may be adapting to altered streamflows and water temperatures. If a species can adapt to a threat in one place it may not be necessary to translocate it to someplace else. In many situations, however, translocations may need to be ongoing if a species is to be maintained in the wild. This is the case for the Kihansi spray toad, other populations of salmon, and the California condor.

On Santa Catalina Island in California, Endangered island foxes were threatened by predation from golden eagles. Golden eagles were translocated from the island to other areas and bald eagles (which do

[1] www.massey.ac.nz/~darmstro/nz_projects.htm#kakapo.

not prey on foxes) were brought in to forestall the return of the golden eagles. However, high concentrations of dichlorodiphenyldichloro-ethylene (DDE) in the food chain caused the translocated bald eagles to produce eggs that broke before they could hatch. By replacing the fragile eggs with artificial eggs, artificially incubating and hatching the removed eggs, and then returning the healthy chicks back to their nests, the bald eagle population was maintained from 1989 to 2006. By then, DDE concentrations had decreased enough for eggs to hatch without human intervention (Sharpe and Garcelon 2005). Additional translocations of bald eagles were made to Santa Cruz Island in the hope that the food chain there would be less contaminated. From these two translocations, the bald eagle population has expanded to breed on five of the eight Channel Islands—and the island fox is recovering.

Translocation is especially challenging for species that migrate between breeding and non-breeding areas. Suitable habitat must be available in both areas and at stopover sites along the way, but individuals must also know how to navigate to the translocation sites. One of the most innovative approaches to this challenge involves the use of ultralight aircraft. In 2001, the conservation group Operation Migration began a program at a reserve in Wisconsin in which they conditioned young whooping cranes (an Endangered species) to follow an ultralight aircraft. In autumn, the aircraft led the flock of young cranes along a migratory route to a new wintering area in Florida (Figure 7.1). Many of the yearling birds returned to Wisconsin on their own the following spring and some then migrated back to Florida in autumn. The program continued until 2016, when 93 of the 250 birds that had been released in 2001 were still alive. However, only 10 young had been produced in Florida. Concerns were raised that the artificial rearing conditions and conditioning to an ultralight aircraft impaired the ability of the cranes to learn the parenting skills necessary to raise chicks in the wild. The US Fish and Wildlife Service halted the ultralight-assisted migration program in 2016. Operation Migration was dissolved in 2018, replaced by a program of using adult

FIGURE 7.1. Captive-raised whooping cranes following an ultralight aircraft to learn their migratory route from Wisconsin to Florida. (A black and white version of this figure will appear in some formats. For the color version, please refer to the plate section.)
Photo: US Fish and Wildlife Service.

whooping cranes and surrogate sandhill cranes to raise young whooping cranes. There has been talk of translocating the remaining cranes from Florida to Louisiana. The search for something that works goes on.

The idea of using ultralight aircraft to teach birds a migratory pathway hasn't died, however. In Europe, captive-bred northern bald ibis have been reintroduced to areas from which they had been absent for four centuries and are being taught to migrate south by following an ultralight aircraft to a reserve in Tuscany.[2] The project has been criticized as being excessively interventionist and expensive (funding has come from private donors and the European Union). Maintaining such approaches over a long time can be difficult, so the effectiveness

---

[2] e360.yale.edu/features/after-a-400-year-absence-waldrapp-rare-ibis-returns-to-european-skies

of using aircraft for conservation-reliant species is up in the air (so to speak). But it illustrates the value of bringing innovative tools to bear on conservation problems.

It is not just extreme interventions that have been criticized; the very idea of translocation is controversial. Critics worry that catching, confining, and releasing individuals in strange places erases all semblance of naturalness. There are also concerns about releasing individuals into novel habitats or new areas. Will a self-sustaining population become established or will continuing introductions and reintroductions be needed? And what about the effects on other species that are already there—does translocation create a new invasive species? Translocation also assumes that there is a suitable reception site and habitat, which requires that the factors that previously threatened a species be left behind. As Seddon (2010: 796) observed, "Without a clear long-term strategy for mitigating limiting factors and/or sustaining intensive management, [translocation] would literally be pouring new animals down the sink."[3]

### CAPTIVE BREEDING FOR SPECIES IN CRISIS

Captive breeding and nursery propagation are often the last resort for saving a vanishing species (McGowan et al. 2017). Here is another story from Christmas Island. The five lizard species that occurred there were common until at least the late 1970s. Introduced predators and yellow crazy ants took their toll, however, and by 2013 four species were extinct in the wild. Alerted to the rapid declines, conservationists had proactively initiated captive-breeding programs for these species in 2009. Captive populations are now well established for two of the species, whose extinction has been averted for now (Andrew et al. 2018). The conservation efforts came too late for the other two species, however, and no individuals remain.

The stories we told earlier about the Christmas Island pipistrelle, dusky seaside sparrow, po'ouli, and vaquita are depressingly

---

[3]  A reference to population sinks in source–sink population dynamics (Liu et al. 2011).

similar. When too few individuals remain, captive breeding faces a formidable challenge. The last Pinta Island tortoise, Lonesome George, spent his final 40 years in a corral at the Galapagos National Park's Fausto Llerena Breeding Center on Santa Cruz Island in the Galapagos.[4] He died of natural causes in 2012 at an age of 120–130 years. But no others were left and attempts to breed him with females from closely related species had failed. A similar fate befell a Hawaiian tree snail (known only by its scientific name, *Achatinella apexfulva*), whose last remaining individual (named George after the tortoise) died in 2019 after living alone in captivity for 14 years.[5] A lonely march to extinction.

Sometimes, however, captive breeding works spectacularly well. Peregrine falcons are no longer endangered because a well-designed (and well-funded) captive-breeding program was initiated before the population was reduced to a handful of individuals. Robbins' cinquefoil responded well to nursery propagation, as many plants do (see Loyal Mehrhoff's Essay 8.1). It could be released (planted) into protected habitat. The species for which captive breeding has worked best are generally fecund (producing lots of potential colonists), can adjust behaviorally to captivity (a cage or aquarium does not keep them from breeding), are easy to maintain in captivity (a broad diet helps), are small (less space is needed), and resonate with the public (which helps to generate funding). Because captive breeding is expensive, requires a facility that can provide adequate space, and needs staff who can provide suitable husbandry, it may not be feasible when a long-term program is needed to keep a species going.

Keeping a species going, however, is exactly the rationale behind the Amphibian Ark. The Amphibian Ark is a global partnership of the World Association of Zoos and Aquariums, the IUCN Conservation Planning Group for Species, and the Amphibian

---

[4] John recalls visiting Lonesome George in his corral in 2004. The visit was uneventful. Lonesome George did nothing, which reinforced the sobering realization that he was alone, the sole survivor of his species.

[5] therevelator.org/hawaii-snail-extinction-crisis.

Specialist Group.[6] To prevent additional extinctions of amphibians, the organization keeps amphibians afloat in captive populations at conservation centers around the world. As Brian Gratwicke discusses in Essay 7.1, this buys time while conservationists seek to eliminate threats or find and establish safe havens in the wild to which animals can be returned. Priority is placed on conserving species that cannot be protected in their natural environment and whose only hope for survival lies in establishing an insurance population at an amphibian-breeding center. The demand for this space, however, far exceeds the capacity of the world's aquariums, zoos, and captive-rearing centers. Over 500 of the world's toad, frog, and salamander species face threats that cannot currently be mitigated, but globally there is room to establish insurance populations for perhaps 50 species—just 10% of the space that is needed.[7] Lack of space and infrastructure is often a physical constraint on captive-breeding programs.

There are also biological constraints. The longer a captive-breeding program continues, the more likely that inbreeding will lead to a loss of genetic diversity and a shift in the evolutionary trajectory of a species. To mitigate this, some captive-breeding programs conduct genetic screening of all individuals and arrange matings to ensure as much outbreeding as possible. In the breeding facilities for Delta smelt in California, for example, each individual is tagged, its genotype is known, and matings are carefully monitored. Lots of smeltlings are produced, but provisions of the Endangered Species Act prevent their release into the wild to replenish a population that is perilously close to extinction. There are also concerns that, after many generations of managed reproduction, the captive-bred smelt are no longer the same as wild smelt. The plight of the smelt also highlights another issue with captive breeding: If a species is to be re-established, offspring must be introduced back into the wild. There must be someplace to go, a reintroduction landscape (Dunham et al. 2016).

---

[6] www.amphibianark.org/

[7] www.amphibianark.org/the-crisis/frightening-statistics/

ESSAY 7.1    **Building an Amphibian Ark in Panama**

*Brian Gratwicke*

"The problem with putting frogs in glass boxes is that it does not mitigate the actual threat!" I stated very matter-of-factly to Mike Hoffman in the Q&A after his pitch for the IUCN Global Amphibian Conservation Action Plan. The year was 2007, and I was attending a conservation biology meeting in South Africa. I was working as a program officer for the National Fish and Wildlife Foundation, searching for winning ideas that might solve big environmental problems while giving us the best return on investment. Though Mike was an old friend of mine from Oxford, I was skeptical of his pitch to build a decentralized global Amphibian Ark for the world's most endangered amphibians. My skepticism proved prescient, as 6 months later I was recruited to lead the Smithsonian National Zoo's amphibian conservation program as part of this broader global effort to save amphibians. Mike's challenging pitch became my new work plan.

Trained as a fish biologist, I was impressed by the Global Amphibian Assessment and by how such a large group of people had organized on a truly global scale. Alas, despite strong academic advances toward understanding the global amphibian crisis, very few conservationists were dedicated full-time to mitigating threats to amphibians. Why was there no BirdLife or Audubon Society for amphibians? My own research revealed that very little money was being invested in saving frogs—the average listed amphibian under the US Endangered Species Act receives a fourth of the funding compared to the average listed bird, reptile, or mammal—not to mention that very few at-risk amphibians even make it onto the endangered species list in the first place.

From the start, my job required figuring how to leverage existing resources and focus them on conserving amphibians. Back then, one of the most urgent threats to amphibians was the chytrid fungus spreading through Latin America. This unusual pathogen affects a large number of different species, sometimes leading to the rapid disappearance and extinction of entire species. In Panama alone, nine frog species are already lost. Like the Monte Verde golden toad

ESSAY 7.1   **(cont.)**

highlighted at the beginning of this book, these amphibian species have vanished and are now very likely extinct. In rapid response to the crisis, and with support from the Houston Zoo, some conservationists in Panama had already begun building an Amphibian Ark. By the time I started in 2008, the amphibian chytrid fungus had just reached the Panama Canal. The fungus had already decimated amphibians in western Panama and was now threatening to inflict the same havoc in eastern Panama. We faced a doomsday scenario.

We knew the most critical task was building new facilities and capacity in Panama to create captive-assurance colonies for amphibians from sites where they were still healthy and abundant. To that end, and in partnership with Houston Zoo, Zoo New England, and the Cheyenne Mountain Zoo, we created the Panama Amphibian Rescue and Conservation Project. Today, the project cares for captive populations of 12 species in a 450-m$^2$ facility with 11 full-time staff members (Figure E7.1.1). We selected these 12 priority species out of Panama's amazing diversity of 214 amphibian species by considering several factors, including: susceptibility to the amphibian chytrid fungus, extinction risk, the likelihood of locating founding populations, and the chances of breeding them in captivity. Currently, we maximize our ability to sustain genetically representative captive populations by conducting ongoing research into husbandry, nutrition, and reproduction. Although these captive populations do not directly mitigate the disease threat, they do buy us some time, which matters in this race against extinction.

The amphibian chytrid fungus has spread around the globe largely unchecked—the one exception is on the island of Majorca, where an extraordinarily determined group of biologists successfully eradicated the fungus by literally draining and scrubbing out the five known infected ponds with antifungal chemicals (Bosch et al. 2015). Without a silver bullet to mitigate the threat in other wild amphibian populations, *ex situ* conservation is really the only conservation tool at our disposal to prevent further extinctions. In my role as a program officer for the National Fish and Wildlife Foundation, I often thought of

ESSAY 7.1  **(cont.)**

FIGURE E7.1.1. Smithsonian Tropical Research Institute Biologist Jorge Guerrel working inside one of seven modified shipping containers designed to house captive amphibians at the Panama Amphibian Rescue and Conservation Project. (A black and white version of this figure will appear in some formats. For the color version, please refer to the plate section.)
Photo: Brian Gratwicke.

conservation-reliant species as species facing persistent threats in the wild that required constant action and vigilance to hold back the tide. However, captive populations of species that have disappeared in the wild are the ultimate expression of conservation reliance. They are entirely dependent upon long-term institutional commitments and uninterrupted funding, and their caretakers assume an unparalleled burden of responsibility.

Given the huge costs, responsibilities, and risks associated with captive collections, it is in our best interest to deal with the threat and re-establish wild, self-sustaining populations of these species as soon as possible. Fortunately, we humans are adept at addressing the problems of disease—since its discovery in 1998, the amphibian chytrid fungus

ESSAY 7.1   **(cont.)**

has been the subject of more than 1000 scientific papers. Our own efforts at the National Zoo have focused on trying to manipulate the skin microbiome of susceptible amphibians by supplementing them with bacteria that produce antifungal metabolites. Despite one promising initial experiment using mountain yellow-legged frogs, we have not yet successfully established proof of concept for this approach using Panamanian frogs.

Our second line of research has examined differential gene expression to understand the genetic basis for survival that may allow us to breed for resistance. Other talented researchers also continue to move the ball down the field by investigating vaccines, managing the pathogen in the environment, improving our understanding of disease dynamics, and selecting reintroduction sites that may act as climatic refuges from disease. One particularly exciting discovery from Panama is that some of the frog populations that had severely declined from the fungus are now recovering. Amazingly, they appear to have evolved antifungal skin peptides.

Cynics may argue that there is little point in trying to beat back the tide of invasive pathogens, and that natural selection should be free to pick the winners and losers. That would certainly be the path of least resistance, but a similar argument could be made against any conservation project—why bother? As conservationists who understand our own impacts on the environment, we have an ethical responsibility to ensure that there is a future for all species on our shared planet. Without these captive populations, there would be a lot more stories like the Monte Verde golden toad, in which case there would not be much point in continuing to look for a cure. But who knows? The lessons we learn from helping frogs may ultimately help us to save ourselves.

Often the place to go is a protected area or reserve, but sometimes suitable release habitat must be manufactured. The spray that maintains habitat for the Kihansi spray toads is provided by a sprinkler system (Figure 4.1B). In Australia, the iconic southern corroboree

FIGURE 7.2. Artificial pools used to protect captive-bred eggs and tadpoles of the southern corroboree frog from fungal disease and drought when they are released in Kosciuszko National Park in New South Wales, Australia. (A black and white version of this figure will appear in some formats. For the color version, please refer to the plate section.)
Photo: David Hunter, New South Wales Office of Environment and Heritage.

frog is restricted to high elevations in Kosciuszko National Park in southeastern New South Wales, where it is considered Critically Endangered by both IUCN and the Australian EPBC Act. Various recovery measures have been proposed (OEH NSW 2012), chief among them captive breeding and releases in the wild. Captive-breeding programs in several locations have been successful in preventing the species' extinction, but survival in the wild requires protection from the amphibian chytrid fungus and from drying of their pond habitat as a result of climate change. To give the eggs and the tadpoles they produce a chance to survive, captive-bred eggs are being released in artificial pools designed to be fungus and drought proof (Figure 7.2). Additionally, a large disease-free enclosure has been built at Kosciuszko to shelter an on-site breeding colony. These measures provide secure release habitats, but it takes 4–5 years for the tadpoles to

FIGURE 7.3. Thousands of masked bobwhite quail have been released in Arizona, but livestock grazing has destroyed their habitat and the reintroductions have failed to produce a sustainable population. (A black and white version of this figure will appear in some formats. For the color version, please refer to the plate section.)
Photo: Steve Hillebrand, US Fish and Wildlife Service.

mature, so whether they will enable the corroboree frog to persist in the wild remains to be seen.

The story of the masked northern bobwhite quail (hereafter, masked bobwhite)[8] illustrates all too well the disconnect between using captive breeding to re-establish populations of an imperiled, conservation-reliant species and having someplace for the offspring to go (Brown and Clark 2017). Masked bobwhite quail (Figure 7.3) were first discovered in southern Arizona in 1884; by the early 1900s they were feared to be extinct in Arizona. This led to multiple efforts to find and capture wild birds in Mexico to establish captive-breeding flocks for later release in Arizona. Livestock grazing had

---

[8] The masked bobwhite quail is a distinctive subspecies of the northern bobwhite quail, which is abundant and widely distributed (and prized by hunters).

destroyed most of the species' natural habitat and other areas provided little food or cover from predators, however, so the released birds soon disappeared. By the early 1950s, expeditions to Mexico failed to find any wild birds and the species was thought to be extinct there also.

Then in 1964 a new population of wild quail was found in Sonora. Efforts to save the species redoubled. Agencies, conservation organizations, and local ranchers collaborated to restore habitat, establish a captive flock, and release birds in new areas—again without success. Continued searches in Sonora in the late 1960s resulted in the capture of 60 birds, which were sent to a US Fish and Wildlife breeding center in Maryland. Captive-bred birds were conditioned to human disturbance and predators before being released and the program finally seemed to be working. Between 1970 and 1982, over 7000 birds were released at Buenos Aires Ranch in Arizona.[9] Some individuals survived and some chicks were seen, but the population was dependent on continuing replenishment by captive-bred birds. The ranch population peaked at 74 calling males in 1979, then plummeted because of a prolonged drought and severe overgrazing; only nine individuals could be found in 1982.

Releases of birds from captive-breeding facilities continued. From 1989 to 1995, over 17 000 quail were released on the refuge. Yet numbers in the wild continued to dwindle; only five released birds were recorded to be alive in 2001–2011. There were too few wild birds left to replenish the captive-breeding stock (the last confirmed sighting of a wild masked bobwhite was in 2007) and the captive-bred birds were beginning to show abnormal behavior and signs of disease. Captive releases were suspended in 2004.

A review in 2014 concluded that the program was insufficient to conserve masked bobwhite in the wild or even in captivity. It called for new protocols for captive-rearing and release programs, better ways of determining population status and habitat, and a new recovery plan with additional funding. A new recovery team was appointed

---

[9] The ranch was purchased and made a National Wildlife Refuge in 1985, primarily to protect the quail.

but a revised recovery plan has yet to be written. New breeding facilities have been established to reduce the chances of catastrophic losses. Large-scale releases of captive-bred birds were resumed in 2017 and several hundred were released in 2018; 85 individuals were still alive in May 2019. There were indications that pairs were beginning to form. In 2019, what could be calling masked bobwhite quail were recorded by automated devices in Sonora, fueling hopes that wild birds might still be found.

Eighty years of effort and multiple attempts at releasing captive-bred individuals have failed to establish a viable population of masked bobwhite quail in the wild, primarily because habitat requirements and threats were not adequately addressed prior to reintroduction. Few recommendations of the initial recovery plan were implemented and there was insufficient coordination among bureaucracies at different levels and between nations. Additionally, prescribed fire regimes on the refuge that were intended to benefit endangered Sonoran pronghorn conflicted with those that would benefit the quail. Brown and Clark (2017) suggested interbreeding masked bobwhite quail with another subspecies of bobwhite, as has been done with Florida panthers (and was briefly attempted for dusky seaside sparrows). To increase public awareness and interest in masked bobwhite, some people have advocated releasing birds on golf courses and in public parks.

Although the story of the masked northern bobwhite quail is one of decades of ineffectiveness and frustration, it is also one of dogged persistence by dedicated professionals. Rearing and release techniques are being improved and potential habitat is being better managed. Conservation efforts are increasingly focused on managing the factors affecting post-release survival. But the masked bobwhite, like other species that rely on captive breeding, will likely remain conservation reliant for a long time if it is to avoid extinction.

## TRACKING MOVEMENTS AND REMOTE SENSING

Knowing whether a translocation or captive-breeding program is successful requires that we know where individuals go once they are

FIGURE 1.1. The golden toad, discovered in Costa Rica in 1964, was briefly conservation reliant. It is now extinct.

Photo: Charles H. Smith, US Fish and Wildlife Service.

FIGURE 1.3. An Endangered California condor soaring in Bitter Creek National Wildlife Refuge, California. All free-ranging birds are individually marked (note the wing tag) and monitored.
Photo: US Fish and Wildlife Service Pacific Southwest Region.

FIGURE 2.2. An Oregon chub. The chub was declared recovered and removed from the US endangered species list in 2015.
Photo: Rick Swart, Oregon Department of Fish and Game.

FIGURE 2.3 The Aleutian cackling goose, a species once thought extinct, has recovered to become an agricultural pest.
Photo: Elizabeth Neipert, ERDC, US Army.

FIGURE 2.4. An adult southern white rhinoceros and calf, considered Near Threatened by IUCN.

Photo: Renauld Fulconis, Awely.

FIGURE 2.5. The black-capped vireo, formerly listed as Endangered, was removed from the endangered species list in 2018, although the species remains conservation reliant.

Photo: Joe Grzybowski/US Army.

FIGURE 2.6. Robbins' cinquefoil, originally listed as Endangered, was declared recovered and delisted in 2002. It remains conservation reliant.
Photo: US Fish and Wildlife Service.

FIGURE 2.7. The Oregon silverspot butterfly is listed as Threatened under the Endangered Species Act.
Photo: NatPar Collection/Alamy.

FIGURE 2.8. The Chatham Island black robin is considered Endangered by the IUCN.

Photo: Leon Berard.

FIGURE 2.9. The woylie (brush-tailed bettong) is considered Critically Endangered by the IUCN.

Photo: © Wayne Lawler/AWC.

FIGURE 2.10. Armed rangers keeping watch over Sudan. Until he died in 2018, Sudan was the world's last male northern white rhinoceros.
Credit: Martin Harvey/Gallo Images/Getty Images Plus.

FIGURE 2.11. A male Guam kingfisher, listed as Endangered under the Endangered Species Act.
Photo: Eric Savage/Creative Commons.

FIGURE 2.12. The extinct po'ouli.
Photo: Paul E. Baker, US Fish and Wildlife Service.

FIGURE 2.13. The extinct dusky seaside sparrow.
Photo: P.W. Sykes, US Fish and Wildlife Service.

FIGURE 2.14. The extinct Christmas Island pipistrelle.
Photo: Lindy Lumsden.

FIGURE 3.1. An Endangered palila selects a seedpod from a māmane tree high on the western slope of Mauna Kea, Hawai'i.
Photo: © Jack Jeffrey Photography.

FIGURE E3.1.1. Aaron Penney, a member of the NimíiPuu (Nez Perce Tribe), dip-net fishing for Chinook salmon in the Middle Fork of the Salmon River, Idaho.
Photo: Zach Penney.

FIGURE 4.1. (A) A Kihansi spray toad with a toadlet. The species is considered Extinct in the Wild by the IUCN. Photo: Julie Larson Maher © Wildlife Conservation Society. (B) The sprinkler spray system at the Mhalala Bridge over the Kihansi River, Tanzania.
Photo: William Newmark.

FIGURE E4.1.1. Magellanic penguins are curious about and tolerant of the thousands of tourists who visit Punta Tombo, Argentina, every year.
Photo: P.D. Boersma.

FIGURE 4.3. A peregrine falcon.
Photo: Roy W. Lowe, US Fish and Wildlife Service.

FIGURE E4.2.1. White-rumped vultures attending a cow carcass in Nepal.
Photo: Chris Bowden/RSPB.

FIGURE 4.6. Tibetan antelope in Zanda County, Tibet Autonomous
Region, China, 2015.
Photo: Panda Eye/Alamy.

FIGURE 4.7. A vaquita, the world's most endangered marine mammal, entangled in a gillnet.
Photo: Flip Nicklin/Minden Pictures.

FIGURE E4.3.1. An adult and juvenile vaquita photographed in the Gulf of California on October 18, 2018. Adults with calves were again sighted in autumn 2019 (Barbara Taylor, personal communication).
Photo: Paula Olson/NOAA.

FIGURE 4.8. A Chinook salmon jumps falls at Ship Creek, Anchorage, Alaska.
Credit: Calvin Hall/First Light/Getty Images Plus.

FIGURE 4.9. Wisdom, a Near Threatened (IUCN) Laysan albatross, is the world's oldest known bird, here shown nesting (successfully) on Midway Atoll in 2018.
Photo: Eric Vanderwerf.

FIGURE 4.10. Borax Lake, Oregon, is fed by a thermal vent deep beneath the surface. The endemic Borax Lake chub (inset) persists along the margins of the lake despite high temperatures and high levels of arsenic and lead.
Photo: The Nature Conservancy.

FIGURE 5.1. The white form of the lemuroid ringtail possum. This form may be extinct, although the lemuroid ringtail possum as a species is considered Near Threatened by the IUCN.
Photo: Mark Ziembicki.

FIGURE 5.2. The extinct Bramble Cay melomys lived only on Bramble Cay, a tiny islet in the Torres Strait north of Queensland, Australia (inset). Rising seas and storm surges led to its extinction.

Photo: Ian Bell, Government of Queensland, Australia, Department of Environment and Heritage Protection.

FIGURE 5.3. Laysan albatrosses and chicks nesting on Midway Atoll. The low elevation of the atoll makes it vulnerable to storm surges, tsunamis, and sea-level rise.

Photo: J. Klavitter, US Fish and Wildlife Service.

FIGURE 5.4. The Puerto Rican parrot is Endangered and is being bred in captivity. It is particularly vulnerable to the increased frequency of hurricanes in the Caribbean.
Photo: US Fish and Wildlife Service.

FIGURE 5.5. An Attwater's prairie chicken male defending its territory at a lek on the Attwater's Prairie Chicken National Wildlife Refuge in Texas.
Photo: John Magera.

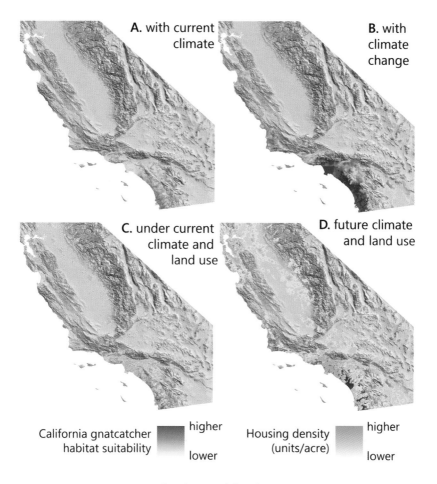

California gnatcatcher habitat suitability — higher / lower

Housing density (units/acre) — higher / lower

FIGURE 5.6. Current distribution of the Threatened California gnatcatcher in southern California (A), projected distribution with climate change (B), and current (C) and future (D) distributions with projected changes in land use superimposed.

Source: D. Jongsomjit, Point Blue Conservation Science.

FIGURE E5.1.1. A Mono checkerspot butterfly, free-flying in its natural habitat. One of the few remaining populations at Schneider's ranch (near Carson City, Nevada) was extinct by 2008 owing to rapidly changing land use. Only five populations of this subspecies are currently known to exist. Photo: Michael C. Singer.

FIGURE 5.7. Research biologist Maya Legrande uses climbing gear to hand-pollinate an Endangered pua'ala (Moloka'i ohaha) plant growing on a cliff face on Moloka'i in the Hawaiian Islands. There are fewer than 200 individuals growing in the wild. Photo: Ken Wood/Maya Legrande.

FIGURE 6.2. The island night lizard, a small lizard restricted to three Channel Islands off the coast of southern California, remains conservation reliant. Color patterns vary among islands; this individual is from San Clemente Island.
Photo: Lawrence L.C. Jones.

FIGURE 7.1. Captive-raised whooping cranes following an ultralight aircraft to learn their migratory route from Wisconsin to Florida.
Photo: US Fish and Wildlife Service.

FIGURE E7.1.1. Smithsonian Tropical Research Institute Biologist Jorge Guerrel working inside one of seven modified shipping containers designed to house captive amphibians at the Panama Amphibian Rescue and Conservation Project.

Photo: Brian Gratwicke.

FIGURE 7.2. Artificial pools used to protect captive-bred eggs and tadpoles of the southern corroboree frog from fungal disease and drought when they are released in Kosciuszko National Park in New South Wales, Australia.

Photo: David Hunter, New South Wales Office of Environment and Heritage.

FIGURE 7.3. Thousands of masked bobwhite quail have been released in Arizona, but livestock grazing has destroyed their habitat and the reintroductions have failed to produce a sustainable population.
Photo: Steve Hillebrand, US Fish and Wildlife Service.

FIGURE 7.5. An Endangered black-footed ferret in a prairie-dog burrow. The species was once thought to be extinct but was later rediscovered.
Credit: Wendy Shattil and Bob Rozinski/Oxford Scientific/Getty Images Plus.

FIGURE 7.6. The Threatened i'iwi is the last of the "sickle-billed" Hawaiian honeycreepers. Its long, downcurved bill is a perfect match for the tubular flowers of the Endangered 'ōhā wai (*Clermontia lindseyana*), which it pollinates.

Photo: © Jack Jeffrey Photography.

FIGURE E8.1.1. The National Tropical Botanical Garden's conservation nursery for endangered Hawaiian plants. At least 15 highly endangered endemic species can be seen in this photograph, with most of these having fewer than 50 plants remaining in the wild.

Photo: Michael J. DeMotta, National Tropical Botanical Garden.

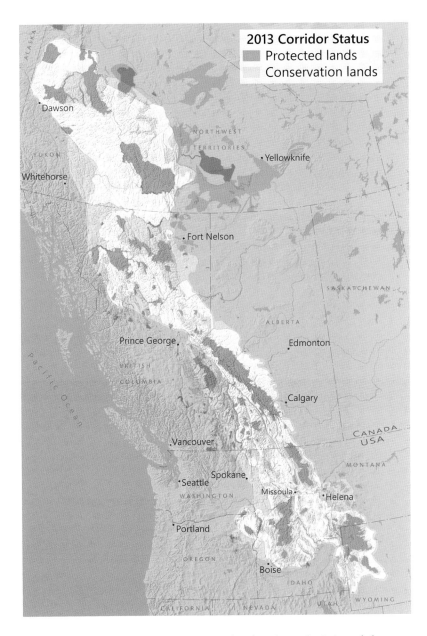

FIGURE 8.1. The Yellowstone to Yukon (Y2Y) corridor is intended to connect isolated populations of wide-ranging predators, such as mainland grizzly bears and wolves, and herbivores, such as moose and elk.
Source: Jodi Hilty, Y2Y.

FIGURE 8.2. A greater yellowlegs and several dunlins feeding in a rice field in California. Under the BirdReturns program, rice fields are flooded in spring to maintain wetland habitat for migratory shorebirds.
Photo: Greg Golet.

FIGURE E8.2.1. Exclosures barring introduced cats and foxes now provide the only mainland havens for many highly threatened Australian-endemic mammal species.
Photo: © Wayne Lawler/Australian Wildlife Conservancy.

FIGURE 8.3. When Hawai'i Volcanoes National Park was established in 1916, feral goats were already decimating native plants, critically imperiling endemic birds and other vulnerable native species.
Photo: National Park Service courtesy of Don Reeser and Bryan Harry.

FIGURE 8.4. A goat exclosure in Hawai'i Volcanoes National Park, showing the lush regrowth of native vegetation only 2 years after the fence was constructed.
Photo: National Park Service courtesy of Don Reeser and Bryan Harry.

FIGURE 8.5. Poisoned bait being dropped onto Rábida Island, Galapagos, to eradicate invasive rats.
Credit: Rodrigo Buendia/AFP/Getty Images.

FIGURE 8.6 Aboriginal use of fire to hunt kangaroos in Australia. From a painting by Joseph Lycett, c. 1820.
Photo courtesy National Library of Australia.

FIGURE 9.2. Members of a local community help to construct beehive fences for deterring elephants from crossing the Pungue River to raid crops. The river forms the southern boundary of Gorongosa National Park, Mozambique.

Photo: Paola Branco.

FIGURE 9.3. Endangered African wild dogs ignoring tourists in a safari vehicle at Duma Tau Camp, Botswana.

Photo: Wilderness Safaris.

FIGURE E9.1.1. The famous tree-climbing lions of Ishasha are under threat from snaring and trade in body parts. Photo taken in the southern sector of Queen Elizabeth National Park, Uganda, during routine lion monitoring. Photo: Mustafa Nsubuga.

FIGURE E9.2.1. The Wolong Nature Reserve breeding center was a crowd pleaser for those eager to see giant pandas. The 2008 Wenchuan earthquake damaged this center, which is now a site to train pandas to be reintroduced into the wild. A new breeding center nearby allows tourists a chance to see the pandas.

Photo: Wei Liu, Michigan State University Center for Systems Integration and Sustainability.

FIGURE 9.5. Greater sage grouse on a Colorado lek during the springtime mating season.

Credit: milehightraveler/iStock/Getty Images Plus.

released. The technologies of remote sensing, monitoring locations, and tracking movements are rapidly expanding in sensitivity, power, miniaturization, and the kinds of information they can provide. All California condors that are released into the wild, for example, are outfitted with global positioning system (GPS) units and radio transmitters that provide information on where they are, where they move, their vital signs, and (as Mike's story in Chapter 3 related) where they die.

Monitoring individual movements, however, is not new. In the Middle Ages, falconers placed identification bands on the legs of birds to establish ownership. This soon yielded unexpected information: A peregrine banded in France by Henry IV in 1595 later showed up in Malta, some 2200 km away. Banding birds (or labeling fish, butterflies, or other animals) has become commonplace.

Gleaning information from such marked individuals, however, depends on where they happen to be when they are encountered. Most of the time their whereabouts are unknown. Remote sensing fills this knowledge gap. Movement patterns, habitat use, and individual home ranges can be tracked to reveal whether conservation practices are working as planned. For example, radio telemetry helped to determine if captive-bred black-footed ferrets fared as well as wild-born ferrets when translocated to a black-tailed prairie-dog colony (they did not; Biggins et al. 2011). Tracking has been used to determine whether individuals are staying in protected areas; whether they use a habitat corridor; what migration routes, wintering and breeding areas, and stopover locations they use; and where they die. Light-level geolocators add even greater spatial and temporal resolution.

One of the most renowned individuals to be tracked is a gray wolf called OR-7. Wolves were reintroduced into Idaho in 1995 and before long had wandered into the Wallowa Mountains of northeastern Oregon, where OR-7 was born in 2009. In the summer of 2011, OR-7 was captured and outfitted with a radio collar that transmitted his location to a satellite.[10] He left his natal pack that fall and began to

---

[10] Hence his name, OR-7: the seventh wolf radio-collared in Oregon.

wander in search of a mate. Over the next 2 years, he traveled over 1600 km (Figure 7.4), moving to southern Oregon and then into northern California, becoming the first gray wolf to be recorded in the state since 1924. He then returned to southern Oregon, found a mate, and fathered a litter in 2013. OR-7 sired his fifth litter of pups in 2018; by then, his offspring had founded two new wolf packs in northern California. None of this history would have been known without the technology to track OR-7's movements—or without sufficient habitat connectivity to make his journey possible.

In situations where attaching a tracking device to an individual is not possible, genetic analyses of urine, feces, feathers, fur, eggshell fragments, shed skin, or other sources of DNA can be used to detect the presence of a species. Environmental DNA (eDNA) is DNA in tissues or cells that have been sloughed off an animal in freshwater, seawater, permafrost, air, or the soil. Samples of eDNA obtained from aquatic environments have helped document habitat use by species such as the European weather loach, which is nearly extinct in Denmark but common elsewhere in Europe (Sigsgaard et al. 2015). They have also been used to detect invasive species such as Asian carp in the rivers and canals around Chicago (Jerde et al. 2011) and to monitor aquatic biodiversity (Valentini et al. 2016).

Knowledge of where animals move is critical for conserving conservation-reliant species, but it is equally important to know something about the places they occupy during their movements. This information can help determine where to establish protected areas, whether the areas are connected by corridors, whether they are large enough to include dispersal travels and movements within a home range, or whether the surroundings of an area facilitate or impede movement. Remote sensing of landscape features—land uses, development, topography, vegetation cover, soils, productivity, and a host of other features—enables data to be collected quickly and inexpensively, especially from places that are difficult to reach in person. The US Navy, for example, is exploring uses of drones to monitor the distribution and status of conservation-reliant plants on San

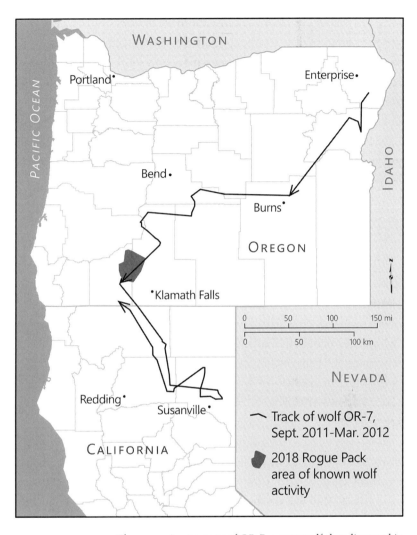

FIGURE 7.4. The approximate route of OR-7, a gray wolf that dispersed in 2011 from the Imnaha pack of wolves in northeastern Oregon. The map covers the journey from 10 September 2011, through 6 March 2012, and shows where OR-7 established a pack.

*Source:* Modified from Wikimedia Commons with added information from Oregon Department of Fisheries and Wildlife.

Clemente Island in areas that are otherwise inaccessible because they are part of an active bombing range. In Hawai'i, drones are used to survey hazardous cliff faces for rare plants. In southern Africa, drones are used to detect potential wildlife poachers so nearby rangers can be alerted.[11] To control ravens that cause substantial mortality of juvenile desert tortoises (an Endangered species) at Marine Corps Logistics Base Barstow in California, drones are being deployed to coat eggs in raven nests with a silica-based oil that deprives the developing young of oxygen. Rather than abandoning their nests, the ravens continue to sit on the eggs for the entire breeding season.

## USING A SPECIES-CENTERED APPROACH TO BENEFIT MULTIPLE SPECIES

Tools such as translocation, captive breeding, and tracking are generally applied to the conservation of an individual species, and their effectiveness is gauged by how well that species responds. But many of the species occupying an area often face the same threats. In such situations the benefits of conserving a single species may extend to an entire suite of species.

The use of surrogate, umbrella, indicator, or focal species that are selected to represent a group of species with similar ecological characteristics is well established in conservation (Wiens et al. 2008; Caro 2010).[12] For example, many species that depend on sagebrush expanses may benefit from protection and management of greater sage grouse (Knick and Connelly 2011). Although there are differences among the approaches, all assume that what works for the representative species will work for the others. The life history and ecology of the other species may not match perfectly with such umbrella species, of course (vertebrates may be poor surrogates for invertebrates or plants), but the hope is that they will be similar enough for most.

---

[11] airshepherd.org.

[12] Lindenmayer and Burgman (2005) list a dozen versions of indicator species, and Marcot and Flather (2007) provide a useful table of approaches and their assumptions.

FIGURE 7.5. An Endangered black-footed ferret in a prairie-dog burrow. The species was once thought to be extinct but was later rediscovered. (A black and white version of this figure will appear in some formats. For the color version, please refer to the plate section.)
Credit: Wendy Shattil and Bob Rozinski/Oxford Scientific/Getty Images Plus.

In other situations, a species may be singled out for conservation attention because it plays a pivotal or "keystone" role in ecosystem processes or provides important ecosystem services to other species or to people. In the tropical rainforests of northern Queensland, for example, southern cassowaries are the sole agent for dispersing over a hundred plant species that have very large fruits. In the shortgrass prairies of North America, black-tailed prairie dogs construct burrows that shelter dozens of other species, including Endangered black-footed ferrets (Figure 7.5). The ferret has been brought back from apparent extinction by captive breeding and releases into prairie-dog colonies. The prairie dogs, however, are threatened by sylvatic plague,[13] which is spread by fleas and can wipe out entire

---

[13] Infection by the same bacterium that causes bubonic plague in humans, *Yersinia pestis*.

colonies. Fleas can be controlled by dusting burrows with deltamethrin, an insecticide (Seery et al. 2003). Both the ferret and the prairie dog are conservation reliant. Populations of cassowaries and prairie dogs are rapidly declining. Conserving such keystone species helps to maintain broader ecosystem composition and functioning.

An even greater interdependency exists between plants and their pollinators. Over 85% of the world's flowering plants depend on pollinators to carry out their reproduction, and many pollinators depend on the nectar or other resources provided by the plants. When either the plant or its pollinators becomes imperiled, the linkage begins to unravel. This is especially likely where the plant and pollinator have become intertwined by coevolution.

Many imperiled Hawaiian plants and their pollinators exemplify such coevolved mutualism, perhaps none more visibly than the i'iwi (a Hawaiian honeycreeper) and most of Hawai'i's endemic lobelias. One of these, *Clermontia lindseyana* (one of several lobelias known in Hawaiian as 'ōhā wai), depends on the i'iwi to disperse its pollen, whereas the bird benefits from feeding on the nutrient-rich, high-energy nectar and the occasional insects it encounters while foraging (Figure 7.6). Historically the i'iwi was abundant and widespread across the main islands of the Hawaiian Archipelago. The 'ōhā wai was known only from two volcanoes on Hawai'i and Maui. Populations of both have declined: The i'iwi is considered Vulnerable and the 'ōhā wai Critically Endangered by IUCN. Both species are conservation reliant, the plant because it is being maintained by propagation and planting in Hakalau Forest National Wildlife Refuge and the i'iwi because the 'ōhā wai is one of the plants on which it depends. Both species also need suitable forest habitat, which requires that non-native herbivores be controlled (Chapter 8).

Sometimes the surrogate, indicator, keystone, or plant/pollinator species we have described are conservation reliant. The necessary management may then be ongoing and other species will benefit from the management actions. Some of these species may also be conservation reliant. Using particular conservation-reliant species as

FIGURE 7.6. The Threatened i'iwi is the last of the "sickle-billed" Hawaiian honeycreepers. Its long, downcurved bill is a perfect match for the tubular flowers of the Endangered 'ōhā wai (*Clermontia lindseyana*), which it pollinates. (A black and white version of this figure will appear in some formats. For the color version, please refer to the plate section.) Photo: © Jack Jeffrey Photography.

surrogates or umbrellas for other species may therefore be an effective way to extend management to the growing number of conservation-reliant species. However, if the surrogate species do not adequately represent the ecological requirements of these other species, the other species may disappear even as the surrogate flourishes. Continued monitoring is essential in such situations.

Another approach focuses on multiple species from the outset. When a variety of imperiled species that face similar threats occur together in a restricted area, they can be managed as a group. In 1977, for example, three animal and four plant species occurring on San Clemente Island were simultaneously listed as Threatened or Endangered. A 1984 Recovery Plan for all eight Channel Islands that applied collectively to 10 species noted that, unlike plans that address the recovery of a single listed species, the plan dealt with the recovery of entire insular ecosystems.

As another example, Ash Meadows is an oasis of springs and wetlands in the expanse of the Mojave Desert in Nevada and California that harbors many endemic species. A National Wildlife refuge was established in part of the area in 1984. The Recovery Plan (USFWS 1990) included 12 Threatened and Endangered species and an additional 21 candidate species in a single package. A similar multi-species recovery plan has been developed for the Channel Islands. Thus, even though the primary focus of the Endangered Species Act is on single species, several listed species may be considered together when they occur in the same management area and are threatened by similar factors.

Such recovery plans assume that what works for one species will work for others. This assumption is based on limited data. An analysis of multi-species recovery plans showed that they contained less information on species-specific biology and were less likely to include management guidance than were single-species plans (Clark and Harvey 2002). Only half of the species covered by the multi-species plans shared threats. Listing several species together can improve management efficiency but does not by itself ensure that more effective conservation will follow.

The species in these multi-species listings and recovery plans include diverse taxa that occur together and are similarly imperiled. In other cases, species have been grouped in multi-species plans based on taxonomic criteria. Collectively, Old World vultures are the most threatened group of terrestrial migratory birds on the planet. Populations of most species have been declining rapidly: 8 of the 16 species are considered Critically Endangered by IUCN and only 2 (the griffon vulture and the non-migratory palm-nut vulture) are of Least Concern. As discussed in Chapter 4, poisoning is the most critical threat to all of the migratory species, whereas collisions with power lines or wind turbines are secondary threats. Because of their precarious status, shared threats, and ecological similarities, it makes sense to consider the conservation of these species in aggregate. Additionally, because the species are migratory and are distributed over large areas of Africa and Eurasia, the approach needs to be multinational as well as multi-species.

This is the basis for the Multi-species Action Plan to Conserve African-Eurasian Vultures (Vulture MsAP; Botha et al. 2017). Developed under the Convention on the Conservation of Migratory Species of Wild Animals, the plan aims to develop a comprehensive approach to address the threats, forestall population declines, and lead to recovery for all 15 migratory vulture species in 128 African, European, and Asian countries. Given the geographic, political, and cultural scope of the plan and of the threats facing vultures, multiple stakeholders must be involved.[14] The plan is intended to coordinate efforts among national and international conservation NGOs, academic and research institutions, government ministries, the private sector, and local communities. Not all of these groups are directly concerned with vulture conservation, but their interests often overlap. Health-care workers, for example, may find themselves dealing with the secondary poisoning of people from the use in belief-based practices of vulture body parts obtained from poisoned birds.

Although the Vulture MsAP considers differences in the threats faced by each of the vulture species, the plan applies to multiple species. The challenge, of course, is to implement the recommended actions across the many countries of Africa and Eurasia that must become involved. Although the plan has been formally adopted, it has yet to attract the attention of most governments, much less the resources needed to coordinate implementation. Developing multi-species plans like the Vulture MsAP or the recovery plans mentioned earlier is the (relatively) easy part; actually implementing actions is much more difficult.

---

[14] The Saving Asia's Vultures from Extinction consortium described by Chris Bowden in Essay 4.2 is one of these collaborators.

## EMERGING TECHNOLOGIES

The effectiveness of imperiled-species conservation can be increased by improving the approaches we have described and by making use of emerging technologies such as the drones or eDNA we mentioned earlier. Even more innovative approaches are being considered or developed.

Of the new genetic tools, the CRISPR-Cas9/gene drive approach may have the greatest potential (Webber et al. 2015; Esvelt and Gemmell 2017). The CRISPR-Cas9 gene-editing technology can be used to modify, add, or delete specific genes from the genome of an individual or group of individuals. In theory, genes could be inserted that could help vulnerable species adapt by widening their thermal tolerance or could eradicate a threatening species by inhibiting its reproduction, reducing survival, or producing infertile offspring. The challenge would then be to infuse the altered genes throughout the target population.

This is where gene drives come in. A gene drive vastly increases the probability that offspring will receive only the altered gene. Because those individuals will then pass only that gene on to their offspring, the altered gene will spread rapidly, especially in species that have short generation lengths and mature rapidly. By using CRISPR-Cas9 and gene drives together, it might be possible to eradicate mosquitoes, rats, and other invasive species from Hawai'i, New Zealand, and elsewhere.

These and other genetic technologies are already being applied in agriculture, where the use of genetically modified organisms has generated intense international debate. Their use in conservation is still being discussed but is likewise controversial. Coincident with the IUCN World Conservation Congress in 2016, a group of scientists, conservationists, lawyers, and policy makers called for restraint. They argued that the emerging genetic tools provide "the ability to intervene in evolution, to engineer the fate of an entire species, to dramatically modify ecosystems, and to unleash large-scale environmental changes, in ways never thought possible before."[15] Once tools like CRISPR-Cas9/gene drive are unleashed, it may be difficult to reverse course if there are unintended negative consequences, or to define the boundaries between applications that are ethical and those that are not.

Artificial intelligence (AI) is another emerging technology that has potential uses in conservation. The power of AI is in its capacity to make sense of an overwhelming amount of information by using machine-learning algorithms, game theory, Big Data screening protocols, pattern recognition, and other ways of fine-tuning analyses as more analyses are done—that is, to learn. Advances in sensor technology and environmental genetics are generating deluges of data on animal movements and occurrences, plant distributions, water quality, habitats, and much else. An AI system called Protection Assistant for Wildlife Security[16] uses information about past wildlife-poaching activity and enforcement patrolling to anticipate the future reasoning and route-planning of poachers. It then calculates which patrol routes might have the greatest probability of successfully intersecting with poachers. Poachers sometimes coordinate their activities and sales through social media, which could also be probed and interpreted by AI (Di Minin et al. 2018). AI can be used to sort through automated camera records to recognize relevant information, such as the spot patterns of individual jaguars being tracked, learning about what could be "relevant" as it goes. More speculatively, AI might help conservation managers imagine which species would fit together in an area to best deal with future conditions (Cantrell et al. 2017).

AI may have great potential as a tool in conservation, but the intelligence is, after all, artificial. To realize that potential, engineers and programmers will need to collaborate with individuals who know natural history.

---

[15] http://www.etcgroup.org/files/files/final_gene_drive_letter.pdf
[16] https://www.cais.usc.edu/projects/wildlife-security/

## MEETING THE NEEDS OF CONSERVATION-RELIANT SPECIES

Ideally, conservation actions should completely eliminate a threat or at least reduce it to such a low level that it no longer matters. When that is not possible, translocations may enable a species to leave a threat behind and establish a viable population elsewhere. When a species has declined to catastrophically low numbers, captive breeding may be the only way to help it achieve sufficient numbers for individuals to be released back into the wild. Tracking and remote sensing can then be used to assess whether translocations or releases of individuals from captive breeding have enabled a species to become established in a new area.

All of these conservation measures are expensive. They may be feasible for short-term rescue efforts, but they will likely need to be continued for a long time for most conservation-reliant species. As expenses mount, resources may be stretched thin and the public may become fatigued by ongoing conservation efforts that do not seem to solve the problem. Funding may wither.

The efficiency and cost effectiveness of conservation measures need to be improved. Some of the emerging genetic technologies may help species cope with threats or reduce the threats themselves, whereas other tools, such as eDNA or AI, may help to reduce the costs of monitoring management outcomes. When conservation actions are applied to a single surrogate species or multiple species as a group, the benefits may extend to other species that share the same habitats or locations with few additional costs. Whether conservation-reliant species will benefit from these spillover actions may depend on how long the management continues. If the target species are themselves conservation reliant, the management may continue for a long time. When the target species recover, however, the dedicated management may end, and with it whatever benefits other species derive.

The utility of conservation actions should be assessed by considering their feasibility, immediate and long-term costs, likelihood of success (or risk of failure), and levels of societal and financial support. Ultimately, however, the effectiveness of any conservation measure requires that species have some place to live—suitable habitat that is free of devastating threats. There may be value, then, in expanding the conservation toolbox to include approaches based on locations and ecosystem processes, to go beyond species. This is the subject of the next chapter.

# 8  Expanding the Conservationist's Toolbox: Going Beyond Species

Every species is part of a larger community or ecosystem, what Darwin referred to as "an entangled bank."[1] Conserving any at-risk or conservation-reliant species depends on understanding its habitat needs and the forces that threaten its existence. But these needs and threats are usually considered from the perspective of the species of interest rather than from the broader ecological context in which it lives.

There are compelling reasons for expanding the scope of conservation beyond species and taking a broader, more holistic approach (Franklin 1993; Orians 1993). An overemphasis on individual species may result in parts of ecosystems being seen as "unimportant" and ignored. Such has been the fate of many communities of invertebrates and microbes, what E.O. Wilson (1987) called "the little things that run the world." Delving into the details of demography, distribution, and threats for any one of the growing number of imperiled species requires information that is hard to come by, especially for little-studied species in remote areas. Inequities in funding among at-risk species and the attraction of the public to large charismatic species exacerbate the challenges. Approaching conservation more comprehensively than one species at a time may lead to more effective

---

[1] In the concluding paragraph of *On the Origin of Species* (1859), Charles Darwin emphasized the evolutionary and ecological connectedness of species:

*"It is interesting to contemplate an entangled bank, clothed with many plants of many kinds, with birds singing on the bushes, with various insects flitting about, and with worms crawling through the damp earth, and to reflect that these elaborately constructed forms, so different from each other, and dependent upon each other in so complex a manner, have all been produced by laws acting around us."*

By which he meant the evolutionary process of natural selection.

conservation, produce better outcomes at a lower cost, and capture a greater spectrum of biological diversity (see Loyal Mehrhoff's Essay 8.1).

In this chapter, we consider how the scope of conservation may be broadened beyond species. There are several ways of doing this (Marcot and Flather 2007; Marcot and Sieg 2007). One is a location-based approach that focuses on places and landscapes by establishing protected areas or eradicating non-native species. Another approach emphasizes the composition, structure, or functioning of entire eco-systems. Such "ecosystem-based management" has become a guiding paradigm for managing broad-scale terrestrial, marine, and freshwater ecosystems (Levin et al. 2009). This approach moves even farther beyond species to emphasize interactions and feedbacks among elements of the biological, physical, and social environments.

## PROTECTING PLACES

Rather than targeting selected species for conservation attention, location-based conservation involves addressing the factors that threaten the conservation value of a particular place. Often this requires an initial investment to buy and set aside an area as a park, refuge, or nature reserve. Then the place must be managed: predators and invasive species must be controlled, fences must be maintained, ownership and responsibility for management must be ensured, human disturbances or incompatible land uses reduced, or agricultural practices adjusted. Many of these actions will be ongoing.

Sometimes areas are protected to conserve a particular species—for example, the Attwater's Prairie Chicken National Wildlife Refuge in the United States or the Wolong National Nature Reserve to protect giant pandas in China (see Jianguo Liu's Essay 9.2). Most often, however, protected areas are set aside to protect habitats that support multiple species. The Hakalau Forest National Wildlife Refuge in Hawai'i provides habitat for 36 Endangered, Threatened, or Candidate species listed under the Endangered Species Act and an additional 44 species of Conservation Concern.

ESSAY 8.1    **Conservation Reliance in the Real World: Lessons from Hawai'i**

*Loyal A. Mehrhoff*

With over 500 native species listed as threated or endangered, Hawai'i is correctly regarded as the endangered species capital of the United States and a bellwether of future conservation issues. Many of the conservation challenges that were recognized in Hawai'i decades ago have emerged in other regions. Like climate change, the concept of conservation-reliant species is forcing us to revisit how we do conservation planning, make decisions, and define success (Figure E8.1.1).

FIGURE E8.1.1.   The National Tropical Botanical Garden's conservation nursery for endangered Hawaiian plants. At least 15 highly endangered endemic species can be seen in this photograph, with most of these having fewer than 50 plants remaining in the wild. (A black and white version of this figure will appear in some formats. For the color version, please refer to the plate section.)

Photo: Michael J. DeMotta, National Tropical Botanical Garden.

ESSAY 8.1 **(cont.)**

So, what can we learn by looking at conservation reliance through the lens of Hawai'i's experiences?

First, until the root causes of endangerment and extinction are reversed, more and more species will be at risk and in need of conservation. At some point, a species-by-species-only approach becomes unmanageable. Hawai'i has long struggled with the sheer magnitude of threats facing its biodiversity and the lack of resources to address those threats. These challenges have spurred innovative conservation efforts. The large numbers of endangered Hawaiian species have forced the use of ecosystem approaches to the listing of species under the US Endangered Species Act, the preparation of recovery plans, land management, and even species management. The more at-risk species that can be covered by large ecosystem-management efforts, the less species-specific efforts are needed. Three statewide conservation efforts have played especially important roles: emergency extinction-prevention programs targeted at hundreds of the most at-risk plants, snails, and birds; watershed partnerships covering nearly half a million hectares of private, state, and federal lands; and island-specific invasive species committees that tackle invasive pests—one of the main causes of species endangerment.

Climate change is a game changer. The long-practiced strategy of saving endangered Hawai'i forest birds by establishing protected areas at elevations above the range of disease-carrying mosquitoes will eventually fail. It is already failing on Kaua'i, where two formerly common birds have recently been listed as Endangered as avian malaria has expanded across the top of the island. Eventually, all of Hawai'i's wet and mesic forests will warm sufficiently to support mosquitoes and malaria. Saving most forest birds will require controlling mosquitoes or malaria—or magically accelerating the resistance of dozens of bird species to a highly fatal disease. Modeling projects that climate change will cause hundreds of plants to undergo major range shifts, with over 40 species losing all potential habitat. The uncertainty of future conditions resulting from a changing climate and the continued introduction of new invasive species will make it harder

ESSAY 8.1    **(cont.)**

to assess the conservation value of an area to a species. As a result of habitat shifts or loss, many hundreds of species that might not have been conservation reliant under a stable climate may be so far into the future. While we continue to strive for species to be self-sustaining on their own, we may need to be satisfied with getting some species to the point where they can persist with our help. Managers will need to develop robust management plans and flexible contingency plans if projections turn out to be inaccurate.

Decision making gets more strategic. Conservation in Hawai'i is already occurring on a shoestring budget (Hawai'i has 30% of all US endangered species yet receives only 9% of the federal funding for recovery). Many Hawaiian species are not just declining—they are on the very brink of extinction. Over 200 species have fewer than 50 individuals remaining in the wild. Virtually every funding decision can become a life-or-death decision for species. The recent defunding of extinction-prevention programs in Hawai'i is heading us in the wrong direction.

Successful biodiversity conservation in Hawai'i will require, first, preventing imminent extinctions, and then, a combination of landscape-level ecosystem stewardship and species-specific efforts to make sure that individual species do not fall through the ecosystem cracks. Funding must follow this same strategy, going first to those species most vulnerable to extinction, and then to protecting key high-diversity ecosystems to help endangered species recover and preclude the need for additional listings. Leadership will need to redirect funds from non-critical species to those species and ecosystems most in need. When I was the US Fish and Wildlife Service's field supervisor responsible for endangered species management in Hawai'i, I chose to move funds away from species like nēnē or lower-priority projects like the reintroduction of Hawaiian crows to ensure that funding was available to prevent imminent extinctions. These are not easy decisions, and they will not get easier in the future.

Funding strategies also affect whether species will become or remain conservation reliant. For example, on many Pacific Islands, land

ESSAY 8.1 **(cont.)**

managers can decide to control invasive species like rats when they reach a threshold level, or they can undertake eradication programs to remove all rats permanently. Although knocking back rat numbers may benefit at-risk species, those species will be reliant on continued control efforts. Eradication would likely result in fewer conservation-reliant species. Eradication, though, is more expensive in the short term, and if funding is limited, other species may be lost in order to provide a more secure future for a lucky few.

People, technologies, laws, and activities set the local conservation context or conservation baseline. This context creates winners and losers, with some species increasing, others declining, and some remaining stable. The local conservation context can vary spatially, among islands or countries, and temporally, as local practices change over time. An island that shifts from industrial pineapple production to organic farming, for example, offers better prospects for pesticide-sensitive species than one that remains in industrial pineapple. Islands with a tradition of hunting sea turtles will have a different conservation context than islands that do not hunt sea turtles. If international trade treaties effectively reduce invasive species introductions, then current conservation conditions may improve. Laws like the Endangered Species Act improve the conservation context for many species.

Conservation-reliant species require actions above and beyond the local conservation context in order to be self-sufficient. Recovery efforts should aim to improve this local conservation context so that the needs of a species will be met and it will no longer be conservation reliant after it is delisted. Improving the conservation context will also increase societal confidence in delisting decisions, which becomes crucial when states assume responsibility for the management and funding of delisted species.

As other areas follow in Hawai'i's footsteps, several thoughts come to mind. Priorities matter. Conservation laws matter—if they are implemented and enforced. Preventing extinctions is more important than delisting species close to recovery or funding popular projects on

ESSAY 8.1 **(cont.)**

non-critical species. Partnerships focused on preventing extinctions, restoring watersheds, and combating invasive species are efficient and effective management tools. Key ecosystem-killing threats must be managed or there will be an ever-increasing number of endangered species. Today's management decisions may determine if a species will or will not be conservation reliant in the future. Climate change and invasive species are changing old conservation goals and strategies. Effective conservation will require a combination of ecosystem and species-specific management.

All but a few of these species are conservation reliant. Although some specific threats differ among taxa (only birds are threatened by avian malaria), all of the species are threatened by habitat loss and degradation caused by invasive species. Thus, the benefits of protecting habitat extend to at least 80 species.

Protected areas are central to the United Nations' Convention on Biological Diversity. When the 194 signatories to the Convention met in Japan's Aichi Prefecture in 2010, they pledged to protect at least 17% of terrestrial and inland water and 10% of coastal and marine areas by 2020.[2] Whether these percentages are enough is debatable; E.O. Wilson (2016) has argued that no less than half the planet should be dedicated to nature.

More important than the proportion of the Earth's surface that is under some form of protection, however, is ensuring that the places we strive to protect actually protect what they are intended to protect. This is the goal of conservation planning and spatial conservation prioritization (Groves 2003; Moilanen et al. 2009; Groves and Game 2016). One way to prioritize areas for protection is to ask how well existing protected areas match the distributions and needs of imperiled species. This is the aim of gap analysis (Scott et al. 1993). Gap

[2] www.cbd.int/sp/targets/

analysis was developed following the Hawaiian Forest Birds Survey (Chapter 3). By overlaying maps of existing protected areas with the distributions of endangered birds, scientists found that there was little overlap between the areas under protection and where the birds actually were. These findings led to the establishment of several new refuges and reserves in Hawai'i. More broadly, gap analysis has shown that protected areas are often located in areas with poor soils, swamps and marshes, or high elevations that may be favored for recreation or scenic qualities but have low value for human development or habitation: the "rocks and ice" syndrome (Terborgh 1999; Scott et al. 2001).

Another way to determine which areas to protect is to focus on places with the richest store of species. Noting that some areas in the tropics supported a high diversity of vascular plants but suffered severe habitat loss, Myers (1988) identified 10 so-called "hotspots" that were extraordinarily diverse and also highly threatened. Myers et al. (2000) subsequently defined hotspots as biogeographic regions with more than 1500 endemic vascular plant species and less than 30% of the original primary habitat remaining. Globally, 35 regions meet these criteria: areas like the Cerrado of Brazil or the Cape Floristic Region of South Africa. Collectively, these hotspots contain 77% of the Earth's endemic plant species and 43% of its vertebrates (including 80% of all threatened amphibians), all in only 17.3% of the Earth's land-surface area.

The argument that focusing conservation on these hotspots would be an efficient use of resources has proved compelling. Several conservation organizations (e.g. the Critical Ecosystem Partnership Fund, Birdlife International, the Alliance for Zero Extinction, Conservation International) have adopted hotspots or similar concepts to guide their programs and investments. In the United States, national assessments have been conducted using counties (Flather et al. 2008) or equal-area hexagons (Chaplin et al. 2000) to identify hotspots of terrestrial species richness and rarity. The latter analysis identified hotspots in the San Francisco Bay and southern coastal and interior regions of California, Death Valley, the Florida panhandle, the southern Appalachians, and Hawai'i. A similar analysis based on watersheds revealed hotspots of at-risk fish and mussel species in two river basins in southeastern United States. Regardless of the scale, the message seems to be that protecting biodiversity hotspots may require only a small proportion of the world's land area.

Like most ideas in conservation, however, the notion of hotspots has its critics. Kareiva and Marvier (2003) pointed out that an overemphasis on hotspots can lead to a neglect of "coldspots," regions of the globe that support low but distinctive biodiversity. Because these ecosystems can be spatially extensive but species poor, individual species, such as polar bears, can play an outsized role in structuring food webs despite being imperiled. Using plant and vertebrate species richness, endemism, and extinction risk to define hotspots may also divert attention from invertebrates, aquatic species, or widespread vertebrate herbivores or predators. Loss of such species would jeopardize entire ecosystems and the services they provide.

Globally defined hotspots may be useful for general planning purposes, but the scale may not match that at which conservation actions are usually implemented. Additionally, by basing hotspots primarily on species richness, the importance of phylogenetic or genetic diversity and evolutionary potential may be neglected. More to our point in this book, the hotspot approach does not explicitly consider threats other than habitat loss. It is therefore unlikely to factor the need for long-term management investment (i.e. conservation reliance) into calculations of the cost effectiveness of conservation actions based on hotspots.

Regardless of how protected areas are determined, they may be of limited effectiveness if they are ecologically isolated. Conserving corridors to join protected areas to one another or to the surrounding landscape may be critical for species with large ranges or necessary to foster genetic diversity. Although there is debate about the efficacy of corridors in enabling movements of plants or animals among places, their management has become a major aim of both landscape ecologists and conservationists (e.g. Crooks and Sanjayan 2006; Worboys et al. 2010).

Some of the most ambitious efforts aim to establish linkages that will enable movements over vast areas. The Yellowstone to Yukon Conservation Initiative (Y2Y)[3] is a joint United States–Canada conservation NGO that aims to connect and protect habitats along the spine of the Rocky Mountains (Locke 2010). This area stretches over 3000 km from Yellowstone National Park in the United States to Yukon Territory in Canada (Figure 8.1). The initiative brings together over 300 partners and stakeholders: conservation groups, local landowners, businesses, government agencies, donors and supporters, Native American and First Nations communities, and scientists. Additionally, the geographic and elevation span of Y2Y is intended to provide places for plants and animals to relocate as climate change causes their habitats to shift. Between 1993 and 2013, Y2Y and its partners increased protected areas in the region from 11% to 21%. Combined with better practices on an additional 30% of the lands, progress toward the goal of an interconnected landscape has been impressive. Many species will benefit from these efforts, including mainland grizzly bears, boreal woodland caribou, and wolverines, all of which are imperiled in the contiguous United States and rely on the network of protected and conservation lands.

Yellowstone to Yukon is not the only effort to establish broad-scale connectivity among protected and other conservation areas. In Australia, the Australian Alps to Atherton (A2A) conservation corridor would conserve and manage habitats and ecosystems over a 2800-km stretch of eastern Australia that spans 21 degrees of latitude (Pulsford et al. 2010). Like Y2Y, A2A is envisioned to connect an array of protected areas, state forests, and government, indigenous, and private lands to facilitate the movements of plants and animals, particularly in response to climate change.

[3] y2y.net/

FIGURE 8.1. The Yellowstone to Yukon (Y2Y) corridor is intended to connect isolated populations of wide-ranging predators, such as mainland grizzly bears and wolves, and herbivores, such as moose and elk. (A black and white version of this figure will appear in some formats. For the color version, please refer to the plate section.)

Source: Jodi Hilty, Y2Y.

Worboys et al. (2010) describe similar broad-scale connectivity conservation plans to knit together existing or planned conservation areas in South Africa, the eastern Himalayas, Sumatra, Mesoamerica, the central Andes, the European Alps, and elsewhere. Many of these involve multiple countries and collaborations among a host of governments, NGOs, partners, and stakeholders. All recognize the importance of integrating conservation objectives with the activities, needs, and cultures of the people living in the regions. Although some have made substantial progress, others are still in the planning phase.

Protected areas represent only one point on a spectrum of location-based conservation. Protected areas usually prohibit other human land uses, such as agriculture and forestry; such prohibitions often hurt local economies and can generate backlash. Conservation easements are one way to continue land use while protecting habitat. A landowner who sells or donates an easement to an NGO or government retains ownership of the property; only the uses incompatible with conservation (e.g. development, surface mining) are restricted. The easement conditions are specified "in perpetuity" and remain with the property even if ownership changes (Byers and Ponte 2005).

Another way to protect places is with conservation reserve contracts. In the United States, the Conservation Reserve Program compensates landowners for taking land out of production by fallowing agricultural fields or planting land cover that will improve soil conditions or restore wildlife habitat.[4] The landowner receives a yearly rent for a contracted time period (generally 10–15 years) after which the contract may be renewed or the land returned to its former or other uses. If markets change and land use or development becomes more profitable than what the Conservation Reserve Program can offer, however, conservation gains can be quickly undone in a way that easements prevent.

---

[4] www.fsa.usda.gov/programs-and-services/conservation-programs/conservation-reserve-program/

As with protected areas, these types of partial protection are tied to a fixed location. If environmental conditions vary, the location may meet the needs of only some species only some of the time. For example, along the Western Flyway of North America, most of the wetlands that historically supported vast numbers of migratory waterfowl, wading birds, and shorebirds have been drained and converted to agriculture. Multiple species now depend not only on protected or partially protected reserves, but also on where and how water availability is managed across the larger landscape. They have become reliant on conservation actions that are undertaken outside protected locations.

In California, a novel approach to wetland conservation allows flexibility in which locations are protected while simultaneously retaining land for agriculture. Rice fields in the Sacramento Valley are flooded a few centimeters deep during the growing season and then again in fall to decompose rice stubble that remains after harvesting. The fields often remain flooded during fall and winter to support the millions of ducks, geese, and swans that use them as surrogate wetlands during their annual migrations. Waterfowl hunting is an important recreational and economic activity at this time. After the hunting season ends, however, farmers usually dry their fields to prepare for planting. This is the time when hundreds of thousands of shorebirds pass through on their spring migration (Figure 8.2). During droughts, such as occurred from 2012 through 2015, the rice fields may remain dry for much or all of the year.

Recognizing this problem, several organizations collaborated with citizen birdwatchers in 2014 to launch a program to provide flooded rice fields to shorebirds. The BirdReturns program has three components. First, in order to target conservation activities, it is necessary to know where and when shorebirds are most likely to occur. Scientists use a large database of observations from birdwatchers (eBird)[5] to predict the distribution of shorebirds of multiple species at the rice-field scale of resolution. Second, the distribution information is combined with satellite

---

[5] ebird.org/home

FIGURE 8.2.  A greater yellowlegs and several dunlins feeding in a rice field in California. Under the BirdReturns program, rice fields are flooded in spring to maintain wetland habitat for migratory shorebirds. (A black and white version of this figure will appear in some formats. For the color version, please refer to the plate section.)
Photo: Greg Golet.

data from NASA that show where and when temporary wetland shorebird habitat is available. Third, TNC compensates selected farmers for the costs of water and management to maintain the very shallow water depths optimal for shorebirds. To select locations, TNC uses a reverse-auction process in which farmers submit bids for the costs of providing habitat based on their own economic considerations. TNC then evaluates bids to obtain the greatest amount of high-quality habitat for the lowest total cost. Importantly, the selection of which fields to flood is flexible depending on circumstances; when more habitat was available in the wet year of 2017, for example, the program was scaled back.

The program has been a resounding success. Since 2014, the BirdReturns program has created over $200 \, \text{km}^2$ of high-quality habitat for shorebirds in California during critical periods of spring and autumn migration at a fraction of the cost of in-perpetuity protection. During the spring of 2014, shorebird density was five-times greater and species richness three-times greater on enrolled fields than in comparable fields (both flooded and dry) not enrolled in the program; 57 shorebird species used the enrolled fields (Reynolds et al. 2017; Golet et al. 2018). During the drought that ended in 2016, BirdReturns fields provided 30–70% of the wetland habitat available for migrating shorebirds. Economic analyses suggest that providing temporary habitat by flooding fields for 8 weeks every spring for 25 years would cost only 10% of the cost of buying, restoring, and maintaining those locations as protected areas, in addition to the local economic benefits of keeping the fields in agricultural production.

The dynamic approach to conserving locations applied to the California rice fields is best regarded as a complement to the permanent protection of places of conservation value. It has the advantages of involving stakeholders in the program on their own terms and bringing together the expertise and data of multiple collaborators. It is most appropriate where the use of habitats by species is seasonal or ephemeral or where environmental conditions are especially variable. Where the conservation value of a place is consistently high, more stable long-term protection may justify the greater initial cost.

Whether it be by protecting areas from human uses or intrusion, establishing restrictions that permit some compatible human uses to continue, or adjusting land-use practices to increase the conservation value of places, managing locations for conservation can benefit multiple species. Some of these species are likely to be imperiled and some conservation reliant, but even common species may come to rely on the habitat, resources, and protection that such places provide.

## RECOVERING PLACES BY ERADICATING INVASIVE SPECIES

The benefits of reserves and protected areas to conservation do not arise solely from their establishment. The benefits are realized only when the locations are adequately and appropriately managed for the entities they are intended to conserve. For imperiled and conservation-reliant species, this usually entails reducing or eliminating threats.

Protected areas often contain habitat that has been lost from the surroundings, reducing one of the threats to imperiled species. But these areas can also include introduced or invasive plants or animals that degrade the habitats and impair the species the protected areas are intended to conserve. In areas without natural boundaries, fencing can be an effective way to keep out unwanted predators, competitors, or herbivores. John Woinarski discusses how fencing has been used to protect imperiled Australian mammals in Essay 8.2.[6]

When Hawai'i Volcanoes National Park was established in 1916, pigs and (especially) goats were destroying native vegetation. Deputized citizens, private-party contractors, and park personnel mounted campaigns to hunt and kill goats. These efforts went on for decades. Thousands of goats were killed, but others moved in and those that remained reproduced faster than they could be removed. The goats were winning (Figure 8.3).

The goal of eradicating goats from the park was controversial. Hunting groups argued for managing the goats as a recreational resource. In response, park personnel worked with hunting groups to draft a new goat-management plan focused on restoring the park's natural resources. The plan proposed rebuilding the park's perimeter fences and then erecting interior fences, one paddock at a time, to create enclosures of hundreds of hectares. As a test, a small area was fenced to exclude goats.

---

[6] The standard in protective fencing was set in Australia more than a century ago with the construction of a 3256-km rabbit-proof fence to protect crops and pasture lands in western Australia from rabbits (featured in the 2002 film *Rabbit-Proof Fence*) and a 5614-km dingo fence, built to protect sheep in southeast Queensland's fertile grazing areas. Where the fence excludes dingoes, kangaroo numbers have increased, overgrazing native vegetation; where dingoes are present, fox activity is inhibited and small mammals have benefitted. Conservation actions often have unanticipated consequences.

ESSAY 8.2   **Resurrecting a Lost World: The Tenuous Return of the Australian Mammal Fauna**

*John Woinarski*

In the little more than two centuries since European settlement of Australia in 1788, its distinctive mammal fauna has been subverted. At least 32 Australian-endemic mammal species were rendered extinct over this period. Many of these species were formerly abundant, widespread, and ecologically important; many also had profound cultural significance to Indigenous Australians. The extinctions are continuing, with another two endemic Australian mammal species lost in the last decade. Many surviving species are imperiled and continue to decline. In many regions of Australia, the current mammal fauna comprises fewer than half of the species present barely a century ago. An early witness to the decline portrayed these losses as the erosion of the essence and spirit of the continent:

> The old Australia is passing. The environment which moulded the most remarkable fauna in the world is beset on all sides by influences which are reducing it to a medley of semi-artificial environments, in which the original plan is lost and the final outcome of which no man may predict. (Finlayson 1935)

Many factors contributed to the transformation of the continent and its biota. These included the removal of long-established indigenous fire management, habitat destruction, ecological degradation due to the extensive spread of imported livestock and feral herbivores (notably rabbits), and, particularly, the introduction of two predator species, the European red fox and feral cat. Singly or collectively, these factors affected almost all of the continent and many of its 8000-odd islands. However, there were some exceptions, as some offshore islands escaped the novel threats. Happily, those islands allowed the persistence of some mammal species that were extirpated from their formerly much more extensive mainland range. For example, the fascinating and formerly highly successful greater stick-nest rat was extirpated from its range of $>1$ million $km^2$ in continental Australia,

ESSAY 8.2  **(cont.)**

but by serendipity persisted (only) on the 5-km$^2$ Franklin Islands off South Australia.

From these surviving populations, conservation managers have made strategic and dedicated efforts to reverse the declines. This has mostly involved numerous translocations to increase the number of populations and the overall population size. Many of these translocations have been to other islands where threats, notably foxes and cats, happened to be absent or were eradicated. But there has also been a concerted effort to return many of the much-dwindled mammal species to vestiges of their former continental ranges. Early attempts almost invariably foundered, as the re-colonists proved incapable of surviving cats and foxes, even where these were reduced in abundance by baiting campaigns. Subsequently, however, there has been almost invariable success when the native mammals have been returned to fenced areas that have been cleared of foxes and cats, and where managers have vigilantly maintained such predator-free status (Figure E8.2.1).

Those predator exclosures now offer an astonishing window through which the country and its wildlife can be viewed as it was before the fall. Outside the exclosures, the mammal fauna is dominated by introduced species with a few resilient native species, such as the large kangaroos. But open the locked gates and step inside the exclosures and the contrast is stark—the native mammal fauna is diverse and abundant: there are bilbies, bettongs, potoroos, woylies, and quolls. The ecology is different and healthier, as many of the mammal species were critical contributors to seed dissemination and germination, and to soil fertility. For an ecologist, this is a tantalizing image of how the country was and should be—a second chance, an opportunity to resurrect an extraordinary mammal fauna. For the community generally, it is about recognizing that the now-familiar pervasive landscape largely devoid of native mammals is an altered and degraded state. For Indigenous Australians, the mammal returns are a cause for joy and cultural restoration.

However, it is a tenuous advance. The exclosures require continued surveillance to maintain their predator-proof status. The establishment

ESSAY 8.2  **(cont.)**

FIGURE E8.2.1. Exclosures barring introduced cats and foxes now provide the only mainland havens for many highly threatened Australian-endemic mammal species. (A black and white version of this figure will appear in some formats. For the color version, please refer to the plate section.)
Photo: © Wayne Lawler/Australian Wildlife Conservancy.

of predator-proof fencing is costly and this resourcing demand has limited the number and size of exclosures to a current set of 17 separate exclosures tallying 337 km$^2$. Many Australian native mammal species susceptible to cats and foxes are not yet represented in these exclosures and others have to date been reintroduced to only a single or few exclosures. Although the network is growing, it represents only a minute proportion of the vast former ranges, populations, and ecological contributions of most of the predator-susceptible native mammal species.

The future of much of the wonderful Australian-endemic mammal fauna is reliant on this conservation mechanism. For every species in this large set of imperiled predator-susceptible mammals, the exclosure network and reintroduction program are vital for averting extinction.

ESSAY 8.2  **(cont.)**

The conservation benefits are far more generic than for these species alone. Their success also offers our community a glimpse of the far more diverse past, a signpost to a future environmental state that can be much better than the present, a stark demonstration of the impacts of ill-advised introductions and of the potential benefits that well-considered conservation management can achieve, and a part of the fabric of restoring and respecting our country's indigenous land management and culture. Hopefully the network is a transitory stage, and ultimately the cause of the long-term decline (foxes and feral cats) can be more permanently erased, the fences no longer necessary, and the native mammal fauna restored more pervasively across the country.

FIGURE 8.3. When Hawai'i Volcanoes National Park was established in 1916, feral goats were already decimating native plants, critically imperiling endemic birds and other vulnerable native species. (A black and white version of this figure will appear in some formats. For the color version, please refer to the plate section.)

Photo: National Park Service courtesy of Don Reeser and Bryan Harry.

FIGURE 8.4. A goat exclosure in Hawai'i Volcanoes National Park, showing the lush regrowth of native vegetation only 2 years after the fence was constructed. (A black and white version of this figure will appear in some formats. For the color version, please refer to the plate section.)
Photo: National Park Service courtesy of Don Reeser and Bryan Harry.

In only 2 years, the plot was covered by a lush growth of native plants, including a previously unknown 'āwikiwiki (lavafield jackbean) (Figure 8.4). The demonstration plots, new information about goat diets, and involvement of the hunting community changed the conversation about goat removal.

By the early 1980s, only a few dozen goats remained in the entire park. These last goats had become wary of hunters, dogs, and helicopters, and were nearly impossible to remove. So Judas goats were enlisted to help. Judas goats are goats that are collared with radio transmitters so they can be released and then tracked. When the Judas goat joins other goats, the entire group can be located and removed, leaving the Judas goat free to find more companions.[7]

[7] The Judas concept has been extended to control other social animals: pigs, rats, raccoon dogs, and dromedary camels; see Spencer et al. (2015) and Robertson et al. (2017).

As a result of the fencing and control programs, goats were eradicated from 55 400 ha of the Park by 1984. Pigs were eliminated from 16 180 ha of the Park by 2007 (Hess and Jacobi 2011). The native plants and animals in the park rebounded in numbers and distribution, although many of them remain conservation reliant. Goats and pigs are still common in areas surrounding the park, so keeping the park free of these and other threats requires constant monitoring, repair of fences, and removal of animals when they breach the fence.

Less than 60 km to the north, Hakalau Forest National Wildlife Refuge faces many of the same threats. The refuge was established in 1985 to protect an area with more endangered species than almost anywhere in the Hawaiian Islands (Scott et al. 1987). Management efforts were focused on high-elevation areas where a malaria-free refuge for endangered forest birds might be created by removing feral cattle and pigs (whose wallowing produced breeding pools for mosquitoes) and restoring the native forest. The area was fenced, the ungulates removed, and refuge staff and volunteers planted more than 400 000 native plants to restore a multi-layered forest.

The results were impressive. Populations of native plants and animals were restored and a native ecosystem re-established. It remains a work in progress, but Hakalau is now the only place in Hawai'i where populations of endangered forest birds, such as the endangered honeycreepers 'alawī (Hawai'i creeper), Hawai'i 'akepa, and 'akiapōlā'au, are stable or increasing (Paxton et al. 2017).

Conservation efforts will continue because the fencing must be maintained and stray ungulates removed. Additionally, invasive plants that encroach from unmanaged surrounding areas must be controlled. A gap in federal funding from 2009 to 2011 emphasized the reliance on continuing management. Fences at Hakalau went unattended during the gap and fell into disrepair. Pigs and cattle moved back in, uprooting, trampling, or eating many endangered plants. When funding was restored in 2012, management efforts were renewed. By 2013, the fences were again intact. During the funding gap, however, people had noticed how inconsistent government support jeopardized conservation gains. In response, a citizen group created a conservation-management endowment to fill funding gaps when federal funding falls short.[8]

Efforts to eradicate non-native species have been extended to islands throughout the Hawaiian Archipelago. Non-native mammals, such as rabbits and rats, were eliminated from most of the northwestern islands by 1995. European rabbits were eliminated from Lehua in the southern Hawaiian chain by 2006, but an attempt at rat eradication in 2009 failed. After several delays, poisoned bait was again distributed in late 2017. In early December 2018, additional rats were detected on Lehua. Eradication efforts were intensified and the clock was reset. The rat watch continues.

Oceanic islands are naturally isolated, surrounded by seas that are inhospitable to most terrestrial species. Since Darwin's time it has been widely recognized that islands are hotspots of evolution. They are hotspots of extinction as well. Comprising only 5% of Earth's landmass, islands account for 61% of all recently extinct species and 31% of all critically endangered species. Much of this dismal record is due to the direct and indirect actions of humans, particularly our role in fostering the spread of rats and other invasive species.

Darwin's laboratory of evolution—the Galapagos Archipelago—exemplifies the perils and promise of eradication efforts on islands. Black rats, brought in on privateers' ships in the seventeenth century, initially occurred only on Santiago Island.[9] As boat traffic among the islands increased, however, they eventually spread throughout most of the archipelago. Rats ate the eggs and hatchlings of endemic birds and reptiles.

The situation was especially dire on the island of Pinzón. By the 1960s, the iconic Pinzón tortoises had failed to reproduce for over a

---

[8] Friends of Hakalau Forest National Wildlife Refuge: www.friendsofhakalauforest.org
[9] Where Darwin collected the first specimen of an introduced rat in 1835.

FIGURE 8.5. Poisoned bait being dropped onto Rábida Island, Galapagos, to eradicate invasive rats. (A black and white version of this figure will appear in some formats. For the color version, please refer to the plate section.)
Credit: Rodrigo Buendia/AFP/ Getty Images.

century.[10] A tortoise-rearing program was initiated to maintain the population until the rats could be eradicated. An early attempt to eradicate rats failed. By one estimate there were 180 million rats on Pinzón (an island of only 1815 ha) in the early 2000s. In 2012, several organizations came together to provide funding for helicopters, poisoned bait, and research on the risks of the bait to native species (Figure 8.5).[11] Rats were eradicated from Pinzón, and within 2 years the tortoises were again producing hatchlings.

The Galapagos are plagued by more than rats. Large herbivores— goats, pigs, and donkeys—were introduced at various times over the last two centuries. Goats eat pretty much anything, so their effects on Galapagos species and ecosystems were especially devastating. By the

---

[10] Tortoises can live for over two centuries, so they can wait. But not forever.
[11] www.galapagos.org/conservation/our-work/ecosystem-restoration/rat-eradication/

late 1990s, there were estimated to be 100 000 goats on the northern portion of Isabela Island (approximately 250 000 ha). In 1997, Project Isabela was launched to eliminate goats, pigs, and donkeys from Pinta, Santiago, and the northern part of Isabela Island using a combination of ground and helicopter-based sharpshooting, ably assisted by Judas goats. All large herbivores had been eradicated from the three areas by 2005 (Carrion et al. 2011).

The eradication efforts on the Hawaiian and Galapagos islands relied mainly on hunting and poisoning to remove unwanted species. New tools are now emerging. In Hawai'i, avian malaria confines native birds to high elevations where the mosquito vectors cannot complete their life cycle. A warming climate will allow mosquitoes and the malaria parasites to expand to higher and higher elevations. In the long term, protecting habitat or places at higher elevations for honeycreepers and other native birds will not suffice; the mosquitoes must be eradicated (Fortini et al. 2015).

This prospect, along with growing concerns about the human-health impacts of mosquito-borne diseases such as West Nile virus, dengue fever, and Zika virus, has prompted discussions about the possibility of creating a "mosquito-free Hawai'i."[12] Male mosquitoes could be sterilized by irradiation or by infecting them with new strains of the bacteria *Wolbachia* and then allowing them to mate with wild mosquitoes, greatly reducing the numbers of disease-spreading mosquitoes. Genomic technology could be used to create genetically self-limiting males whose offspring would not survive to reproduce. Use of the CRISPR-Cas9/gene drive technology described in Chapter 7 is also a possibility. Although these would be major undertakings, eliminating mosquitoes island- or archipelago-wide would remove a major threat to native species and human health and free up funding for other conservation or social projects.

---

[12] www.cpc-foundation.org/uploads/7/6/2/6/76260637/report_on_mosquito_free_workshop.pdf

The stories from Hawai'i and the Galapagos islands illustrate five points relevant to managing protected areas for conservation-reliant species.

First, the challenge of complete eradication becomes exponentially more difficult as the size of an island or area to be fenced increases. The eradication of rats from Rábida (499 ha) was relatively quick and easy; the elimination of goats from all of Isabela (458 812 ha) is considerably more challenging and expensive, and is a work in progress. New Zealand's proposal to eradicate several non-native predator species from the entire country (66 229 120 ha) by 2050 will require even more resources.

Second, the cost and effectiveness of eradication from an area depends on the surroundings. Maintenance of fencing and monitoring to detect new arrivals will be more demanding if the surrounding area supports large numbers of invasive plants or animals.

Third, eradication does not always work the first time around. The first attempts to eliminate rats from Pinzón Island and Lehua Island failed, but people incorporated the lessons from those failures into later attempts.

Fourth, eradication only works if all the offending individuals are removed or neutralized. In Chapter 4, we described what happened on Macquarie Island when a program to eradicate European rabbits stopped prematurely—the rabbits produced more and more rabbits, unleashing a cascade of indirect effects. Similarly, rat eradication on Henderson Island, one of the British Pitcairn Islands, stopped short of complete elimination and the rats returned. In fact, the costs and difficulty of complete eradication of rats from Henderson have led those supporting the program to conclude that it is not feasible using currently available technology. Eradication efforts have been suspended.[13]

Finally, early engagement with stakeholders and the public can prevent delays and backlash later on. The ethical issues raised by

---

[13] datazone.birdlife.org/site/factsheet/henderson-island-iba-pitcairn-islands-(to-uk)/text.

killing animals such as cats, goats, and rats need to be made transparent and fully addressed. Conservation actions require broad public support and involvement to work through such concerns. In planning for the countrywide elimination of invasive predators, for example, New Zealand convened a diverse panel including an ecologist, a geneticist, a lawyer, a hunter, and a Māori leader to discuss the ethical and social challenges.[14]

## RESTORING PLACES BY MANAGING FIRE REGIMES

Places such as protected areas provide many species with a place to live and conservationists with a defined area in which to apply their management tools. These locations are also subject to disturbances that alter habitats and threaten species. We mentioned the effects of hurricanes and tsunamis in Chapters 4 and 5; here we comment on the role of fire as an ecosystem process that can benefit as well as threaten imperiled species. Management of fire can therefore contribute to the conservation reliance of a species.

Many people think of wildfires as unnatural events that disturb or destroy ecosystems and threaten human lives and property. Recent conflagrations in the western United States, Canada, Australia, Borneo, Brazil, and elsewhere reinforce that view. Droughts linked to changing climate are increasing the frequency, intensity, size, and impacts of wildfires, leading to calls for even more fire suppression than occurred over much of the last century.

In many ecosystems, however, fires are a natural process to which many plants and animals have evolved. When a series of fires in Yellowstone National Park burned over $3000\,km^2$ in 1988, scientists documented a reset in forest succession and an overall increase in landscape heterogeneity and biodiversity (Turner et al. 2003). Some of the world's most diverse plant assemblages, such as the Cape Floristic Province of South Africa or the *Banksia* and *Eucalyptus*

---

[14] www.sciencemag.org/news/2017/07/new-zealand-aims-eradicate-invasive-predators-winning-public-support-may-be-big

woodlands of southwestern Australia, are composed of fire-adapted species. Several pine species (and most *Banksia* species) have serotinous cones or seed capsules that open and release seeds only when exposed to fire. The longleaf pine forests that once covered much of the southeastern United States evolved to depend on frequent fires to maintain an open parkland understory, suppress invasive species, and foster forest regeneration.

When humans alter fire regimes, fire-adapted species become reliant on people to replace the missing process. In longleaf pine ecosystems, humans have replaced the natural fire regime with carefully planned prescribed burning to maintain conditions for the pines and some 29 federally listed Endangered and Threatened species, such as red-cockaded woodpeckers, gopher tortoises, and Cooley's meadowrue.[15] These species are now conservation reliant.

The reliance of species and ecosystems on fire management is not a recent development. Native Americans used fire in hunting game, clearing underbrush, and nurturing food plants well before Europeans arrived (Nowacki et al. 2012; Hummel and Smith 2017). In Australia, indigenous peoples have used fire with expertise since they came to the continent some 50 000–60 000 years ago. What we know about indigenous Australian fire practices derives mostly from the accounts of European explorers in the eighteenth and nineteenth centuries and from traditional practices that still occur in some areas (Bowman 1998). Over tens of thousands of years of continual practice and refinement, fire management evolved into a precise art form tuned to the landscape, the timing of seasons, variations among places, and differences among plant species (Figure 8.6). Fire was used to clear tracks for driving game and hunting, to encourage the growth of palatable bush plants, to open the canopy in woodlands, to increase populations of open-country prey like kangaroos, to send signals among groups, and to make it easier to walk from place to place

---

[15] Connor et al. (2001) provide an in-depth review of how fire is used to manage the longleaf pine ecosystem and conserve the woodpecker.

FIGURE 8.6 Aboriginal use of fire to hunt kangaroos in Australia. From a painting by Joseph Lycett, c. 1820. (A black and white version of this figure will appear in some formats. For the color version, please refer to the plate section.)
Photo courtesy National Library of Australia.

(and avoid poisonous snakes!). Burning also had a spiritual role, to cleanse the land of bad spirits.

Extending over many millennia, indigenous Australian fire regimes became an evolutionary force that reorganized the biota of the continent. The flora of many parts of Australia is now dominated by fire-resistant and fire-dependent species. Many of Australia's most iconic plants, such as grass trees, are well adapted to fire, and several require fire to blossom. Indigenous fire regimes were carefully orchestrated and typically fine scale, allowing cooler fires at their margins to be used to protect fire-sensitive vegetation, such as rainforests and *Acacia* woodlands. Together with lightning-caused fires, these practices created a patchwork of fire sizes and histories across the landscape.

When Europeans arrived and dispossessed the indigenous peoples, such fire-management practices were lost. In the tropical savannas, fires were started late in the dry season (when more fuel was available), leading to very hot fires that reached the canopy and burned into fire-sensitive vegetation patches. Fire was actively suppressed in many areas to protect livestock and property. As a consequence, ecosystem composition and processes were altered and indigenous culture was further diminished. Many plant communities and species are now in decline; for example, Garnett (1992) tallied 50 Australian bird taxa that are threatened by inappropriate (i.e. modern) fire regimes (see Woinarski 1999).

In recent years, the consequences of inappropriate fire management have become more widely recognized. In Australia, some managers are attempting to mimic indigenous fire regimes, especially in the northern savannas. Whether European or indigenous Australian fire practices are followed, however, much of the biota of large parts of Australia has become reliant on human fire management or is affected by its mismanagement (or the absence of any management). The same is true of many forested and grassland ecosystems in North America and elsewhere in the world.

## WHAT ABOUT ECOSYSTEMS?

Consideration of ecosystem processes such as fire can help us uncover some of the root causes of conservation reliance. But beyond such processes, should ecosystems themselves be targets of conservation and management?

In the previous chapter, we mentioned the Ash Meadows Recovery Plan as an example of multi-species planning. The recovery plan went further, to emphasize that the recovery effort must be "strongly oriented toward recovering the entire Ash Meadows ecosystem rather than individual species" (USFWS 1990: 1). This emphasis on ecosystems is also explicit in the language of the Endangered Species Act, whose purpose is "to provide a means whereby the ecosystems upon which endangered species and threatened species depend may be conserved."[16] This purpose was reaffirmed when the agencies responsible for administering the act announced a joint policy in 1994 to incorporate ecosystem considerations into actions under the act. The Integrated Natural Resource Management Plan

---

[16] Endangered Species Act, 16 USC § 1531 et seq.

developed by the US Navy for San Clemente Island explicitly calls for the implementation of "an ecosystem restoration program that provides for conservation and rehabilitation of natural resources and that is consistent with the military mission."[17] In 2008, Secretary of the Interior Dirk Kempthorne proposed listing 48 species endemic to Kaua'i in a single action, touting it as an ecosystem-based approach to species conservation. "By addressing the common threats that occur across these ecosystems," he noted, "we can more effectively focus our conservation efforts on restoring the functions of these shared habitats." The actions would "benefit the recovery of the listed species and also all the species within the native ecological community."[18]

Secretary Kempthorne used the term "ecosystem" to refer to the multiple species and habitats associated with a specific place. The term may also refer to a general ecosystem type, such as mountain rainforest, moist lowland, or estuarine mudflat. Such ecosystem types can be mapped (e.g. United States: Sayre et al. 2009; Africa: Sayre et al. 2013). More generally, "ecosystem" encompasses the webs of interactions among species, processes of energy and material transfer, and spatial and temporal dynamics that make nature function.

Ecosystems throughout the world have undergone massive changes. Some have disappeared, while others have become so diminished in their extent or compromised in their composition and functioning that they can be considered endangered. An analysis by Noss et al. (1995) concluded that 27 ecosystem types in the United States, such as sedge meadows in Wisconsin and longleaf pine forests and savannas in the southeastern coastal plain, were Critically Endangered (>98% decline). In Australia, where protection of threatened ecological communities is written into the EPBC Act (Chapter 6), more than 80 communities are now listed.[19]

---

[17]  tierradata.com/sci/wp-content/uploads/2012/10/2002-INRMP.pdf

[18]  www.fws.gov/news/ShowNews.cfm?ref=kempthorne-announces-proposal-to-protect-48-hawaii-species&_ID=5975

[19]  www.environment.gov.au/cgi-bin/sprat/public/publiclookupcommunities.pl

At a global scale, IUCN is developing a Red List of Ecosystems that uses reduction in geographic distribution and degradation of key ecosystem components and processes as criteria to assess the risk of collapse of an ecosystem (Bland et al. 2016).[20] The giant kelp forests of Alaska and tapia forests of Madagascar are considered globally Endangered, whereas the Meso-American reef in Central America and the ironstone shrublands of Australia are assessed regionally as Critically Endangered. The Aral Sea, which has largely disappeared, is categorized as a Collapsed ecosystem.

It is clear that many ecosystems are imperiled at local to global scales. Yet ecosystems are not like species. When we talk of conserving the longleaf pine ecosystem, we have in mind the multitude of species that are parts of the processes and dynamics in a place dominated by longleaf pines. If the environment changes, the pines may vanish and the species composition and processes may be altered. The longleaf pine ecosystem as we have defined it may disappear, having been transformed into a different ecosystem. Nitrogen will continue to cycle and food webs will exist. Although the changed habitats will be unsuitable for some species, they may be ideal for others. The transformation of the Sacramento–San Joaquin Delta in California that we describe in Chapter 9 has favored non-native fish over native species, leading to novel ecosystems with different processes and dynamics (Moyle 2014).

It is different with species. Species may change or evolve over time, but when a species vanishes its extinction creates a gap in nature that will persist forever (Flannery and Schouten 2001). Conservation of species therefore aims to prevent extinction and foster recovery; conservation of ecosystems strives to maintain processes and functions. Applying the ecosystem concept in conservation draws attention to the importance of interactions, processes, and dynamics

---

[20] iucnrle.org/about-rle/rle/. The categories of risk for ecosystems are the same as those in the IUCN Red List of Threatened Species (Box 6.3) with "Collapsed" replacing "Extinct."

as key features of species' habitats and highlights the services that ecosystems provide to people. But an emphasis on ecosystems may lead to a failure to manage threats that could change the composition of ecological communities irreparably before we realize the damage.

## DO BROADER APPROACHES BENEFIT CONSERVATION-RELIANT SPECIES?

Agencies, conservation organizations, scientists, and the public are taking a greater interest in the multi-species and location-based approaches to conservation we have discussed in this and the previous chapter. One reason is their potential cost effectiveness. Although joining several species together in a listing under the Endangered Species Act does not save much other than the administrative costs of listing, other approaches that group species together in plans or places can enable multiple species to benefit from a single conservation action—there are economies of scale. Because species do not need to be treated individually, less information is required and fewer conservation actions may be needed, potentially speeding up management. Efforts to protect large areas may protect a broader array of biodiversity, especially if the areas are located in biodiversity hotspots. Ecosystem- or biodiversity-based parks and nature reserves allow people to see iconic species like pandas or lions, and the other species that support such icons. They also provide local human communities with an economic benefit from ecotourism. Appreciation for nature beyond the iconic species can build public support for conservation and increase public, private, corporate, and institutional stakeholder involvement.

Because conservation-reliant species require long-term management, they incur long-term costs. The greater cost effectiveness of broadened approaches may benefit such species, especially ones that have been largely overlooked. Species that are not at immediate risk or are often neglected in conservation efforts, such as many invertebrates and microbes, may also benefit. Management efforts directed toward keystone species, developing multi-species recovery plans, protecting natural areas or hotspots, or managing fire regimes may help to attack some of the most important threats to diverse species.

Of course, there are tradeoffs. Which human activities are permitted in protected areas and, indeed, the continued existence of these areas are subject to political whims and economic forces. Even if the areas are reasonably secure they may not retain the composition, functions, and values that people had in mind when the areas were established. Locations that help conserve species change over time in response to management and other human actions; societal and political forces; disturbances such as fire, drought, or hurricanes; and climate change. The larger the area or broader the scope of conservation and management, the more likely such forces will produce unforeseen consequences. Protected areas may provide long-term security of place, but they do not ensure content.

Conversely, conserving imperiled or conservation-reliant species one at a time may be effective but it is costly. Maximizing the probability of success requires information on distribution, habitat preferences, demography, population trends, food habits, threats from predators or competitors, and a host of other factors. As conservation plans and management actions become more general to accommodate more species, some of this detailed knowledge will be sacrificed. Thus, a conundrum: Will broad approaches be good enough to buy time for many imperiled species, or is a species or population focus essential to crafting conservation approaches that will really work?

As with most things in conservation, the choice is not between species-centered or broader approaches. The focus may shift over time from an initial effort to rescue an imperiled species to a multi-species approach that could include designation of protected areas or management of ecosystem processes. Ultimately, the balance between single- and multi-species approaches, and the broader roles of protected areas and ecosystem management, rests on how we answer the question we posed earlier in this book: What is it we are trying to conserve? There is no single or simple answer, yet this question is central to how we think about addressing the challenge of conservation and conservation reliance.

# 9 Conservation Reliance Is a Human Issue

Successful conservation depends on an understanding of the ecology and biology of the species and ecosystems to be conserved. It also depends on understanding how people relate to nature. Conservation is carried out in a societal context, but societies are not homogeneous. Different groups of people have different values and objectives that lead them to weight the economic, social, political, and ecological costs and benefits of conservation differently. The benefits of protecting species, for example, may be greater for residents near where the conservation efforts take place but may seem irrelevant to people in distant urban areas. Conversely, species protection may be viewed as an unaffordable luxury by people struggling to support themselves and their families. When costs to people are too high, saving species will not succeed, no matter what the laws may say or how strong the counter arguments.

Tradeoffs are inevitable. Balancing conservation with social, cultural, political, and economic concerns is especially difficult when species are critically imperiled or conservation reliant and their needs are unrelenting. Conflicts often result. For conservation to succeed, however, scientists, managers, decision makers, and other stakeholders must work together to cultivate a shared vision of how conservation can be integrated with societal concerns at multiple levels.

There is a burgeoning literature dealing with the social and economic context of conservation.[1] In this chapter, we use several case studies to explore how the conservation of species and places intersects with what people and organizations do, their values, and

---

[1] See, for example, Conservation Measure Partnership (2013), Groves and Game (2016), and Rahman et al. (2017).

their politics. These case studies illustrate both conflicts and collaboration—the real-world context of conservation.

## GORONGOSA NATIONAL PARK: INTEGRATING CONSERVATION WITH LOCAL COMMUNITIES

Gorongosa National Park in central Mozambique is a beacon of hope for supporting conservation-reliant species in a developing country. In the park, health concerns and economic stresses on the local communities are evident—yet multiple imperiled species are being conserved over an area of more than 4000 km². The park is a hotspot of biodiversity where conservation prospects are improving rather than declining.[2]

When it was established as a national park in 1960, Gorongosa contained a rich abundance of wildlife. There were more than 200 lions and thousands of elephants, African buffalo, blue wildebeests, Crawshay's and plains zebras, waterbuck, impala, and hippos—along with many herds of eland, sable, and hartebeest. Shortly after gaining independence in 1976, however, Mozambique became embroiled in civil war. Most of the elephants were killed during the war to feed soldiers and fund the purchase of arms and ammunition through the sale of ivory. The park was ransacked and abandoned. Hippo, African buffalo, zebra, and lion numbers were reduced by 95%, and cheetahs, leopards, hyenas, African wild dogs, and rhinos were largely extirpated from the Park (Stalmans et al. 2019).

Relative political stability returned in 1994. This, along with support of the African Development Bank, the European Union, and the IUCN, provided an opportunity to re-establish the park with enough protection from poaching to prevent additional wildlife declines. Beginning in 2004, the Government of Mozambique partnered with the US-based Carr Foundation to invest in the park and rebuild its ecological communities. Significant investments (some of which are mapped in Figure 9.1) included armed guards, translocations of large animals from elsewhere in southern Africa, a safari camp

---

[2] https://www.gorongosa.org/our-story.

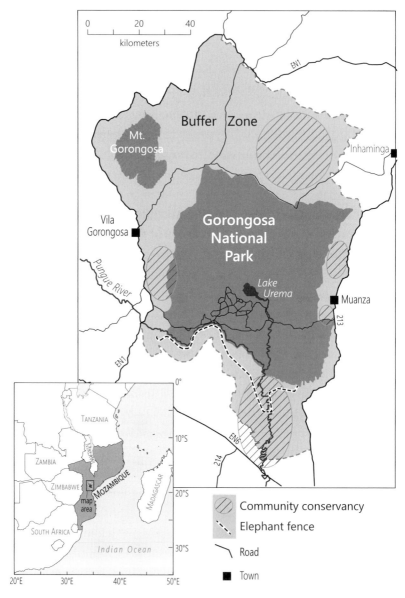

FIGURE 9.1. Gorongosa National Park, Mozambique, showing the park and the Mount Gorongosa extension, the surrounding buffer zone, proposed community conservancies, local villages, and the approximate location of fencing to keep elephants away from crops.

*Source*: Marc Stalmans, Gorongosa National Park.

for tourists, plant propagation facilities to support revegetation efforts, and a biological station[3] to support scientific research.

These efforts have been successful in part because investment in local communities has happened alongside investment into the park. The management plan for the park included social and economic objectives from the outset. A 3300-km$^2$ sustainable-development zone around the park includes 26 000 local families organized into 16 community conservancies that plan and help to implement projects to improve local economics and ecological sustainability. Community projects are supported in part by Park entrance fees. The United States Agency for International Development (USAID) and the Institute Portuguese de Apoio ao Desenvolvimento fund education. USAID and the US President's Emergency Plan for AIDS Relief support health care, including training for community health workers and traditional birth attendants, mobile medical clinics, and improved food security.

Despite such forward-looking efforts, it became apparent after several years that tourism levels would not reach the goals that were originally set. The park is too remote and does not have the right combination of major attractions, including the five most iconic African wildlife species. The recent emphasis on building scientific capacity, however, seems to be working. During much of the summer, the park is at peak capacity with a large number of scientists working there. Researchers working in the park spend money locally and are strongly encouraged to hire local community members. Some community members are trained as research technicians by local park science staff. The research has included cataloging flora and fauna in the park to reveal which species are unique to the area, which are imperiled, and which are known or unknown. Expeditions to Mount Gorongosa since 2010 have discovered several new species, including the Mount Gorongosa crab, two endemic katydids, and a gecko, *Arodedura gorongosa*. There are doubtlessly many other endemic plants

---

[3] Named in honor of E.O. Wilson and supported in part by the E.O. Wilson Biodiversity Foundation.

FIGURE 9.2. Members of a local community help to construct beehive fences for deterring elephants from crossing the Pungue River to raid crops. The river forms the southern boundary of Gorongosa National Park, Mozambique. (A black and white version of this figure will appear in some formats. For the color version, please refer to the plate section.)
Photo: Paola Branco.

and insects.[4] Annual biodiversity surveys and biannual aerial counts of game species are now part of the park's management plan..

Other research projects explicitly engage local people at the community–conservation interface. As the population of elephants in Gorongosa has continued to recover following the war, elephants have begun raiding crops in the park's buffer zone. As part of an experimental evaluation of community-based techniques for reducing crop-raiding, Rui Branco and others hired over a dozen community members to aid in data collection and maintenance of mitigation measures (e.g. beehive fences, Figure 9.2) over a 2-year period. Each

[4] www.gorongosa.org/sites/default/files/research/041-bfa_no.23_gorongosa_vegetation_survey.pdf

individual received a bicycle to facilitate access to their designated work area and was paid a full-time salary (King et al. 2017).

The progress in Gorongosa demonstrates how conserving imperiled species in places with widespread poverty benefits from strong support from local residents and decision makers, and a vision that includes economic security. External funding from multiple sources is needed for protected areas, management of species, and building infrastructure, administration, socioeconomic projects, education, and health care.

Although Gorongosa is an exciting case study, it is one point within a continent of need. There are more than 1100 other national parks and reserves across sub-Saharan Africa, of which 36 are designated World Heritage Sites. Since 1970, the total protected area of terrestrial and marine habitats in Africa has increased nearly two-fold and now encompasses more than 3 million $km^2$. Yet the conservation status of many species is often difficult to determine and can change rapidly. Protecting preserves from subsistence hunting, poaching for illegal markets, logging, burning, mining, and other illegal activities is also a challenge. Virunga National Park in the Democratic Republic of the Congo, for example, is known internationally for its population of mountain gorillas, but poaching and civil unrest threaten both gorillas and those who protect them. More than 170 rangers have been killed there over the last 20 years. Such instability threatens parks and their funding sources, especially tourism.

Like Gorongosa, most African parks require external funding, whether from their own governments, international aid, tourism, international NGOs, or dedicated donors. Since 2000, the conservation NGO African Parks has provided stability to park management by partnering with African and international governments, other NGOs, private foundations, and local communities to assume responsibility for the rehabilitation and long-term management of 14 national parks that represent diverse ecoregions.[5] Although these

[5] www.africanparks.org/our-work/community-development

efforts are substantial, they have reached less than 2% of Africa's parks and reserves. An analysis by Lindsey et al. (2018) suggests that funding for the effective conservation of lions in the national parks of Africa (as a proxy for park management in general) faces a shortfall of at least US$900 million per year. Funding sources fluctuate according to local and global economies and politics, adding to the challenge.

Tourism can be a particularly potent initial catalyst for building local support to protect wildlife and natural habitats, not just in Africa but in other developing countries as well (Leung et al. 2018).[6] Tourists are drawn to places that are beautiful, have substantial biodiversity, or support iconic animals that are easy to see (see Essay 4.1 by Dee Boersma, Essay 9.1 by Timothy Tear and Simon Nampindo and Essay 9.2 by Jianguo Liu). The Neotropics and sub-Saharan Africa are favorite destinations for ecotourism or safaris. Because these places often are in developing countries, tourism may be a significant source of revenue. In Botswana, for example, tourism generated over US$1 billion in 2016. Foreign-owned safari companies and investors dominate Botswana's tourism industry (Mbalwa 2017), but local communities benefit as well. Northern Botswana contains several national parks, game reserves, and forest reserves and numerous community concession areas, which are managed by and for the benefit of local communities. Safaris are ubiquitous in the Okavango Delta and Chobe River areas, so much so that many animals have become habituated to safari vehicles and blithely ignore them (so long as tourists remain in the vehicles) (Figure 9. 3).

Tourism is sensitive to economic changes, the stability of local governments, and the availability of infrastructure for safe and convenient travel. Like NGO funding, these things may vary from year to year, so the reliability of support for the ongoing needs of conservation-reliant species may be uncertain. Even small gaps in funding and support can cause a severe setback for an imperiled species.

---

[6] IUCN has developed guidelines for tourism and protected areas; see portals.iucn.org/library/node/47918.

FIGURE 9.3. Endangered African wild dogs ignoring tourists in a safari vehicle at Duma Tau Camp, Botswana. (A black and white version of this figure will appear in some formats. For the color version, please refer to the plate section.)
Photo: Wilderness Safaris.

ESSAY 9.1   **Conservation Reliance in Africa: Uganda and the Ishasha Lions as a Window to the Future**

*Timothy H. Tear and Simon Nampindo*

As human civilization emerges as the dominant ecological driver on the planet—a period now called the Anthropocene—a dynamic and complex context is set for all conservation efforts. In Africa, this is manifested at multiple spatial scales. At the continental scale, many global macro-economic forces are altering Africa's vast landscapes at a startling pace. Many developed nations are turning to Africa to meet their natural-resource needs, as there are still vast tracts of undeveloped land that can be exploited for everything from raw timber to rare metals or precious stones. In addition, sub-Saharan Africa remains the only large area on the planet where human population growth rates are still increasing. Although urbanization is drawing more people to cities, there is still intense pressure on the land in

ESSAY 9.1   **(cont.)**

remote rural areas where Africa's most poverty-stricken people live, sometimes in very close contact with its most iconic wildlife.

Uganda ranks second among African countries for biodiversity, including iconic savanna species, such as elephants, black rhinos, giraffes, and buffaloes, as well as forest-dwelling primates, like mountain gorillas and chimpanzees. Uganda is also home to 50% of Africa's bird species. Uganda benefits from tourism to see this wildlife living in the protected areas that sustain them, to the tune of nearly US$1.35 billion per year. However, much of the natural land cover outside protected areas has been lost over the last few decades. Between 1990 and 2005, over one-fourth of Uganda's forest cover was converted to other land uses, and forest-cover loss continues each year at four times the rate of forest cover planted. Meanwhile the human population continues to grow at a staggering rate of 3.6% per year, more than double the global average and one of the 10 highest rates on the planet. What emerges is conflict where people who live around protected areas interact with the wildlife species these areas support.

Our story of one small population of lions in Uganda illustrates some of the challenges and opportunities that society will need to balance over the next several decades. In Queen Elizabeth National Park (QENP) in southwest Uganda, a small but important group of lions have captured the attention of international tourism. They are called the tree-climbing lions of Ishasha (Figure E9.1.1). This small group of fewer than 100 lions developed the unusual behavior of living in trees and other large vegetation, providing interesting opportunities to watch them. A single lion in Uganda has been estimated to earn US$13 500 per year from photographic tourism.

The biggest threats to lions in and around QENP include incidental death from bushmeat snares and retaliatory killing for livestock losses. Each year, at least three lions die as a result of snaring and five lions die from retaliatory killing. As Uganda's human population continues to expand, many people still rely on wild bushmeat from protected areas for protein, mostly captured with wire snares and spears. The snares indiscriminately kill lions as they hunt

ESSAY 9.1   **(cont.)**

FIGURE E9.1.1. The famous tree-climbing lions of Ishasha are under threat from snaring and trade in body parts. Photo taken in the southern sector of Queen Elizabeth National Park, Uganda, during routine lion monitoring. (A black and white version of this figure will appear in some formats. For the color version, please refer to the plate section.)
Photo: Mustafa Nsubuga.

for prey. In addition, there is less and less land for grazing outside protected areas and those who own or manage livestock are increasingly turning to grazing their animals in protected areas. Local Basongora pastoralists, for whom QENP was once a historical grazing area, returned to this area in 2007 from the neighboring Democratic Republic of the Congo (DRC), claiming their ancestral grazing lands. Unfortunately, the rangelands and water sources outside the park are proving to be insufficient, leading pastoralists to illegally graze their cattle inside the park. This has resulted in both daytime lion predation in the park and nighttime predation in nearby villages (night is the time when lions rule). Lions learned that livestock are an easy meal, and communities retaliated against the lions by poisoning livestock carcasses. Additionally, a new tea factory was opened in the area, attracting more people looking for employment and livestock herders from outside the region who brought with them with ~40 000 cattle. As these pressures mounted, the Uganda

ESSAY 9.1   **(cont.)**

Wildlife Authority, which manages QENP, was forced to divert its ranger force to query illegal settlement of pastoralists inside the park, leaving the key lion conservation area in Ishasha sector that borders DRC unmanned. This combination of events led to an increase in lion killings. At one point, four lion carcasses were found to be missing heads and parts of their limbs, probably killed for traditional local medicinal purposes or for a new and growing illegal wildlife trade in lion parts as a substitute for tiger parts in the Asian market. The list of threats increases while lion numbers decrease. The conservation-reliance race is on.

The loss of lions is not just a problem of loss of tourism revenue. As top-level predators in this system, their loss would likely result in significant ecological changes, as was dramatically illustrated by the loss and subsequent reintroduction of the gray wolf to Yellowstone National Park in the United States. Recent estimates (Riggio et al. 2013; Bauer et al. 2015) suggest that lion numbers in Africa have decreased by almost half (43%) over the past two decades, and this rate is expected to continue. Understanding the plight of the Ishasha lions graphically illustrates why.

Yet we know that lions have very high reproductive rates and can bounce back quickly if protected. Several strategies to protect lions have worked for varying periods of time, including increased law enforcement, a variety of benefit-sharing programs and compensation schemes, and special efforts such as providing guards to follow lions to warn local communities of their presence or supporting the construction of lion-proof enclosures to keep livestock safe at night.

Uganda will have to balance the importance of lions for sustaining tourism revenue with the conflicts they create with local communities. Lindsey et al. (2018) estimated that 88–94% of protected areas with lions are insufficiently funded and that saving lions in Africa will require over US$1 billion of new money annually to better manage the protected areas where they persist. The cost is likely to increase if the effects of climate change are not addressed.

The case of the Ishasha lions illustrates how most African lion populations today will rely on conservation efforts to persist into the next century.

DELTA SMELT: IT'S ALL ABOUT THE WATER

The interdependence of ecological and economic security is also evident in wealthier parts of the world, although it may be expressed differently. The delta smelt is a small (5–7 cm), minnow-like fish that is endemic to the California Delta, where the Sacramento and San Joaquin rivers meet before emptying into San Francisco Bay. The smelt is now on the brink of extinction. The threats to its survival are ultimately about one thing: water—and the political, socio-economic, legal, and ecological conflicts over who gets it.[7]

---

ESSAY 9.2   **Pandas and People in China**

*Jianguo "Jack" Liu*

The giant panda is China's national treasure and a global conservation icon. It has received exceptional support from the Chinese government and international organizations in the past half-century. Since the first nature reserve for panda conservation was established in the early 1960s, the number of panda reserves has increased to 67, covering more than half of current panda habitat and including about two-thirds of wild pandas. Thanks to these reserves and several other conservation programs, panda habitat has been recovering since 2001. The government's surveys document that panda numbers in the wild increased from 1596 to 1864 during 2003–2013.[7] A successful captive-breeding program has produced several hundred pandas and has provided pandas to several dozen zoos in China and a number of foreign countries. Several pandas have been reintroduced from captivity into the wild. In 2016, IUCN moved the panda from Endangered to Threatened status.[8]

---

[7] State Council Information Office of China. 2015. www.scio.gov.cn/xwfbh/gbwxwfbh/fbh/Document/1395514/1395514.htm [in Chinese].

[8] International Union for the Conservation of Nature. 2016. *Ailuropoda melanoleuca* (Giant Panda). www.iucnredlist.org/details/712/0

ESSAY 9.2   **(cont.)**

However, changing the panda's status does not mean that they no longer need conservation. There are still many threats to panda survival, including climate change, human activities, and diseases. Some old threats have been reduced, but new threats have emerged. For instance, although fuelwood collection and timber harvesting have declined substantially, livestock grazing has increased. Illegal poaching has diminished, but climate change is becoming a potential threat that could cause a drastic reduction in bamboo—the staple food for the panda.

To ensure long-term panda sustainability, we must view panda conservation not just as a local problem or a China problem, but one that truly is connected to the entire world—one with solutions embedded in both nature and people. The framework of metacoupled (intertwined) human and natural systems offers a systematic tool to address these complex interconnections because it integrates human–nature interactions within a focal area such as a nature reserve or panda distribution range; between the focal area and adjacent areas; and between the focal area and distant areas (Liu 2017).

Unlike nature reserves in the United States, some panda reserves are home to local residents whose activities affect panda habitat and populations. Most people in the panda's range believe killing a panda will bring misfortune (not to mention jail time), so killing pandas is rare. However, for lack of affordable alternatives, some local people still need to cut down forests in panda habitat for fuelwood and timber. For example, in Wolong Nature Reserve of southwestern China, where my colleagues and I have been doing research since 1996, there are more than 5000 local residents (Liu et al. 2016). The vast majority of them are farmers. Besides farming, they also collect fuelwood, harvest timber, rear livestock, and collect herbal medicines. In 2001, we reported in *Science* that panda habitat in Wolong was destroyed faster after the reserve was established in 1975 than before (Liu et al. 2001). At first, the government, World Wildlife Fund, and some researchers did not believe our results. Although substantial investments were made in this "flagship" reserve for panda conservation, there were

ESSAY 9.2   **(cont.)**

hidden increases in resource consumption because both the human population and the number of households kept rising. After the government realized that the panda habitat had indeed experienced accelerated loss, several actions were taken. One of our co-authors of the *Science* paper was promoted to director of the reserve. A new "eco-hydropower plant" was built to provide electricity for local residents to minimize the use of fuelwood. A natural-forest conservation program provides local residents with money to monitor and prevent illegal logging and a grain-to-green program encourages farmers to convert their cropland to forests by giving farmers incentives, including grains and cash. Since then, the reserve has been transformed from decades of habitat loss to recovery.

As for most nature reserves elsewhere, residents live next to Wolong. Many cross the boundary to collect fuelwood and other resources. Wild pandas may also travel beyond the reserve boundaries, as there are no fences to prevent their movement. Furthermore, nature reserves are under human influences from distant places: tourism, trade, species invasion, and investments in infrastructure construction and conservation. In the early 1980s, tourism began in Wolong; it now attracts visitors from around the world (Figure E9.2.1). Tourism has many socioeconomic and environmental effects, such as generating income for local households, stimulating construction of tourism facilities, and adding to the disturbance of panda habitat. Farmers in Wolong also sell cash crops to people in cities. Income from tourism and agriculture, as well as conservation subsidies from the central government and international organizations, help farmers afford more electricity and minimize the collection of fuelwood in panda habitat.

Human–nature interactions within, near, and far away from the panda's distribution range shape the future of the panda and its reliance on conservation. The solutions can be found in effective policies guided by interdisciplinary science. Government policies are crucial, as they influence culture and human behaviors, which in turn affect panda habitat and populations. Changes in panda habitat and populations prompt the government to develop new policies, which further affect

ESSAY 9.2   **(cont.)**

FIGURE E9.2.1. The Wolong Nature Reserve breeding center was a
crowd pleaser for those eager to see giant pandas. The 2008 Wenchuan
earthquake damaged this center, which is now a site to train pandas to
be reintroduced into the wild. A new breeding center nearby allows
tourists a chance to see the pandas. (A black and white version of this
figure will appear in some formats. For the color version, please refer to
the plate section.)
Photo: Wei Liu, Michigan State University Center for Systems Integration and
Sustainability.

people's attitudes and social norms. Complex feedback loops like these
demonstrate the need for long-term and proactive solutions to reduce
conservation reliance. For example, road construction has been a major
contributor to panda habitat fragmentation; more underground tunnels
are needed in and near panda habitat to prevent habitat fragmentation and
disturbances. Continued urbanization and improved school education
can enable more young people living in the panda's range to seek jobs and
move to cities, reducing direct impacts on panda habitat and populations.
To address the effects of climate change, creating nature reserves in areas
where no pandas currently live but that will become suitable in the future
may offer a safer and cheaper haven for pandas.

ESSAY 9.2   **(cont.)**

The two-pronged truth is stark: wild pandas cannot thrive nor will captive-bred pandas survive in the wild unless suitable habitat is available to them, and panda habitat is not sustainable unless the people who live there can also thrive. Even if all local and national issues are addressed, global collective actions are required to mitigate climate change for pandas and people now and into the future.

The California Delta of today is nothing like the delta in which the smelt evolved and thrived. At the time of the California gold rush in the mid-nineteenth century, the California Delta was a vast wetland, laced with waterways that meandered through freshwater and tidal marshes. Over the years, the inflowing rivers and tidal sloughs were channelized, levees were built to control floods, and marshes were drained and converted to agricultural fields. Today, the Central Valley and State Water projects pump water out of the delta and shunt it through a network of aqueducts to the urban centers of southern California and the San Francisco Bay area and to the agricultural fields of the San Joaquin Valley. There is substantial variation in water inflows to the delta from the Sacramento and San Joaquin rivers and in water exports by the pumps (Mount et al. 2018). In some years, the pumps are powerful enough to pull water flow from the delta upstream toward the pumps instead of downstream to the bay. Additionally, there is substantial variation in the seasonal releases of fresh water that are required to keep intrusion of tidal saltwater at bay, maintaining brackish conditions in the low-salinity zone preferred by the smelt and ensuring the quality of fresh water for within-delta agricultural use and export.

Freshwater releases are also critical for the delta smelt. From spring through autumn, smelt occupy the low-salinity, open-water areas where tidal and fresh waters mix. In the winter, the smelt move upstream into fresh water to spawn. Other traits make the smelt vulnerable to changing conditions, including a sensitivity to warm

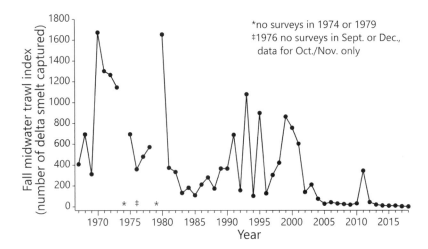

FIGURE 9.4. Index of Threatened delta smelt abundance in fall midwater trawl surveys in the Sacramento–San Joaquin Delta of California, 1967–2018.
Data courtesy Peter Moyle.

water temperatures (>22°C), a life span of only 1 year, and low fecundity. The invasion of an Asian clam that devours the plankton on which smelt feed and a regime shift in salinity and water clarity that favors non-native fish (Moyle and Bennett 2008) have magnified the smelt's vulnerability to altered hydrology.

The delta smelt was listed as Threatened under the Endangered Species Act in 1993. Protection under the act prompted restrictions on water exports to ensure that there was enough for the fish. The act, after all, confers priority to endangered species over human economic interests (this was at the core of the snail darter decision discussed in Chapter 6). After much legal wrangling, court rulings affirmed that sufficient water must be allocated for the smelt. The wheels of law turn slowly, however, and in the interim the status of the smelt only worsened (Figure 9.4).

The problem is that there simply is not enough water to go around. Rising sea levels are pushing saltwater from San Francisco Bay farther into the delta. Because more water then has to be released from the dams into the delta to prevent saltwater intrusion, less is available for export by the pumps. But there are 25 million people in southern California who depend on water from the delta. Irrigated farms in the Central Valley produce more than half of the fruits, vegetables, and nuts grown in the United States. Many of these farms have been in the same families for generations, so the attachment to the delta and its water runs deep. Droughts exacerbate the challenges by reducing freshwater inflow to the delta but increasing the demand on water exports for people and agriculture.

The most recent severe drought in California (2011–2016) threatened the livelihoods of farmers and their communities—indeed, their way of life. As water became scarce, public outrage grew. Some people turned their anger on the smelt and the laws and court decisions that protected it, saying that restrictions on water use had not resulted in recovery of the fish so the water should be given to the farmers where it would do some good. Politicians blamed a "stupid little fish" or a "worthless little worm that needs to go the way of the dinosaurs." When the drought broke during the winter of 2016, people complained that the bounty of water was being "wasted" and allowed to run out to sea unused rather than captured and stored (Cloern et al. 2017; Mount et al. 2018). The federal government has recently proposed loosening the restrictions of the Endangered Species Act to allow more water to be diverted from the delta for agricultural uses. The water wars described by Marc Reisner in *Cadillac Desert* (1993) are not over.

All of this ignores a basic reality. The releases of fresh water are primarily driven by the need to maintain water quality for human uses. During the 2011–2016 drought, the delta smelt accounted for perhaps 1% of the restrictions on pumping exports (Moyle et al. 2018). The smelt figures so prominently in the management of the delta, however, because it is a symbol of the overall decline in the condition of the delta as an estuarine ecosystem. This decline is felt by people and by many other imperiled native fishes: winter-run Chinook salmon, longfin smelt, and green sturgeon are also utterly dependent on delta water and its management. There is much more than science involved here. As Alagona (2013: 222) observed, the story of the smelt "is not a tale of animal versus people but rather a case of people versus people, with some unsuspecting species stuck in the middle." A solution currently seems out of reach—unless extinction of the smelt is regarded as one.

## WOLVES, GRIZZLIES, AND PEOPLE

Delta smelt create conflicts with people because they need what we want—water. The conflicts with wolves and grizzly bears in North America are more direct—they prey on livestock and are dangerous to people, generating anger and fear.

Three wolf taxa occur in North America: the red wolf, the gray wolf, and the Mexican gray wolf (a subspecies of gray wolf) (NAS 2019). The red wolf was once common throughout the southeastern United States, but by the 1960s only a remnant population remained along the Gulf coast of Texas and Louisiana. Red wolves were extinct in the wild by 1980, but a breeding program had been founded with 14 captive wolves. The program was successful—as of 2018, there were 3 breeding pairs and 44 individuals in the wilds of northeastern North Carolina and about 200 in the captive-breeding program. Because of conflicts with sportsmen and state agencies over hunting regulations and concerns about wolf predation on domestic animals, there have been proposals to restrict red wolves only to federal property. A 2018 status review notes that "[F]undamental change is needed in the way stakeholders are engaged in management of wild-ranging red wolf populations."[9] The wild population is threatened by sea-level rise, suburban development, and interbreeding with coyotes. The red wolf is currently listed as Endangered under the Endangered Species Act and Critically Endangered by IUCN.

The Mexican gray wolf once ranged widely from central Mexico through the southwestern United States. It was eradicated from the United States and most of Mexico by the mid-1900s and was listed as Endangered under the Endangered Species Act in 1976. The first individuals were released from a captive-breeding program in Arizona in 1998. By 2017, 114 Mexican gray wolves were living in the wild in Arizona and New Mexico. Inbreeding is a persistent concern.

---

[9] ecos.fws.gov/docs/five_year_review/doc5714.pdf

By far the greatest attention is focused on the several other subspecies of gray wolf that occur in North America. Thousands of wolves were shot during the nineteenth and twentieth centuries to protect domestic animals and the bison, elk, moose, and deer people hunted. Government control programs offered bounties for wolf pelts until 1965. The gray wolf was exterminated from all of the United States except Alaska and northern Minnesota by 1960. In 1974, the gray wolf was listed as Endangered in the contiguous 48 United States and in Mexico.[10] In 1995 and 1996, wolves from Canada were reintroduced into Yellowstone National Park and onto US Forest Service lands in central Idaho. In 2003, populations of most gray wolves were downlisted to Threatened status.

As wolf populations began to recover, depredations on domestic livestock became more frequent. In response, in 2005 the federal government authorized livestock owners in Montana and Idaho to kill wolves without a permit if the wolves were chasing livestock. It also gave states authorization to kill wolves if they were the primary reason for decline of deer or elk populations. There followed a period of court challenges by western states seeking an end to protections and by conservation NGOs seeking to reinstate full protections. Different populations of gray wolves were listed, downlisted, delisted, and then listed again—sometimes in a matter of months.[11] Through all of this legal jockeying, wolf populations continued to increase; by 2018 there were over 4000 wolves in the Western Great Lakes region.

---

[10] Healthy populations persist in Canada and Alaska, where many feed on caribou.

[11] The effect was dizzying, nothing like the linear process we describe in Chapter 6 for the island night lizard. In 2008, the Northern Rockies wolves were delisted, but they were relisted 4 months later just before the opening of hunting seasons. In 2009, they were again delisted. In 2010, protections were reinstated for Idaho and Montana wolves. In 2011, a rider on a budget bill removed protections of the Endangered Species Act for wolves in Montana, Idaho, Washington, Oregon, and Utah and banned legal challenges to the delisting. The Obama administration then removed Endangered Species Act protections for wolves in the Great Lakes region as well. Wolves in Wyoming remained protected because state management plans were inadequate and wolf populations were lower than those in Idaho or Montana, but in 2013 the protections were removed. In 2015, protections were reinstated for Wyoming and Great Lakes wolves, but these were removed for the gray wolf in Wyoming in 2017.

Wolves have also expanded from Montana and Idaho into southeastern Washington and eastern and central Oregon.

Managing wolves means managing their interactions with people. As wolves have re-established themselves in the western United States, ranchers are once again losing livestock to wolf packs. Hunters blame them for declines in elk and mule deer. Across Montana, Idaho, and Wyoming, hundreds of wolves are killed annually to protect herds. In Oregon and Washington, wolf populations are much smaller, but a fragile truce between wildlife managers and ranchers is constantly tested. Various arrangements have been made to compensate ranchers for documented wolf kills or unusually high losses of calves, although compensation requires ranchers to provide evidence that they have undertaken deterrence measures to protect their herds.

There is little doubt that as wolf populations increase there will be more conflicts with people. More wolves will have to be removed to protect livestock or grazing on public land will have to be restricted. In Washington state, a Wolf Advisory Group has brought together a wide range of stakeholders to influence policies for wolf management.[12] Continued success in managing free-ranging wolves depends on wolf managers, NGOs, politicians, and the public paying attention to the voices, cultures, and livelihoods of local residents. But managing wolves across land ownerships is difficult; young wolves leave their natal pack at 1 or 2 years of age in search of mates and may cover large distances (as did the wolf OR-7, as we describe in Chapter 7). Given the difficulties of coexisting with humans, free-ranging gray wolves are likely to require intensive management (including the selective removal of problem wolves or packs) even after management responsibilities are transferred to the states.

Gray wolves and grizzly bears differ in their interactions with humans in two important ways. First, grizzly bears are more likely to avoid human activity and infrastructure, such as roads and highways, which makes it difficult to maintain habitat connectivity. Second,

---

[12]  wdfw.wa.gov/about/advisory/wag/

bears are omnivores that may seek stored human food or garbage, leading to encounters around human habitations and recreation sites. Grizzly bears also prey upon domestic animals and consequently run afoul of ranching communities.

There were perhaps 50 000 bears in the contiguous United States in the early 1800s; by 2018, the remaining population was estimated at 1200–1400.[13] In 1975, the US Fish and Wildlife Service listed the grizzly bear as Threatened. Grizzly bears are more solitary than wolves and have fewer offspring, so their potential for recovery is lower; of the 37 grizzly populations that existed in 1922, only 6 remained in 2018. One of these, the Greater Yellowstone population, had recovered from 136 bears in 1975 to 700 bears when the population was delisted in 2017. This decision lasted only a year. In September 2018, a court directed that the bear be relisted. This brought an abrupt halt to regulated hunts planned for later that fall but it also prompted legislation to be introduced that would delist the grizzly bear and prohibit further judicial reviews.

Grizzly bear management includes compensating ranchers for missing calves, working with ranchers to avoid depredation, helping recreationists and rural residents manage garbage and stored food-stuffs, and transporting or killing bears when they become a problem. In some cases, individuals may need to be moved among populations to maintain genetic diversity.

The emphasis in management of both gray wolves and grizzly bears is shifting from recovery to control. Because both species range over wide areas, conflicts with people are likely. The Blackfoot Challenge[14] is one example of what can be accomplished when people in rural communities seek to share the land with predators. Efforts to create "coexistence landscapes" in which people and their livestock can coexist with predators are gaining force (Oriol-Cotterill et al.

---

[13] In 2018, there were estimated to be 30 000 brown or grizzly bears in Alaska and 25 000 in Canada.

[14] www.blackfootchallenge.org

2015). The experience of Europeans in living with bears may also offer some lessons to North Americans (Linnell et al. 2001).

## THE ROLE OF THE MILITARY

The US Fish and Wildlife Service and NOAA Fisheries have the primary responsibility for implementing and enforcing the Endangered Species Act, but other government agencies also play an active role in conservation, especially on the lands and waters they manage (Stein et al. 2008). One does not usually think of the mission of the US Department of Defense as having much to do with conservation of imperiled species, but the density of at-risk species on its lands is actually greater than that of any other US federal agency, even the US Fish and Wildlife Service and its National Wildlife Refuge System.

Most military installations adjust their training activities to avoid disturbing endangered species and some make additional investments in management and monitoring. On US Marine Corps Base Camp Lejeune in North Carolina, for example, foraging habitat used by family groups of Endangered red-cockaded woodpeckers is managed by prescribed burning to clear mid-story vegetation. Military activities are scheduled to avoid nesting areas at critical times. Eglin Air Force Base in Florida undertakes similar management and has also supported research and incorporated the findings into practice. At Fort Hood in Texas, fire is used to create suitable habitat for black-capped vireos. The US Department of Defense, US Fish and Wildlife Service, and state wildlife agencies in Alabama, Florida, Georgia, and South Carolina have adopted a collaborative conservation plan to protect at-risk gopher tortoises while maintaining training on military bases.

These military efforts are driven in part by the requirement to follow the dictates of the Endangered Species Act. But they are also an expression of the military tradition of responding to a mission challenge. Military teams and installations compete for the Secretary of Defense Environmental Awards, which recognize outstanding efforts to conserve natural resources. Because of the demanding nature of the primary military mission and turnover of base personnel, however, long-term planning for conservation-reliant species can be difficult. Several installations have formed partnerships with citizen groups or NGOs to provide continued monitoring of the species and their responses to management practices. In collaboration with Nature-Serve, the Department of Defense has prepared a handbook to guide biodiversity conservation efforts on military lands (Benton et al. 2008).

## SAGE GROUSE: POLITICAL CONTEXT CAN CHANGE, BUT CONSERVATION RELIANCE DOES NOT

Collaboration is also the key to efforts to conserve the greater sage grouse in the western United States, but the story illustrates how politics can intercede. After all, the needs of conservation are unrelenting but political systems and priorities change over time. Unfortunately, conservation measures are often easy prey for politicians anxious to cut programs or please their most vocal constituents. Although legislation may dictate what should be done to protect and restore imperiled species, politics plays a large role in determining whether funds will be available to implement the actions called for by the laws. In addition, politicians can take away what they once gave by altering or suspending regulations or passing new laws (as in the case of gray wolf protection). This is what happened in the United States with the Northwest Forest Plan (Chapter 4) and the conflict over the snail darter and the Tellico Dam (Chapter 6). It is also central to the saga of the greater sage grouse.

The sage grouse (Figure 9.5) is a large, strikingly plumaged bird with spectacular courtship displays. Historically, the sagebrush-dominated expanses of the western United States where the sage grouse lives have been considered of low value for agriculture and grazing and have largely been left under government management. However, the recent development of oil and gas leases and other types of land conversion (particularly to irrigated crops such as alfalfa) have changed economic values and led to widespread habitat loss. Sage grouse numbers are declining rapidly. As numbers have dwindled,

FIGURE 9.5. Greater sage grouse on a Colorado lek during the springtime mating season. (A black and white version of this figure will appear in some formats. For the color version, please refer to the plate section.)
Credit: milehightraveler/iStock/Getty Images Plus.

calls to list the species under the Endangered Species Act have intensified.

To forestall listing of the species (and avoid the restrictions on land use that would come with it), several state governments worked with a diverse array of stakeholders—Native American tribes, NGOs, ranchers, other agriculturalists, oil and gas developers, scientists, community leaders, and the federal government—to develop a comprehensive agreement and conservation plan. The agreement was finalized in 2015 after more than a decade of highly collaborative efforts. It offered some uniformity of regulations across state boundaries and prevented development on the most critical habitat areas, while allowing a variety of land uses to continue in other areas. It was an agreement that most parties felt they could live with. In 2018, however, the Trump administration proposed replacing the agreement with management plans friendlier to industry and passing decision making for protection of the sage grouse and the sagebrush ecosystem it occupies back to the states.

This abrupt loss of agreed-upon protections has resulted in disappointment among multiple stakeholders and a loss of trust that will make it much more difficult to negotiate future collaborative agreements. It illustrates the fragility of such agreements in the face of powerful special interests and the importance of trust in gaining local support for conservation (Bennett et al. 2019).

## PACIFIC NORTHWEST SALMON AND INDIGENOUS RIGHTS

Indigenous tribes have an increasingly important role in the politics of long-term conservation. In Canada, for instance, indigenous people—particularly the Indigenous Circle of Experts—provide advice and recommendations for achieving Canada's goals for protected areas under the 2010 Convention on Biological Diversity.[15] Canada's indigenous people, like those in many areas, have not been treated well by history, so trust is in short supply. To help build trust and mutual respect, the process creates an "ethical space" in which indigenous and non-indigenous peoples can gather as equals to share different systems of knowledge and collaborate to provide advice on conservation goals.

In some instances, tribes have longstanding treaties that include rights to hunt or fish for species that are now imperiled. Salmon have long been at the core of tribal and individual spiritual and cultural identity for the Nez Perce and other tribes of the Columbia River basin (see Joseph Oatman's Essay 3.1). Salmon are used in religious services. The time when the first salmon of the season return each year is a time of renewed hope and harvest ceremonies. The annual

---

[15] We Rise Together. Achieving Pathway to Canada Target 1 through the creation of Indigenous Protected and Conserved Areas in the spirit of practice and reconciliation, March 2018. Available at: static1.squarespace.com/static/ 57e007452e69cf9a7af0a033/t/5ab94aca6d2a7338ecb1d05e/1522092766605/PA234- ICE_Report_2018_Mar_22_web.pdf

First Salmon Ceremony brings together tribal nations, federal and state agencies, and NGOs from throughout the Columbia River basin and provides an opportunity for families to return to their traditional fishing grounds.

The long-term sustainability of natural and cultural resources is integral to indigenous interests. Demands that longstanding treaty rights be respected may give rise to conflicts over the long-term needs of imperiled species. For instance, tribal rights as well as endangered species law support restoring or maintaining runs of several endangered stocks of Chinook salmon in rivers of the Pacific Northwest, but this can conflict with energy generation through hydroelectric dams or with commercial and recreational fishing interests. Resolving such conflicts is expensive. In fiscal year 2016, federal and state agencies spent nearly US$180 million on four evolutionarily significant units of Chinook salmon in the Columbia and Snake river basins. This was 12.2% of the total government expenditures on all endangered species in the United States that year.[16] Some people see the expenditures as justified. But when water is released from a dam to create favorable water conditions for salmon passage or to improve water conditions downstream, farmers, ranchers, and municipalities that use river water complain about water being lost rather than used productively.

Traditional practices and treaty rights lie at the heart of such debates. For example, in 2018, the US Supreme Court heard a case brought by 21 tribes against the state of Washington to fix culverts that block salmon access to spawning streams. In 1855, tribes had sold their land to the government in exchange for the right to fish at their usual places; the question is now whether the right to fish refers to the right to put a net in the water or the right for there to be fish to catch. Because of a tie vote, the lower court decision in favor of the tribes stands. The issue of what fishing rights really mean, however, remains unresolved.

[16] www.fws.gov/Endangered/esa-library/pdf/2016_Expenditures_Report.pdf

## KIRTLAND'S WARBLER: A MODEL FOR COLLABORATION WITH NGOS

State and federal government agencies have the legal responsibility for managing imperiled species, but they cannot do it alone. NGOs actively promote conservation interests, especially by identifying populations of at-risk species and preserving and managing their habitats. Although they cannot control and regulate the use of wildlife as governments do, NGOs mobilize public support for conservation of species and protected areas. Because they depend on the support of their members and donors they must navigate multiple perspectives about what should be conserved, and where. Scientists may help to determine priorities for actions and funding, but often a single donor may exert a strong influence by donating land for a preserve or because the donor wants to earmark a substantial gift for a particular species. To attract donors, NGOs often promote the conservation of species that are large, attractive, need emergency assistance, or are likely to respond to conservation actions. Because NGOs need to show near-term results to justify their budgets or risk losing support, it may be difficult to make a long-term commitment to a conservation-reliant species.

The story of the Kirtland's warbler illustrates one way to deal with this difficulty by involving multiple agencies, NGOs, and citizens to ensure long-term management. Kirtland's warblers are migratory songbirds that breed in a small area of young jack pine habitat, primarily in northern Michigan. They winter (sensibly) in the Bahamas. Historically, periodic fires created a patchwork of young jack pine stands across the landscape, but as wildfire suppression gained force in the 1900s, warbler habitat disappeared. Nest parasitism by brown-headed cowbirds added another threat to the mix and warbler populations crashed (Rapai 2013). Fewer than 500 singing males were estimated to exist when the species was listed as Endangered under the precursor of the Endangered Species Act in 1967; 4 years later there were only 201. A program was launched to trap large numbers of cowbirds, dramatically lowering the rate of nest parasitism. Yet,

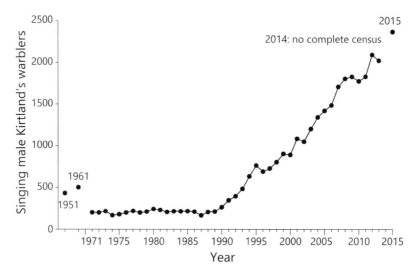

FIGURE 9.6. Kirtland's warbler population trends, 1951–2015. The species was listed as Endangered under the Endangered Species Act in 1973. Numbers increased in response to habitat management and removal of brown-headed cowbirds, and the species was delisted in 2019.
Data from US Fish and Wildlife Service.

warbler numbers continued to decline. Only 167 singing males were found in 1987 (Figure 9.6).

Then, in the 1980s, prescribed burning, timber cutting, and several large wildfires increased available habitat. By 2001, there were over 1000 singing males and recovery goals were exceeded. In 2007, Kirtland's warblers were found nesting in Wisconsin and Ontario for the first time. People began to talk about removing the species from the endangered species list.

Funding under the Endangered Species Program will go away if the species is delisted, however, even though the Kirtland's warbler still relies on timber clearcuts, replanting jack pine seedlings, and cowbird control for survival.[17] (The use of prescribed burns is limited

---

[17] Cowbird control may not be as necessary as it once was. During 2015–2017, managers reduced cowbird trapping by 20–30% and found just three cases of parasitism. In 2018, no cowbird trapping occurred in the Lower Peninsula of

because of public resistance.) To ensure the warbler's future, NGOs and citizen groups (including the National Fish and Wildlife Foundation and the Kirtland's Warbler Alliance) have stepped in to identify and coordinate partners, conduct public education and outreach, and build an endowment to provide funding for the continued management of the warbler. State and federal government agencies, including the US Fish and Wildlife Service and Michigan Department of Natural Resources, have agreed to continue conservation management regardless of the species' future legal status. In 2016, the Kirtland's Warbler Conservation Team was formed to ensure continuing input of science into management. The conservation efforts for the Kirtland's warbler continue to draw new partners into the Alliance, including the American Bird Conservancy, Bahamas National Trust, Cornell Lab of Ornithology, and several state NGOs in Wisconsin and Michigan. The focus has shifted from recovery to continuing conservation, emphasizing adaptive management (Cooper et al. 2019). In November 2019, Kirtland's warbler was delisted.[18]

The recovery of the warbler shows what is possible when the threats to a species are manageable, governmental agencies at multiple levels partner to achieve shared conservation goals, steps are taken to ensure that the necessary conservation actions will continue, and citizen groups educate the public and generate support. All of these measures make it possible to relax legal protections for a species while addressing its conservation reliance through a Conservation Management Agreement (CMA) (Bocetti et al. 2012). CMAs provide a way to transfer management responsibility for a conservation-reliant species from government agencies to other entities (see Chapter 6). Such agreements also foster collaboration and communication among diverse stakeholder groups, facilitating the integration of societal and conservation concerns and mobilizing public support.

Michigan for the first time since 1972; 4 of 514 nests monitored in 2015–2018 (<1%) were parasitized. Cowbird populations, and thus the incidence of nest parasitism, seem to be decreasing locally and nationally.

[18] US Fish and Wildlife Service 2019 Federal Register 84, 54436–24463.

There may be drawbacks to CMAs, however. Critics argue that CMAs can facilitate the erosion of protections for endangered species by allowing species to be delisted based on uncertain and tenuous long-term management commitments (Rohlf et al. 2014b). For Kirtland's warbler and for many other conservation-reliant species, however, species-specific management agreements, funding endowments, and shared responsibilities, along with education and outreach, may allow the conservation net to be widened to include people who might not otherwise be involved in conservation.

All this collaboration around the warbler's breeding grounds could be for naught if conditions are unsuitable on the wintering grounds in the Bahamas, where the warblers face different threats. The frequent hurricanes that occur in the Caribbean may pose an immediate threat, but hurricane disturbance can also create new habitat over the long term. Feral cats are a growing threat. The US Forest Service, the Institute of Tropical Forestry, and the Bahamas National Trust are collaborating with the Bahamian government to establish better warbler conservation practices on the islands, including feral cat control.

Unfortunately, what has worked for the Kirtland's warbler (and for the black-capped vireo we discussed in Chapter 2) probably will not work for the majority of imperiled and conservation-reliant species. The warbler and vireo are showy birds with appealing songs, making it relatively easy to garner public support. For most imperiled species that don't attract so much attention, such conservation actions or CMAs may be more difficult to achieve, especially when they require a long-term commitment.

## WHO CAN TAKE ON CONSERVATION RELIANCE? WILL THEY?

In this chapter, we have only touched on some of the many issues involved in the complex and evolving interplay between conservation and people. What insights can we glean from these stories? There are several. Broad-based, financially supported programs that involve multiple parties in discussions and decisions, as at Gorongosa, are a start. But where the factors that threaten a species are closely intertwined with economic and social forces, conflicts are likely to develop. Such conflicts can place an additional burden on releasing a species from conservation reliance, as they must be addressed in addition to the biological challenges, which are already formidable. Resistance to conservation of imperiled species and the laws that protect them deepens when a way of life is threatened and no alternatives seem available. Distrust among those involved can harden the resistance. Some conflicts may be difficult to resolve, even with transparency and trust. Is there an acceptable balance between the needs of native fish and those of farmers or urban dwellers for the California Delta's limited water? What formula will foster coexistence of wolves and ranchers as wolf populations grow and expand and external economic forces and shifting political winds threaten rural ways of life? Will lions and other wide-ranging predators require efforts similar to intensive wolf and grizzly bear management as African countries develop? Are they already there?

The stories in this chapter illustrate problems and solutions found on every continent. Protected areas, for example, require the support of neighboring communities, not just initially but through time. As long as protected areas prevent some human uses, fish need water, and predators impinge on places where livestock graze, imperiled species will come up against human interests.

Consequently, conservation must involve people. People support, legislate, and legally defend conservation laws; government or tribal staff decide upon specific conservation actions or monitoring; landowners care for the lands or waters where the actions take place; and people implement the actions and, ultimately, pay the bills. Some people value nature for what it provides, whereas others value it for its own sake. Conservation takes a collaborative community of people willing to share their opinions but also listen to those of others.

Because people have different objectives, conservation will entail tradeoffs that consider social, economic, and political factors and multiple sources of knowledge. Science alone is not sufficient. These tradeoffs affect how we prioritize conservation efforts, which we consider in the following chapter.

**Making Tough Decisions: Prioritizing Species for Conservation**

Saving the California condor is a conservation priority. Millions of dollars have been spent on captive breeding and taking care of the birds living in the wild. Scientists and government agencies have probed every aspect of the species' biology. Citizens and conservation NGOs have mounted major efforts to raise awareness and money. The efforts have indeed prevented the condor's extinction (as we describe in Chapter 1). But why did the California condor become a conservation priority and why does it remain so?

There are several reasons. The condor was perilously close to becoming extinct and it was imperative to do something quickly. As the condor's plight became better known, the species captured the public's imagination and it became an icon of the conservation movement—and the subject of intense debate. Condors have no discernible economic value, but they are large, spectacular in flight, and long-lived; a soaring California condor with its 3 m wingspan is at once graceful and awe-inspiring. Additionally, the condor lives in an environmentally progressive state with a powerful Congressional delegation.[1] As more money has been invested in condor conservation (leading to greater management intervention and increasing the species' conservation reliance) more money has followed—an expression of the Concorde Fallacy.[2] The condor became a conservation priority not because of an objective analysis,

---

[1] California was the home state of President Nixon, who encouraged and signed the Endangered Species Act under which the condor received full protection and agency attention.

[2] Or, more properly, the "sunk cost fallacy": the tendency to keep investing in something because so much has already been invested in it, rather than evaluating expected future benefits (Curio 1987). To many, forestalling the condor's extinction was benefit enough.

but largely because, as Small (2012: 41) put it, "tugging at the heart-strings loosens the purse strings."

The condor story is not unique. In countries that have laws and funding directed toward rescuing imperiled species, the process of determining which species to rescue often depends on influences that are seldom acknowledged. How NGOs choose which species to invest in is similarly opaque. Managers may prioritize species for which success is likely to be quick and can be achieved using existing tools. Species whose habitat requirements conflict with energy development, irrigation, or other economic activities may be passed over as too difficult—or they may receive excessive attention in the hope that a balanced solution can be found. These and other influences on conservation decisions are not necessarily wrong, but they are rarely stated explicitly.

Conservation reliance heightens the need to prioritize the investment of time, effort, and money in conservation. To do so in a way that is scientifically sound requires information and analysis. But the decisions involve much more than science. As the previous chapter illustrated, prioritizing efforts must also acknowledge what people want conservation to do. Decisions must be based on a transparent process that engages multiple stakeholders, viewpoints, and values from the outset.

## WHY PRIORITIZE?

Why is prioritization even necessary? Don't endangered species laws mandate the prevention of extinction for all imperiled species?

Unfortunately, the reality is there are too many species needing help and not enough money or people to do everything. "Save all species" is not a realistic goal when conservation of even the most deserving species is woefully underfunded. As Keith Schreiner, first administrator of the Endangered Species Act in the US Fish and Wildlife Service, lamented in 1975, "[W]e can only do so much, and I have to set priorities. Many people do not agree with my priorities but if we shift money into one area we have to take away from another."[3] This has not changed.

People's support for the conservation of so many species and ecosystems will likely falter in the face of escalating demands. Climate change, destabilized economies, armed conflicts, human population growth and migrations, and a host of other forces all compete for resources. If many at-risk species are also conservation reliant, then managing those species will stretch resources ever thinner. The patience of those who expect an end to conservation reliance of these species will be sorely tested.

So, decisions must be made about what to do and what not to do. But even among conservationists there are different perceptions about what is important, which leads to different goals and objectives. Should priorities be based on species vulnerability; biological uniqueness; responsiveness to management; or some measure of ecological, social, or economic value? There is no single "best" way to prioritize among species; rather, each approach must be evaluated by how well it addresses particular goals and objectives for a particular time and place and suite of species. Nonetheless, there are some common elements to the prioritization process. So let's begin there.

### SETTING BOUNDARIES: WHAT SPECIES AND WHAT GOALS?

Conservation prioritization is about making decisions—which species or habitats to manage, which actions to take, over what time period, and so on—so that more species can be conserved more effectively with the resources that are available. The process is intended to be informed and transparent, explicitly recognizing assumptions, values, preferences, tradeoffs, and consequences. Some of the earliest applications of conservation prioritization were in the selection of nature reserves and protected areas (e.g. Margules et al. 1988; Pressey and Nicholls 1989). Prioritization has since been applied to targeting river

---

[3] *New York Times*, December 30, 1975.

catchments to enhance fish diversity (Grantham et al. 2016), land-scapes for conservation restoration (Rappaport et al. 2015), islands for eradication of invasives (Dawson et al. 2015), or other places for conservation investments (e.g. Dinerstein and Wikramanayake 1993; Kiester et al. 1996). Hotspots (Chapter 8) prioritize locations based on biodiversity and habitat loss.

Because our emphasis in this book is on species (however defined; see Chapter 3), we focus on how conservation reliance can be incorporated in the process of prioritizing species. Species prioritization begins by specifying what is to be prioritized (the species pool), over what scale, to achieve what goals and objectives (Figure 10.1).

Only the species that are included in the species pool are prioritized: if a species is not included in the pool, it automatically fails to be considered for conservation action. Identifying the species pool is therefore perhaps the most basic decision in the process. Most conservation prioritizations begin by identifying which species are of conservation concern and should therefore be considered for inclusion in the pool. But given this, should the pool of species include all species designated by a jurisdictional listing process (e.g. state, provincial, territorial, national, international) as threatened or at-risk, only species of economic value, only species occurring in some administrative unit, only birds of prey, or some other grouping? Determining the species pool may include assessing the current population status of each species: which species are critically endangered, which are common now but rapidly declining in abundance, which are stable but rare, and so on.

The species to be prioritized are delimited by boundaries. Some boundaries are natural: ecological boundaries may define vegetation types, watersheds, ecoregions, or biomes; physical boundaries separate land from water. Other boundaries are established by people: political and jurisdictional boundaries define states, provinces, and nations, and thus the purviews and missions of agencies charged with conservation or resource management; legal boundaries define the

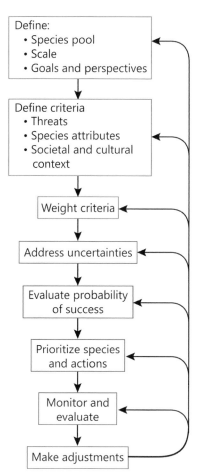

FIGURE 10.1. A process for prioritizing species for conservation activities. Adaptive management (the feedback arrows) requires continuous monitoring of the effectiveness of activities and a willingness to change strategies in response to new information.

framework of laws and regulations that bound conservation actions. Regardless of the type of boundary, larger areas usually contain more species than smaller areas and thus increase the size of the species pool. Because prioritization makes comparisons among species in a pool to determine their priority rankings, the larger a species pool the less sensitive are the rankings to the inclusion or exclusion of a particular species (Kujala et al. 2017).

Identifying the species pool and scale for a prioritization is incomplete without a clear statement of what is to be accomplished. Differences in goals and objectives drive variations in approaches.

A prioritization aiming to minimize the risk of extinction is more likely to emphasize different traits of species than one intended to maximize the probability of recovery, leading to different actions. Avoiding extinction may end up prioritizing the species that are most difficult to save, whereas optimizing recovery may shift the focus to those that are easiest to recover. Attaining long-term demographic viability may require ensuring distribution throughout a species' range, maintaining ecological functions, fostering sustainable use, restoring historical numbers, or something else.

Goals and objectives are scale-dependent. Conservation at different scales may draw on different methods, different information, or different sources of support. Conservation at a global scale, for example, may prioritize areas that harbor high biodiversity or numbers of endemic species, whereas a focus on a regional or local scale may emphasize particular species or species groups. Time scales are also important. Species with different generation lengths, for example, will differ in their rate of recovery. Some of the species in the species pool may also be conservation reliant. Consequently, prioritization must consider the duration and long-term costs of management.

As we explored in Chapter 9, conservation is carried out in a social, political, and economic context. Consequently, determinations of the species pool, the spatial and temporal scales, and the goals and objectives of a prioritization exercise must acknowledge the differing perspectives of involved stakeholders. If scientists, conservationists, managers, policy makers, landowners, tribal members, and other groups (much less the decision makers) cannot agree about the basic elements of a prioritization, implementing the results will be difficult (Tear et al. 2005; Nicholson and Possingham 2006).

## DEFINING THE PRIORITIZATION CRITERIA

Once the scope of a prioritization exercise has been determined, the next step is to decide on the criteria that will be used to prioritize the species (Figure 10.1). Which criteria are used and how they are weighted determine the priority rank of a species in relation to other species in the pool. The more specific the criteria, the more likely that distinctions can be drawn among species. Consequently, this is where the demand for species-specific information is the greatest and where gaps in knowledge are most likely to create uncertainty in the priorities.

Most prioritization approaches include information about the threats facing the species, characteristics of the species that affect their risk of extinction or their probability of successful recovery, an assessment of taxonomic or evolutionary distinctiveness, the cost of recovery efforts, and (in some cases) various societal factors that influence whether conservation actions are realistic. In the United States, government agencies charged with implementing the Endangered Species Act consider the degree of threat, recovery potential, genetic distinctiveness of species, and conflicts with development in prioritizing species for conservation. McCarthy et al. (2008) prioritized Australian bird species based on the efficiency and cost of management, importance of the species, level of threat, and time frame over which results are expected. In New Zealand, the Threatened Species Strategy gives weight to a species' social contribution to the people of New Zealand, its contribution to ensuring a wide range of taxonomic lineages, its conservation status and rate of decline, and its conservation dependency (i.e. conservation reliance).

Threats are the starting point for most prioritization approaches, as they are what cause a species to become imperiled and of conservation interest in the first place. Threats differ in their magnitude, manageability, scale, duration, and number, all of which can enter into prioritization calculations. The magnitude of a threat affects how imperiled a species is and the feasibility of sustaining species that rely on conservation management. The threat of habitat loss, for example, may become important in assessing the priority of a species for conservation only when it reaches a threshold where the habitat has become too fragmented or too little is left, increasing the vulnerability of a species to extinction (Opdam and Wiens 2002). Species imperiled by threats that can be easily addressed might be given a high priority for conservation because success seems imminent, or species threatened by large-magnitude factors might rank high because even a slight reduction in the threat level could yield significant benefits to the species. Species that face unmanageable threats, on the other hand, might have a low priority because management is not feasible or is too costly. And as we point out in Chapters 4 and 5, species facing threats from multiple sources are often (but not always) more vulnerable than those threatened by a single factor. Conservation-reliant species tend to rank low on a prioritization list that favors short-term, easily managed threats.

The vulnerability of a species to threats is a function of its sensitivity, exposure, and adaptive capacity (Pacifici et al. 2015; Foden and Young 2016). In general, the attributes that heighten the risk of extinction of a species are the opposite of those that may hasten its recovery under management (Box 10.1). It might seem straightforward to use the listing status of a species (such as the IUCN Red List) as a measure of vulnerability in setting priorities. In a case study from Australia, for example, Szabo et al. (2006) assigned a threat level of critically endangered a value of 0.7, endangered a value of 0.5, and vulnerable a value of 0.3. Although the status of a species may provide a useful starting point, by itself it is inadequate (Possingham et al. 2002).

A valid prioritization will incorporate a variety of species traits. As the stories in this book illustrate, species are especially prone to extinction if they occupy small ranges and are endemic to an area, are declining in abundance throughout their range, have limited capacity to move elsewhere, are physiologically challenged, have little behavioral or phenotypic or genetic flexibility to adjust to changing conditions, or are restricted to a specific habitat or feeding on particular prey. But because species do not live in isolation and are embedded in webs of interactions, how they relate to other species may also be important. Interdependencies among species, such as those between black-tailed prairie dogs and black-footed ferrets or i'iwis and lobelias (Chapter 7), are not usually included as prioritization criteria. The ferret, for example, is assigned a high priority and is listed as

BOX 10.1. **Examples of Criteria that Have Been Used to Prioritize Species for Conservation**

Attributes of species, taxonomy, threats, and societal considerations may be scored and weighted in different ways to rank species for conservation priority.

**Species Factors**

| Species factor | Extinction risk | Recovery potential |
|---|---|---|
| Listing status | Threatened or Endangered | Least Concern or unlisted |
| Range size | Small, endemic | Large, widespread |
| Population distribution | Fragmented, disjunct | Connected, metapopulation |
| Population size | Small, rare | Large, common |
| Population trend | Declining | Stable, increasing |
| Population age structure | Skewed | Balanced |
| Mobility, dispersal | Sedentary, resident | Mobile, migratory |
| Reproductive rate | Low | High |
| Physiological tolerance | Narrow, close to threshold | Broad, far from threshold |
| Phenotypic plasticity | Limited | Broad |
| Genetic diversity | Low, inbred | High, outbred |
| Ecological specialization | Specialist | Generalist |
| Ecological role | Relies on other species | Facilitated by other species |

**Taxonomic Factors**

- Phylogenetic distinctiveness
- Genetic distinctiveness

BOX 10.1.  (cont.)

**Threat Attributes**

- Level—high to low, continuous vs. intermittent
- Manageability—e.g. by legal mechanisms or management actions
- Scale—local, regional, global
- Changeability—such as disturbance, sea-level rise
- Number—single vs. multiple threats

**Societal Factors**

- Direct costs of conservation actions (short-term, long-term)
- Willingness to pay for an action or plan
- Management capacity, funding
- Conflicts or tradeoffs with economic interests
- Other societal values (e.g. recreation, ecosystem services)
- Lost or gained conservation and economic opportunity costs
- Cultural values (e.g. spiritual)
- Attractiveness, beauty (e.g. iconic or charismatic species)
- Political support

Endangered under the Endangered Species Act, whereas the black-tailed prairie dog is not listed and is, in fact, considered a varmint by many ranchers.

Species can also be characterized by their phylogenetic, evolutionary, or genetic distinctiveness. Those species that are hanging alone on branches of a phylogenetic tree, are sole members of a genus or family, or are genetically unique may be evolutionary dead ends—or they may have the greatest potential to adapt as conditions change. In either case, such species may be a higher priority to protect and nurture than other, less distinctive species. The New Zealand Threatened Species Strategy, for example, begins by optimizing taxonomic representation to include as many orders, families, and genera as possible from the pool of species to be prioritized and only then selects the most threatened species within a lineage.

Such taxonomic or phylogenetic categorizations address evolutionary potential only at a broad level, however, and what is considered distinctive may change depending on what other species are included in the pool. Increasingly, genomic information is being promoted as a more reliable assay of the genetic distinctiveness of species or populations than morphological distinctiveness (Volkmann et al. 2014). We noted in Chapter 3 how different populations of salmon are listed separately as "evolutionarily significant units" under the Endangered Species Act. Recent studies suggest that differences in migration timing between spring-run and fall-run populations of Chinook salmon in the Klamath River Basin are attributable to a single gene (Prince et al. 2017). As genomic methods become more widely applied in conservation, debates will no doubt intensify about how much genetic differentiation justifies recognition of a population as genetically distinct or evolutionarily significant.

Chinook salmon also illustrate the need to include social and economic considerations in prioritization. On the west coast of North America, salmon support commercial and recreational fishing and are also highly valued by Native American tribes (Chapter 9). Spring-run Chinook salmon on the Klamath River figure prominently in the traditions of the Karuk Tribe of northern California. As the salmon runs have diminished, the tribe has petitioned the federal government to list the salmon under the Endangered Species Act. Listing the salmon could trigger restrictions on water allocations for agricultural and municipal uses on the Klamath, leading to conflicts.

The reality is that prioritization must consider societal and cultural values, costs of conservation actions, capacity to take on management challenges, and other societal factors from the outset (e.g. Naidoo and Ricketts 2006). After all, society will bear the costs of conservation in one way or another, and it may make little sense to develop a conservation priority list if there are slim prospects that the investments will be made. African baobab trees have attracted conservation attention because of the girth of their trunks and their importance in local cultures, Komodo dragons because of their size and value to ecotourism, and Asian openbill storks because of their association with a Buddhist temple (Small 2012). The public's willingness to pay for conservation may be more closely related to a species' charismatic features or its instrumental value to people than to biological assessments (Martín-López et al. 2008).

Societal factors are difficult to turn into quantifiable criteria. Some prioritization approaches address this challenge by monetizing the costs and benefits of conducting conservation actions. This facilitates cost–benefit or return-on-investment analyses that may resonate with the public, conservation NGOs, and politicians. However, it is incorrect to assume that the most important societal factors influencing a species are those with a high dollar value. Dollars are only one measure of value.

### WEIGHTING THE CRITERIA

The criteria to be used in a prioritization are not necessarily of equal importance in ranking species for conservation attention. A trend in population numbers, for example, may be more important than the size of the population. Or it may not be. How the factors are weighted relative to one another is a critical step and depends on the conservation goals, the overall characteristics of the pool of species to be prioritized, and the appropriateness of particular criteria for an assessment.

Assigning weights to factors is a critical step in the prioritization process. The US Fish and Wildlife Service applies one of three weightings (high, moderate, or low) to each of several criteria.[4] Similarly, Reece and Noss (2014) assign a weight of 1, 2, 3, or 4 to each of their criteria, achieving only marginally better resolution.

Using an even wider range of values would allow scores to be expressed with greater precision, but whether this improves accuracy depends on the information available and on the process used to derive the scores and weightings. Marsh et al. (2007) used panels of

[4] Federal Register 82 FR 24944; May 31, 2017.

technical experts, policy makers, and stakeholders to distribute points among the components of several criteria to prioritize Australian species for resource allocation. For example, one criterion considered the consequences should a species become extinct. Out of 100 points available, loss of its ecological role received a maximum weight of 34; loss of social value, 33; loss of genetic and taxonomic distinctiveness, 11 each; and consequences to those responsible for conserving the species, 11. The resulting score was combined with information on the probability of successful recovery (scored similarly) and probability of extinction (a species' listing status) to derive an overall priority. Importantly, the priority rankings did not always agree with the listing status of a species: the Endangered cascade treefrog, for example, was not among the species identified as high priority; but the holy cross frog, a species of Least Concern, was, largely because of its greater probability of successful recovery.

## DEALING WITH UNCERTAINTY

Assigning numerical values to weightings and criteria conveys precision and certainty. But the scores can change depending on the information available, the way that criteria are translated into numerical values, and who determines the weightings (Hemming et al. 2018). Consequently, the priority rankings of species can change as factor weightings change, so there is a possibility of conscious or unconscious bias. The importance of criteria or their components can also vary among locations or over time, yet prioritization calculations generally do not include estimates of spatial or temporal variance.

The less information that is available to inform a prioritization process, the more uncertain the results will be. For those averse to taking risks, uncertainty can be an excuse for inaction. There are always tradeoffs in balancing the need to take quick action with the need for better knowledge on which to base decisions. For many imperiled species, however, waiting for better knowledge is not an option. Marcot et al. (2015) provide an excellent example of a method for testing the sensitivity of demographic metrics for Threatened northern spotted owls to alternative designs for habitat protection. Expert workshops can generate information or reach consensus opinions about critical components of a prioritization. Even in the absence of actual data on population trends, a panel of experts might still be able to conclude if a population is declining, stable, or increasing with a high degree of certainty.

The opinions of experts, although often well informed, may nonetheless contain biases. Turning their consensus into a hard numerical value may mask the underlying uncertainties in the opinions or the differences among experts. Consensus is more readily reached among like-minded people (or with a dominant personality on an expert panel), so the composition of an expert panel (e.g. only scientists versus a broader representation of stakeholders) can affect the outcome. Consequently, prioritization numbers may convey a false sense of certainty, instilling a greater degree of confidence in the results of a prioritization than is warranted. Early involvement in a prioritization process of those who will be affected by the prioritization decisions will increase the likelihood that the results will be accepted, or at least understood.

## PROBABILITY OF SUCCESS

The overall aim of a prioritization process is to increase the probability of conservation success in meeting the initial goal, be it protecting the most imperiled species, maximizing the number of species protected, or something else. Gauging the probability of success is important in part because success generates public support for conservation. A prioritization based on preventing extinction is likely to emphasize different traits of species than one intended to maximize the probability of recovery, driving different actions as a result.

How much is invested in recovery of a species directly influences the probability of success (Waldron et al. 2017). Conservation-reliant species require long-term management and funding, which may deprive other vulnerable species of the management and funding they need—more tradeoffs. How do we balance the benefits of protecting populations of an imperiled species in multiple locations against the costs of missed opportunities to invest in other imperiled species? The process of prioritization, and the actions that follow as a result of the process, can be thought of as a way to explicitly recognize and manage risks, costs, and benefits.

Determining whether the actions taken to conserve the priority species have been successful requires follow-up monitoring and evaluation. In some cases, this may lead to a modification of actions, re-evaluation of priorities, or even a revision of the goals—the cycle of adaptive management (Gregory et al. 2006; Westgate et al. 2013).

## HOW HAS PRIORITIZATION BEEN DONE?
### FOUR EXAMPLES

Many systems have been proposed for prioritizing species for conservation and management, with different goals and objectives. To see how conservation reliance might be incorporated into prioritizations, we briefly describe four approaches.

Our first example, the Project Prioritization Protocol (PPP), was developed at the University of Queensland, Australia, to facilitate decisions about allocating resources among threatened species (Szabo et al. 2006; Joseph et al. 2008; Kilham and Reinecke 2015). The objective was to maximize the recovery (or minimize the extinction) of threatened species within a limited budget—in other words, to allocate available funds in the most cost-effective manner. Weitzman (1998) originally framed this as the "Noah's Ark Problem": Which species should Noah take onto the Ark? Weitzman's approach to this problem was abstract and mathematical, but it established the foundation for the more pragmatic approach taken by Joseph et al. (2008). Joseph et al. used a variation on Weitzman's approach to prioritize 32 threatened species in New Zealand for conservation, using the formula:

$$E_i = \frac{W_i \times B_i \times S_i}{C_i}$$

where $E_i$ is the cost efficiency of measures to protect species $i$ (i.e. its priority rank), $W_i$ is the weight given to the species (the species' value), $B_i$ is the biodiversity benefit of protecting the species, $S_i$ is the probability of success, and $C_i$ is the cost of the conservation actions. Species weight ($W_i$) could be based on factors such as cultural or economic importance, ecological role, or endemicity; Joseph et al. used a measure that combined the taxonomic distinctiveness of a species with overall species richness. Biodiversity benefit ($B_i$) was evaluated as the probability of the species surviving into the future (Joseph et al. used 50 years). $S_i$ was estimated as the probability that the conservation actions could be implemented successfully and would ensure the security of the species (i.e. a measure of the successful application of management actions). Costs ($C_i$) were estimated over the 50-yr period based on discounted future expenditures. For many species, values of these components of $E_i$ were not available, so they were estimated by a panel of experts.

Joseph et al. ranked species by their cost-efficiency values ($E_i$); the top 15 species are shown in Table 10.1. With a fixed budget of somewhat more than NZ\$20 million, funds were available to meet the needs of the first 11 species. If one followed the priorities, the remaining species would receive no funding. Joseph et al. also considered how the species would rank if they were prioritized without weighting (i.e. $W_i$ not included) or based only on cost, taxonomic distinctiveness, or their status in New Zealand's Classification Species List. Not surprisingly, the rankings changed (Table 10.1): For example, the North Island brown kiwi, one of New Zealand's iconic species, ranked fifth using the weighted efficiency value but much lower when evaluated by the other approaches; only with the weighted value would it qualify for conservation funding.

The PPP has been adopted to guide conservation investments in New Zealand and in New South Wales, Australia, where it is a central part of the "Saving our Species" conservation program. In both countries, some iconic species such as the koala or southern and northern corroboree frogs are designated for conservation management

Table 10.1. *Calculations of priority rankings of conservation efforts for 15 of 32 New Zealand species based on weighted cost efficiency, unweighted cost efficiency, and cost, taxonomic distinctiveness, or threat status alone. Bold face ranks indicate the species that would receive funding using the different criteria, given a budget of slightly over NZ$20 million (see text). Based on data from Joseph et al. (2008).*

| Species | Weighted efficiency rank | Unweighted efficiency rank | Cost rank | Distinctiveness rank | Threat status rank |
|---|---|---|---|---|---|
| *Dactylanthus* (flower of Hades) | **1** | **2** | 6 | 1 | 27 |
| Maud Island frog | 2 | 6 | **15** | 4 | 20 |
| Shrubby tororaro | 3 | 9 | 7 | 3 | 26 |
| Hamilton's frog | 4 | **10** | **16** | 5 | 7 |
| North Island brown kiwi | 5 | 18 | 30 | 2 | 28 |
| Climbing everlasting daisy | 6 | **1** | 3 | 13 | 17 |
| Hochstetter's frog | 7 | 13 | **2** | 6 | 31 |
| New Zealand shore plover | 8 | **11** | **10** | 10 | **3** |
| *Pittosporum patulum* | 9 | **12** | 21 | 9 | 21 |
| *Oreomyrrhis* sp. nov. (= *O. aff. rigida*) | **10** | 3 | **4** | 17 | 18 |
| *Pachycladon exilis* | **11** | 7 | **12** | 12 | **5** |
| Archey's frog | 12 | 17 | 23 | 7 | **11** |
| Canterbury mudfish | 13 | **16** | **13** | **8** | 19 |
| Holloway's broom | 14 | 5 | 5 | 24 | **1** |
| *Poa spania* | 15 | **4** | 9 | 25 | **2** |

regardless of where they might rank on a PPP. Of the remaining species, those for which managing a particular place is likely to support recovery are designated "site-managed species" and subjected to a variation of PPP (lacking the weighting function, $W_i$) to determine their priority. Resources are then allocated accordingly.[5]

Critics of PPP argue that it is too difficult to predict how species will respond to conservation actions ($S_i$) and that there is too much uncertainty in the data that feed the PPP for the rankings to be valid. They may also disagree with the criteria used to calculate the priorities or the species included in the analysis. Some distrust the professional judgments used to set values, the difficulty of including conflicting societal values, or the lack of acceptance by managers or policy makers (Soderquist 2011; Kilham and Reinecke 2015). The PPP does not adjust priorities when multiple species could benefit from a single management action and it ignores interactions among species, such as predation or competition.[6]

Our second example highlights how a priority ranking of species based on multiple criteria may not translate directly into the allocation of resources. The procedures used by the US Fish and Wildlife Service and NOAA Fisheries to guide recovery of species listed under the Endangered Species Act differ not only in the species under their jurisdictions, but also in the criteria used to assign priorities.

In the US Fish and Wildlife Service approach,[7] species are assigned a priority rank (1–18) based on the degree of threat confronting the species, its potential for successful recovery, and its taxonomic

---

[5] Details are in the *Saving our Species Technical report* (2013), available at www.environment.nsw.gov.au/resources/threatenedspecies/SavingOurSpecies/130699sostech.pdf.

[6] Courtois et al. (2014) addressed the latter problem mathematically by incorporating the effects of species interactions on survival probabilities into a revision of Weitzman's Noah's Ark parable. The approach provides a glimpse of how PPP could be extended, but the arguments are mathematically dense and require translation before they can be applied to real-world situations.

[7] 48 FR 43098 (September 21, 1983); see www.gao.gov/cgi-bin/getrpt?GAO-05-211 (2005).

distinctiveness. The degree of threat to a species is categorized as high, moderate, or low based on the immediacy of extinction risk. Recovery potential is ranked high or low depending on how well the threats are understood, how easily they can be alleviated, and whether intensive management is needed for recovery. Taxonomic distinctiveness is used as a surrogate for genetic distinctiveness, giving a higher ranking to a monotypic genus over species and subspecies. Because species are ranked independently of one another, multiple species can have the same priority rank; one species is then given priority over another with the same rank if its conservation would conflict with economic activities such as development.

Although the NOAA guidelines[8] use the same broad prioritization criteria as the US Fish and Wildlife Service, they establish 24 priority rankings and do not consider potential economic conflicts (even as a tie-breaker). Threats to species are evaluated in terms of demographic risk based on listing status, productivity, distribution, abundance, and population trend. Whether the threats occur in areas under United States jurisdiction is included among the factors determining recovery potential in the NOAA system (as is appropriate for the marine species it manages).

Typically, the agencies use prioritization systems as only one of several inputs when deciding on conservation actions and funding allocations. The US Fish and Wildlife Service, for example, is hierarchically organized into a single headquarters, eight regions, and many field offices. Rather than allocating funds based on the priority ranks, headquarters allocates most of the recovery budget to the regional offices based on their workload—the number of listed species the region is responsible for and the cost to recover each species. The regions, in turn, allocate funds to the field offices, emphasizing opportunities to work with partners who can bring additional funding and

---

[8] 82 FR 24944 (May 31, 2017); see www.federalregister.gov/documents/2017/05/31/2017-11157/endangered-and-threatened-species-listing-and-recovery-priority-guidelines

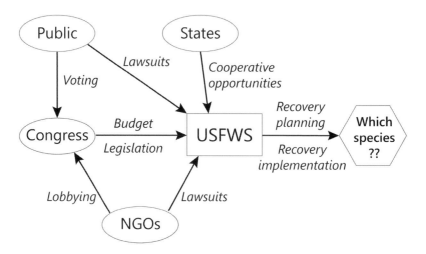

FIGURE 10.2. Allocations of efforts and expenditures for recovery of at-risk species by the US Fish and Wildlife Service (USFWS) are influenced by Congress, the states, non-governmental organizations (NGOs) and the public. After Restani and Marzluff (2002).

resources to the recovery program. Consequently, funds may be directed to projects where there is a willing partner rather than to species based on their priority rankings alone.

This is how funding is determined administratively; ultimately, the determination of how funds are allocated among species is influenced by a broader array of societal and political forces (Figure 10.2). Congressional actions influence the budget the US Fish and Wildlife Service has to work with and legislation may require that funds be spent in certain ways. In turn, the US Congress is subjected to lobbying by conservation NGOs and other special-interest groups, which affects both legislation and the budgeting process. The public and NGOs may influence decisions in the agency by filing lawsuits and instigating court actions. State governments may also share responsibilities (and financial support) for conservation and management.

As a consequence, disparities in funding among species can be huge and at odds with their rankings. Of the total expenditures by US federal and state agencies on Threatened and Endangered species in fiscal year 2016, the top 1% received 39% of the funding. Of these 16 taxa, 13 are fish (only 3 of them Endangered). Of the 13 fish, 11 are distinct population segments or evolutionarily significant units of salmonids and all but 3 are found in the Columbia River watershed.[9] By way of comparison, the northern spotted owl ranked 20th for funding, the Delta smelt 25th, and the California condor 192nd. The highest ranked non-vertebrate to receive funding, the Cumberlandian combshell, was 59th, and the highest ranked plant, the small whorled pogonia,[10] did not appear until 201st place. Even though plants comprise the majority of listed species, Threatened and Endangered plants received less than 5% of the overall recovery funding from 2007 to 2011 (Negrón-Ortiz 2014).

In general, wide-ranging mainland species (especially birds and mammals) are disproportionately given more funding in the United States relative to island species (Restani and Marzluff 2002), in part because they have a larger constituency. Hawai'i stands out as having particularly low funding relative to the species in need. Although Hawaiian species represent about a third of the 96 listed bird species, they received only 4% of the total expenditures in 1996–2004 (Leonard 2008). The priority ranks for Hawaiian species are similar to those of mainland listed species, but the mainland species received over 15 times the funding of Hawaiian birds. In his essay (Essay 8.1), Loyal Mehrhoff offers a perspective on the lessons Hawai'i has to offer; how to get a fair share of conservation funding is not one of them.

Most prioritization approaches do not consider conservation reliance, at least explicitly. The PPP and the US Fish and Wildlife Service guidance, for example, assign high priority to species with a

---

[9] Total expenditures were US$1.48 billion (93% federal) on 1605 of the 1703 species listed at that time (litigation expenses not included). www.fws.gov/endangered/esa-library/pdf/2016_Expenditures_Report.pdf

[10] Upon seeing a reference to this species when reviewing this chapter, Bruce Marcot mentioned that he had once written a poem about the small whorled pogonia. You can find it at www.plexuseco.com/The%20Plexus/po_pagon.htm

high potential for recovery. This emphasizes short-term results. Factoring in the need for ongoing management may reduce the priority ranking of conservation-reliant species. On the other hand, if a species' greater vulnerability to threats increases its priority, conservation-reliant species would rank higher because they generally lack adaptive capacity and continue to be exposed to threats that cannot be eliminated. Costs may be considered over a designated time frame (e.g. McCarthy et al. 2008) or as a factor influencing the likelihood of conservation success (e.g. the PPP approach; Joseph et al. 2008), but prioritization protocols generally do not assess how differences between short-term and long-term management needs might affect priorities. Conservation reliance is considered in the New Zealand Threatened Species Strategy[11] but only when, other things being equal, a conservation-dependent species gets a higher priority than another species to break a tie.

Our third example, the approach developed by Marsh et al. (2007), explicitly incorporates several elements of conservation reliance. In their system, species are prioritized based on three broad criteria: the threat category, the ecological and social consequences should the species become extinct, and the potential for successful recovery. A species' listing status is used as a surrogate for the threat criterion; the remaining two criteria are scored on a 1–100 scale based on several components. Conservation reliance enters into calculations of recovery potential through the inclusion of the capacity to control (or eliminate) a threat, the need for ongoing management and financial support, and the level of public support for implementing management actions. Each is scored on a 1–4 scale; collectively, these three attributes account for 60% of the total weighting for recovery potential.

In our fourth example, Akçakaya et al. (2018) have suggested an approach based on "counterfactuals"—the difference between the current status of a species and what would happen if ongoing conservation

---

[11] www.doc.govt.nz/tss-algorithm.

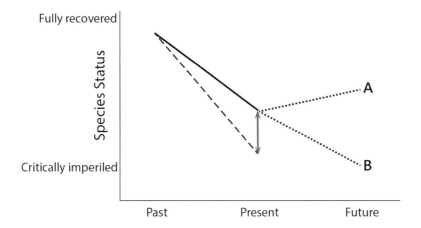

FIGURE 10.3. Hypothetical changes in the status of a species over time, showing the observed change in status (solid line), the past change expected in the absence of past conservation efforts (the counterfactual, dashed line), and future scenarios of change expected with increased future conservation efforts (A) and without any additional future conservation efforts (B) (dotted lines). After Akçakaya et al. (2018).

efforts were to cease or not begin. Future conservation gains could then be measured as the improvement in the status of a species were the ongoing and planned conservation actions to continue (Figure 10.3). A species with a high degree of conservation reliance (a large counterfactual) and high recovery potential (high conservation gain) would be likely to yield substantial payoffs for conservation investments and therefore have a high-priority ranking in most protocols.

The case study of saiga antelope used by Akçakaya et al. (2018) to demonstrate the feasibility of the approach, however, also illustrates a weakness: what would have happened without past management or what will happen in the future are both unobservable. Akçakaya et al. do suggest a procedure for using expert judgment to set bounds on the projections. The fact remains, however, that making decisions based on uncertain projections about the long-term consequences of conservation reliance requires accepting some degree of risk (Falcy 2016).

When a prioritization assessment accounts for conservation reliance, it expands the species pool by drawing attention to additional species that are not listed under the Endangered Species Act or other legal vehicles. Examples are the California bird species of special concern considered by Wiens and Gardali (2013) or the thousands of species that have been identified as of conservation concern by state fish and game departments across the United States.

Conservation reliance affects species' rankings by including criteria that describe the long-term management and funding that will be needed to maintain or recover a species and the attendant risk of failure. Consequently, conservation-reliant species may rank lower in priority than other species offering more immediate prospects for successful recovery (i.e. a higher value of $S_i$ in PPP). Because investments in conservation depend on public support, the societal and political commitments to conservation-reliant species may wane the longer conservation efforts continue without yielding success. If conservation reliance is not incorporated into prioritization, however, we may risk overinvesting in species that are unlikely to survive at the cost of underinvesting in species that have a real chance. Decision makers need to know whether conservation will require a huge annual budget for a year or two and not much thereafter, or a smaller annual budget that goes on and on. This long-term evaluation is not the only criterion on which decisions should be made, but it needs to be in the mix.

## IF WE CAN'T SAVE EVERYTHING, WHAT SHOULD WE SAVE? CONSERVATION TRIAGE

One reason prioritization is controversial among conservationists is that it explicitly acknowledges that funding is inadequate to save all species. If decision makers allocate funding according to the rankings, then at some point a line will be drawn below which species will be abandoned. In the (hypothetical) New Zealand example of PPP (Table 10.1), the top 11 species in the priority rankings received funding but the remaining  species were left to fend for themselves. With PPP now being used to set conservation priorities in New Zealand, New South Wales, and elsewhere, the prospect of this kind of triage becomes very real.

There is a significant ethical dilemma associated with prioritization. Some conservationists worry that prioritization approaches contain too much uncertainty, raising the possibility that a species that might persist with conservation actions could be left behind—no species should be considered a lost cause. Noss (1996) called triage an "ethically pernicious and politically defeatist" concept that is "a convenient escape from our moral duties to other creatures." Fitzpatrick (2018) opined that "deriving algorithms and promoting conservation triage miss the point entirely…wrapped under the guise of rational decision making, they provide defense and cover for the status quo." The issue has even made it into the popular media (e.g. Nijhuis 2012; Kahn 2018).

But the reality is that we are already investing in some species and abandoning others. As we describe above in this chapter, even though the US Fish and Wildlife Service ranks species, the funding does not directly correspond to the rankings because of Congress, US Fish and Wildlife Service's administrative structure, and other factors. To address these mismatches, Gerber (2016) compared the allocation of funding for species listed under the Endangered Species Act against the funding that was proposed for those species in recovery plans. Gerber's concern was with "costly failures," species with little prospect of recovery that were substantially overfunded, and "injurious neglect" species that were declining but woefully underfunded. Her study suggests that reallocating funding for 50 costly failures to injurious neglect species could allow 180 species to be funded to the full extent of their recovery plans. The costly failure species would receive less funding and likely continue to decline—triage by budget compression—but a considerably greater number of recovery plans would be adequately funded. This approach, however, does not incorporate the long-term costs or benefits associated with conservation reliance.

Prioritization offers the opportunity to make decisions in a way that is participatory, transparent, science-based, and acknowledges the full range of costs and benefits. The rankings that determine winners and losers in the race for resources depend on what goes into the prioritization protocol: the species pool, scale, prioritization criteria, and weightings. Equally important is the commitment to follow a prioritization. The more closely funding allocations match a prioritization, the farther down in the rankings funding will stretch and the fewer species will suffer triage. The funding for each species that makes the cutoff must also be adequate to maintain populations or the result is still a disguised form of triage. In addition, the results of a prioritization must align with the missions, responsibilities, and administrative structures of the relevant agencies or organizations or they will be of little use (Joseph et al. 2009). There must also be a way to ensure that the commitment by these organizations will continue.

### WHERE DOES THIS LEAVE US?

Conservation reliance affects costs and risk, so choices will be made. The question is how? Unfortunately, prioritization does not provide a definitive answer. Prioritization protocols can be expressed with mathematical sophistication (e.g. Weitzman 1998; Courtois et al. 2014) but, as with any mathematical formulations or models, they are sensitive to what goes into them and how they are calculated. What is the species pool? Which variables are used as prioritization criteria and how are they determined and weighted? Are the costs of conservation included, and what do the costs encompass, over what time frame? What are the roles of expert panels and who is an "expert"? How are uncertainty and the risk of failure treated? And, beneath it all, what are the goals and objectives?

Such questions and concerns could easily lead one to wonder whether prioritization provides anything more than coarse guidance for making conservation decisions. We believe it does, and see at least two significant advantages. First, properly conducted, prioritizations involve diverse stakeholders in the deliberations to discuss and agree upon goals and objectives and to establish prioritization criteria and weightings. This increases the likelihood that the results of a prioritization exercise will fairly represent the concerns of multiple stakeholders, enhancing public and institutional support for conservation plans. Second, a protocol stipulates what has gone into the calculations, so the basis of the resulting priority rankings is transparent. This enables people to determine why one species ranks higher or lower than another, which in turn may help to focus conservation efforts on actions that best meet their goals and objectives.

Conservation reliance needs to be considered in prioritizing species to direct greater attention to the factors that threaten the species, what it will require to eliminate or mitigate them, and how long it is likely to take. As the magnitude of conservation reliance grows and its implications become more apparent, prioritization of species and conservation efforts may lead to conflicts among people with different perspectives and values. Agreement may be elusive, but with a robust and participatory prioritization effort, we will at least have a structure that may foster compromise or consensus.

# 11  Being a Good Shepherd

We have reached a critical point in caring for the Earth's biota. Worldwide, one-fourth of the plant and animal species that have been assessed are on the pathway toward extinction.[1] Many of these species are threatened by forces that cannot be eliminated. They will need our help if they are to survive. We must be their shepherds, perhaps for a very long time.

The challenge of conservation reliance is daunting, but not hopeless. In earlier chapters we told the success stories of species such as the black-capped vireo, Oregon chub, island night lizard, southern white rhinoceros, and Robbins' cinquefoil. There are many others. These stories are as much about the people doing the conservation work as they are about the plants and animals they conserved. They give us renewed hope.

But dealing with the growing ranks of conservation-reliant species will take more than hope. Conservationists talk of "protecting" or "preserving" species. We must also be good shepherds of nature. As it is generally used, "shepherding" means watching over and caring for a flock or group. Shepherding nature is about taking responsibility for watching over and caring for species and the Earth's biodiversity. It is also about shepherding how people and societies relate to nature.

How we shepherd nature depends on how we answer several questions that shape all conservation efforts.

## WHY SHOULD WE CONSERVE?

How this question is answered determines how people will become engaged in shepherding nature and whether there will be support for

---

[1] According to the Intergovernmental Science-Policy Platform on Biodiversity and Ecosystem Services (IPBES 2019).

conservation-reliant species. Ultimately, the answer depends on values. Values determine which species are important and what it is about nature that should be conserved. Do we believe nature has intrinsic value, that every species is important no matter what? Or do we believe nature has only instrumental value, that species and ecosystem services matter only inasmuch as they are useful to people? Should we conserve nature for its immediate value, or for its long-term value to future generations?

People differ in how they answer these questions. Their values are shaped by their culture, religion, politics, heritage, social standing, income, profession, closeness to nature, and many other factors. Consequently, people may have contrasting perspectives on the importance of species and their conservation. Even when people share broadly defined values, differences in their priorities and interests can create conflicts. For example, farmers, ranchers, indigenous people, and urban conservationists may all agree about the value of species and nature expressed in the intent of various laws and regulations. They may differ sharply, however, when it comes to deciding which species to conserve, which areas to protect, or which activities to prohibit, depending on how those laws and regulations align with their individual or group interests.[2] A pastoralist in India and a conservationist in North America may both value tigers intrinsically, but regard them quite differently. Because values are immediate and powerful motivators, such differences can lead to controversy and conflict, as the stories we told of the gray wolf and delta smelt illustrate.

## WHAT IS IT THAT SHOULD BE CONSERVED?

How we answer the "why" question leads to the "what" question. The focus of conservation has usually been on species, including subspecies, discrete population segments, evolutionarily significant units, or demographic units such as isolated populations. Genetic

---

[2] See Schmidtz (2017) for a discussion of this issue from an ethical perspective.

technology now enables us to identify specific genetic variants to conserve. Alternatively, conservation efforts may focus on entire habitats, system processes, or ecosystems. There are multiple answers to the "what" question, including "all of the above."

Regardless of how it is defined, people must be clear and agree about what is being conserved in order to begin, as this determines all else that follows. The focal units of conservation dictate the management methods used; the local, regional, or global scales of application; the legal statutes enabling protection; the costs and how fundraising efforts are designed; and public and political support for conservation.

What we choose to conserve also determines how we address the mismatch between conservation needs and available funding. We have argued throughout this book that comprehensive prioritization is the best way to use the available resources to achieve desired outcomes in a way that is transparent and fair. Because conservation reliance often lengthens the duration of conservation actions, how it is weighted will strongly influence how priorities are determined.

## WHAT ARE WE TRYING TO ACCOMPLISH?

If we know why and what we are trying to conserve, then we can set goals. Usually, the goal of conserving a species depends on its current status. If the population is stable but at risk, there is likely time to develop and implement a recovery plan. If a species is declining but still reasonably abundant over much of its range, managers may aim to halt the decline and ensure that sufficient habitat remains to sustain a viable population. If the species is critically endangered, however, there must be immediate action to protect the remaining individuals and their habitat or to mount rescue efforts.

The array of tools to accomplish conservation goals is large and growing. Protected areas and managed habitat are widely viewed as some of the most cost-effective ways to conserve multiple species, habitats, and ecosystems. When these approaches are insufficient, more aggressive measures may be called for, including translocations, captive breeding, or eradication of invasive plants or animals. In addition, newer tools are being used, such as medicine to treat diseases that threaten broad taxonomic groups, genomic technologies that may help expand the scale and scope of eradication efforts, artificial intelligence to track down poachers, or drones to survey inaccessible places. Although the conservation approaches differ, all aim to prevent extinction and promote recovery or, if a species is conservation reliant, to reach a point where long-term management can be sustained or the species emerges from conservation reliance.

## WHO WILL UNDERTAKE THE CONSERVATION ACTIONS?

Conservation and management don't just happen; they must be undertaken by actors and supporters. Someone must plan and implement the management actions and conduct the monitoring to know when a species is in trouble or recovering. Little can happen without support. For many endangered species, government agencies may draw on public funds (e.g. user fees or taxes) to undertake management. These funds are usually inadequate, so conservation often becomes a collaborative effort involving NGOs, local communities, and donors operating at multiple scales. Governments can play an important role by offering incentives for ongoing conservation efforts; the Department of Agriculture in the United States supports several programs that pay farmers and landowners for protecting important habitats. Adding a small surcharge to oil and gas leases or coupling conservation with international human aid programs can provide a significant boost to conservation funding and community development and help to maintain a continuing commitment. Ensuring that adequate support is stable and reliable is essential if conservation efforts are to be carried through to completion.

For conservation to be successful, the actors must have the capacity to act and the responsibility to do so. Legal responsibility for conservation varies among states, territories, provinces, and nations; it also varies across types of land ownership. The dynamics and needs of species do not respect political or legal boundaries, however, especially for wide-ranging animals (and even less so as the climate changes). Consequently, multiple actors may then need to collaborate in carrying out the necessary actions. Expectations for long-term commitments must be explicit, especially when conservation-reliant species are involved.

## WHO ARE THE SHEPHERDS?

Despite their differences, most people in all parts of the world share a belief that humans have a responsibility to see that nature persists. There are many shepherds. Thousands upon thousands of individuals play the role of shepherd from local to international scales. A colleague of ours has restored half of his Oregon farm into habitat for the Endangered Fender's blue butterfly. His actions, along with those of several dozen others, have enabled a species once thought to be extinct to recover and spread.

There are many, many other examples. In Chapter 4, we describe how Phil Pister and his buckets saved the Owens pupfish from certain extinction. Tom Cade founded The Peregrine Fund and was the driving force in making the recovery of the peregrine falcon in the United States one of conservation's greatest success stories; Carl Jones has played a similar role in the recovery of the Mauritius kestrel. In Mozambique, Greg Carr and his team are building communities and supporting scientific research while making Gorongosa National Park a showplace for progressive conservation. Chico Mendes alerted the world to the wanton destruction of Brazilian rainforests, and Archie Carr drew attention to the perilous plight of sea turtles throughout the world. Wangari Maathai was instrumental in founding the Green Belt Movement in Africa. Aldo Leopold, Rachel Carson, Jane Goodall, George Schaller, and E.O. Wilson—to name just a few— have advanced awareness of conservation through their inspirational writing, speaking, and actions.

Sometimes groups of people step up to become shepherds. Community-based conservation in many parts of the world aims to integrate the conservation of species and biodiversity with the well-being of the people who share the landscape. Communities have come together to promote conservation of the Araripe manakin in Brazil. In Botswana, concession areas adjacent to parks and reserves give local communities responsibility for management and conservation of wildlife resources. A consortium of individuals, local communities, NGOs, and government agencies has banded together to support Haka-lau Forest National Wildlife Refuge in Hawai'i; a similar consortium has assumed responsibility for management of the Kirtland's warbler in the Great Lakes region of the United States. A few dedicated individuals have started groups like the Amphibian Ark or Saving Asia's Vultures from Extinction (SAVE), which now have growing international support. The Svalbard Global Seed Bank, which cares for the seeds and germ-plasm of nearly a million plant varieties (many of agricultural import-ance), was started by one individual, Cary Fowler, in collaboration with the Consultative Group on International Agricultural Research.

Although the approaches, focus, and reach of these individuals and groups vary, all have a deeply held belief in the value of nature to current and future generations. They recognize that people are not apart from nature, that even critically imperiled species and people must coexist. They take on a personal and shared responsibility for species and their habitats. Many of them are leaders, generating enthusiasm and commitment among others. They recognize that individuals can make a difference. And they know that there are no quick solutions when so many species are conservation reliant.

## WHAT WILL IT TAKE?

Conservation must counter the escalating impacts of the uses of lands and waters, the increasing exploitation of plant and animal species, and the accelerating climate changes that are the underlying causes of extinction, imperilment, and conservation reliance. Addressing the magnitude and scale of these conservation challenges demands that we reach beyond the heroic shepherds to change how we, as a society, view conservation. We must move away from short-term approaches that often become embroiled in conflict and compromise toward a long-term perspective that is transparent about costs and tradeoffs, acknowledges other pressing societal concerns, and realistically assesses the consequences of global changes.

Doing this will take nothing less than a transformative change in how people relate to the environment, nature, and one another.[3] Business as usual or slow, incremental change will not get us there. We need new ways of integrating economic, social, political, and technological demands with conservation that can show a path toward achieving natural and human communities that have long-term sustainability. We need broader agreement on our conservation priorities and a willingness to take action on our priorities. And we need to remove impediments to taking quick and decisive action when it is needed, but do so in a way that is consistent with agreed-upon conservation goals and objectives. Recently introduced legislation in the US Congress, the Recovering America's Wildlife Act, provides an encouraging glimpse of the sort of transformative actions that are needed. The act would provide US$1.4 billion to states and tribes for the management of at-risk species, many of them conservation reliant—a 28-fold increase over the funds allocated in fiscal year 2019. The act has bipartisan support, but whether the legislation will be enacted, much less funded, is subject to political uncertainties.

For meaningful change to be successful, conservation actions must have a firm ethical foundation. Ethics are beliefs about how people should regard and treat species, nature, and one another, now and in the future. Many cultures regard the sanctity of life as an ethical imperative. Indigenous peoples are perhaps the most explicitly connected to nature and the Earth, through traditions that seamlessly combine their values and ethics with a sense of community that includes past and future generations. The Anchorage Declaration, adopted in 2009 by indigenous representatives from throughout the world, reaffirms "the unbreakable and sacred connection between

---

[3] Tallis et al. (2018) and IPBES (2019) also highlight the need for such a transformative change in how we think and act for conservation.

land, air, water, oceans, forests, sea ice, plants, animals and our human communities to the material and spiritual basis for our existence."[4]

Even when there is agreement about our ethical responsibility for nature, however, ambiguities can stymie conservation. In Chapter 1, we described the debate between those who agreed with the decision to capture the last free-living California condors for captive breeding and those who objected, arguing that the birds should be allowed "extinction with dignity." Both groups defended their positions based on ethical arguments: saving the species versus allowing individuals to live out their lives roaming freely. Neither had exclusive claim to being right (or righteous).

Conservation is full of such ethical conundrums. Is it ethical to kill individuals of one species to save individuals of another, as we have done by killing feral cats or rats to save endemic island species, killing barred owls to save northern spotted owls, or killing wolves to protect ranch and game animals? Do animal rights supersede conservation needs? Are all species valuable, or just those we care about? Should we give up on species that are unlikely to survive climate change? As more species become conservation reliant, will we be forced to abandon more species to their fate, or should we hold fast to the aspiration of saving all species?

Shepherding nature is about caring for nature, watching out for nature. The writer and environmentalist Wallace Stegner put it this way:

> *We are the most dangerous species of life on the planet, and every other species, even the earth itself, has cause to fear our power to exterminate. But we are also the only species which, when it chooses to do so, will go to great effort to save what it might destroy.* (Stegner 1955)

We must choose to do so, for nature and for one another. The future of many species, including humans, hangs in the balance.

---

[4] *Indigenous Peoples' Global Summit on Climate Change Consensus Agreement.* unfccc.int/resource/docs/2009/smsn/ngo/168.pdf.

# Appendix A
## National Wildlife Statutes

Most nations have statutes that govern the management and use of "wildlife" (broadly defined). There are 101 statutes in English that are summarized on Endangered Earth.[1] These statutes fall into seven relatively distinct, non-exclusive categories:

### A.1 COMPREHENSIVE AT-RISK SPECIES STATUTES

Six nations have enacted comprehensive statutes: Australia, Bermuda, Canada, Macedonia, United States, and Vietnam. Statutes in this category share three types of provisions:

1. Processes and standards for listing species as at-risk. There are various categories: extinct in the wild, critically endangered, endangered, vulnerable, critically endangered communities, and endangered communities (Australia); critically endangered, endangered, or vulnerable (Bermuda); data deficient, special concern, threatened, endangered, extirpated, and extinct (Canada); species in danger of extinction, endangered species, vulnerable species, rare species, and relict species (Macedonia); endangered or threatened (United States); and endangered, precious and rare forest plants and animals (Vietnam).
2. Delegation of the power to take protective actions to prevent listed species from continuing to decline toward extinction: e.g. prohibiting take or habitat degradation, prohibitions on commerce.
3. Delegation of the power to take affirmative actions to increase a species' numbers and distribution: e.g. developing recovery plans, designating critical habitat, translocating species.

### A.2 AT-RISK AS A CATEGORY IN A WILDLIFE-MANAGEMENT STATUTE

Seventeen nations have wildlife-management statutes that include at-risk categories. The statutes in this category differ from the first category by the lack of affirmative recovery actions.

---

[1] www.endangeredearth.com/endangered-species-laws/

Armenia ("vanishing animal species")

Bhutan ("endangered species")

China ("rare or near extinction")

Costa Rica ("species threatened with extinction")

Cuba ("endemic, endangered, or threatened, or in the process of extinction")

Georgia ("endangered species")

Indonesia ("endangered species [and] rare species")

Kazakhstan ("rare and ... under threat of disappearance")

Lao People's Democratic Republic ("rare and near extinct species")

Latvia ("endangered, disappearing, or rare species")

Liberia ("rare, threatened and endangered species")

Lithuania ("rare and vanishing species")

Malawi ("rare, endangered, and endemic species")

Malta ("endangered species")

Mongolia ("extremely rare animals and rare animals")

Philippines ("endangered species" and "threatened species")

Taiwan ("endangered species, rare and valuable species, and other conservation-deserving species")

## A.3   STATUTES ENACTED TO COMPLY WITH CITES

Nineteen nations have statutes that were enacted to comply with the Convention on International Trade in Endangered Species of Wild Flora and Fauna (CITES):

| | |
|---|---|
| Botswana | Montserrat |
| Fiji | Philippines |
| Hong Kong | Saint Christopher and Nevis |
| Japan* | Singapore |
| Jersey | Solomon Islands |
| Lao People's Democratic Republic | Tanzania |
| Liberia | Uganda |
| Malaysia | United Kingdom |
| Malta | Vanuatu |
| Mongolia | |

* Isozaki (1989)

## A.4   GENERAL WILDLIFE-MANAGEMENT STATUTES

Sixty-eight nations have general wildlife-management statutes that include hunting regulations, reserves, and the like:

| | |
|---|---|
| Albania | Malaysia |
| Bahamas | Malta |
| Bangladesh | Mauritius |
| Belize | Mongolia |
| Bhutan | Montserrat |
| Botswana | Myanmar |
| Bulgaria | Namibia |
| China | New Zealand |
| Cook Islands | Nigeria |
| Costa Rica ("biodiversity") | Niue |
| Dominica | Norway |
| Eritrea | Pakistan |
| Estonia | Palau |
| Finland | Papua New Guinea |
| Gambia | Romania |
| Georgia | Saint Lucia |
| Ghana | Saint Vincent and the Grenadines |
| Grenada | Samoa |
| Hong Kong | Seychelles |
| India | Sierra Leone |
| Indonesia | Solomon Islands |
| Ireland | Somalia |
| Jamaica** | Sri Lanka |
| Japan | Sudan |
| Jersey | Swaziland |
| Jordan | Taiwan |
| Kenya | Tajikistan |
| Kiribati | Tanzania |
| Lao People's Democratic Republic | Thailand |
| Latvia | Trinidad and Tobago |
| Lesotho | Tuvalu |
| Liberia | Uganda |
| Macedonia | Zambia |
| Malawi | Zimbabwe |

** Blackhall's Laws of Jamaica, http://www.jamaicalawonline.com/revised-laws/statutes/642-WILD LIFE PROTECTION ACT.html.

## A.5   LIMITED WILDLIFE-MANAGEMENT STATUTES

Fifty-one nations have enacted wildlife-management statutes that are limited to specific types of wildlife. Some nations have enacted more than one statute. The protected species are often economically important.

Antigua and Barbuda: birds; mongoose population
Bahamas: fisheries
Barbados: fisheries
Belize: fisheries
Belize: deer and antelope
Bermuda: fisheries
Bonaire: turtles
British Indian Ocean Territory: fisheries
Brunei: buffaloes
Cambodia: fish
Cayman Islands: turtles; marine species
Cook Islands: whales
Estonia: fish
Falkland Islands: fisheries
Fiji: fisheries
Grenada: fisheries
Guam: deer
Iceland: birds; fisheries
Indonesia: fishery resources
Kenya: fish
North Korea: fish
Maldives: fish
Mauritius: protected wildlife
Micronesia, Federated States of: marine species
Montserrat: fisheries
Myanmar: fisheries
Namibia: fisheries
Nauru: fisheries
New Zealand: marine mammals
Norfolk Island: birds
Papua New Guinea: crocodiles
St. Helena: fisheries
St. Lucia: turtles, lobsters, and fish
St. Vincent and the Grenadines: fisheries and wildlife
Samoa: fisheries

Seychelles: bird eggs

Sierra Leone: fisheries

Singapore: fisheries

South Africa: elephants

Sri Lanka: fisheries

Sudan: freshwater fisheries

Swaziland: birds

Taiwan: fisheries

Tonga: fisheries

Trinidad and Tobago: conservation of marine turtles

Turks and Caicos Islands: fisheries

Tuvalu: fisheries

United Kingdom: fisheries

United States: marine mammals; Bald and Golden Eagle Protection Act

Vanuatu: enumerated birds; turtles

Virgin Islands (British): fisheries; turtles

Zambia: sport hunting elephants

## A.6  ANTI-CRUELTY STATUTES

Nine nations have enacted anti-cruelty statutes that include wild animals:

| | |
|---|---|
| Bangladesh | Norfolk Island |
| Barbados | Poland |
| Belize | South Africa |
| Grenada | United Kingdom |
| Guernsey | |

## A.7  NO RELEVANT STATUTE

Four nations had not enacted any relevant statute:

Kuwait

Marshall Islands

South Korea

Tokelau

# Appendix B
## Common and Scientific Names of Species Mentioned in the Text

| Common Name | Scientific Name |
| --- | --- |
| **Trees** | |
| alder, red | *Alnus rubra* |
| banksia | *Banksia* spp. |
| baobab | *Adansonia digitata* |
| eucalyptus | *Eucalyptus* spp. |
| mahogany | *Swietenia* spp. |
| māmane | *Sophora chrysophylla* |
| naio | *Myoporum sandwicense* |
| pine, jack | *Pinus banksiana* |
| pine, longleaf | *Pinus palustris* |
| pine, Torrey | *Pinus torreyana* |
| sandalwood, mountain ('iliahi) | *Santalum paniculatum* |
| tapia | *Uapaca bojeri* |
| torreya, Florida | *Torreya taxifolia* |
| **Shrubs** | |
| broom, Holloway's | *Carmichaelia hollowayi* |
| pitpat | *Pittosporum patulum* |
| sagebrush, big | *Artemisia tridentata* |
| tororaro, shrubby | *Muehlenbeckia astonii* |
| **Herbs** | |
| aster, Georgia | *Symphyotrichum georgianum* |
| 'āwikiwiki (lavafield jackbean) | *Canavalia pubescens* |
| bamboo | Family Poaceae, Subfamily Bambusoideae |
| bluegrass, Sandberg | *Poa secunda* |
| cactus | Family Cactaceae |
| cattail | *Typha* spp. |
| cinquefoil, Robbins' | *Potentilla robbinsiana* |

*(cont.)*

| Common Name | Scientific Name |
| --- | --- |
| cordgrass | *Spartina* spp. |
| dactylanthus | *Dactylanthus* spp. |
| daisy, climbing everlasting | *Helichrysum dimorphum* |
| jackbean, lavafield ('āwikiwiki) | *Canavalia pubescens* |
| lobelia, giant | *Lobelia rhynchopetalum* |
| meadowrue, Cooley's | *Thalictrum cooleyi* |
| 'ōhā wai (some members of genus) | *Clermontia lindseyana* |
| oreomyrrhis | *Oreomyrrhis* sp. nov. (*O.* aff *rigida*) |
| pachycladon | *Pachycladon exilis* |
| plantain, narrowleaf | *Plantago lanceolata* |
| poa, awahokomo | *Poa spania* |
| pogonia, small whorled | *Isotria medeoloides* |
| pua'ala (Moloka'i ohaha) | *Brighamia rockii* |
| rice-flower, Wimmera (spiny rice-flower) | *Pimelea spinescens* ssp. *pubiflora* |
| rose, wood (pua o te reinga, flower of Hades) | *Dactylanthus taylorii* |
| sedge | *Carex* spp. |
| violet, early blue (hookedspur) | *Viola adunca* |

### *Algae*

| | |
| --- | --- |
| kelp, giant (giant bladder kelp) | *Macrocystis pyrifera* |

### *Arthropods*

| | |
| --- | --- |
| ant, yellow crazy | *Anoplolepis gracilipes* |
| butterfly, checkerspot | *Euphydryas* spp. |
| butterfly, Edith's checkerspot | *Euphydryas editha* |
| butterfly, Fender's blue | *Icaricia icarioides fenderi* |
| butterfly, monarch | *Danaus plexippus* |
| butterfly, Mono Lake checkerspot | *Euphydryas editha monoensis* |
| butterfly, Oregon silverspot | *Speyeria zerene hippolyta* |
| butterfly, Quino checkerspot | *Euphydryas editha quino* |
| crab, Mount Gorongosa | *Potamonautes gorongosa* |

*(cont.)*

| Common Name | Scientific Name |
| --- | --- |
| katydid | Family Tettigonioidea |
| louse, Califonia condor | *Colpocephalum californici* |
| mosquito | Family Culicidae |
| mosquito, Asian tiger | *Stegomyia albopicta (Aedes albopictus)* |
| mosquito, southern house | *Culex quinquefasciatus* |
| stick insect, Lord Howe Island | *Dryococelus australis* |

### *Mollusks & Other Non-Arthropod Invertebrates*

| | |
| --- | --- |
| combshell, Cumberlandian | *Epioblasma brevidens* |
| coral | Class Anthozoa |
| clam, Asian | *Corbicula fluminea* |
| mussel, zebra | *Dreissena polymorpha* |
| oyster | Most in Superfamily Ostreoidea |
| sea urchin | Class Echinoidea |
| tree snail, Hawaiian (Lonesome George) | *Achinatella apexfulva* |

### *Fish*

| | |
| --- | --- |
| anchovy | Family Engraulidae |
| barramundi | *Lates calcarifer* |
| bass, smallmouth | *Micropterus dolomieu* |
| carp, Asian | Usually refers to *Hypophthalmichthys* spp. |
| chub, Borax Lake | *Siphateles boraxobius* |
| chub, Oregon | *Oregonichthys crameri* |
| cod, Atlantic | *Gadus morhua* |
| darter, snail | *Percina tanasi* |
| lamprey, Pacific | *Entosphenus (Lampetra) tridentata* |
| loach, European weather | *Misgurnus fossillis* |
| mudfish, Canterbury | *Neochanna burrowsius* |
| pupfish, Owens | *Cyprinodon radiosus* |
| salmon, Atlantic | *Salmo salar* |
| salmon, Chinook | *Oncorhynchus tshawytscha* |
| salmon, coho | *Oncorhynchus kisutch* |
| salmon, sockeye | *Oncorhynchus nerka* |
| smelt, delta | *Hypomesus transpacificus* |

*(cont.)*

| Common Name | Scientific Name |
| --- | --- |
| steelhead | Sea-run (anadromous) *Onchorhynchus mykiss* |
| sturgeon, green | *Acipenser medirostris* |
| totoaba | *Totoaba macdonaldi* |
| trout (stocked from hatcheries) | Can be rainbow trout (*Onchorhynchus mykiss*), brown trout (*Salmo trutta*), or brook trout (*Salvelinus fontinalis*) |
| tuna, southern bluefin | *Thunnus maccoyii* |

### Amphibians

| | |
| --- | --- |
| frog, Archey's | *Leiopelma archeyi* |
| frog, corroboree, northern | *Pseudophryne pengilleyi* |
| frog, corroboree, southern | *Pseudophryne corroboree* |
| frog, Hamilton's | *Leiopelma hamiltoni* |
| frog, Hochstetter's | *Leiopelma hochstetteri* |
| frog, holy cross | *Notaden bennettii* |
| frog, Maud Island | *Leiopelma pakeka* |
| frog, mountain yellow-legged | *Rana muscosa* |
| toad, cane | *Rhinella marina* |
| toad, golden | *Incilius periglenes* |
| toad, Kihansi spray | *Nectophrynoides asperginis* |
| tree frog, cascade | *Litoria pearsoniana* |

### Reptiles

| | |
| --- | --- |
| alligator, American | *Alligator mississippiensis* |
| crocodile, Nile | *Crocodylus niloticus* |
| crocodile, saltwater | *Crocodylus porosus* |
| gecko (from the Gorongosa region) | *Afroedura gorongosa* |
| Komodo dragon | *Varanus komodoensis* |
| lizard, island night | *Xantusia riversiana* |
| sea turtle, green | *Chelonia mydas* |
| snake, brown tree | *Boiga irregularis* |
| snake, Indian wolf | *Lycodon aulicus* (*L. capucinus*) |
| tortoise, Galapagos | *Chelonoidis* spp. (*C. nigra* for extant species) |

*(cont.)*

| Common Name | Scientific Name |
| --- | --- |
| tortoise, gopher | *Gopherus polyphemus* |
| tortoise, Pinta Island | *Chelonoidis abingdonii* |
| tortoise, Pinzón giant | *Chelonoidis duncanensis* |
| turtle, western pond | *Actinemys marmorata* |
| turtle, western swamp | *Pseudemydura umbrina* |

### *Birds*

| Common Name | Scientific Name |
| --- | --- |
| 'akepa, Hawai'i | *Loxops coccineus* |
| 'akepa, Maui | *Loxops ochraceus* |
| 'akialoa, Kaua'i | *Akialoa stejnegeri* |
| 'akiapōlā'au | *Hemignathus wilsoni* |
| 'alalā (Hawaiian crow) | *Corvus hawaiiensis* |
| 'alauahio, O'ahu (O'ahu creeper) | *Paroreomyza maculata* |
| 'alawī (Hawai'i creeper) | *Loxops mana* |
| albatross, black-footed | *Phoebastria nigripes* |
| albatross, Laysan | *Phoebastria immutabilis* |
| albatross, short-tailed | *Phoebastria albatrus* |
| 'amakihi, Hawai'i | *Chlorodrepanis virens* |
| 'a'o (Newell's shearwater) | *Puffinus newelli* |
| bobwhite, masked northern | *Colinus virginianus ridgwayi* |
| capercaillie, western | *Tetrao urogallus* |
| caracara, northern crested | *Caracara cheriway* |
| cassowary, southern | *Casuarius casuarius* |
| condor, California | *Gymnogyps californianus* |
| cormorant, double-crested | *Phalacrocorax auritus* |
| cowbird, brown-headed | *Molothrus ater* |
| crane, sandhill | *Antigone canadensis* |
| crane, whooping | *Grus americana* |
| crow, Banggai | *Corvus unicolor* |
| crow, Hawaiian ('alalā) | *Corvus hawaiiensis* |
| dodo | *Raphus cucullatus* |
| dunlin | *Calidris alpina* |
| eagle, bald | *Haliaeetus leucocephalus* |
| eagle, golden | *Aquila chrysaetos* |
| falcon, peregrine | *Falco peregrinus* |

(cont.)

| Common Name | Scientific Name |
| --- | --- |
| flycatcher, Guam | *Myiagra freycineti* |
| gnatcatcher, California | *Polioptila californica* |
| goose, Aleutian cackling | *Branta hutchinsii leucopareia* |
| grouse, greater sage | *Centrocercus urophasianus* |
| honeycreeper, Laysan | *Himatione fraithii* |
| ibis, northern bald | *Geronticus eremita* |
| i'iwi | *Vestiaria coccinea* |
| 'io (Hawaiian hawk) | *Buteo solitarius* |
| kākāpō | *Strigops habroptilus* |
| kāma'o | *Myadestes myadestinus* |
| kestrel, Mauritius | *Falco punctatus* |
| kingfisher, Guam | *Todiramphus cinnamominus cinnamominus* |
| kiwi, North Island brown | *Apteryx mantelli* |
| manakin, Araripe | *Antilophia bokermanni* |
| moa | Order Dinornithiformes |
| nēnē | *Branta sandvicensis* |
| nightjar, European | *Caprimulgus europaeus* |
| nukupu'u, Kaua'i | *Hemignathus hanapepe* |
| oloma'o (Moloka'i thrush) | *Myadestes lanaiensis* |
| 'ō'ō, Kaua'i | *Moho braccatus* |
| openbill (stork), Asian | *Anastomus oscitans* |
| 'ō'ū | *Psittirostra psittacea* |
| owl, barn | *Tyto alba* |
| owl, barred | *Strix varia* |
| owl, California spotted | *Strix occidentalis occidentalis* |
| owl, Mexican spotted | *Strix occidentalis lucida* |
| owl, northern spotted | *Strix occidentalis caurina* |
| palila | *Loxioides bailleui* |
| parrot, Puerto Rican | *Amazona vittata* |
| penguin, Magellanic | *Spheniscus magellanicus* |
| petrel, Bonin | *Pterodroma hypoleuca* |
| pigeon, common | *Columba livia* |
| pigeon, passenger | *Ectopistes migratorius* |

*(cont.)*

| Common Name | Scientific Name |
| --- | --- |
| plover, shore | *Thinornis novaeseelandiae* |
| po'ouli (po'o-uli) | *Melamprosops phaeosoma* |
| prairie-chicken, Attwater's | *Tympanuchus cupido attwateri* |
| pygmy-owl, ferruginous | *Glaucidium brasilianum* |
| quelea, red-billed | *Quelea quelea* |
| rail, Guam | *Gallirallus owstoni* |
| rail, Laysan | *Porzana palmeri* |
| rail, Ridgway's | *Rallus obsoletus obsoletus* |
| robin, Chatham Island black | *Petroica traversi* |
| shearwater, Newell's ('a'o) | *Puffinus newelli* |
| sparrow, dusky seaside | *Ammospiza maritima nigrescens* |
| starling, European | *Sturnus vulgaris* |
| storm-petrel, Tristram's | *Oceanodroma tristrami* |
| tern, Caspian | *Hydropogne caspia* |
| tomtit, Chatham Island | *Petroica macrocephala chathamensis* |
| vireo, black-capped | *Vireo atricapilla* |
| vulture, bearded | *Gypaetus barbatus* |
| vulture, Cape | *Gyps coprotheres* |
| vulture, griffon | *Gyps fulvus* |
| vulture, hooded | *Necrosyrtes monachus* |
| vulture, Indian | *Gyps indicus* |
| vulture, lappet-faced | *Torgos tracheliotos* |
| vulture, palm-nut | *Gypohierax angolensis* |
| vulture, red-headed | *Sarcogyps calvus* |
| vulture, slender-billed | *Gyps tenuirostris* |
| vulture, turkey | *Cathartes aura* |
| vulture, white-backed | *Gyps africanus* |
| vulture, white-rumped | *Gyps bengalensis* |
| warbler, Kirtland's | *Setophaga kirtlandii* |
| woodlark | *Lullula arborea* |
| woodpecker, ivory-billed | *Campephilus principalis* |
| woodpecker, red-cockaded | *Leuconotopicus (Picoides) borealis* |
| wren, Pacific | *Troglodytes pacificus* |
| yellowlegs | *Tringa melanoleuca* |

(cont.)

| Common Name | Scientific Name |
| --- | --- |
| **Mammals** | |
| antelope, giant sable | *Hippotragus niger variani* |
| antelope, roan | *Hippotragus equinus* |
| antelope, sable | *Hippotragus niger* |
| antelope, saiga | *Saiga tatarica* |
| antelope, Tibetan (chiru) | *Pantholops hodgsonii* |
| bear, brown | *Ursus arctos* |
| bear, grizzly | *Ursus arctos horribilis* |
| bear, short-faced | *Arctodus* spp. |
| beaver, giant | *Castoroides* spp. |
| bettong | *Bettongia* spp. |
| bilby, greater | *Macrotis lagotis* |
| bison, American | *Bison bison* |
| brushtail possum, common | *Trichosurus vulpecula* |
| buffalo, African (Cape) | *Syncerus caffer* |
| caribou, boreal woodland | *Rangifer tarandus caribou* |
| cat, feral (domestic) | *Felis catus* |
| cat, saber-tooth | *Smilodon* spp. |
| cattle, feral | *Bos taurus* |
| cheetah | *Acinonyx jubatus* |
| chimpanzee, common | *Pan troglodytes* |
| cottontail, New England (rabbit) | *Sylvilagus transitionalis* |
| cougar | *Puma concolor* |
| coyote | *Canis latrans* |
| deer, feral | Family Cervidae |
| deer, mule | *Odocoileus hemionus* |
| deer, Père David's | *Elaphurus davidianus* |
| dingo | *Canis lupus dingo* |
| dog, feral | *Canis lupus familiaris* |
| donkey, feral | *Equus asinus* |
| eland, common | *Taurotragus oryx* |
| elephant (African species) | *Loxodonta* spp. |
| elk, American | *Cervus canadensis* |
| ferret, black-footed | *Mustela nigripes* |

(*cont.*)

| Common Name | Scientific Name |
| --- | --- |
| flying fox, Christmas Island | *Pteropus natalis* |
| flying fox, gray-headed | *Pteropus poliocephalus* |
| fox, Arctic | *Vulpes lagopus* |
| fox, island | *Urocyon littoralis* |
| fox, red | *Vulpes vulpes* |
| fox, San Miguel Island | *Urocyon littoralis littoralis* |
| fox, Santa Catalina Island | *Urocyon littoralis catalinae* |
| fur seal, Guadalupe | *Arctocephalus townsendi* |
| giraffe | *Giraffa* spp. |
| goat, feral | *Capra hircus* |
| gorilla, mountain | *Gorilla beringei beringei* |
| ground squirrel, Piute | *Urocitellus mollis* |
| hartebeest, Lichtenstein's | *Alcelaphus buselaphus lichtensteinii* |
| hippopotamus | *Hippopotamus amphibius* |
| hyena, spotted | *Crocuta crocuta* |
| impala | *Aepyceros melampus* |
| kangaroo | Family Macropodidae |
| kangaroo rat, giant | *Dipodomys ingens* |
| koala | *Phascolarctos cinereus* |
| leopard | *Panthera pardus* |
| lion | *Panthera leo* |
| mammoth, wooly | *Mammuthus primigenius* |
| marten, European pine | *Martes martes* |
| melomys, Bramble Cay | *Melomys rubicola* |
| monk seal, Hawaiian | *Neomonachus schauinslandi* |
| mongoose | *Herpestes* spp. |
| mongoose, Javan | *Herpestes javanicus* |
| moose | *Alces alces* |
| mouse, house | *Mus musculus* |
| panda, giant | *Ailuropoda melanoleuca* |
| panther, Florida | *Puma concolor couguar* |
| pig, feral | *Sus scrofa* |
| pika, American | *Ochotona princeps* |
| pipistrelle, Christmas Island | *Pipistrellus murrayi* |
| potoroo | *Potorous* spp. |

*(cont.)*

| Common Name | Scientific Name |
| --- | --- |
| prairie dog, black-tailed | *Cynomys ludovicianus* |
| quoll | *Dasyurus* spp. |
| quoll, northern | *Dasyurus hallucatus* |
| rabbit, European | *Oryctolagus cuniculus* |
| rabbit, New England cottontail | *Sylvilagus transitionalis* |
| rat | *Rattus* spp. |
| rat, black | *Rattus rattus* |
| rat, bulldog (Christmas Island burrowing rat) | *Rattus nativatatus* |
| rat, Maclear's | *Rattus macleari* |
| rhinoceros, black | *Diceros bicornis* |
| rhinoceros, northern white | *Ceratotherium simum cottoni* |
| rhinoceros, southern white | *Ceratotherium simum simum* |
| ringtail possum, lemuroid | *Hemibelideus lemuroides* |
| ringtail possum, white lemuroid | *Hemibelideus lemuroides* |
| rock wallaby, black-footed | *Petrogale lateralis* |
| sea lion, California | *Zalophus californianus* |
| sea lion, Steller's | *Eumetapias jubatus* |
| seal, harbour | *Phoca vitulina* |
| seal, Hawaiian monk | *Neomonachus schauinslandi* |
| sheep, European mouflon | *Ovis gmelini musimon* |
| sheep, feral | *Ovis aries* |
| shrew, Christmas Island | *Crocidara trichura* |
| sloth, giant ground | *Megatherium* spp. |
| stick-nest rat, greater | *Leporillus conditor* |
| stoat | *Mustela erminea* |
| tiger | *Panthera tigris* |
| vaquita | *Phocoena sinus* |
| vole, northern red-backed | *Myodes rutilus* |
| waterbuck | *Kobus ellipsiprymnus* |
| whale, gray | *Eschrichtius robustus* |
| wild dog, African | *Lycaon pictus* |
| wildebeest, blue | *Connochaetes taurinus* |

*(cont.)*

| Common Name | Scientific Name |
| --- | --- |
| wolf, gray | *Canis lupus* |
| wolf, Mexican gray | *Canis lupus baileyi* |
| wolf, red | *Canis rufus* |
| wolverine | *Gulo gulo* |
| wombat, northern hairy-nosed | *Lasiorhinus krefftii* |
| woylie (brush-tailed bettong) | *Bettongia penicillata* |
| zebra, Crawshay's | *Equus quagga crawshayi* |
| zebra, plains | *Equus quagga* |

### Disease Organisms

| | |
| --- | --- |
| bacterium, plague (cause of sylvatic and human plague) | *Yersinia pestis* |
| fungi, amphibian chytrid (cause of chytridiomycosis) | *Batrachochytrium dendrobatidis*; *Batrachochytrium salamandrivorans* |
| fungus, white-nose (cause of white-nose syndrome) | *Pseudogymnoascus destructans* |

# Essay Contributors

**Michael J. Bean** directed the wildlife conservation activities of the Environmental Defense Fund for over 30 years. He served during the Obama Administration as the Principal Deputy Assistant Secretary for Fish and Wildlife and Parks. He is the author of *The Evolution of National Wildlife Law* and many essays, op-eds, and journal articles about wildlife conservation.

**P. Dee Boersma** is Director, Center for Ecosystem Sentinels, University of Washington, where she holds the Wadsworth Endowed Chair in Conservation Science. Her work on Magellanic and Galapagos penguins helped to secure Marine Protected Areas in Argentina and the Galapagos and resulted in moving oil tanker lanes farther from the coast of Chubut, Argentina, to reduce the oiling of penguins during their migration. She is an editor of *Penguins: Natural History and Conservation* and *Invasive Species of the Pacific Northwest* (both University of Washington Press).

**Christopher G.R. Bowden** has been Asian Vulture Programme manager for the Royal Society for the Protection of Birds (RSPB) since 2004. He also manages SAVE (Saving Asia's Vultures from Extinction), a consortium of 24 regional and international organizations committed to the conservation of vultures in South Asia (http://www.save-vultures.org/). Chris has co-chaired the IUCN Vulture Specialist Group since its formation in 2011. His experience over the past 35 years is mainly with Critically Endangered bird species, particularly northern bald ibis, but has also included various species in Africa, Asia, the UK, and the Caribbean.

**Brian Gratwicke** is a conservation biologist leading amphibian conservation programs at the Smithsonian Conservation Biology

Institute. His focus has been on building capacity to conserve amphibians in Appalachia and in the tropics through the Panama Amphibian Rescue and Conservation Project, which is based at the Smithsonian Tropical Research Institute.

**Jianguo "Jack" Liu** is a human-environment scientist and sustainability scholar. He holds the Rachel Carson Chair in Sustainability and is University Distinguished Professor at Michigan State University. He and his collaborators have been working on an interdisciplinary project, "Pandas, People, and Policies," since 1995. He has recently developed an integrated framework of metacoupling (human–nature interactions within as well as between adjacent and distant systems) for global sustainable development and conservation.

**Loyal A. Mehrhoff** has been involved in the conservation of endangered species for over 40 years. He has worked to prevent the extinction of endangered plants and animals at the Center for Biological Diversity, US Fish and Wildlife Service, National Park Service, US Geological Survey, and the Bishop Museum. His expertise includes conservation policy and Hawaiian plants.

**Simon Nampindo** has been the Country Director of the Wildlife Conservation Society's Uganda Country Program since 2015. He has 15 years of conservation work experience in Eastern Africa, Eastern Democratic Republic of Congo, Rwanda, and South Africa, and collaborates extensively with various universities and research institutions globally in the fields of wildlife conservation, climate change, human dimensions of conservation, and sustainable conservation financing.

**Joseph Y. Oatman** is a Nez Perce tribal member who comes from the Chief Looking Glass Band of the Nez Perce and is a descendant of A-Pus-Wyekt (Flint Necklace, also known as Chief Looking Glass), a principal signatory for the Tribe for the Treaty of 1855. His family, people, land, and the Tribe's reserved treaty rights are very important to who he is and what he does. Joe holds a BS degree in fishery resources and a Masters of Natural Resources from the University of Idaho. He is currently the deputy program manager for the Nez Perce Tribe's Department of Fisheries Resources Management, where he oversees the harvest management of the Tribe's treaty mainstem Columbia River and tributary fisheries and seasons for salmon and steelhead. He serves as US member to the Southern Panel of the Pacific Salmon Treaty and as Tribal Representative to the Pacific Fishery Management Council.

**Camille Parmesan**'s research focuses on the impacts of climate change on wild plants and animals, spanning fieldwork on butterflies to synthetic analyses of global impacts on a broad range of species across terrestrial and marine biomes. She is also involved in developing conservation assessment and planning tools for preserving biodiversity in the face of climate change and is currently lead author for the chapter on "Terrestrial Ecosystems" for the IPCC 6th Assessment Report. She was awarded the Conservation Achievement Award in Science by the National Wildlife Federation (2007), was an official Contributor to IPCC's Nobel Peace Prize (2007), and is a "Make Our Planet Great Again" Laureate, awarded by President Emmanuel Macron (France). She is primarily based at CNRS in France.

**Lorenzo Rojas-Bracho** has been working with vaquitas since 1997. He was joint chief scientist on the 1997, 2008, and 2015 vaquita surveys. He chairs the International Committee for the Recovery of the Vaquita (CIRVA) to advise the Government of Mexico on conservation measures for the vaquita's recovery. He is a member of the Convention for MS Scientific Council's Aquatic Mammals Working Group, the IUCN's Cetacean Specialist Group, The Red List Authority, and the Marine Mammal Protected Areas Task Force. He chairs the International Whaling Commission's Conservation Committee.

**Barbara Taylor** has conducted conservation research on marine mammals for over 30 years, working for US National Marine Fisheries Service. Her focus has been on risk analysis and conservation genetics. She oversees IUCN Cetacean Red List assessments and chairs the Society for Marine Mammalogy's Conservation Committee. Conservation of Mexico's vaquita porpoise has been a passion throughout her career.

**Timothy H. Tear** has been the Executive Director of the Wildlife Conservation Society's Africa Program since 2015. He has worked on conservation in Africa, Arabia, and the United States for over three decades. In Africa, in the 1980s he lived and worked in Mt. Kenya National Park in Kenya and on the establishment of Boma National Park in South Sudan, and in the 1990s and 2010s worked in Tanzania conserving the Serengeti Ecosystem.

**John Woinarski** has many decades of experience in research, policy, and management relating to Australia's threatened species and the factors that affect them. He is a Deputy Director of the Threatened Species Recovery Hub of the Australian government's National Environmental Science Program. John's recent books include *The Action Plan for Australian Mammals 2012, Recovering Australian Threatened Species: A Book of Hope, A Bat's End: The Christmas Island Pipistrelle and Extinction in Australia*, and *Cats in Australia: Companion and Killer.*

# References

Akçakaya, H.R., E.L. Bennett, T.M. Brooks, et al. 2018. Quantifying species recovery and conservation success to develop an IUCN Green List of Species. *Conservation Biology* 32(5): 1128–1138. https://doi.org/10.1111/cobi.13112

Alagona, P.S. 2013. *After the Grizzly. Endangered Species and the Politics of Place in California.* Berkeley, CA: University of California Press.

Allendorf, F.W., R.F. Leary, P. Spruell, and J.K. Wenburg. 2001. The problem with hybrids: Setting conservation guidelines. *Trends in Ecology and Evolution* 16: 613–622.

Allentoft, M.E., R. Heller, C.L. Oskam, et al. 2014. Extinct New Zealand megafauna were not in decline before human colonization. *Proceedings of the National Academy of Sciences of the United States of America* 111: 4922–4927. https://doi.org/10.1073/pnas.1314972111

Amos, W., H.J. Nichols, T. Churchyard, and M. de L. Brooke. 2016. Rat eradication comes within a whisker! A case study of a failed project from the South Pacific. *Royal Society Open Science* 3: 160110. https://doi.org/10.1098/rsos.160110

Andrew, P., H. Cogger, D. Driscoll, et al. 2018. Somewhat saved: a captive breeding programme for two endemic Christmas Island lizard species, now extinct in the wild. *Oryx* 52: 171–174. https://doi.org/10.1017/S0030605316001071

Balmford, A. 2012. *Wild Hope. On the Front Lines of Conservation Success.* Chicago, IL: Chicago University Press.

Banko, P.C., S.C. Hess, P.G. Scowcroft, et al. 2014. Evaluating the long-term management of introduced ungulates to protect the Palila, an endangered bird, and its critical habitat in subalpine forest of Mauna Kea, Hawai'i. *Arctic, Antarctic, and Alpine Research* 46: 871–889. https://doi.org/10.1657/1938-4246-46.4.871

Barrow, M.V., Jr. 2009. *Nature's Ghosts. Confronting Extinction from the Age of Jefferson to the Age of Ecology.* Chicago, IL: Chicago University Press.

Barrowclough, G.F., J. Cracraft, J. Klicka, and R.M. Zink. 2016. How many kinds of birds are there and why does it matter? *PLoS ONE* 11(11): e0166307. https://doi.org/10.1371/journal.pone.0166307

Bauer H., G. Chapron, K. Nowell, et al. 2015. Lion (*Panthera leo*) populations are declining rapidly across Africa, except in intensively managed areas. *Proceedings of the National Academy of Sciences of the United States of America* 112: 14 894–14 899.

Baumsteiger, J., and P.B. Moyle. 2017. Assessing extinction. *BioScience* 67: 357–366. https://doi.org/10.1093/biosci/bix001

Bennett, N.J., A. Di Franco, A. Calò, E., et al. 2019. Local support for conservation is associated with perceptions of good governance, social impacts, and ecological effectiveness. *Conservation Letters*. Online: e12640. doi: 10.1111/conl.12640.

Benton, N., J.D. Ripley, and F. Powledge (eds). 2008. *Conserving Biodiversity on Military Lands: A Guide for Natural Resources Managers*. Arlington, VA: NatureServe. http://www.dodbiodiversity.org.

Bergstrom, D.M., A. Lucieer, K. Kiefer, et al. 2009a. Indirect effects of invasive species removal devastate World Heritage Island. *Journal of Applied Ecology* 46: 73–81. doi: 10.1111/j.1365-2664.2008.01601.x.

Bergstrom, D.M., A. Lucieer, K. Kiefer, et al. 2009b. Management implications of the Macquarie Island trophic cascade revisited: a reply to Dowding et al. (2009). *Journal of Applied Ecology* 46: 1133–1136. doi: 10.1111/j.1365-2664.2009.01708.x.

Bessesen, B. 2018. *Vaquita. Science, Politics, and Crime in the Sea of Cortez*. Washington, DC: Island Press.

Beurton, P.J. 2002. Ernst Mayr through time on the biological species concept: a conceptual analysis. *Theory in Biosciences* 121: 81–98. doi:10.1078/1431-7613-00050.

Biggins, D.E., J.L. Godbey, B.M. Horton, and T.M. Livieri. 2011. Movements and survival of black-footed ferrets associated with an experimental translocation in South Dakota. *Journal of Mammalogy* 92: 742–750. https://doi.org/10.1644/10-MAMM-S-152.1

Black, S.H., and D.M. Vaughan. 2005. Species profile: *Spyeyeria zerene hippolyta*. Portland, OR: The Xerces Society for Invertebrate Conservation. https://xerces.org/oregon-silverspot/

Bland, L.M., D.A. Keith, R.M. Miller, N.J. Murray, and J.P. Rodriguez (eds). 2016. *Guidelines for the Application of IUCN Red List of Ecosystems Categories and Criteria, Version 1.0*. Gland, Switzerland: IUCN. http://dx.doi.org/10.2305/IUCN.CH.2016.RLE.1.en

Bocetti, C.I., D.D. Goble, and J.M. Scott. 2012. Using Conservation Management Agreements to secure postrecovery perpetuation of conservation-reliant species: the Kirtland's warbler as a case study. *BioScience* 62: 874–879. https://doi.org/10.1525/bio.2012.62.10.7.

Bosch, J., E. Sanchez-Tomé, A. Fernández-Loras, et al. 2015. Successful elimination of a lethal wildlife infectious disease in nature. *Biology Letters* 11(11): https://doi.org/10.1098/rsbl.2015.0874

Botha, A. J., J. Andevski, C. G R. Bowden, et al. 2017. Multi-species Action Plan to Conserve African-Eurasian Vultures. CMS Raptors MOU Technical Publication No. 5. CMS Technical Series No. 35. Coordinating Unit of the CMS Raptors MOU, Abu Dhabi, United Arab Emirates. https://www.cms.int/sites/default/files/document/cms_cop12_doc.24.1.4_annex3_vulture-msap_e.pdf.

Bowman, D.M.J.S. 1998. Tansley Review No. 101: the impact of Aboriginal landscape burning on the Australian biota. *New Phytologist* 140: 385–410.

Bowman, M., P. Davies, and C. Redgwell. 2010. *Lyster's International Wildlife Law*, 2nd edition. Cambridge, UK: Cambridge University Press.

Bradshaw, C.J.A., and P.R. Ehrlich. 2015. *Killing the Koala and Poisoning the Prairie. Australia, America, and the Environment.* Chicago, IL: Chicago University Press.

Brand, S. 2015. Rethinking extinction. *Aeon*, April 21, 2015. https://aeon.co/essays/we-are-not-edging-up-to-a-mass-extinction.

Brown, D.E., and K.B. Clark. 2017. The saga of the masked bobwhite: lessons learned and unlearned. *National Quail Symposium Proceedings* 18(1): Article 102. http://trace.tennessee.edu/nqsp/vol8/iss1/102.

Burgess, M.D., K.W. Smith, K.L. Evans, et al. 2018. Tritrophic phenological match-mismatch in space and time. *Nature Ecology and Evolution* 2: 970–975. doi: 10.1038/s41559-018-0543-1.

Burnham, W., and T.J. Cade (eds). 2003. *Return of the Peregrine: A North American Saga of Tenacity and Teamwork.* Boise, ID: The Peregrine Fund.

Burrows, M.T., D.S. Schoeman, L.B. Buckley, et al. 2011. The pace of shifting climate in marine and terrestrial ecosystems. *Science* 334: 652–655. doi: 10.1126/science.1210288.

Butler D, and D. Merton. 1992. *The Black Robin: Saving the World's Most Endangered Bird.* Oxford, UK: Oxford University Press.

Byers, E., and K.M. Ponte. 2005. *The Conservation Easement Handbook*, 2nd edition. Washington, DC, USA and San Francisco, CA: Land Trust Alliance and Trust for Public Land.

Callaway, E. 2016. Geneticists aim to save rare rhino. *Nature* 533: 20–21. doi:10.1038/533020a

Camacho, A.E., M. Robinson-Dorn, A.C. Yildiz, and T. Teegarden. 2017. Assessing state laws and resources for endangered species protection. *Environmental Law Review* 47: 10 837–10 844.

Cantrell, B., L.J. Martin, and E.C. Ellis. 2017. Designing autonomy: opportunities for new wildness in the Anthropocene. *Trends in Ecology and Evolution* 32: 156–166. https://doi.org/10.1016/j.tree.2016.12.004

Caro, T. 2010. *Conservation by Proxy.* Washington, DC: Island Press.

Carrion, V., C.J. Donlan, K.J. Campbell, C. Lavoie, and F. Cruz. 2011. Archipelago-wide island restoration in the Galápagos Islands: Reducing costs of invasive mammal eradication programs and reinvasion risk. *PLoS ONE* 6(5): e18835. https://doi.org/10.1371/journal.pone.0018835

Carson, R. 1962. *Silent Spring*. Boston, MA: Houghton Mifflin.

Ceballos, G., P.R. Ehrlich, and R. Dirzo. 2017. Biological annihilation via the ongoing sixth mass extinction signaled by vertebrate population losses and declines. *Proceedings of the National Academy of Sciences of the United States of America* 114(30): E6089–E6096. https://doi.org/10.1073/pnas.1704949114

Chala, D., C. Brochmann, A. Psomas, et al. 2016. Good-bye to tropical alpine plant giants under warmer climates? Loss of range and genetic diversity in *Lobelia rhynchopetalum*. *Ecology and Evolution* 6: 8931–8941. doi: 10.1002/ece3.2603

Channing, A., S. Finlow-Bates, S.E. Haarklau, and P.G. Hawkes. 2006. The biology and recent history of the critically endangered Kihansi spray toad *Nectophrynoides asperginis* in Tanzania. *Journal of East African Natural History* 95: 117–138. doi:10.2982/0012-8317(2006)95[117:tbarho]2.0.co;2.

Chaplin, S.J., R.A. Gerrard, H.M. Watson, L.L. Master, and S.R. Flack. 2000. The geography of imperilment: Targeting conservation toward critical biodiversity areas. In B.A. Stein, L.S. Kutner, and J.S. Adams, eds, *Precious Heritage. The Status of Biodiversity in the United States*. Oxford, UK: Oxford University Press, pp. 159–199.

Chessman, B.C. 2013. Identifying species at risk from climate change: Traits predict the drought vulnerability of freshwater fishes. *Biological Conservation* 160: 40–49.

Clark, J.A., and E. Harvey. 2002. Assessing multi-species recovery plans under the Endangered Species Act. *Ecological Applications* 12: 655–662. doi: 10.2307/3060974

Cloern, J.E, J. Kay, W. Kimmerer, et al. 2017. Water wasted to the sea? *San Francisco Estuary and Watershed Science* 15(2): art1. https://doi.org/10.15447/sfews.2017v15iss2art1

Cokinos, C. 2000. *Hope is the Thing with Feathers. A Personal Chronicle of Vanishing Birds*. New York, NY: Jeremy P. Tarcher/Putnam.

Conner, R. N., D. C. Rudolph, and J. R. Walters. 2001. *The Red-cockaded Woodpecker: Surviving in a Fire-maintained Ecosystem*. Austin, TX: University of Texas Press.

Conservation Measures Partnership. 2013. Open Standards for the Practice of Conservation. Version 3.0. Available at: http://cmp-openstandards.org/wp-content/uploads/2014/03/CMP-OS-V3-0-Final.pdf

Cooper, D.S., J. Mongolo, and C. Dellith. 2017. Status of the California gnatcatcher at the northern edge of its range. *Western Birds* 48: 124–140. doi: 10.21199/WB48.2.3

Cooper, N.W., C.R. Rushing, and P.P. Marra. 2019. Reducing the conservation reliance of Kirtland's warbler through adaptive management. *Journal of Wildlife Management* 83(6): 1297–1305.

Cosco, J.M. 1998. NEPA for the Gander: NEPA's application to critical habitat designations and other "benevolent" federal action. *Duke Environmental Law & Policy Forum* 8: 345–385.

Costanza, R. (ed.). 1991. *Ecological Economics: The Science and Management of Sustainability*. New York, NY: Columbia University Press.

Courtois, P., C. Figuieres, and C. Muller. 2014. Conservation priorities when species interact: The Noah's Ark metaphor revisited. *PLoS ONE* 9(9): e106073. doi: 10:1371/journal.pone.0106073.

Crooks, K.R., and M. Sanjayan (eds). 2006. *Connectivity Conservation*. Cambridge, UK: Cambridge University Press.

Crutzen, P.J., and E.F. Stoermer. 2000. The 'Anthropocene'. *Global Change Newsletter* 41: 17–18.

Curio, E. 1987. Animal decision-making and the 'Concorde fallacy'. *Trends in Ecology and Evolution* 2: 148–152. https://doi.org/10.1016/0169-5347(87)90064-4.

Daily, G.C. (ed.). 1997. *Natures Services: Societal Dependence on Natural Ecosystems*. Washington, DC: Island Press.

Darwin, C. 1859. *On the Origin of Species. Or the Preservation of Favoured Races in the Struggle for Life*. London: John Murray .

Davis, R.J., A.N. Gray, J.B. Kim, and W.B. Cohen. 2017. Patterns of change across the forested landscape. In D.H. Olson and B. Van Horne, eds, *People, Forests, and Change. Lessons from the Pacific Northwest*. Washington, DC: Island Press, pp. 91–101.

Dawson, J., S. Oppel, R.J. Cuthbert, et al. 2015. Prioritizing islands for the eradication of invasive vertebrates in the United Kingdom overseas territories. *Conservation Biology* 29: 143–153. doi: 10.1111/cobi.12347

de Queiroz, K. 2005. Ernst Mayr and the modern concept of species. *Proceedings of the National Academy of Sciences of the United States of America* 102 (Supplement 1): 6600–6607. doi:10.1073/pnas.0502030102.

Di Minin, E., C. Fink, T. Hiippala, and H. Tenkanen. 2018. A framework for investigating illegal wildlife trade on social media with machine learning. *Conservation Biology* 33(1): 210–213. doi: 10.1111/cobi.13104

Diamond, J. 2005. *Collapse. How Societies Choose to Fail or Succeed*. New York, NY: Viking Penguin.

Diller, L.V., K.A. Hamm, D.A. Early, et al. 2016. Demographic response of northern spotted owls to barred owl removal. *Journal of Wildlife Management* 80: 691–707. doi:10.1002/jwmg./1046.

Dinerstein, E., and E.D. Wikramanayake. 1993. Beyond "Hotspots": How to prioritize investments to conserve biodiversity in the Indo-Pacific region. *Conservation Biology* 7: 53–65. doi: 10.1046/j.1523-1739.1993.07010053.x

Donlan, C.J. (ed.) 2015. *Proactive Strategies for Protecting Species. Pre-Listing Conservation and the Endangered Species Act.* Oakland, CA: University of California Press.

Doremus, H. 2010. The Endangered Species Act: static law meets dynamic world. *Washington University Journal of Law and Policy* 32: 175–235.

Doremus, H., and J. E. Pagel. 2001. Why listing may be forever: Perspectives on delisting under the U.S. Endangered Species Act. *Conservation Biology* 15: 1258–1268.

Dowding, J.E., E.C. Murphy, K. Springer, A.J. Peacock, and C. J. Krebs. 2009. Cats, rabbits, *Myxoma* virus, and vegetation on Macquarie Island: a comment on Bergstrom et al. (2009). *Journal of Applied Ecology* 46: 1129–1132. doi:10.1111/j.1365-2664.2009.01690.x.

Dugger, K.M., E.D. Forsman, A.B. Franklin, et al. 2016. The effects of habitat, climate, and Barred Owls on long-term demography of Northern Spotted Owls. *The Condor* 118: 57–116. https://doi.org/10.1650/CONDOR-15-24.1

Duncan, R.P., A.G. Boyerb, and T.M. Blackburne. 2013. Magnitude and variation of prehistoric bird extinctions in the Pacific. *Proceedings of the National Academy of Sciences of the United States of America* 110: 6436–6441. doi: 10.1073/pnas.1216511110.

Dunham, J.B., R. White, C.S. Allen, B.G. Marcot, and D. Shively. 2016. The reintroduction landscape: Finding success at the intersection of ecological, social, and institutional dimensions. In D.S. Jachowski, J.J. Millspaugh, P.L. Angermeier, and R. Slolow, eds, *Reintroduction of Fish and Wildlife Populations.* Berkeley, CA: University of California Press, pp. 79–103.

Elphick, C.S., D.L. Roberts, and J.M. Reed. 2010. Estimated dates of recent extinctions for North American and Hawaiian birds. *Biological Conservation* 143: 617–624. doi:10.1016/j.biocon.2009.11.026.

Esvelt, K.M., and N.J. Gemmell. 2017. Conservation demands safe gene drive. *PLoS Biology* 15(11): e2003850. doi.org/10.1371/journal.pbio.2003850

Evans, D.M., J.P. Che-Castaldo, D. Crouse, et al. 2016. Species recovery in the United States: Increasing the effectiveness of the Endangered Species Act. *Issues in Ecology Report Number 20.* Washington, DC: Ecological Society of America.

Ewen, J.G., L. Adams, and R. Renwick. 2013. New Zealand Species Recovery Groups and their role in evidence-based conservation. *Journal of Applied Ecology* 50: 281–285. doi: 10.1111/1365-2664.12062.

Fabinyi, M., and N. Liu. 2014. Seafood banquets in Beijing: consumer perspectives and implications for environmental sustainability. *Conservation and Society* 12: 218–228. www.conservationandsociety.org/text.asp?2014/12/2/218/138423.

Falcy, M. 2016. Conservation decision making: integrating the precautionary principle with uncertainty. *Frontiers in Ecology and the Environment* 14: 499–504. doi: 10.1002/fee.1423

FAO (Food and Agriculture Organization of the United Nations). 2002. Legal Trends in Wildlife Management. FAO Legislative Study 74, FAO, Rome, Italy. www.fao.org/docrep/005/Y3844E/Y3844E00.HTM.

Finkelstein, M.E., D.F. Doak, D. George, et al. 2012. Lead poisoning and the deceptive recovery of the critically endangered California condor. *Proceedings of the National Academy of Sciences of the United States of America* 109: 11 449–11 454. doi: 10.1073/pnas.1203141109.

Finlayson, H.H. 1935. *The Red Centre: Man and Beast in the Heart of Australia.* Sydney, Australia: Angus & Robertson.

Finney, S.C., and L.E. Edwards. 2016. The "Anthropocene" epoch: scientific decision or political statement? *GSA Today* 26(3). doi: 10.1130/GSATG270A.

Fischer J., and D.B. Lindenmayer. 2000. An assessment of the published results of animal relocations. *Biological Conservation* 96: 1–11.

Fisher, H.I., and P.H. Baldwin. 1946. War and the birds of Midway Atoll. *Condor* 48: 3–15.

Fitzpatrick, J.W. 2018. Analysis: Failing to invest in endangered species is a Tragedy of the Commons. *Living Bird*. Summer 2018. https://www.allaboutbirds.org/analysis-failing-to-invest-in-endangered-species-is-a-tragedy-of-the-commons/

Fitzpatrick, J.W., M. Lammertink, M.D. Luneau, Jr., et al. 2005. Ivory-billed woodpecker (*Campephilus principalis*) persists in continental North America. *Science* 308: 1460–1462.

Flannery, T. 1994. *The Future Eaters. An Ecological History of the Australasian Lands and People.* New York, NY: Grove Press.

Flannery, T. 2012a. Unmourned death of a sole survivor. *The Sydney Morning Herald*, November 17, 2012.

Flannery, T. 2012b. *After the Future. Australia's New Extinction Crisis.* Quarterly Essay No. 48. Buxton, Victoria, Australia: Nokomis Publications.

Flannery, T., and P. Schouten. 2001. *A Gap in Nature. Discovering the World's Extinct Animals.* New York, NY: Atlantic Monthly Press.

Flather, C.H., M.S. Knowles, and J. McNees. 2008. *Geographic pattern of at-risk species: A technical document supporting the USDA Forest Service Interim Update of the 2000 RPS Assessment.* General Technical Report RMRS-GTR-211. Fort Collins, CO: US Department of Agriculture, Forest Service, Rocky Mountain Research Station.

Flessa, K.W., and D. Jablonski. 1983. Extinction is here to stay. *Paleobiology* 9: 315–321.

Fluker, S., and J. Stacey. 2012. The basics of Species at Risk legislation in Alberta. *Alberta Law Review* 50: 95–113.

Foden, W.B., and B.E. Young (eds). 2016. IUCN SSC Guidelines for Assessing Species' Vulnerability to Climate Change. (Version 1.0). Occasional Paper of the IUCN Species Survival Commission No. 59. Gland, Switzerland and Cambridge, UK: IUCN Species Survival Commission. http://dx.doi.org/10.2305/IUCN.CH.2016.SSC-OP.59.en.

Foden, W.B., S.H.M. Butchart, S.N. Stuart, et al. 2013. Identifying the World's most climate change vulnerable species: a systematic trait-based assessment of all birds, amphibians and corals. *PLoS ONE* 8(6): e65427. https://doi.org/10.1371/journal.pone.0065427

Foley, C.M., M.A. Lynch, L.H. Thorne, and H.J. Lynch. 2017. Listing foreign species under the Endangered Species Act: a primer for conservation biologists. *BioScience* 67: 627–637. doi:10.1093/biosci/bix027.

Fordham, D.A., H.R. Akçakaya, M.B. Araújo, D.A. Keith, and B.W. Brook. 2013. Tools for integrating range change, extinction risk and climate change information into conservation management. *Ecography* 36: 956–964.

Fortini, L.B., A.E. Vorsino, F.A. Amidon, E.H. Paxton, and J.D. Jacobi. 2015. Large-scale range collapse of Hawaiian forest birds under climate change and the need [for] 21st century conservation options. *PLoS ONE* 10(10): e0140389. https://doi.org/10.1371/journal.pone.0140389

Foster, J.T., B.L. Woodworth, L.E. Eggert, et al. 2007. Genetic structure and evolved malaria resistance in Hawaiian honeycreepers. *Molecular Ecology* 16: 4738–4746. doi:10.1111/j.1365-294X.2007.03550.x

Franklin, J.F. 1993. Preserving biodiversity: species, ecosystems, or landscapes? *Ecological Applications* 3: 202–205. https://doi.org/10.2307/1941820

Fraser, D.J., and L. Bernatchez. 2001. Adaptive evolutionary conservation: towards a unified concept for defining conservation units. *Molecular Ecology* 10: 2741–2752. doi:10.1046/j.0962-1083.2001.01411.x

Freyfogle, E.T., and D.D. Goble. 2009. *Wildlife Law: A Primer.* Washington, DC: Island Press.

Fulton, G.R. 2017. The Bramble Cay melomys: the first mammalian extinction due to human-induced climate change. *Pacific Conservation Biology* 23: 1–3. http://dx.doi.org/10.1071/PCv23nl_ED.

Galbreath, R. 1993. *Working for Wildlife: A History of the New Zealand Wildlife Service*. Wellington, NZ: Bridget Williams Books.

Gardali, T., N.E. Seavy, R.T. DiGaudio, and L.A. Comrack. 2012. A climate change vulnerability assessment of California's at-risk birds. *PLoS ONE* 7(3): e29507. doi: 10.1371/journal.pone.0029507.

Gardiner, S.M., and A. Thompson (eds). 2017. *The Oxford Handbook of Environmental Ethics*. Oxford, UK: Oxford University Press.

Garnett, S. 1992. *Threatened and Extinct Birds of Australia*. Melbourne, VIC, Australia: Royal Australasian Ornithologists Union.

Garnett, S., P. Latch, D. Lindenmayer, and J. Woinarski (eds). 2018. *Recovering Australian Threatened Species. A Book of Hope*. Clayton South, VIC, Australia: CSIRO Publishing.

Gerber, L.R. 2016. Conservation triage or injurious neglect in endangered species recovery. *Proceedings of the National Academy of Sciences of the United States of America* 113: 3563–3566. doi: 10.1073/pnas.1525085113.

Gese, E.M., F.F. Knowlton, J.R. Adams, et al. 2015. Managing hybridization of a recovering endangered species: the red wolf *Canis rufus* as a case study. *Current Zoology* 61: 191–205.

Gleaves, K., M. Kurue, and P. Monatanio. 1992. The meaning of species under the Endangered Species Act. *Public Land and Resources Law Review* 13: 25–50.

Goble, D.D. 2006. Evolution of at-risk species protection. In J.M. Scott, D.D. Goble, and F.W. Davis, eds, *The Endangered Species Act at Thirty. Volume 2. Conserving Biodiversity in Human-dominated Landscapes*. Washington, DC: Island Press, pp. 6–23.

Goble, D.D. 2009a. The Endangered Species Act: what we talk about when we talk about recovery. *Natural Resources Journal* 49: 1–44.

Goble, D.D. 2009b. Endangered Species Act. In J.B. Callicott and R. Frodeman, eds, *Encyclopedia of Environmental Ethics and Philosophy*. Detroit, MI: Macmillan Reference USA, pp. 300–305.

Goble, D.D. 2010. A fish tale: a small fish, the ESA, and our shared future. *Environmental Law* 40: 339–362.

Goble, D.D., and J.M. Scott. 2006. Recovery Management Agreements offer alternative to continuing ESA listings. *Fisheries* 31: 35–36.

Goble, D.D., S.M. George, K. Mazaikac, J.M. Scott, and J. Karle. 1999. Local and national protection of endangered species: an assessment. *Environmental Science & Policy* 2: 43–59. https://doi.org/1016/S1462-9011(98)00041-0.

Goble, D.D., J.A. Wiens, J.M. Scott, T.D. Male, and J.A. Hall. 2012. Conservation-reliant species. *BioScience* 62: 869–873.

Goble, D.D., E.T. Freyfogle, E. Biber, F. Cheever, and A. Wiersema. 2017. *Wildlife Law, Cases and Materials*, 3rd edition. St Paul, MN: Foundation Press.

Goettsch, B., C. Hilton-Taylor, G. Cruz-Piñón, et al. 2015. High proportion of cactus species threatened with extinction. *Nature Plants* 1: Article 15142. doi:10.1038/nplants.2015.142.

Golet, G.H., C. Low, S. Avery, et al. 2018. Using ricelands to provide temporary shorebird habitat during migration. *Ecological Applications* 28: 409–426. doi: 10.1002/eap.1658.

Goulding, M., N.J.H. Smith, and D.J. Mahar. 1996. *Floods of Fortune. Ecology and Economy along the Amazon.* New York, NY: Columbia University Press.

Graber, J.W. 1961. Distribution, habitat requirements, and life history of the black-capped vireo (*Vireo atricapilla*). *Ecological Monographs* 31: 313–336. doi: 10.2307/1950756.

Grant, P.R., and B.R. Grant. 2014. *40 Years of Evolution. Darwin's Finches on Daphne Major Island.* Princeton, NJ: Princeton University Press.

Grantham, T.E., K.A. Fesenmyer, R. Peek, et al. 2016. Missing the boat on freshwater fish conservation in California. *Conservation Letters* 10(1): 77–85. https://doi.org/10.1111/conl.12249|

Green, D.M. 2005. Designatable units for status assessment of endangered species. *Conservation Biology* 19: 1813–1820. doi: 10.1111/j.1523-1739.2005 .00284.x

Green, R.E., I. Newton, S. Shultz, et al. 2004. Diclofenac poisoning as a cause of vulture population declines across the Indian subcontinent. *Journal of Applied Ecology* 41: 793–800.

Greenwald, N., K.F. Suckling, B. Hartl, and L. Markoff. 2019. Extinction and the US Endangered Species Act. *Peer Preprints* 7: e27471v2. https://doi.org/10.7287/ peerj.preprints.27471v2

Gregory, R., D. Ohlson, and J. Arvai. 2006. Deconstructing adaptive management: Criteria for applications to environmental management. *Ecological Applications* 16: 2411–2425.

Groves, C.P., P. Fernando, and J. Robovsky. 2010. The sixth rhino: a taxonomic reassessment of the critically endangered northern white rhinoceros. *PLoS ONE* 5 (4): e9703. https://doi.org/10.1371/journal.pone.0009703.

Groves, C.R. 2003. *Drafting a Conservation Blueprint. A Practitioner's Guide to Planning for Biodiversity.* Washington, DC: Island Press.

Groves, C.R., and E.T. Game. 2016. *Conservation Planning. Informed Decisions for a Healthier Planet.* Greenwood Village, CO: Roberts and Company.

Grzybowski, J.A. 1991. Black-Capped Vireo Recovery Plan. Endangered Species Bulletins and Technical Reports (USFWS). 26. http://digitalcommons.unl.edu/endangeredspeciesbull/26

Grzybowski, J.A. 1995. Black-capped Vireo (*Vireo atricapilla*). In P.G. Rodewald, ed., *The Birds of North America*. Ithaca, NY: Cornell Lab of Ornithology. doi: 10.2173/bna.181. Available at: https://birdsna.org/Species-Account/bna/species/bkcvir1

Gumbs, R., C.L. Gray, O.R. Wearn, and N.R. Owen. 2018. Tetrapods on the EDGE: overcoming data limitations to identify phylogenetic conservation priorities. *PLoS ONE* 13(4): e194680. https://doi.org/10.1371/jpoournal.pone.0194680.

Guthery, F.S., and B.K. Strickland. 2015. Exploration and critique of habitat and habitat quality. In M.L. Morrison and H.A. Mathewson, eds, *Wildlife Habitat Conservation. Concepts, Challenges, and Solutions*. Baltimore, MD: Johns Hopkins University Press, pp. 9–18.

Gynther, I., N. Waller, and L.K.-P. Leung. 2016. Confirmation of the extinction of the Bramble Cay melomys *Melomys rubicola* on Bramble Cay, Torres Strait: Results and conclusions from a comprehensive survey in August–September 2014. Unpublished report to the Department of Environment and Heritage Protection, Queensland Government, Brisbane.

Hanski, I., and O.E. Gaggiotti (eds). 2004. *Ecology, Genetics, and Evolution of Metapopulations*. Amsterdam, Netherlands: Elsevier Academic Press.

Hemming, V., T.V. Waische, A.M. Hanea, F. Fidler, and M.A. Burgman. 2018. Eliciting improved quantitative judgments using the IDEA protocol: A case study in natural resource management. *PLoS ONE* 13(6): e0198468.

Hess, S.C., and J.D. Jacobi. 2011. The history of mammal eradications in Hawai'i and the United States associated islands of the Central Pacific. In C.R. Veitch, M.N. Clout, and D.R. Townsend, eds, *Proceeding of the International Conference on Island Invasives*. Christchurch, NZ: The Caxton Press, pp. 67–73.

Hitchmough, R. 2013. Summary of changes to the conservation status of taxa in the 2008–11 New Zealand Threat Classification System listing cycle. New Zealand Threat Classification Series 1. Wellington, NZ: Department of Conservation.

Hobbs, C.I. 1955. Hybridization between fish species in nature. *Systematic Zoology* 4: 1–20.

Hobbs, R.J., E.S. Higgs, and C.M. Hall (eds). 2013. *Novel Ecosystems. Intervening in the New Ecological World Order*. Chichester, UK: Wiley-Blackwell.

Holdgate, M. 1999. *The Green Web: A Union for World Conservation*. London: Earthscan Publications Ltd.

Holdo, R.M., A.R.E. Sinclair, A.P. Dobsono, et al. 2009. A disease-mediated trophic cascade in the Serengeti and its implications for ecosystem C. *PLoS Biology* 7(9): e1000210. https://doi.org/10.1371/journal.pbio.1000210.

Holen, S.R., T.A. Demére, D.C. Fisher, et al. 2017. A 130 000-year-old archaeological site in southern California, USA. *Nature* 544: 479–483. doi: 10.1038/nature22065.

Hume, J.P. 2017. Undescribed juvenile plumages of the Laysan rail or crake (*Zapornia palmeri*: Frohawk, 1892) and a detailed chronology of its extinction. *The Wilson Journal of Ornithology* 129: 429–445.

Hummel, S.S., and J.E. Smith. 2017. People and forest plants. In D.H. Olson and B. Van Horne, eds, *People, Forests and Change. Lessons from the Pacific Northwest*. Washington, DC: Island Press, pp. 33–46.

Hunter, M.L., Jr. 1993. Of puffins and parochialism: why is it important to conserve species that are locally rare, but globally common? *Maine Naturalist* 1: 39–42.

International Center for Environmental Management (ICEM). 2010. Mekong River Commission (MRC) Strategic Environmental Assessment (SEA) for Hydropower on the Mekong Mainstream: Fisheries Baseline Assessment Working Paper. Vientiane, Lao PDR: MRC. http://www.mrcmekong.org/about-the-mrc/programmes/initiative-on-sustainable-hydropower/strategic-environmental-assessment-of-mainstream-dams/.

International Union for the Conservation of Nature (IUCN). 2013. Guidelines for Reintroductions and Other Conservation Translocations. Version 1.0. Gland, Switzerland: IUCN Species Survival Commission, International Union for the Conservation of Nature.

International Union for the Conservation of Nature (IUCN). 2019. Threats classification scheme. Version 3.2. Gland, Switzerland: IUCN. https://www.iucnredlist.org/resources/threat-classification-scheme.

IPBES (Intergovernmental Science-Policy Platform on Biodiversity and Ecosystem Services). 2019. Summary for policymakers of the global assessment report on biodiversity and ecosystem services. Bonn, Germany: IPBES. https://www.ipbes.net/news/ipbes-global-assessment-summary-policymakers-pdf

Isozaki, H. 1989. Japan's new law on endangered species. *Boston University International Law Journal* 7: 211–221.

James, F.C. 1980. Miscegenation in the dusky seaside sparrow? *BioScience* 30: 800–801. https://doi.org/10.2307/1308366

Jaramillo-Legorreta, A.M., G. Cardenas-Hinojosa, E. Nieto-Garcia, et al. 2016. Passive acoustic monitoring of the decline of Mexico's critically endangered vaquita. *Conservation Biology* 31:183–191. https://doi.org/10.1111/cobi.12789

Jaramillo-Legorreta, A.M., G. Cardenas-Hinojosa, E. Nieto-Garcia, et al. 2019. Decline towards extinction of Mexico's vaquita porpoise (*Phocoena sinus*). *Royal Society Open Science* 6. http://doi.org/10.1098/rsos.190598

Jerde, C.L., A.R. Mahon, W.L. Chadderton, and D.M. Lodge. 2011. "Sight-unseen" detection of rare aquatic species using environmental DNA. *Conservation Letters* 4: 150–157. doi: 10.1111/j.1755-263x.2010.00158.x.

Jewett, L. and A. Romanou. 2017. Ocean acidification and other ocean changes. In D.J. Wuebbles, D.W. Fahey, K.A. Hibbard, et al., eds, *Climate Science Special Report: Fourth National Climate Assessment*, Volume I. US Global Change Research Program, Washington, DC, USA, pp. 364–392. doi: 10.7930/J07S7KXX

Johnson, M.D. 2007. Measuring habitat quality: a review. *Condor* 109: 489–504.

Johnson, W.E., D.P. Onorato, M.E. Roelke, et al. 2010. Genetic restoration of the Florida panther. *Science* 329: 1641–1645. doi: 10.1126/science.1192891.

Jongsomjit, D., D. Stralberg, T. Gardali, L. Salas, and J. Wiens. 2012. Between a rock and a hard place: the impacts of climate change and housing development on breeding birds in California. *Landscape Ecology* 28: 187–200. doi: 10.1007/s10980-012-9825-1.

Joseph, L.N., R.F. Maloney, S.M. O'Connor, et al. 2008. Improving methods for allocating resources among threatened species: the case for a new national approach in New Zealand. *Pacific Conservation Biology* 14: 154–158.

Joseph, L.N., R.F. Maloney, and H.P. Possingham. 2009. Optimal allocation of resources among threatened species: a project prioritization protocol. *Conservation Biology* 23: 328–338. https://doi.org/10.1111/j.1523-1739.2008.01124.x

Juvik, J.O., and S.P. Juvik. 1984. Mauna Kea and the myth of multiple use: Endangered species and mountain management in Hawaii. *Mountain Research and Development* 4: 191–202. doi: 10.2307/3673140.

Kahn, J. 2018. Should some species be allowed to die out? *New York Times Magazine*, March 13, 2018. https://nyti.ms/2GnLsoT.

Kannan, P.M. 2009. United States law and policies protecting wildlife. The 2009 Colorado College State of the Rockies Report Card. Faculty Overview. Available at: https://www.coloradocollege.edu/dotAsset/fc919f40-c24a-4287-ab6c-d649e4dca7a6.pdf.

Kareiva, P., and M. Marvier. 2003. Conserving biodiversity coldspots. *American Scientist* 91: 344–351.

Kareiva, P., S. Watts, R. McDonald, and T. Boucher. 2007. Domesticated nature: shaping landscapes and ecosystems for human welfare. *Science* 316: 1866–1869.

Kiester, A.R., J.M. Scott, B. Csuti, et al. 1996. Conservation prioritization using GAP data. *Conservation Biology* 10: 1332–1342. doi: 10.1046/j.1523-1739.1996.10051332.x

Kilham, E., and S. Reinecke. 2015. *"Biggest Bang for Your Buck": Conservation Triage and Priority-Setting for Species Management in Australia and New*

*Zealand.* INVALUABLE Policy Brief, 0115. Freiburg, Germany: Albert-Ludwigs-Universität Freiburg.

King, L.E., F. Lala, H. Nzumu, E. Mwambingu, and I. Douglas-Hamilton. 2017. Beehive fences as a multidimensional conflict-mitigation tool for farmers coexisting with elephants. *Conservation Biology* 31: 743–752. doi: 10.1111/cobi.12898

Klein, N. 2014. *This Changes Everything: Capitalism vs. the Climate.* New York, NY: Simon & Schuster.

Knick, S.T., and J.W. Connelly (eds). 2011. *Greater Sage-grouse/ Ecology and Conservation of a Landscape Species and its Habitats.* Berkeley, CA: University of California Press.

Knight, M.H., R.H. Emslie, R. Smart, and D. Balfour. 2015. *Biodiversity Management Plan for the White Rhinoceros* (Ceratotherium simum) *in South Africa 2015–2020.* Pretoria, South Africa: Department of Environmental Affairs.

Koch, P.L., and A.D. Barnosky. 2006. Late Quaternary extinctions: state of the debate. *Annual Review of Ecology, Evolution, and Systematics* 37: 215–250. https://doi.org/10.1146.annurec.ecolsys.34.011802.132415.

Koford, C.B. 1953. *The California Condor.* National Audubon Society Research Report No. 4. New York, NY: National Audubon Society.

Koh, L.P., R.R. Dunn, N.S. Sodhi, et al. 2004. Species coextinctions and the biodiversity crisis. *Science* 305: 1632–1634. doi: 10.1126/science.1101101.

Kossin, J.P., T. Hall, T. Knutson, et al. 2017. Extreme storms. In D.J. Wuebbles, D.W. Fahey, K.A. Hibbard, et al., eds, *Climate Science Special Report: Fourth National Climate Assessment,* Volume I. Washington, DC: US Global Change Research Program, pp. 257–276. doi: 10.7930/J07S7KXX

Kovach, R.P., J.E. Joyce, J.D. Echave, M.S. Lindberg, and D.A. Tallmon. 2013. Earlier migration timing, decreasing phenotypic variation, and biocomplexity in multiple salmonid species. *PLoS ONE* 8(1): e53807. https://doi.org/10.1371/journal.pone.0053807.

Kujala, H., A. Moilanen, and A. Gordon. 2017. Spatial characteristics of species distributions as drivers in conservation prioritization. *Methods in Ecology and Evolution* 2017: 1–12. doi: 10.1111/2041-210X.12939.

Kumar, L., and M.S. Tehrany. 2017. Climate change impacts on the threatened terrestrial vertebrates of the Pacific Islands. *Nature Scientific Reports* 7: art 5030.

Kurlansky, M. 1997. *Cod. A Biography of the Fish that Changed the World.* New York, NY: Penguin Books.

Lafferty, K.D., J.P. McLaughlin, D.S. Gruner, et al. 2018. Local extinction of the Asian tiger mosquito (Aedes albopictus) following rat eradication on Palmyra Atoll. *Biology Letters* 14. doi: 10.1098/rsbl.2017.0743

Lausche, B.J. 2008. *Weaving a Web of Environmental Law.* Gland, Switzerland: International Union for the Conservation of Nature.

Lawrence, C., D. Paris, J.V. Briskie, and M. Massaro. 2017. When the neighbourhood goes bad: can endangered black robins adjust nest-site selection in response to the risk of an invasive predator? *Animal Conservation* 20: 321–330. doi: 10.1111/acv.12318.

Laws, R.J., and D.C. Kesler. 2012. A Bayesian network approach for selecting translocation sites for endangered island birds. *Biological Conservation* 155: 175–178.

Lawton, J.H., and R.M. May (eds). 1995. *Extinction Rates.* Oxford, UK: Oxford University Press.

Leclerc, C., C. Bellard, G.M. Luque, and F. Courchamp. 2015. Overcoming extinction: Understanding processes of recovery of the Tibetian antelope. *Ecosphere* 6 (9): 171. http://dx.doi.org/10.1890/ES15-00049.1.

Lenoir J., J.C. Gegout, P.A. Marquet, P. de Ruffray, and H. Brisse. 2008. A significant upward shift in plant species optimum elevation during the 20th century. *Science* 320: 1768–1771. doi: 10.1126/science.1156831.

Leonard, D.L., Jr. 2008. Recovery expenditures for birds listed under the US Endangered Species Act: The disparity between mainland and Hawaiian taxa. *Biological Conservation* 141: 2054–2061. doi:10.1016/j.biocon.2008.06.001.

Leopold, A. 1934. Conservation economics. *Journal of Forestry* 32: 537–544.

Leopold, A. 1949. *A Sand County Almanac: And Sketches Here and There.* Oxford, UK: Oxford University Press.

Leslie, D.M., Jr., and G.B. Schaller. 2008. *Pantholops hodgsonii* (Artiodactyla: Bovidae). *Mammalian Species* 817: 1–13.

Lesmeister, D.B., R.J. Davis, P.H. Singleton, and J.D. Wiens. 2018. Northern spotted owl habitat and populations: status and threats. In T.A. Spies, P.A. Stine, R. Gravenmier, J.W. Long, and M.J. Reilly, technical coordinators, *Synthesis of Science to Inform Land Management Within the Northwest Forest Plan Area.* General Technical Report PNW-GTR-966. Portland, OR: US Department of Agriculture, Forest Service, Pacific Northwest Research Station, pp. 245–299.

Leung, Y.-F., A. Spenceley, G. Hvenegaard, and R. Buckley (eds). 2018. Tourism and visitor management in protected areas: guidelines for sustainability. *Best Practice Protected Area Guidelines Series No. 27.* Gland, Switzerland: International Union for the Conservation of Nature.

Levin, P.S., M.J. Fogarty, S.A. Murawski, and D. Fluharty. 2009. Integrated ecosystem assessments: Developing the scientific basis for ecosystem-based management of the ocean. *PLoS Biology* 7(1): e1000014. doi: 10.1371/journal. pbio.1000014.

Lewis, S.L., and M.A. Maslin. 2015. Defining the Anthropocene. *Nature* 519: 171–180.

Lindenmayer, D., and M. Burgman. 2005. *Practical Conservation Biology*. Collingwood, VIC: CSIRO Publishing.

Lindsey, P.A., J.R.B. Miller, L.S. Petracca, et al. 2018. More than $1 billion needed annually to secure Africa's protected areas with lions. *Proceedings of the National Academy of Sciences of the United States of America* 115(45): E10 788–E10 796. https://doi.org/10.1073/pnas.1805048115

Linhares, K.V., F.A. Soares, and I.C.S. Machado. 2010. Nest support plants of the Araripe manakin *Antilophia bokermanni*, a Critically Endangered endemic bird from Ceará, Brazil. *Cotinga* 32: 121–125.

Linnell, J.D.C., J.E. Swenson, and R. Andersen. 2001. Predators and people: conservation of large carnivores is possible at high human densities if management policy is favourable. *Animal Conservation* 4: 345–349.

Liu, J. 2017. Integration across a metacoupled world. *Ecology and Society* 22(4):29. https://doi.org/10.5751/ES-09830-220429

Liu, J., M. Linderman, Z. Ouyang, et al. 2001. Ecological degradation in protected areas: the case of Wolong Nature Reserve for giant pandas. *Science* 292: 98–101.

Liu, J., V. Hull, A.T. Morzillo, and J.A. Wiens (eds). 2011. *Sources, Sinks and Sustainability*. Cambridge, UK: Cambridge University Press.

Liu, J., V. Hull, W. Yang, et al. (eds). 2016. *Pandas and People: Coupling Human and Natural Systems for Sustainability*. Oxford, UK: Oxford University Press.

Livezey, K.B. 2009. Range expansion of barred owls, Part II: facilitating ecological change. *American Midland Naturalist* 161: 323–349. https://doi.org/10.1674/0003-0031-161.2.323.

Livezey, K.B., T.L. Root, S.A. Gremel, and C. Johnson. 2008. Natural range expansion of barred owls? A critique of Monahan and Hijmans (2007). *The Auk* 125: 230–232. doi: 10.1525/auk.2008.125.1.230.

Loarie, S.R., P.B. Duffy, H. Hamilton, et al. 2009. The velocity of climate change. *Nature* 462: 1052–1055. doi: 10.1038/nature08649.

Locke, H. 2010. Yellowstone to Yukon connectivity conservation initiative. In G.L. Worboys, W.L. Francis, and M. Lockwood, eds, *Connectivity Conservation Management. A Global Guide*. London: Earthscan, pp. 161–181.

Loehle, C., and W. Eschenbach 2012. Historical bird and terrestrial mammal extinction rates and causes. *Diversity and Distributions* 18: 84–91. https://doi.org/10.1111/j.1472-4642.2011.00856.x

Lomborg, B. 2001. *The Skeptical Environmentalist. Measuring the Real State of the World*. Cambridge, UK: Cambridge University Press.

Lumsden, L., and M. Schulz. 2009. Captive breeding and future in-situ management of the Christmas Island pipistrelle, *Pipistrellus murrayi*. A report to the Director of National Parks. Melbourne, Australia: Arthur Rylah Institute, Department of Sustainability and Environment.

Lumsden, L., P.A. Racey, and A.M. Hutson. 2010. *Pipistrellus murrayi*. The IUCN Red List of Threatened Species 2010: e.T136769A4337617. http://dx.doi.org/ 10.2305/IUCN.UK.2010-2.TLTS.T136769A4337617.en.

Lunstrum, E. 2014. Green militarization: anti-poaching efforts and the spatial contours of Kruger National Park. *Annals of the Association of American Geographers* 104: 816–832. doi: 10.1080/00045608.2014.912545.

Mace, G.M., N.J. Collar, K.J. Gaston, et al. 2008. Quantification of extinction risk: IUCN's system for classifying threatened species. *Conservation Biology* 22: 1424–1442. doi: 10.1111/j.1523-1739.2008.01044.x.

Malcom, J.W., and Y.-W. Li. 2015. Data contradict common perceptions about a controversial provision of the US Endangered Species Act. *Proceedings of the National Academy of Sciences of the United States of America* 112: 15 844–15 849. https://www.pnas.org/cgi/doi/10.1073/pnas.1516938112.

Mann, C.C., and M.L. Plummer. 1995. *Noah's Choice: The Future of Endangered Species*. New York, NY: Alfred Knopf.

Marcot, B.G., and C.H. Flather. 2007. Species-level strategies for conserving rare or little-known species. In M.G. Raphael and R. Molina, eds, *Conservation of Rare or Little-Known Species: Biological, Social, and Economic Considerations*. Washington, DC: Island Press, pp. 125–164.

Marcot, B.G., and C.H. Sieg. 2007. System-level strategies for conserving rare or little-known species. In M.G. Raphael and R. Molina, eds, *Conservation of Rare or Little-Known Species: Biological, Social, and Economic Considerations*. Washington, DC: Island Press, pp. 165–186.

Marcot, B. G., P. H. Singleton, and N. H. Schumaker. 2015. Analysis of sensitivity and uncertainty in an individual-based model of a threatened wildlife species. *Natural Resource Modeling* 28: 37–58.

Margules, C.R., A.O. Nicholls, and R.L. Pressey. 1988. Selecting networks of reserves to maximize biological diversity. *Biological Conservation* 43: 63–76.

Marinelli, J. 2018. For endangered Florida tree, how far to go to save a species? *Yale Environment* 360, March 27, 2018. https://e360.yale.edu/features/for-endangered-florida-tree-how-far-to-go-to-save-a-species-torreya.

Markandya, A., T. Taylor, A. Longo, et al. 2008. Counting the cost of vulture decline: an appraisal of the human health and other benefits of vultures in India. *Ecological Economics* 67: 194–204. https://doi.org/10.1016/j.ecolecon .2008.04.020.

Marsh H, A. Dennis, H. Hines, et al. 2007. Optimizing allocation of management resources for wildlife. *Conservation Biology* 21: 387–399. doi: 10.1111/j.1523-1739.2006.00589.x

Martin, T.G., S. Nally, A.A. Burbidge, et al. 2012. Acting fast helps avoid extinction. *Conservation Letters* 5: 274–280.

Martín-López, B., C. Montes, and J. Benayas. 2008. Economic valuation of biodiversity conservation: the meaning of numbers. *Conservation Biology* 22: 624–635. https://doi.org/10.1111/j.1523-1739.2008.00921.x

Massaro M., R. Sainudiin, D. Merton, et al. 2013. Human-assisted spread of a maladaptive behavior in a critically endangered bird. *PLoS ONE* 8(12): e79066. https://doi.org/10.1371/journal.pone.0079066

Mathewson, H.A., and M.L. Morrison. 2015. The misunderstanding of habitat. In M.L. Morrison and H.A. Mathewson, eds, *Wildlife Habitat Conservation. Concepts, Challenges, and Solutions*. Baltimore, MD: Johns Hopkins University Press, pp. 3-8.

Matthews, O.P. 1986. Who owns wildlife? *Wildlife Society Bulletin* 14: 459–465.

Matthews, S.N., L.R. Iverson, A.M. Prasad, and M.P. Peters. 2011. Changes in potential habitat of 147 North American breeding bird species in response to redistribution of trees and climate following predicted climate change. *Ecography* 33: 933–945. https://doi.org/10.1111/j.1600-0587.2011.06803.x|

Mayr, E. 1942. *Systematics and the Origin of Species*. New York: Columbia University Press.

Mbalwa, J.E. 2017. Poverty or riches: who benefits from the booming tourism industry in Botswana? *Journal of Contemporary African Studies* 35: 93–112. doi: 10.1080/02589001.2016.1270424

McCarthy, M.A., C.J. Thompson, and S.T. Garnett. 2008. Optimal investment in conservation of species. *Journal of Applied Ecology* 45: 1428–1435. https://doi.org/10.1111/j.1365-2664.2008.01521.x

McGowan, P. J., K. Traylor-Holzer, and K. Leus. 2017. IUCN Guidelines for determining when and how ex situ management should be used in species conservation. *Conservation Letters* 10: 361–366. doi: 10.1111/conl.12285.

McMenamin, S.K., and L. Hannah. 2012. First extinctions on land. In L. Hannah, ed., *Saving a Million Species. Extinction Risk from Climate Change*. Washington, DC: Island Press, pp. 89–101.

Meltzer, D.J. 2015. Pleistocene overkill and North American mammalian extinctions. *Annual Review of Anthropology* 44: 33–53. https://doi.org/10.1146/annurev.anthro-102214-013854.

Millennium Ecosystem Assessment. 2005. *Millennium Ecosystem Assessment. Summary for Decision Makers*. Washington, DC: Island Press.

Miller, G.H., M.L. Fogel, J.W. Magee, et al. 2005. Ecosystem collapse in Pleistocene Australia and a human role in megafaunal extinction. *Science* 309: 287–290. doi: 10.1126/science.1111288.

Mini, A.E., and R. LeValley. 2006. *Aleutian Cackling Goose Agricultural Depredation Plan for Del Norte County, California.* San Francisco, CA: California Coastal Conservancy.

Mini, A.E., D.C. Bachman, J. Cocke, et al. 2011. Recovery of the Aleutian cackling goose *Branta hutchinsii leucopareia*: 10-year review and future prospects. *Wildfowl* 61: 3–29.

Moilanen, A., K.A. Wilson, and H.P. Possingham. 2009. *Spatial Conservation Prioritization. Quantitative Methods & Computational Tools.* Oxford, UK: Oxford University Press.

Molloy, J., B. Bell, M. Clout, et al. 2002. Classifying species according to threat of extinction. A system for New Zealand. *Threatened Species Occasional Publication 22.* Wellington, NZ: Department of Conservation.

Monahan, W.B., and R.J. Hijmans. 2007. Distributional dynamics of invasion and hybridization by *Strix* spp. in western North America. In C. Cicero and J. V. Remsen Jr., eds, *Festschrift for Ned K. Johnson: Geographic Variation and Evolution in Birds. Ornithological Monographs No. 63*, pp. 55–66.

Mooers, A.O., D.F. Doak, C.S. Findlay, et al. 2010. Science, policy, and species at risk in Canada. *BioScience* 60: 843–849.

Moritz, C. 1994. Defining 'evolutionarily significant units' for conservation. *Trends in Ecology and Evolution* 9: 373–375.

Mount, J., E. Hanak, G. Gartrell, and B. Gray. 2018. Accounting for water "Wasted to the Sea". *San Francisco Estuary & Watershed Science* 16(1): Article 1. https://doi.org/a0.15447/sfews.2018v16iss1/art1.

Moyle, P.B. 2014. Novel aquatic ecosystems: The new reality for streams in California and other Mediterranean climate regions. *River Research and Applications* 30: 1335–1344. doi: 10.1002/rra.2709

Moyle, P.B., and W.A. Bennett. 2008. The future of the Delta ecosystem and its fish. Technical Appendix D in J.R. Lund, E. Hanak, W.E. Fleenor, eds, *Comparing Futures for the Sacramento-San Joaquin Delta.* Berkeley, CA: University of California Press and Public Policy Institute of California. https://www .waterboards.ca.gov/waterrights/water_issues/programs/bay_delta/docs/cmnt081 712/sldmwa/moyleandbennett2008.pdf.

Moyle, P.B., J.D. Kiernan, P.K. Crain, and R.M. Quiñones. 2013. Climate change vulnerability of native and alien freshwater fishes of California: a systematic assessment approach. *PLoS ONE* 8(5): e63883. https://doi.org/10.1371/journal.pone.0063883

Moyle, P.B., J.A. Hobbs, and J.R. Durand. 2018. Delta smelt and water politics in California. *Fisheries* 43: 42–60. doi: 10.1002/fsh.10014

Murchison, K.M. 2007. *The Snail Darter Case. TVA Versus the Endangered Species Act*. University Press of Kansas, Lawrence, KS, USA.

Myers, N. 1988. Threatened biotas: "hot spots" in tropical forests. *Environmentalist* 8: 187–208.

Myers, N., R.A. Mittermeier, C.G. Mittermeier, G.A.B. da Fonseca, and J. Kent. 2000. Biodiversity hotspots for conservation priorities. *Nature* 403: 853–858.

Nahonyo, C.L., E.M. Goboro, W. Ngalason, et al. 2017. Conservation efforts of Kihansi spray toad *Nectophryoides aspersinis*: Its discovery, captive breeding, extinction in the wild and re-introduction. *Tanzania Journal of Science* 43: 23–35.

Naidoo, R., and T.H. Ricketts. 2006. Mapping the economic costs and benefits of conservation. *PLoS Biology* 4(11): e360. https://doi.org/10.1371/journal.pbio.0040360

NAS (National Academies of Sciences, Engineering, and Medicine). 2016. *Attribution of Extreme Weather Events in the Context of Climate Change*. Washington, DC: The National Academies Press. doi: 10.17226/21852.

NAS (National Academies of Sciences, Engineering, and Medicine). 2019. *Evaluating the Taxonomic Status of the Mexican Gray Wolf and the Red Wolf*. Washington, DC: The National Academies Press. https://doi.org/10.17226/25351.

Neel, M.C., A K. Leidner, A. Haines, D.D. Goble, and J.M. Scott. 2012. By the numbers: how is recovery defined by the US Endangered Species Act? *BioScience* 62: 646–657.

Negrón-Ortiz, V. 2014. Pattern of expenditures for plant conservation under the Endangered Species Act. *Biological Conservation* 171: 38–43. http://dx.doi.org/10.1016/j.biocon.2014.01.018.

Nelson, E., J.C. Withey, D. Pennington, and J.J. Lawler. 2014. Identifying the opportunity cost of Critical Habitat designation under the U.D.S. Endangered Species Act. *Economics Department Working Paper Series*, Paper 11. Bowdoin Digital Commons. http://digitalcommons.bowdoin.edu/econpapers/11

Nicholson, E., and H.P. Possingham. 2006. Objectives for multiple-species planning. *Conservation Biology* 20: 871-881. https://doi.org/10.1111/j.1523-1739.2006.00369.x

Nicotra, A.B., E.A. Beever, A.L. Robertson, G.E. Hofmann, and J. O'Leary. 2015. Assessing the components of adaptive capacity to improve conservation and management efforts under global change. *Conservation Biology* 29: 1268–1278. https://doi.org/10.1111/cobi.12522

Nie, M., C. Barns, J. Haber, et al. 2017. Fish and wildlife management on federal lands: debunking state supremacy. *Environmental Law* 47: 797–932.

Nijhuis, M. 2012. Conservationists use triage to determine which species to save and not. *Scientific American* 307(2). August.

Noss, R.F. 1996. Conservation or convenience? *Conservation Biology* 10: 921–922. doi: 10.1046/j.1523-1739.1996.10040921.x

Noss, R.F., E.Y. LaRoe III, and J.M. Scott. 1995. Endangered ecosystems of the United States: A preliminary assessment of loss and degradation. Biological Report 28. Washington, DC: US Department of the Interior, National Biological Service. http://sciences.ucf.edu/biology/king/wp-content/uploads/sites/106/2011/08/Noss-et-al-1995.pdf.

Nowacki, G.J., D.W. MacCleery, and F.K. Lake. 2012. Native Americans, ecosystem development, and historical range of variation. In J.A. Wiens, G.-D. Hayward, H.D. Safford, and C.M. Giffen, eds, *Historical Environmental Variation in Conservation and Natural Resource Management*. Chichester, UK: Wiley-Blackwell, pp. 76–91.

OEH NSW. 2012. National Recovery Plan for the Southern Corroboree Frog, *Pseudophryne corroboree*, and the Northern Corroboree Frog, *Pseudophryne pengilleyi*. Hurstville, NSW: Australia Office of Environment and Heritage (NSW).

Olive, A. 2014a. *Land, Stewardship, and Legitimacy: Endangered Species Policy in Canada and the United States*. Toronto, Canada: University of Toronto Press.

Olive, A. 2014b. The road to recovery: comparing Canada and US recovery strategies for shared endangered species. *The Canadian Geographer* 58: 263–275. doi: 10.1111/cag.12090.

Olive, A. 2016. It is just not fair: the Endangered Species Act in the United States and Ontario. *Ecology and Society* 21(3):13. http://dx.doi.org/10.5751/ES-08627-210313.

Olson, D.H., and B. Van Horne (eds). 2017. *People, Forests, and Change. Lessons from the Pacific Northwest*. Washington, DC: Island Press.

Opdam, P., and J.A. Wiens, 2002. Habitat loss, fragmentation and landscape management. In K. Norris and D. Pain, eds, *Conserving Bird Biodiversity*. Cambridge, UK: Cambridge University Press, pp. 202–223.

Orians, G.H. 1993. Endangered at what level? *Ecological Applications* 3: 206–208.

Oriol-Cotterill, A., M. Valeix, L.G. Frank, C. Riginos, and D.W. Macdonald. 2015. Landscapes of coexistence for terrestrial carnivores: the ecological consequences of being downgraded from ultimate to penultimate predator by humans. *Oikos* 124: 1263-1273. doi:10.1111/oik.02224

Pacifici, M., W.B. Foden, P. Visconti, et al. 2015. Assessing species vulnerability to climate change. *Nature Climate Change* 5: 215–225.

Paravisini-Gebert, L. 2018. The parrots of the Caribbean. Facing the uncertainties of climate change. *ReVista* Spring/Summer. https://revista.drclas.harvard.edu/book/parrots-caribbean

Parmesan, C., and G. Yohe. 2003. A globally coherent fingerprint of climate change impacts across natural systems. *Nature* 421: 37–42. http://dx.doi.org/10.1038/nature01286

Parmesan, C., A. Anderson, A.S. Mikheyev, M. Moskwik, and M.C. Singer. 2015. Climate change success story? The endangered Quino checkerspot butterfly. *Journal of Insect Conservation* 19: 185–204. doi: 10.1111/oik.01490.

Patten, M.A. 2015. Subspecies and the philosophy of science. *The Auk, Ornithological Advances* 132: 481–485. doi: 10.1642/AUK-15-1.1.

Paxton, E.H., R.J. Camp, P.M. Gorresen, et al. 2016. Collapsing avian community on a Hawaiian island. *Science Advances* 2(9): e1600029. doi: 10.1126/sciadv.1600029.

Paxton, E.H., S.G. Yelenik, T.E. Borneman, et al. 2017. Rapid colonization of a Hawaiian restoration forest by a diverse avian community. *Restoration Ecology* 26: 165–173. https://doi.org/10.1111/rec.12540

Peterson, A.T. 2001. Endangered species and peripheral populations: Cause for reflection. *Endangered Species Update* 18: 30–31.

Phippen, J.W. 2016. Busting cactus smugglers in the American West. How undercover agents infiltrated the global black market for cacti. *The Atlantic*. February 22, 2016. https://www.theatlantic.com/science/archive/2016/02/cactus-thieves/470070/.

Pister, E.P. 1993. Species in a bucket. *Natural History* (January). Reprinted in *American Currents* 40: 15–20 (2015).

Pitelka, F.A. 1981. The condor case: an uphill battle in a downhill crush. *Point Reyes Bird Observatory Newsletter* 53: 4–5.

Plater, Z.J.B. 2014. *The Snail Darter and the Dam. How Pork-Barrel Politics Endangered a Little Fish and Killed a River*. New Haven, CT: Yale University Press.

Possingham, H.P., S.J. Andelman, M.A. Burgman, et al. 2002. Limits to the use of threatened species lists. *Trends in Ecology and Evolution* 17: 503–507.

Powell, A. 2008. *The Race to Save the World's Rarest Bird: The Discovery and Death of the Po'ouli*. Mechanicsburg, PA: Stackpole Books.

Prakash V., M.C. Bishwakarma, A. Chaudhary, et al. 2012. The population decline of *Gyps* vultures in India and Nepal has slowed since veterinary use of diclofenac was banned. *PLoS ONE* 7(11): e49118. https://doi.org/10.1371/journal.pone.0049118.

Pressey, R.L., and A.O. Nicholls. 1989. Application of a numerical algorithm to the selection of reserves in semi-arid New South Wales. *Biological Conservation* 50: 263–278.

Prince, D.J., S.M. O'Rourke, T.Q. Thompson, et al. 2017. The evolutionary basis of premature migration in Pacific salmon highlights the utility of genomics for informing conservation. *Science Advances* 3(8): e1603198. https://advances.sciencemag.org/content/3/8/e1603198.full

Pulsford, I., G.L. Worboys, and G. Howling. 2010. Australian Alps to Atherton connectivity conservation corridor. In G.L. Worboys, W.L. Francis, and M. Lockwood, eds, *Connectivity Conservation Management. A Global Guide.* London: Earthscan, pp. 96–106.

Punt, A.E., and G.P. Donovan. 2007. Developing management procedures that are robust to uncertainty: lessons from the International Whaling Commission. *ICES Journal of Marine Science* 64: 603–612. https://doi.org/10.1093/icesjms/fsm035

Quammen, D. 1997. *The Song of the Dodo. Island Biogeography in an Age of Extinctions.* New York, NY: Simon & Schuster.

Rahman, M.M., M.A. Al Mahmud, and M. Shahidullah. 2017. Socioeconomics of biodiversity conservation in the protected areas: A case study in Bangladesh. *International Journal of Sustainable Development & World Ecology* 24: 65–72. doi: 10.1080/13504509.2016.1169453

Rapai, W. 2013. *The Kirtland's Warbler. The Story of a Bird's Fight Against Extinction and the People Who Saved It.* Ann Arbor, MI: University of Michigan Press. doi: 10.3998/mpub.4072745.

Rappaport, D.I., L.R. Tambosi, and J.P. Metzger. 2015. A landscape triage approach: combining spatial and temporal dynamics to prioritize restoration and conservation. *Journal of Applied Ecology* 52: 590–601. doi: /10.1111/1365-2664.12405.

Redford, K.H., G. Amato, J. Baillie, et al. 2011. What does it mean to successfully conserve a (vertebrate) species? *BioScience* 61: 39–48. https://doi.org/10.1525/bio.2011.61.1.9

Reece, J.S., and R.F. Noss. 2014. A flexible tool for prioritizing species by conservation value and vulnerability to multiple threats. *Natural Areas Journal* 34: 31–45.

Reed, J.M., D.W. DesRochers, E.A. VanderrWerf, and J.M. Scott. 2012. Long-term persistence of Hawaii's endangered avifauna through conservation-reliant management. *BioScience* 62: 881–892.

Régnier, C., B. Fontaine, and P. Bouchet. 2009. Not knowing, not recording, not listing: numerous unnoticed mollusk extinctions. *Conservation Biology* 23: 1214–1221. https://doi.org/10.1111/j.1523-1739.2009.01245.x

Reich, D.E., R.K. Wayne, and D.B. Goldstein. 1999. Genetic evidence for a recent origin by hybridization of red wolves. *Molecular Ecology* 8: 139–144.

Reisner, M. 1993. *Cadillac Desert. The American West and its Disappearing Water.* New York, NY: Penguin Books.

Restani, M., and J.M. Marzluff. 2002. Funding extinction? Biological needs and political realities in the allocation of resources to endangered species recovery. *BioScience* 52: 169–177.

Reynolds, M.D., B.L. Sullivan, E. Hallstein, et al. 2017. Dynamic conservation for migratory species. *Science Advances* 3(8): e1700707. doi:10.1126/sciadv.1700707

Reynolds, M.H., K.N. Courtot, P. Berkowitz, et al. 2015. Will the effects of sea-level rise create ecological traps for Pacific Island seabirds? *PLoS ONE* 10(9): e0136773. https://doi.org/10.1371/journal.pone.0136773

Rhymer, J.M., and D. Simberloff. 1996. Extinction by hybridization and introgression. *Annual Review of Ecology and Systematics* 27: 83–109.

Richardson, M.G., and J.P. Croxall., 2019. Achieving post eradication biosecurity on South Georgia Island. In C.R. Veitch, M.N. Clout, A.R. Martin, J.C. Russell, and C.J. West, eds, *Island Invasives: Scaling Up to Meet the Challenge*. Occasional Paper SSC No. 62. Gland, Switzerland: IUCN, pp. 482–493.

Rideout, B.A., I. Stalis, R. Papendick, et al. 2012. Patterns of mortality in free-ranging California condors (*Gymnogyps californianus*). *Journal of Wildlife Diseases* 48: 95–112.

Riggio J., A. Jacobson, L. Dollar, et al. 2013. The size of savannah Africa: a lion's (*Panthera leo*) view. *Biodiversity Conservation* 22:17–35.

Ripley, S.D. 1981. Take the ultimate risk. *Point Reyes Bird Observatory Newsletter* 53: 1–3.

Robertson, B.A., R. S. Ostfeld, and F. Keesing. 2017. Trojan females and Judas goats: evolutionary traps as tools in wildlife management. *BioScience* 67: 983–994. https://doi.org/10.1093/biosci/bix116.

Robinson, J.G. 2011. Ethical pluralism, pragmatism, and sustainability in conservation practice. *Biological Conservation* 144: 958–965. doi:10.1016/j.biocon.2010.04.017.

Roemer, G.W., T.J. Coonan, D.K. Garcelon, J. Bascompte, and L. Laughrin. 2001. Feral pigs facilitate hyperpredation by golden eagles and indirectly cause the decline of the island fox. *Animal Conservation* 4: 307–318.

Rohlf, D.J., C. Carroll, and B. Hartl. 2014a. Conservation-reliant species: Toward a biology-based definition. *BioScience* 64: 601–611.

Rohlf, D.J., C. Carroll, and B. Hartl. 2014b. Reply to Goble and colleagues. *BioScience* 64: 859–860.

Rojas-Bracho, L., F.M.D. Gulland, C. Smith, et al. 2019. A field effort to capture critically endangered vaquitas (*Phocoena sinus*) for protection from entanglement in illegal gillnets. *Endangered Species Research* 38: 11–27.

Rolston, H. III. 2012. *A New Environmental Ethics. The Next Millennium for Life on Earth*. New York, NY: Routledge.

Ruhl, G.B. 2008. Climate change and the endangered species act: building bridges to the no-analog future. *Boston University Law Review* 88: 1–62.

Russell, J.C., and K.G. Broome. 2016. Fifty years of rodent eradication in New Zealand: another decade of advances. *New Zealand Journal of Ecology* 40: 197–204. doi: 10.20417/nzjecol.40.22.

Russell, J.C., J.G. Innes, P.H. Brown, and A.E. Byrom. 2015. Predator-free New Zealand: Conservation country. *BioScience* 65: 520–525. doi: 10.1093/biosci/biv012.

Sandler, R.L. 2012. *The Ethics of Species. An Introduction.* Cambridge, UK: Cambridge University Press.

Saragusty, J., S. Diecke, M. Drukker, et al. 2016. Rewinding the process of mammalian extinction. *Zoo Biology* 35: 280–292. doi: 10.1002/zoo.21284.

Savidge, J.A. 1987. Extinction of an island forest avifauna by an introduced snake. *Ecology* 68: 660–668.

Sayre, R., P. Comer, H. Warner, and J. Cress. 2009. A new map of standardized terrestrial ecosystems of the conterminous United States. *Professional Paper* 1768. Reston, VA: US Geological Survey. https://pubs.usgs.gov/pp/1768.

Sayre, R.G., P. Comer, J. Hak, et al. 2013. A new map of standardized terrestrial ecosystems of Africa. *African Geographical Review.* Washington, DC: Association of American Geographers.

Schaller, G.B., and J. Ren. 1988. Effects of a snowstorm on Tibetan antelope. *Journal of Mammalogy* 69: 631–634.

Scheffers, B.R., D.I. Yong, J.B.C. Harris, X. Giam, and N.S. Sodhi. 2011. The world's rediscovered species: back from the brink? *PLoS ONE* 6(7): e22531. https://doi.org/10.1371/journal.pone.0022531.

Schmidtz, D. 2017. Environmental conflict. In S.M. Gardiner and A. Thompson, eds, *The Oxford Handbook of Environmental Ethics.* Oxford, UK: Oxford University Press, pp. 517–527.

Schoepf, V., C.P. Jury, R.J. Toonen, and M.T. McCulloch. 2017. Coral calcification mechanisms facilitate adaptive responses to ocean acidification. *Proceedings of the Royal Society B* 284: 20172117. doi: 10.1098/rspb.2017.2117.

Schwartz, M.W. 2008. The performance of the Endangered Species Act. *Annual Review of Ecology, Evolution, and Systematics* 39: 279–299. doi: 10.1146/annurev.ecolsys.39.110707.173538.

Scott, J.M., S. Mountainspring, F.L. Ramsey, and C.B. Kepler. 1986. Forest bird communities of the Hawaiian Islands: their dynamics, ecology, and conservation. *Studies in Avian Biology* 9: 1–431.

Scott, J.M., B. Csuti, J.D. Jacobi, and J.E. Estes. 1987. Species richness. *BioScience* 37: 782–788.

Scott, J.M., F. Davis, B. Csuti, et al. 1993. Gap Analysis: a geographic approach to protection of biological diversity. *Wildlife Monographs* 123: 3–41. http://www.jstor.org/stable/3830788.

Scott, J.M., F.W. Davis, R.G. McGhie, et al. 2001. Nature reserves: Do they capture the full range of America's biological diversity? *Ecological Applications* 11: 999–1007. doi: 10.1890/1051-0761(2001)011[0999:NRDTCT]2.0.CO;2.

Scott, J.M., D.D. Goble, J.A. Wiens, et al. 2005. Recovery of imperiled species under the Endangered Species Act: the need for a new approach. *Frontiers in Ecology and the Environment* 3: 383–389.

Scott, J.M., D.D. Goble, A.M. Haines, J.A. Wiens, and M.C. Neel. 2010. Conservation-reliant species and the future of conservation. *Conservation Letters* 3: 91–97.

Scudder, G.G.E. 1999. Endangered species protection in Canada. *Conservation Biology* 13: 963–965. doi: 10.1046/j.1523-1739.1999.099i3.x.

Seabrook-Davison, M.N.H., W. Ji, and D.H. Brunton. 2010. New Zealand lacks comprehensive threatened species legislation: comparison with legislation in Australia and the USA. *Pacific Conservation Biology* 16: 54–65.

Seasholes, B. 2007. Bad for species, bad for people: What's wrong with the Endangered Species Act and how to fix it. *NCPA Policy Report No. 303*. Dallas, TX: National Center for Policy Analysis. www.ncpa.org/pub.st.st303.

Seddon, P.J. 2010. From reintroduction to assisted colonization: moving along the conservation translocation spectrum. *Restoration Ecology* 18: 796–802.

Seery, D.B., D.E. Biggins, J.A. Montenieri, et al. 2003. Treatment of black-tailed prairie dog burrows with deltamethrin to control fleas (Insecta: Siphonaptera) and plague. *Journal of Medical Entomology* 40: 718–722. https://doi.org/10.1603/0022-2585-40.5.718.

Sharpe, P.B., and D.K. Garcelon. 2005. Restoring and monitoring bald eagles in southern California: the legacy of DDT. In D.K. Garcelon and C.A. Schwemm, eds, *Proceedings of the Sixth California Islands Symposium, Ventura, California, December 1–3, 2003*. Service Technical Publication CHIS-05-01. Arcata, CA: National Park Institute for Wildlife Studies, pp. 323–330.

Sigsgaard, E.E., H. Carl, P.R. Møller, and P.F. Thomsen. 2015. Monitoring the near-extinct European weather loach in Denmark based on environmental DNA from water samples. *Biological Conservation* 183: 46–52. http://dx.doi.org/10.1016/j.biocon.2014.11.023.

Sinclair, A.R.E., and M. Norton-Griffiths (eds). 1979. *Serengeti. Dynamics of an Ecosystem*. Chicago, IL: Chicago University Press.

Singer, M.C., and C. Parmesan. 2018. Lethal trap created by adaptive evolutionary response to an exotic resource. *Nature* 557:238–241. doi:10.1038/s41586-018-0074-6.

Small, E. 2012. The new Noah's Ark: beautiful and useful species only. Part 2. The chosen species. *Biodiversity* 13: 37–51. http://dx.doi.org/10.1080/14888386 .2012.659443.

Smallwood, K. 2003. *A Guide to Canada's Species At Risk Act.* Toronto, Canada: Sierra Legal Defence Fund.

Smith, K.N., J.W. Cain III, M.L. Morrison, and R.N. Wilkins. 2012. Nesting ecology of the black-capped vireo in southwest Texas. *The Wilson Journal of Ornithology* 124: 277–285.

Snyder, N., and H. Snyder. 2000. *The California Condor.* New York, NY: Academic Press.

Snyder, N., and H.A. Snyder. 2005. Introduction to the California condor. *California Natural History Guides No. 81.* Berkeley, CA: University of California Press.

Snyder, N., S.R. Derrickson, S.R. Beissinger, et al. 1996. Limitations of captive breeding in endangered species recovery. *Conservation Biology* 10: 338–348. doi: 10.1046/j.1523-1739.1996.10020338.x.

Snyder, N.F.R., J.W. Wiley, and C.B. Kepler. 1987. *The Parrots of Luquillo: Natural History and Conservation of the Puerto Rican Parrot.* Los Angeles, CA: Western Foundation of Vertebrate Zoology.

Soderquist, T. 2011. What we don't know and haven't learned about cost–benefit prioritisation of rock-wallaby management. *Australian Mammalogy* 33: 202–213. https://doi.org/10.1071/AM10053

Spencer, P.B., J.O. Hampton, C. Pacioni, et al. 2015. Genetic relationships within social groups influence the application of the Judas technique: a case study with wild dromedary camels. *Journal of Wildlife Management* 79: 102–111. doi: 10.1002/jwmg.807.

Spinage, C.A. 2003. *Cattle Plague: A History.* New York, NY: Kluwer Academic/ Plenum Publishers.

Stallcup, R. 1981. Farewell, skymaster. *Point Reyes Bird Observatory Newsletter* 53: 10.

Stalmans, M.E., T.J. Massad, M.J.S. Peel, C.E. Tarnita, and R.M. Pringle. 2019. War-induced collapse and asymmetric recovery of large-mammal populations in Gorongosa National Park, Mozambique. *PLoS ONE* 14(3): e0212864. https:// doi.org/10.1371/journal.pone.0212864.

Steadman, D.W. 2006. *Extinction and Biogeography of Tropical Pacific Birds.* Chicago, IL: Chicago University Press.

Stegner, W. (ed.) 1955. *This Is Dinosaur: Echo Park Country and Its Magic Rivers.* New York, NY: Knopf.

Stein, B.A., C. Scott, and N. Benton. 2008. Federal lands and endangered species: the role of military and other federal lands in sustaining biodiversity. *BioScience* 58: 339–347.

Stralberg, D., D. Jongsomjit, C.A. Howell, et al. 2009. Re-shuffling of species with climate disruption: a no-analog future for California birds? *PLoS One* 4(9): e6825. doc 10.1371/journal.pone.0006825.

Stralberg D., M. Brennan, J.C. Callaway, et al. 2011. Evaluating tidal marsh sustainability in the face of sea-level rise: a hybrid modeling approach applied to San Francisco Bay. *PLoS ONE* 6(11): e27388. doi:10.1371/journal.pone.0027388

Sykes, P.W., Jr. 1980. Decline and disappearance of the dusky seaside sparrow from Merritt Island, Florida. *American Birds* 34: 728–737.

Syverson, V.J., and D.R. Prothero. 2010. Evolutionary patterns in Late Quaternary California condors. *Palarch's Journal of Vertebrate Paleontology* 7:1–18.

Szabo, J., S. Briggs, R. Lonie, et al. 2006. The feasibility of applying a cost-effective approach for assigning priorities for threatened species recovery with a case study from New South Wales, Australia. *Pacific Conservation Biology* 12: 255–258.

Tallis, H.M., P.I. Hawthorne, S. Polasky, et al. 2018. An attainable global vision for conservation and human well-being. *Frontiers in Ecology and the Environment* 16: 563–570. doi: 10.1002/fee.1965.

Taylor, M.F.J., K.F. Suckling, and J. Rachlinski. 2005. The effectiveness of the Endangered Species Act: A quantitative analysis. *BioScience* 55: 360–367. https://doi.org/10.1641/0006-3568(2005)055[0360:TEOTES]2.0.CO;2

Tear, T.H., P. Kareiva, P.K. Angermeier, et al. 2005. How much is enough? The recurrent problem of setting measurable objectives in conservation. *BioScience* 55: 835–849. https://doi.org/10.1641/0006-3568(2005)055[0835:HMIETR]2.0.CO;2

Telwala Y., B.W. Brook, K. Manish, and M.K. Pandit. 2013. Climate-induced elevational range shifts and increase in plant species richness in a Himalayan biodiversity epicentre. *PLoS ONE* 8(2): e57103. https://doi.org/10.1371/journal.pone.0057103

Terborgh, J. 1999. *Requiem for Nature*. Washington, DC: Island Press.

Thomas, C.D. 2012. First estimates of extinction risk from climate change. In L. Hannah, ed., *Saving a Million Species. Extinction Risk from Climate Change*. Washington, DC: Island Press, pp. 11–27.

Thomas, C.D. 2017. *Inheritors of the Earth. How Nature is Thriving in an Age of Extinction*. New York, NY: Public Affairs.

Tingley, M.W., W.B. Monahan, S.R. Beissinger, and C. Moritz. 2009. Birds track their Grinnellian niche through a century of climate change. *Proceedings of the*

*National Academy of Sciences of the United States of America* 106 (Supplement 2): 19 637–19 643. doi: 10.1073/pnas.0901562106.

Tingley, M.W., M.S. Koo, C. Moritz, A.C. Rush, and S.R. Beissinger. 2012. The push and pull of climate change causes heterogeneous shifts in avian elevational ranges. *Global Change Biology* 18: 3279–3290. doi:10.1111/j.1365-2486.2012.02784.x.

Trouwborst, A., A. Blackmore, L. Boitani, et al. 2017. International wildlife law: Understanding and enhancing its role in conservation. *BioScience* 67: 784–790. https://doi.org/10.1093/biosci/bix086

Turner, M.G., W.H. Romme, and D.B. Tinker. 2003. Surprises and lessons from the 1988 Yellowstone fires. *Frontiers in Ecology and the Environment* 1: 351–358. doi: 10.1890/1540-9295(2003)001[0351:SALFTY]2.0.CO;2

Urban, M.C. 2017. Accelerating extinction risk from climate change. *Science* 348: 571–573. doi: 10.1126/science.aaa4984.

USDA and USDI (US Department of Agriculture and US Department of the Interior). 1994. *Record of Decision for Amendments to Forest Service and Bureau of Land Management Planning Documents within the Range of the Northern Spotted Owl*. Washington, DC: US Department of Agriculture and US Department of the Interior. https://reo.gov/riec/newroda.pdf

USEPA (US Environmental Protection Agency). 2009. *A Framework for Categorizing the Relative Vulnerability of Threatened and Endangered Species to Climate Change*. EPA/600/R-09/011. Washington, DC: National Center for Environmental Assessment. www.epa.gov.ncea.

USFWS (US Fish & Wildlife Service). 1990. *Recovery Plan for the Endangered and Threatened Species of Ash Meadows, Nevada*. Portland, OR: US Fish & Wildlife Service.

USFWS (US Fish & Wildlife Service). 1998. *Recovery Plan for the Oregon Chub* (Oregonichthys crameri). Portland, OR: US Fish & Wildlife Service.

USFWS (US Fish and Wildlife Service). 2013. *California Condor* (Gymnogyps californianus) *5-Year Review: Summary and Evaluation*. Sacramento, CA: US Fish and Wildlife Service, Pacific Southwest Region.

Valentini, A., P. Taberlet, C. Miaud, et al. 2016. Next-generation monitoring of aquatic biodiversity using environmental DNA metabarcoding. *Molecular Ecology* 25: 929–942. doi:10.1111/wer.13428.

Van Horne, B. 1983. Density as a misleading indicator of habitat quality. *Journal of Wildlife Management* 47: 893–901.

Van Horne, B., and J.A. Wiens. 2015. Managing habitats in a changing world. In M.L. Morrison and H.A. Mathewson, eds, *Wildlife Habitat Conservation. Concepts, Challenges, and Solutions*. Baltimore, MD: Johns Hopkins University Press, pp. 34–43.

Van Horne, B., G.S. Olson, R.L. Schooley, J.G. Corn, and K.P. Burnham. 1997. Effects of drought and prolonged winter on Townsend's ground squirrel demography in shrubsteppe habitats. *Ecological Monographs* 67: 295–315. doi: 10.2307/2963457.

Van Norman, J. 2017. Response to "Listing foreign species under the Endangered Species Act" (Foley et al. 2017). *BioScience* 67: 873. https://doi.org/10.1093/biosci/bix108.

Vaz Pinto, P., P. Beja, N. Ferrand, and R. Godinho. 2016. Hybridization following population collapse in a critically endangered antelope. *Nature Scientific Reports* 6: Article 18788. doi: 10.1038/srep18788.

Vitousek, P.M. 1994. Beyond global warming: ecology and global change. *Ecology* 75: 1861–1876.

Volkmann, L., I. Martyn, V. Moulton, A. Spillner, and A.O. Mooers. 2014. Prioritizing populations for conservation using phylogenetic networks. *PLoS ONE* 9(2): e88945. https://doi.org/10.1371/journal.pone.0088945

Waldron, A., D.C. Miller, D. Redding, et al. 2017. Reductions in global biodiversity loss predicted from conservation spending. *Nature* 551: 364–367. doi: 10.1038/nature24295.

Wallace, P. 2009. Where the wild things are: examining the intersection between the RMA 1991 and the Wildlife Act 1953. *Resource Management Journal* 2009 (April): 21–25. http://www.rmla.org.nz/wp-content/uploads/2016/07/2009_rmla_april-09.pdf

Wallace, P. J., and S. Fluker. 2016. Protection of threatened species in New Zealand. *New Zealand Journal of Environmental Law* 19: 179–205.

Walters, J.R., S.R. Derrickson, D.M. Fry, et al. 2010. Status of the California condor (*Gymnogyps californianus*) and efforts to achieve its recovery. *Auk* 127: 969–1001.

Walters, M.J. 2007. *A Shadow and a Song: The Struggle to Save an Endangered Species*. White River Junction, VT: Chelsea Green Publishing Company.

Waples, R.S. 1991. Pacific salmon, *Oncorhynchus* spp., and the definition of "species" under the Endangered Species Act. *Marine Fisheries Review* 53(3): 11–22.

Waples, R.S. 2006. Distinct population segments. In J.M. Scott, D.D. Goble, and F.W. Davis, eds, *The Endangered Species Act at Thirty. Conserving Biodiversity in Human-dominated Landscapes,* Volume 2. Washington, DC: Island Press, pp. 127–149.

Waples, R.S., and O. Gaggiotti. 2006. Invited review: What is a population? An empirical evaluation of some genetic methods for identifying the number of gene pools and their degree of connectivity. *Molecular Ecology* 15: 1419–1439. doi: 10.1111/j.1365-294X.2006.02890.x

Waples, R.S., R.W. Zabel, M.D. Scheuerell, and B.L. Sanderson. 2008. Evolutionary responses by native species to major anthropogenic changes to their ecosystems: Pacific salmon in the Columbia River hydropower system. *Molecular Ecology* 17: 84–96. doi: 10.1111/j.1365-294X.2007.03510.x.

Waples, R.S., M. Nammack, J.F. Cochrane, and J.A. Hutchings. 2013. A tale of two acts: endangered species listing practices in Canada and the United States. *BioScience* 63: 723–734. https://doi.org/10.1525/bio.2013.63.9.8.

Waples, R.S., R. Kays, R.J. Fredrickson, K. Pacifici, and L.S. Mills. 2018. Is the red wolf a listable unit under the US Endangered Species Act? *Journal of Heredity* 109: 585–597. https://doi.org/10.1093/jhered/esy020

Ward, P. 1971. The migration patterns of *Quelea quelea* in Africa. *Ibis* 113: 275–297.

Waters, C.N., J. Zalasiewicz, C. Summerhayes, et al. 2016. The Anthropocene is functionally and stratigraphically distinct from the Holocene. *Science* 351 (6269): aad2622. doi: 10.1126/science.aad2622.

Wayne, A.F., M.A. Maxwell, C.G. Ward, et al. 2015. Sudden and rapid decline of the abundant marsupial *Bettongia penicillata* in Australia. *Oryx* 49: 175–185. https://doi.org/10.1017/S0030605313000677

Wayne, A.F., M.A. Maxwell, C.G. Ward, et al. 2017. Recoveries and cascading declines of native mammals associated with control of an introduced predator. *Journal of Mammalogy* 98: 489–501. https://doi.org/10.1093/jmammal/gyw237

Webber, B.L., S. Raghu, and O.R. Edwards. 2015. Opinion: Is CRISPR-based gene drive a biocontrol silver bullet or global conservation threat? *Proceedings of the National Academy of Sciences of the United States of America* 112(34): 10565–10567. http://doi.org/10.1073/pnas.1514258112

Weitzman, M.L. 1998. The Noah's Ark Problem. *Econometrica* 66: 1279–1298.

Westgate, M.J., G.E. Likens, and D.B. Lindenmayer. 2013. Adaptive management of biological systems: a review. *Biological Conservation* 158: 128–139.

Wheeler, D.P., and R.M. Rowberry. 2010. Habitat conservation plans and the Endangered Species Act. In D.C. Baur and W.R Irwin, eds, *The Endangered Species Act: Law, Policy, and Perspectives, Second edition.* Chicago, IL: American Bar Association, pp. 220–243.

Wiens, J.A. 2013. Introduction and background. In J.A. Wiens, ed., *Oil in the Environment. Legacies and Lessons of the* Exxon Valdez *Oil Spill.* Cambridge, UK: Cambridge University Press, pp. 3–36.

Wiens, J. 2016a. Is conservation a zero-sum game? *Bulletin of the British Ecological Society* 47(4): 38–39.

Wiens, J.A. 2016b. *Ecological Challenges and Conservation Conundrums. Essays and Reflections for a Changing World.* Chichester, UK: John Wiley & Sons.

Wiens, J.A., and T. Gardali. 2013. Conservation reliance among California's at-risk birds. *The Condor* 115(3): 1–15.

Wiens, J.A., N.C. Stenseth, B. Van Horne, and R. A. Ims. 1993. Ecological mechanisms and landscape ecology. *Oikos* 66: 369–380.

Wiens, J.A., G.D. Hayward, R.S. Holthausen, and M.J. Wisdom. 2008. Using surrogate species and groups for conservation planning and management. *BioScience* 58: 241–252.

Wiens, J.D., K.M. Dugger, D.B. Lesmeister, K.E. Dilione, and D.C. Simon. 2018. Effects of experimental removal of barred owls on population demography of Northern Spotted Owls in Washington and Oregon: 2017 progress report. *US Geological Survey Open-File Report 2018–1086.* https://doi.org/10.3133/ofr20181086.

Wilcove, D.S., and J. Lee. 2004. Using economic and regulatory incentives to restore endangered species: lessons learned from three new programs. *Conservation Biology* 18: 639–645. doi: 10.1111/j.1523-1739.2004.00250.x

Wilcove, D.S., and L.L. Masters. 2005. How many endangered species are there in the United States? *Frontiers in Ecology and the Environment* 3: 414–420.

Wiles, G.J., J. Bart, R.E. Beck, Jr., and C.F. Aguon. 2003. Impacts of the brown tree snake: patterns of decline and species persistence in Guam's avifauna. *Conservation Biology* 17: 1350–1360.

Wilson, E.O. 1984. *Biophilia*. Cambridge, MA: Harvard University Press.

Wilson, E.O. 1987. The little things that run the world (the importance and conservation of invertebrates). *Conservation Biology* 1: 344–346. doi: 10.1111/j.1523-1739.1987.tb00055.x.

Wilson, E.O 1992. *The Diversity of Life*. Cambridge, MA: Harvard University Press.

Wilson, E.O. 1997. Introduction. In M.L. Reaka-Kudla, D.E. Wilson, and E.O. Wilson, eds, *Biodiversity II. Understanding and Protecting Our Biological Resources*. Washington, DC: Joseph Henry Press, pp. 1–3.

Wilson, E.O. 2002. *The Future of Life*. New York, NY: Alfred A. Knopf.

Wilson, E.O. 2016. *Half-Earth. Our Planet's Fight for Life*. New York, NY: Liveright Publishing Corporation.

Wilson, K. 2004. *Flight of the Huia. Ecology and Conservation of New Zealand's Frogs, Reptiles, Birds, and Mammals*. Christchurch, NZ: Canterbury University Press.

Winemiller, K.O., P.B. McIntyre, L. Castello, et al. 2016. Balancing hydropower and biodiversity in the Amazon, Congo, and Mekong. *Science* 351: 128–129. doi: 10.1126/science.aac7082.

Woinarski, J.C.Z. 1999. Fire and Australian birds: a review. In A.M. Gill, J.C.Z. Woinarski, and A. York, eds, *Australia's Biodiversity: Responses to Fire*.

Biodiversity Technical Paper No. 1. Canberra, ACT: Department of Environment and Heritage, pp. 55–112.

Woinarski, J. 2018. *A Bat's End: The Christmas Island Pipistrelle and Extinction in Australia.* Melbourne, Australia: CSIRO Publishing.

Woinarski, J.C.Z., and A. Fisher. 1999. The Australian Endangered Species Protection Act 1992. *Conservation Biology* 13: 959–962.

Woinarski, J.C.Z., S.T. Garnett, S.M. Legge, and D.B. Lindenmayer. 2017. The contribution of policy, law, management, research, and advocacy failings to the recent extinctions of three Australian vertebrate species. *Conservation Biology* 31: 13–23.

Wojciechowski, S., S. McKee, C. Brassard, C.S. Findlay, and S. Elgie. 2011. SARA's safety net provisions and the effectiveness of species at risk protection on non-federal land. *Journal of Environmental Law and Practice* 22: 203–222.

Worboys, G.L., W.L. Francis, and M. Lockwood (eds). 2010. *Connectivity Conservation Management. A Global Guide.* London: Earthscan.

Wright, S. 1940. Breeding structure of populations in relation to speciation. *American Naturalist* 74: 232–248.

Zalasiewicz, J., C.N. Aaters, M. Williams, et al. 2015. When did the Anthropocene begin? A mid-twentieth century boundary level is stratigraphically optimal. *Quaternary International* 383: 196–203. doi: 10.1016/j.quaint.2014.11.045.

Zavaleta, E.S., R.J. Hobbs, and H.A. Mooney. 2001. Viewing invasive species removal in a whole-ecosystem context. *Trends in Ecology & Evolution* 16: 454–459. https://doi.org/10.1016/S0169-5347(01)02194-2

Zhang, H., and S.M. Gorelick. 2014. Coupled impacts of sea-level rise and tidal marsh restoration on endangered California clapper rail. *Biological Conservation* 172: 89–100. https://doi.org/10.1016/j.biocon.2014.02.016.

# Index

*Page numbers in italic denote photos.*